Lone Star Tarnished

Texas pride, like everything else in the state, is larger than life. So, too, perhaps, are the state's challenges. *Lone Star Tarnished*, Third Edition approaches public policy in the nation's most populous "red state" from historical, comparative, and critical perspectives. The historical perspective provides the scope for asking how various policy domains have developed in Texas history, regularly reaching back to the state's founding and with substantial data for the period 1950 to the present. In each chapter, Cal Jillson compares Texas public policy choices and results with those of other states and the United States in general. Finally, the critical perspective allows us to question the balance of benefits and costs attendant to what is often referred to as "the Texas way" or "the Texas model." This is used best as a supplementary text for instructors of a course on Texas Politics who want to stress history, political culture, and public policy.

Jillson delves deeply into eight substantive policy chapters, covering the most important policy areas in which state governments are active. The third edition includes completely rewritten first and second chapters, as well as updates throughout the book and revised figures and tables. Also new to the third edition is a completely new chapter on higher education in Texas. Through Jillson's lively and lucid prose, students are well equipped to analyze how Texas has done and is doing compared to selected states and the national average over time and today. Readers will also come away with the necessary tools to assess the many claims of Texas's exceptionalism.

New to the Third Edition

- Highlights major new actors in Texas politics, including Governor Greg Abbott, Lt. Gov. Dan Patrick, George P. Bush, and a higher-profile Ted Cruz.
- Notes key policy developments in education, health care, transportation, energy, and more, resulting from the 2015 and 2017 legislative sessions and the arrival of the new Republican Trump administration in Washington.
- Updates all tables and figures in the book, including a dozen new ones, assessing how Texas is doing in income, education, human services, transportation, energy, and the environment.
- Includes an entirely new chapter on "Higher Education in Texas."

Cal Jillson is Professor in the Department of Political Science at Southern Methodist University. He is the author of *American Government: Political Development and Institutional Change; Texas Politics: Governing the Lone Star State; Congressional Dynamics; Constitution-Making: Conflict and Consensus in the Federal Convention of 1787*; and *The American Dream in History, Politics, and Fiction*.

Praise for the Third Edition

Texas and its government face significant, complex challenges. This revised and enhanced edition of Cal Jillson's *Lone Star Tarnished* not only affirms this but also helps us to understand these challenges with an engaging mosaic of history, data, and analysis, and encourages us to work for viable solutions. The new chapter on higher education is an excellent addition. This must-read book is an invitation to learn, to think critically, and to act, and I plan to continue to use it in my state government courses.

Eric V. Morrow, *Tarleton State University*

Lone Star Tarnished is an indispensable resource for students and faculty who want to get beyond the basics of understanding Texas government. Cal Jillson presents the often overlooked roots and development for how our current policies came to be. This eye-opening and unvarnished history enriches classroom discussions and provides a framework for understanding Texas public policy and the serious consequences and disparate impact on contemporary Texans.

Cindy Castañeda, *Eastfield College*

Lone Star Tarnished

A Critical Look at Texas Politics and Public Policy

Third Edition

Cal Jillson

SOUTHERN METHODIST UNIVERSITY

Routledge
Taylor & Francis Group

NEW YORK AND LONDON

Published 2018
by Routledge
711 Third Avenue, New York, NY 10017

and by Routledge
2 Park Square, Milton Park, Abingdon, Oxon, OX14 4RN

Routledge is an imprint of the Taylor & Francis Group, an informa business

First edition published by Routledge 2012
Second edition published by Routledge 2015

Visit the eResources: www.routledge.com/9781138562691

Library of Congress Cataloging in Publication Data
Names: Jillson, Calvin C., 1949- author.
Title: Lone star tarnished : a critical look at Texas politics and public policy /
    Cal Jillson, Southern Methodist University.
Description: Third edition. | New York, NY : Routledge, 2018.
Identifiers: LCCN 2017031660| ISBN 9781138562684 (hardback) | ISBN
    9781138562691 (pbk.) | ISBN 9781315121208 (ebook)
Subjects: LCSH: Political planning—Texas. | Texas—Politics and
    government. | Texas—Social policy. | Texas—Economic policy.
Classification: LCC JK4849.P64 J55 2018 | DDC 320.9764—dc23
LC record available at https://lccn.loc.gov/2017031660

ISBN: 978-1-138-56268-4 (hbk)
ISBN: 978-1-138-56269-1 (pbk)
ISBN: 978-1-315-12120-8 (ebk)

Typeset in Times New Roman
by Swales & Willis Ltd, Exeter, Devon, UK

Remembering
Old Sam Jacinto and Mr. Sam

Contents

List of Illustrations

Figures

Tables

Preface

Lone Star Tarnished describes how the Texas political culture, the Texas way of thinking about and practicing politics, shapes the state's politics and public policy. This book is intended for use in Texas Politics courses in the state's colleges and universities, but it is not a standard textbook. *Lone Star Tarnished* is designed to be used in conjunction with a basic *text*, which will cover political processes and institutions, in courses that want more coverage of Texas political culture, history, and public policy. Blushing only slightly, I suggest my own text, *Texas Politics: Governing the Lone Star State*. Though these books were written for a college audience, Texas politics junkies of any age are, of course, welcome.

Most of *Lone Star Tarnished* is dedicated to describing the meaning of "the Texas way" and tracing its impact on Texas public policy in separate chapters on jobs, income, and poverty, public education, higher education, health care and social services, crime and punishment, transportation, energy and the environment, and tax policy. The thesis of this book is that Texas is in thrall to a myth that blinds it to social and economic changes that threaten its future. We begin with the irrefutable point that there is a romantic reading of Texas history in which most Anglo Texans revel. The myth is that Texas has always been and remains big, bold, open, and vibrant and that these attributes assure dynamism, growth, and prosperity. In Texas history, the defenders of freedom at the Alamo and San Jacinto and the planters, ranchers, wildcatters, and high-tech entrepreneurs who followed in their wake are the exemplars.

The Texas way, as Governor Greg Abbott and former Governor Rick Perry continue to call this distinctive outlook on life, rests on the pillars of individualism, personal responsibility, low taxes, and limited government. The Texas way presumes that individuals build families and businesses and create wealth. Sometimes individuals join together to seize opportunities or solve problems, but they do so on their own terms and usually in their own neighborhoods and communities. There is a place for government where individual and community effort is insufficient to solve pressing problems, but government should limit itself to the essentials, defending persons and property, promoting an economic infrastructure of transportation and utilities, and establishing courts to enforce the rule of law. In this environment of freedom, some will succeed and some will fail, but all will deserve and should own the results that they achieve. In many ways, this is an attractive view of life and politics.

But virtually no one still denies that for most of Texas history the state's commitment to individualism, personal responsibility, and limited government encompassed only white men and served particularly well the needs and interests of wealthy white men. Far fewer recognize that today the Texas way, rather than marking the path forward, obscures growing threats to our future security and prosperity. Touting the Texas way as if it applied to all Texans, when, in fact, it is the heritage of an ever shrinking Anglo portion of the population, is an excuse for political and policy inaction. Anglo Texans have not yet fully realized that the days in which they could succeed even as Texas blacks and Hispanics lagged are fading fast.

The challenges facing Texas are no secret: they involve the interaction of demographic change, educational attainment, and income distribution. Demographic change is an old story in Texas. But once the Anglo majority in Texas was established by the 1830s, it ranged from two-thirds to three-quarters of the total population into the last quarter of the twentieth century. As late as 1980, Anglos accounted for 66 percent of the Texas population, blacks for 12 percent, and Hispanics for a little over 20 percent. By 2050, Anglos are expected to be just 28 percent of the population, blacks will be 10 percent, and Hispanics will account for more than 50 percent. These are massive changes, but massive changes do not have to be worrisome. If Anglos, blacks, and Hispanics in Texas enjoyed equal educations and incomes, there would be no reason to worry, because demographic change would not affect the state's overall competitiveness and productivity. Unfortunately, this happy possibility does not pertain in Texas.

The problems posed by demographic change in Texas emerge most clearly when we look at educational attainment and income by race and ethnicity. In 2015, Texas ranked 49th, next to last among the 50 states, in the proportion of residents 25 and older who held a high school diploma, at 81.9 percent compared to 85.6 percent nationally. High school graduates in Texas by race and ethnicity break down this way—Anglos 91 percent, blacks 84 percent, and Hispanics 57 percent. Because Hispanic educational attainment lags that of Anglos and blacks, so do Hispanic incomes. Median family income in Texas in 2015 for Anglos was $85,797, for blacks $48,761, and for Hispanics $45,959. Unless Hispanic educational attainment and income improve as the Hispanic share of the population grows, Texas will become a poorer, less dynamic, less effective wealth producing state. Not *might* become poorer—*will* become poorer—it is simple math.

Still, for many Anglo Texans, bred in the Texas way of individualism, personal responsibility, and small government, this seems like a boot strap issue. If lack of education limits income potential for many Texas Hispanics, then the answer is to study harder in school, go further in school, and work harder in the private economy once you leave school. Alternatively, to view Hispanic educational attainment as a major public policy problem, requiring significant investments in the state's poorer schools, would be expensive and the money would have to come at least partially from the pockets of wealthier Anglo school districts. The political dilemma is in two parts and is quite simple: (1) nothing in Texas history suggests that Anglos will provide the revenues necessary to support high-quality public schools for minority children, (2) but, if they do not, the state's economic growth and prosperity will decline.

We seek to unravel this dilemma by approaching Texas politics and public policy from historical, comparative, and analytical/critical perspectives. The historical perspective provides the scope for asking how Texas politics and public policy have evolved and developed, often with a qualitative discussion reaching back to the state's founding and with substantial data for the period 1950 to the present. In each chapter we compare Texas public policy choices and results with those of other states, usually including California and Florida as they are similarly situated, and the United States in general. Finally, the analytical/critical perspective allows us to question the balance of benefits and costs attendant to "the Texas way" or "the Texas model" and to think about how we might do better.

All of the tables and graphs in this book have been crafted with teachers and students in mind. Data are usually presented in straightforward numbers, with statistics rarely more complicated than percentages. Students can easily grasp their meaning and teachers can easily introduce them for class discussion. Most importantly, these clear graphic presentations allow class discussions to begin from a foundation of fact. All political discussions end in argument and debate, but they should not and do not have to begin there.

Lone Star Tarnished is comprised of 11 chapters divided into three sections. Part I is entitled "The Great State of Texas?" The goal of Chapter 1, "The Texas Way," is to show that a distinctive view of the role and purpose of government has long, indeed always, characterized Texas. In this new edition, we highlight the work of the prominent cultural geographer Wilbur Zelinsky to better understand the stability so clear in Texas political development. Zelinsky's "Doctrine of First Settlement" helps explain the lasting impact of the early Anglo settlement of Texas out of the American South. The foundation of Anglo dominance laid then helps explain the racial and ethnic tensions that persist in Texas today.

In Chapter 2, entitled "Texas: The Myth vs. the Reality," we highlight and attempt to get control of the boosterism and braggadocio that pervade Texas life in general and Texas politics in particular. In this new edition, we confront one of the broader myths of Texas history—that the state is culturally western or southwestern, rather than southern—with compelling evidence that it is not so. While Texas elites have sought for decades to foster a western image over a southern one, we show that the bulk of the state's population, economic activity, and political weight have always been in the state's most unambiguously southern cultural regions. We also show that while Texas has done very well on population and job growth, its ranking among the states on income, education, social services, criminal justice, and the environment have been stagnant or falling for decades.

Chapter 3 highlights the rapidly changing demographics of Texas. Demographic change is nothing new to Texas, but from the Austin colony of the 1820s through the current decade Anglos (whites to the wider world) were the dominant ethnicity. They still are, but in 2005 Anglos fell below 50 percent of the Texas population, compared to Hispanics at 36 percent, blacks at a little less than 12 percent, and Asians at about 3 percent. By the early 2030s Hispanics will be the majority in Texas, though Anglos will still control the wealth and likely the politics of the state. We ask what these demographic changes mean for Texas politics and public life in the coming decades. The 2010 census and its annual updates provide rich new demographic data for our consideration.

Part II, entitled "The Reality Thus Far," is composed of seven substantive policy chapters. These chapters cover most of the major policy areas in which state governments are active; including the economy, public education, higher education, health and human services, crime and punishment, transportation, and, especially in Texas, energy and the environment. We ask what Texas says it is trying to do, how hard it seems to be trying to do it, with what results, and for whom. In chapters dealing with economic and social policy issues such as income, education, and health care, we have added substantial new detail that highlights troubling differences in opportunity and achievement by race and ethnicity. In each chapter we compare Texas to a relevant selection of states and usually to the national average of all 50 states. We want to know how Texas has done and is doing compared to selected states and the national average over time and today. Is Texas above or below the national average, say in education expenditures or access to health care, and is it falling behind or moving up? What we find is that Texas's firm commitment to low taxes has starved state government funding of programs in most of these policy areas, and comparisons with other states have worsened.

Part III, entitled "The Coming Reality," is composed of one concluding chapter. Chapter 11, entitled "The Way Forward," explores the history of Texas tax policies and asks how Texas might change its revenue system to better confront the problems that loom clearly on the horizon. In recent years, Texas has consistently ranked among the lowest of the low-tax states, ranking 42nd in 2015. We ask what tax reforms and new tax sources would provide the additional revenues needed to bring Texas to the southern average for tax effort, and then to the national average, and to what uses those funds might be put. Since few expect that the Republican Party that now controls Texas will seek new tax revenues—income tax anyone—we ask when two-party competition might arrive in Texas. Hint—the 2030s.

New to the Third Edition

- The manuscript has been revised throughout to highlight major new actors in Texas politics, including Governor Greg Abbott, Lieutenant Governor Dan Patrick, George P. Bush, and a higher profile Ted Cruz, and to note the major policy developments in education, health care, transportation, energy and more resulting from the 2015 and 2017 legislative sessions and the arrival of the new Republican Trump administration in Washington.
- All of the tables and figures in the book, including a dozen new ones, have been revised and updated with the most recent data and information. These data ground our discussion of how Texas is doing in income, education, human services, transportation, energy and the environment and more compared to the past, to other states, and to national averages.
- Chapters 1 and 2 have been completely rewritten to better highlight the continuity in "the Texas way" from first Anglo settlement to today and to show how new actors like Greg Abbott have replaced old actors like Rick Perry without missing a beat. See especially the discussion late in Chapter 2 of Governor Abbott's call for a Convention of the States to amend the U.S. Constitution.
- Chapter 3 has been thoroughly updated as demographic change continues apace in Texas.
- Chapter 4 has been rewritten to include a major new section, including a new table and two new graphs, highlighting the ongoing importance of the energy sector to the Texas economy. Outside the energy sector, where 95 percent of Texans work, the state's workers lag national averages for both productivity and pay.
- Chapter 6 is an entirely new chapter on "Higher Education in Texas." We find that Texas lags national averages for college attendance, state funding, graduation rates, and much more.
- In Chapter 10 we analyze the implications for Texas energy and environmental policies of the transition from the Obama administration to the Trump administration and the EPA now headed by former Oklahoma Attorney General Scott Pruitt.
- Chapter 11 has a new section exploring the pace of a potential Democratic Party return to competitiveness in Texas, often called Purple Texas, as the most likely driver of major tax and policy change in the state.

Books take time and their authors—at least the lucky ones—draw on many kinds of support. I am deeply grateful to Southern Methodist University for its ongoing support of my work. This book originated in conversations with Harold Stanley and matured in daily conversations with Brad Carter, Dennis Ippolito, Joe Kobylka, the recently departed Dennis Simon, and Matt Wilson. I am also grateful to the students in my Texas Politics classes, the journalists with whom I frequently talk Texas politics, and the reviewers who took the time to offer advice and suggestions when the manuscript was in draft. Many of the improvements found in this new edition can be attributed to teachers and students of Texas politics who have used the book and suggested how it might be strengthened. My wife Jane continues to expand the calm in my life. Finally, this is the third of my books that Jennifer Knerr has seen through the production process at Routledge. She is ever faithful. These are the relationships that define and sustain me and upon which I place great value.

Part I

The Great State of Texas?

1   The Texas Way

I ask you today to join me in my fight for the ideals and values of the greatest people ever to inhabit this earth, the people of the great state of Texas.

(Greg Abbott, 2013)

In January 1822, Jared Ellison Groce rumbled into Stephen F. Austin's new colony at the head of 50 covered wagons containing his family, household goods, and agricultural equipment. Behind the wagons some of his 90 slaves drove herds of horses, mules, oxen, cattle, sheep, and hogs. Groce immediately became and long remained the colony's richest citizen. He received the largest land grant in the colony, eventually totaling 11 leagues or 44,000 acres of prime Brazos River bottom land. With ready money and an experienced labor force, he soon had the best of his land in cotton and his famed Bernardo Plantation rose on a bluff overlooking the river.[1]

Jared Groce, like most of the early Austin colonists, called the "the Old Three Hundred" in Texas history, came out of the American South. Groce was born into a prominent Virginia family in October 1782. Eager to make his own mark, Groce acquired a South Carolina plantation in 1802 at the age of 20. In 1804 he moved to Georgia and in 1814 to Alabama where he established a plantation called Fort Groce. Just a little more than six months after Stephen F. Austin arrived in Texas to take over his deceased father's colonization venture, and one month after Austin himself arrived on the Brazos, Groce's party arrived. Austin, the *empresario* or real-estate developer and leader of the colony, needed wealthy immigrants like Groce to bring people, agricultural expertise, and development capital to the colony. Groce generally cooperated with Austin, but always on his own terms. A fellow colonist described Groce as "a warm friend or bitter Enemy Just as his Immidiate Interest is Effected. . . . his Excentricities and Exalted notions of himself is his worst foibles."[2]

Groce's reputation for self-interested aristocratic eccentricity became legendary. In 1828 a proud Mexican official named Jose Maria Sanchez fumed to his diary that Groce had treated him with studied contempt. Sanchez wrote, "They did not deign to offer us shelter in the house, even though they saw us camping under the trees. Later, they asked us into the house for the sole purpose of showing us the wealth of Mr. Groce and to introduce us to three dogs called Ferdinand VII [then King of Spain], Napoleon [former Emperor of the French], and Bolivar [the hero of Latin American independence movements]." But Groce's self-interested hauteur was not reserved for Mexican officials. William Fairfax Gray, a Virginia lawyer, military officer, and land agent, commonly referred to as Colonel Gray, was allowed to stay in the house while visiting Bernardo, but he also used his diary to criticize Groce. Gray attended the Convention of March 1 to 17, 1836, that declared independence and wrote the Texas Constitution, spent March 18 to 21 at Groce's, and prepared to join the "Runaway Scrape" of Texas civilians fleeing east before Santa Anna's advancing armies. As Gray and his party prepared to depart, some were concerned that they had imposed on Groce's hospitality. Colonel Gray reports that, "This delicacy was cured when . . . he presented each with a bill for $3 per day, man and horse."[3]

Another of "the Old Three Hundred," the sugar plantation owner Sterling McNeal, also arrived in Texas in 1822 and took up a land grant in what became Brazoria County. Like Groce, he prospered and his plantation became a common stop for travelers. In 1848–49, future U.S. President Rutherford B. Hayes of Ohio visited the region. He described McNeal as "A shrewd, intelligent, cynical, old bachelor. . . . Very fond of telling his own experience and talking of his own affairs." Hayes went on to observe that "The haughty and imperious part of a man develops rapidly on one of these lonely sugar plantations, where the owner rarely meets with any except his slaves and menials."[4] While comparatively few men arrived as did Groce and McNeal with their fortunes in hand, many assumed that the lush new country would soon yield them a fortune. None other than frontiersman and former Kentucky congressman David Crockett, soon to die at the Alamo, wrote, "I do believe it is a fortune to any man to come here. There is a world of country to settle."[5] Hence, even those not yet wealthy practiced the haughty planter manner in confident anticipation.

A prickly defense of individual interests, a fulsome self-regard, and intolerance of outside authority, whether emanating from near or far, soon came to characterize the white male population of Texas. Several leading mid-twentieth-century scholars have described in very similar terms the mind-set or world view of early Anglo Texans. T.R. Fehrenbach, former head of the Texas Historical Commission and author of the iconic *Lone Star: A History of Texas and the Texans* (1968), argued that, "the poorer whites and larger cotton growers . . . held very similar world views. Both were atomistic, . . . ferociously self-motivated and self-reliant, prideful and intolerant, hard-working and ambitious . . . both were impatient with government (which inevitably followed them) except as it served their wishes and interests."[6] D.W. Meinig, the prominent cultural geographer and author of *Imperial Texas: An Interpretive Essay in Cultural Geography* (1969), made a similar point at greater length, saying:

> The Texan . . . is strongly individualistic and egalitarian, optimistic and utilitarian, volatile and chauvinistic, ethnocentric and provincial. . . . Such a person regards government as no more than a necessary evil, distrusts even informal social action as a threat to his independence, and accepts violence as an appropriate solution to certain kinds of social and group problems. . . . There is an easy acceptance of equality among one's own kind but a rigid sense of superiority over other local peoples, and a deep suspicion of outsiders as threats to the social order.[7]

W.W. Newcomb, the respected mid-twentieth-century anthropologist and Director of the Texas Memorial Museum, wrote that "Texans . . . came to regard themselves as a breed apart, perhaps, too, a chosen people in a chosen land."[8]

In thinking about the three quotes above and many that will follow, the reader is always well advised to keep this question in mind—who are they talking about, who are the Texans that are being described? With a little thought, it will usually become clear that they are not talking about "all" Texans. In fact, they are not talking even about "most" Texans. They are talking about the "iconic" Texan: the "mythic" Texans of John Wayne's *Alamo*, Larry McMurtry's *Lonesome Dove*, and Edna Ferber's *Giant*. Leigh Clemons, a scholar of contemporary media and culture and author of *Branding*

Texas: Performing Culture in the Lone Star State, argued that a "white male, brazenly independent, and typically larger-than-life stereotype has defined the common perceptions of what it means to be a Texan, who does and does not have access to that identity, and what impact . . . that identity has on the state's relationship with the rest of the country and among Texas residents."[9] Texan iconography does not have a place, certainly not an equal place, for blacks, Hispanics, Native-Americans, or women.

Until well into the twentieth century, the reminder that the appellation "Texan" meant whites was unnecessary. Everyone knew that "Texan" referred to white people, though it was occasionally necessary to explain that to Yankees and Europeans. For example, N. Doran Maillard, an Englishman and editor of the Richmond, Virginia, *Telescope*, toured Texas from January through July 1840. In 1842, Maillard published *The History of the Republic of Texas*, explaining to his readers that, "The white population of Texas are called 'Texans' . . . The Texans are generally styled the first offsprings of America, and the grand-children of England."[10] Even in recent decades, scholars have felt the need to remind readers that history changes the meaning even of familiar words. Texas historian Billy D. Ledbetter opened his classic 1973 paper, "White Over Black in Texas: Racial Attitudes in the Antebellum Period," by writing, "In this paper, the word 'Texan' refers only to white Texans—the accepted ante-bellum definition of the word."[11] Our initial inclination might be to think that the word "Texan" is no longer used so narrowly, but would we be right? Let's leave that question open, but front of mind, for now.

In this opening chapter, we trace the origins, development, and political impact of "the Texas way." No one will be surprised to find that the "empresarios" of early Texas and the leaders of the Texas Republic worked hard to attract wealthy white men, their families, property, and capital. From the perspective of white men, women were valued family members, but by no means equals, slaves were useful, even economically essential, while Hispanics, and even more evidently, Indians, were in the way. Yet, many will be surprised to find that the cultural assumptions of early Texas survived robustly into our own time. We trace the southern cultural heritage of early Texas and its evolution through Texas history—always supporting the primacy of male social and economic elites, personal autonomy and individual responsibility, small government and low taxes, and a deep suspicion of foreign, meaning federal as well as international, influence and authority.

The Southern Cultural Matrix of Early Texas

Cultural geographers have long understood that early settlers establish social, cultural, economic, and political matrices into which those who come later must fit. Pennsylvania State University's famous cultural geographer Wilbur Zelinsky initially offered "The Doctrine of First Settlement" in 1973, the year he served as president of the American Association of Geographers. Zelinsky explained that:

> Whenever an empty territory undergoes settlement, or an earlier population is dislodged by invaders, the specific characteristics of the first group able to effect a viable, self-perpetuating society are of crucial significance for the later social and cultural geography of the area, no matter how tiny the initial band of settlers may have been. . . . Thus, in terms of lasting impact, the activities of a few hundred, or even a few score, initial colonizers can mean much more for the cultural geography of a place than the contributions of tens of thousands of new immigrants a few generations later.[12]

Texas was occupied before the Anglo-American influx, but it was very thinly occupied. As late as 1820, Mexican Texas numbered only three or four thousand non-Indian inhabitants, mostly in the San Antonio and Goliad areas, with a smaller mixed Anglo-American and Mexican population at Nacogdoches. But the opening of Texas to Anglo immigration, and especially the founding of the Austin colony in 1821, brought uncontrollable change. By 1835, there were about 25,000 non-Indians in Texas, 80 percent of them Anglo-American, and after independence the Anglo tide rose rapidly. The weight of the population and wealth were in the Austin colony's rich Brazos and Colorado River bottoms. Texas historians report that the bulk of Anglo immigrants were southerners and brought with them southern habits and expectations. Randolph B. Campbell, author of *Gone to Texas: A History of the Lone Star State* (2003), wrote that, "Most of the planters and plain folk who settled in antebellum Texas were southerners, and they built an overwhelmingly agricultural economy highly similar to that found in the older southern states."[13]

D.W. Meinig's well-known description of the cultural geography of antebellum Texas reported that:

> East Texas . . . was entirely Anglo-American and very largely from Alabama and other Gulf states. East Texas was thus the western extension of the older Deep South. . . . It had an economy based upon cotton, corn, cattle, and hogs, a wholly rural society . . . in which slaves, who made up a third or more of the total population, were an integral part of the economic and social structure.[14]

When Meinig and others refer to East Texas, they do not mean just the piney woods of far East Texas adjacent to Louisiana. Rather, they also, even principally, mean the green, well-watered, humid, low lands north of Galveston and Houston, east of Austin, and between the Trinity and Colorado Rivers, centered on the rich Brazos River valley. Michael Lind, like Meinig, described East Texas as "the westernmost extension of the Deep South. The society of East Texas . . . was biracial and hierarchical. . . . It was a clone of the society of Alabama, Mississippi, Georgia, and northern Florida."[15] East Texas was the center of plantation wealth and so set the social and cultural tone for early Texas.[16]

But the plantation aristocracy of early Texas faced a more threatening reality and faced it far longer than did their cousins back home. The courtly plantation life of Virginia and South Carolina, even of Alabama and Mississippi, never really came to Texas. All of Texas, including the Austin colony, was a contested and often bloody frontier in the 1820s and 1830s. Civil institutions remained to be built so order was maintained by voluntary, including vigilante, effort. In 1825 Jared Groce provided 30 armed slaves to Stephen F. Austin to assist in putting down Karankawa raids. In 1833 when Groce divided parts of his original estate among his children and moved several miles north to establish a new plantation at Groce's Retreat, he took 20 armed slaves to deal with Cherokee raids. Even after the brief but bloody fight for independence in 1836, two invasions by Mexican forces, both of which occupied San Antonio briefly, occurred in the early 1840s. Statehood in 1845 was expected to bring peace, but Comanche raids plagued the state's western frontier for three more decades.

The leading early settlers of Texas had the social expectations of plantation aristocrats sharpened by the demands and dangers of frontier life. Many fought Indians across the southern frontier, carried slaves with them to Texas, and fumed at Mexican rule once they arrived. These early settlers "brought with them a long history of dealing with Indians and blacks, while the experience of the Alamo and the Mexican War served to crystallize and affirm anti-Mexican prejudice."[17] The Anglo elite had an unshake-able expectation of social deference and political and economic primacy that they were prepared to enforce. They did not equivocate or compromise with enemies; they pushed most Mexicans, including Tejanos, south of the Rio Grande and exterminated those Indians that refused to leave the state.

The plantation culture of deep racial distinctions and Anglo dominance was entrenched in East Texas before meaningful settlement took place in North Texas and in the broad expanses of West Texas.[18] When settlement did come to North Texas in the 1840s and 1850s, it had a different cultural source and feel than East Texas. Meinig described the Blackland Prairie of North Texas as "distinctly Border South country, drawing most heavily from Missouri, strongly from Arkansas and Tennessee, and significantly from Illinois." There was little cotton, at least initially, and few slaves: "agriculture was more diversified . . .; settlement was more compact; towns a more vital part of social organization; and contrasts between rich and poor rather less promi-nent. In short, there existed here between North and East Texas the same difference as between Kentucky and Alabama."[19] Nonetheless, the Brazos plantation elite assumed the right to lead and the farmers and small town folk of North Texas did not contest it.[20]

As the Civil War approached, Texas elites were unequivocal about their southern roots and cultural assumptions—slavery was a positive good for whites and blacks and they would fight to defend it. In 1856 Lorenzo Sherwood, a Galveston lawyer recently immigrated from New York and even more recently elected to the Texas Legislature, opined that slavery, while perhaps necessary now, sat uncomfortably with democracy and would probably fade away in the next century. The state erupted in outrage. The Dallas *Herald* declared that, "A man, a Texan, a southerner who could get up in the legislature of a southern State, *of the most southern State*, and deliberately outrage the feelings of the whole people without distinction of party, on a question so directly affecting their most vital interests, by uttering sentiments that strike at the foundation of their social and political rights," was not fit to serve.[21] Sherwood resigned his seat. In 1857, the *Galveston Weekly* declared, "Those who are not for us, must be against us. There can be no middle ground. Those who denounce slavery as an evil, in any sense, are enemies of the South, whatever may be their pretended conservatism."[22] Moreover, the Texas Secession Convention, meeting on January 28, 1861, voted 166 to 8 to secede from the Union. The Convention defended its recommendation for secession in its famous "Declaration of Causes." Secession was necessary to protect the "'beneficent and patriarchal system of African slavery' against 'the debasing doctrine of the equal-ity of all men, irrespective of race or color.'" The declaration went on to say that the U.S. and certainly Texas were founded "exclusively by the white race, for themselves and their posterity; that the African race had no agency in their establishment; that they were rightly held and regarded as an inferiorand dependent race, and in that condi-tion only could their existence in this country be rendered beneficial or tolerable." The "Declaration of Causes" barely mentioned issues other than slavery; fully 95 percent of the document was dedicated to a defense of slavery. The remaining 5 percent dealt with border and frontier security. States' rights were mentioned, but barely, and then only as a defense of slavery. Texas approved secession by a vote of 46,154 to 14,747 on February 23, 1861.

Though the Civil War and Reconstruction temporarily loosened the grip of estab-lished elites, they restored their dominance by the early 1870s and fastened it down in the Constitution of 1876. James McEnteer writes that, "the Texas Constitution of 1876 reflects the Alamo values of 1836, affirming states' rights, decentralized government and the supremacy of the white race. Frequently amended, that document has never been rewritten and remains in force."[23] White supremacy remained the dominant Anglo Texan attitude toward others well into the mid-twentieth century.

The last great migration into Texas in the nineteenth century was the post–Civil War exodus of busted whites out of the Old South. Robert Calvert and his colleagues write that,

> Residents of states that had been devastated by the Civil War and post-1865 economic stagnation sought out a fellow ex-Confederate state with cotton lands and similar racial attitudes in which to resettle. . . . Thus (in descending order) Arkansas, Alabama, Mississippi, Tennessee, Missouri, Louisiana, and Georgia sent the majority of the in-migrants to Texas. . . . The influx of new people did little to alter the previously formed cultural regions that had determined the course of prewar politics.[24]

New Texans and old, these defeated southerners had decades of rebuilding to do. They had to regain control of their state and then slowly rebuild it on the old white supremacy model. Slavery was gone, but white supremacy could be restored behind a strict segregation of the races.[25]

The post–Civil War battles for social and political control of the South were fought with all of the weapons that could be brought to hand. The great historian of the South, C. Vann Woodward, wrote that, "Southern whites . . . used craft and guile, force and violence, economic pressure and physical terror, and all the subtle psychological devices of race prejudice and propaganda at their command."[26] By the first decade of the new century, restrictive voter registration, the white primary, and the poll tax were in place, assuring elite Anglo control. T.R. Fehrenbach correctly asserted that, "Texas entered the 20th century" with white supremacy restored but "with its basic society a full two generations, or about sixty years, behind the development of the American mainstream. Industry was in its infancy; among the people themselves the norms and patterns of the industrial society had no root. . . . The early 19th century American values were in no way eroded in Texas."[27] Texas elites wanted to attract northern capital, but not at the expense of southern social and cultural traditions.

West Texas was not cleared of Indians and hence ready for settlement until after the Civil War and Reconstruction. Even then West Texas was an unforgiving land that broke the first generation of farmers before being fenced for ranching in the late 1880s. Critically, as we will see in detail in Chapter 2, there was never anything remotely like a balance between the cultures of southern traditionalism and western individualism, because the vast majority of the population always lived in the region dominated by southern traditionalism. This point was entertainingly made in the sweeping Texas novel by Phillipp Meyer, *The Son*; the patriarch, Eli McCullough, noted of post–Civil War Texas, "our state's reputation as a cattle kingdom is overboiled. Beef was always a poor cousin to the woolly plant and it was not until thirty years after Spindletop that even oil knocked King Cotton from his throne."[28]

In fact, the fundamental social assumptions and commitments of Anglo Texans have been remarkably stable from first settlement to today. Anglo Texans have demanded independence, personal and collective, small government, low taxes, light regulation, and personal responsibility. These ideas were not unusual in nineteenth-century America, though Anglo Texans were keenly aware of differences in emphasis and implementation between North and South. In Texas, as in the South more generally, the idea of freedom, to be unrestrained, was important to whites because its opposite, black slavery, was so immediately before their eyes. What is unusual, however, is that

Anglo Texans have held to these ideas more tenaciously and for longer than others, without seeing, one hopes, that historically they were the underpinnings of the doctrine of white supremacy.

More Freedom Requires Less Government

Many have wrestled with the singularity of Texas and how both Texans and others react to it. Two famous statements by Sam Houston, the dominant figure in Texas from independence to secession, show that the broad confidence that many have seen as hyperbole has surrounded Texas from its earliest days. Sam Houston's first appearance in Texas was widely thought to be as a scout for his close friend and political associate, President Andrew Jackson. In 1833, Houston wrote to Jackson, saying "I have travelled near five hundred miles across Texas, and am now enabled to judge pretty near correctly of the soil, and the resources of the Country, and I have no hesitancy in pronouncing it the finest country of its extent upon the globe."[29] This might be discounted as early Texas bluster, but his declaration that, "Texas could exist without the United States, but the United States cannot, except at very great hazard, exist without Texas," is uninterpretable outside of Texas.[30] What Houston meant—and Texas leaders from that day to this have shared variations on this vision—was that an independent Texas might expand westward to the Pacific faster or simply be so much more dynamic than the U.S., that it might displace it as the continent's dominant republic.

Houston's vision was of two Anglo republics sharing, uncomfortably, the continent, with the Texan Republic more dynamic, more energetic and aggressive, than its elder cousin. Anglo Texans knew the United States; it had been home for most of them. They viewed their new home as freer, more open, more entrepreneurially dynamic, and less burdened by government and regulation than the United States. U.S. President James K. Polk understood, if he did not fully share, this vision and acted to preempt it by welcoming Texas into the American Union. Anglo Texans entered the Union gratefully, aware that their decade of independence had been a struggle, but worried that being embedded in the United States might limit their ability to act at discretion—might limit their freedom.

The first settlers into Texas understood as clearly as any developer does today that land values and commercial opportunities hinged on population growth so they told tales of free land, rich soil, and unlimited opportunity. In the early decades of the Austin colony, the Republic, and statehood, these "tales shone the shimmering image of a fabulous empire, of broad vistas and plateaus where a man could see for miles, of barbaric Indians and millions of buffalo and cattle hardly less wild. This was a country where a man could be a man, and a good man could make himself a king. In these years a lasting legend was born."[31]

The early legends of a rich and expansive land open to domination by strong men was deepened into a founding myth by the events of the Texas Revolution. "Crockett at the Alamo" seems to "set the state's tone, capture its essence . . ., as an expression of the culture's fundamental values, or at least those that it wants to cultivate."[32] Don Graham, a Texana scholar at the University of Texas, reminds us that "the most frequent formulation of the Alamo's great theme is freedom."[33] The power of the "Alamo myth" is both in what it highlights and in what it leaves in shadow. It highlights Anglo sacrifice, courage, and determination. Free men, choosing death over escape, stand against tyranny until overwhelmed. Similarly, Houston's army, civilian recruits collected along the line of retreat, trained only haphazardly as the enemy closes in, astoundingly victorious in less than half an hour over a well-drilled but cowardly Mexican enemy at San Jacinto. Government is in the shadows, squabbling and ineffectual, in fact, barely present, as free men, almost spontaneously, carry the day.

Texas historian T.R. Fehrenbach sharpened this point by writing that, "Until this time," meaning 1835, "self-government in Texas had really meant the absence of government. In a province where everyone had land . . . no government was needed to clear the wilderness and plant cotton."[34] Anglo Texans might come together to confront danger, but when it passed, they adhered to a highly personal view of freedom. As the Englishman William Boellert wrote in 1842, "Their land costs them but little, . . . It is their own and their children's, no proud lord to look up to, no tythes or taxes, no game laws, and to use an American expression, 'One feels freed and one is free.'"[35] This sense of freedom, understandably, still appeals to many in Texas. When then-Governor Rick Perry was questioned in early 2013 about the possibility that Texas Democrats might become competitive as the Hispanic population increased, he rejected the possibility out of hand, saying, "It's because of freedom. People in Texas truly aspire to freedom. They don't want government coming in and telling them how much of this or how much of that. . . . Texans have never been for that, and Texans never will."[36]

For the first Anglo Texans, the fact that there were dangers about did not mean that strong government was needed for protection, it meant that men needed to be determined, even ruthless, in defense of their persons, property, and prospects. Historians Patrick Cox and Michael Phillips contend that, "During the early statehood years (1845–1860), the framers of the Texas Constitution intentionally created a weak central government in order to hamper dissent and ensure the rule of economic elites."[37] Minimizing government maximizes individual freedom and choice, especially for elites.

"We Pay No Taxes"

Like the American Revolution, the Texas Revolution began as a tax revolt.[38] By the early 1820s the Mexican government had concluded that populating its northern frontier would require opening it to Anglo-American settlers on attractive terms. Anglo *empresarios*, led by Stephen F. Austin, negotiated contracts permitting them to bring settlers in, distribute free or cheap land, and suspend taxes, usually for six to ten years, to get the settlement or colony started. Not surprisingly, Texans that paid no taxes in the early years were reluctant to begin paying taxes once the exemption period ended. The most heated anti-tax protests and, eventually, battles took place at Anahuac in the early 1830s. Anahuac was a Mexican town and fort responsible for collecting taxes on goods entering the Austin colony from the gulf. Jim Bowie and William B. Travis entered the Texas resistance to Mexican authority through the anti-tax protests at Anahuac.[39]

Even as tensions built between Texas and Mexican authorities, an Anglo East Texas land commissioner from Nacogdoches wrote in 1834: "Come what may I am convinced that Texas must prosper. We pay no taxes, work no public roads, get our land at cost, and perform no public duties of any kind."[40] Central to the Texas way, both in the early years and thereafter, has been a fierce individualism, free from taxes and public service, allowing men to concentrate on their own interests.

While Texas's decade of independent nationhood was financially troubled, with bankruptcy threatening particularly during President Mirabeau B. Lamar's term, the Republic depended on import fees, business fees, and a few luxury taxes. The terms of Texas's admission to the Union in December 1845 were highly favorable and brought badly needed financial relief. Five million dollars in Republic of Texas debts were assumed by the federal government and Texas retained title to all of its unsettled lands to offset its remaining debts. After admission to the Union, disputes over the boundaries between Texas, New Mexico, and Colorado, provided another opportunity for Texas to benefit. In the Boundary Act of 1850, Senator Sam Houston and the Texas congressional delegation agreed to limit Texas's claims in the Upper Rio Grande in exchange for a payment to the state of $10 million. Debts quickly devoured this $10 million, but a second payment of $7.5 million in 1855 as a final debt payment and reimbursement of state expenditures for frontier defense, left Texas not only debt free for the first time, but with a bankable surplus of $4 million.

Texas historians agree that this federal largesse allowed the state to limit its own tax efforts. George Garrison explained in *Texas: A Clash of Civilizations* (1903) that, "For the six years from 1852 to 1858 nearly all of the taxes collected in the State were given to the counties for local use, the expenses of the state government being paid meanwhile out of the indemnity received from the United States."[41] Fehrenbach quoted the prominent Texas historian Rupert Richardson noting that, "The advantages of such a condition are obvious, but the system may have worked injury as well as benefit. The people learned to look to outside sources rather than to taxation as the means of supporting their government and were not prepared for the day when windfalls would cease."[42] Carl Moneyhon, a noted historian of the Civil War and Reconstruction in Texas, weighed both the good and the bad of federal monies flowing to Texas. He wrote that, "prewar state government attempted to provide for the interests of local businessmen and farmers with minimal claims on their individual financial resources. The result was a tradition of limited public services in areas such as education or charity."[43]

When war came Texas was plunged back into debt. More shocking to Texans was the unprecedented taxing and spending of Governor Edmund J. Davis's Republican Reconstruction government. During Reconstruction, with many whites excluded from the electorate because they had served in the southern armies and governments, Davis and Republican majorities in the Texas House and Senate, elected on the votes of newly enfranchised blacks, increased spending for police and militia, expanded local governments, and provided free public education for all Texas children, black and white. Whites were outraged by armed black police and state militia and by paying taxes to educate black children. When white Democrats returned to power in the mid-1870s, after nearly a decade of U.S. Army and Republican Party rule, they slashed taxes and government, defunded the public schools, and returned control of most government activities to local elites. By 1900, Texas blacks had been moved to the periphery of society where the Civil War promises of equality and opportunity had little meaning.

The conservative "Establishment in Texas Politics," which George Norris Green described as "a loosely knit plutocracy comprised mostly of Anglo businessmen, oilmen, bankers, and lawyers . . . dedicated to a regressive tax structure, low corporate taxes, antilabor laws, political, social, and economic oppression of blacks and Mexican-Americans, alleged states' rights, and extreme reluctance to expand state services," governed Texas, with brief interludes, throughout the twentieth century.[44] Generations of elected political leaders, conservative Democrats and, more recently, Republicans, have eagerly done the establishment's bidding.[45]

The traditional establishment view still holds undisputed sway in Texas. Governor Rick Perry constantly cast Texas as an example to other states and to the federal government. At the Values Voters Conference in Washington in September 2009, Perry declared, "As a Texan, I'm understandably biased, but I think our whole country could use a dose of Texas-style fiscal discipline." In the days leading up to the opening of the

2017 Texas state Legislature, Governor Abbott acknowledged that there would be tight budgets and said, "Texans expect their government to live within its means, and I fully expect to sign a budget that does just that. As fiscal conservatives, we must treat our state budget the way families do—by funding our priorities, while constraining the size and growth of government."[46] Anglo Texans have always evinced an unwillingness to tax some to provide benefits to others. Independence, autonomy, and personal responsibility remain central to the Anglo Texan sense of self. These values also warned them to be alert to threats from beyond their own borders.

An Intrusive and Overbearing National Government

Texans have always believed that distant authority, whether in Mexico City, Washington, D.C., or even Austin, wished them ill out of greed, enmity, and a lust for power. In 1835, as tax protests built inexorably toward revolution, William B. Travis, soon to be fatally in command at the Alamo, wrote to David C. Burnet, soon to be interim president of the Republic of Texas, about the political and financial demands of the Mexican federal government. Travis said, "I wish to know, for whom do I labor— whether for myself or a *plundering* robbing, autocratical, aristocratical jumbled up govt."[47] As soon as Mexican authority was thrown off, Texans looked to the U.S., but warily, for protection. Republic of Texas President Sam Houston and most Texans favored annexation, but his successor, President Mirabeau B. Lamar and others, thought the Republic of Texas might find glory on its own. One of the very first histories of the Texas Revolution, Chester Newell's 1838 *History of the Revolution in Texas* warned of northern animus, saying "There is existing in the minds of the people in many places, if not generally, at the North, a strong and bitter prejudice against Texas."[48]

Southerners arrived in Texas well aware that Americans held conflicting views of federalism. Northerners generally thought in terms of union and southerners in terms of states' rights. Yet, even by southern standards, Texas has been prickly on issues of state sovereignty. While most states entered the Union after a period of territorial tutelage under rules established by Congress, Texas did not. A free-standing republic, Texas entered the Union almost as an equal after negotiations that produced favorable terms. T.R. Fehrenbach reports that as early as 1849, "Texans tended to resent all national interference."[49] From the beginning, Texas governors felt free to address U.S. presidents peremptorily.

> When Texans began to realize that statehood would not provide security, Acting Governor Horton informed President James Polk of the consequences: "The citizens of the frontier will protect themselves, and retaliate whenever occasion offers, and in a very short time a state of things will thus be brought about which will greatly retard, if not entirely defeat, the wish of the general government, to settle a boundary line between us and the Indians, or make any treaty with them."[50]

When the Civil War came, Texas unhesitatingly joined the Confederacy. The Confederacy was structured around state sovereignty and limited national power. Nonetheless, Confederate Senator William Simpson Oldham of Texas warned in March 1862 that, "The tendency to indoctrinate the people into the belief that there was no reliance in the State Government was the bane of the old republic, and would be, if not avoided, the bane of this."[51] Texas Confederate Governor Pendleton Murrah (1863–1865) complained regularly about "federal encroachment" by the Confederate government in Richmond on Texas prerogatives. The Texas aversion to national intrusion was deepened greatly by the Civil War and Reconstruction. Texans saw Reconstruction as harshly punitive treatment of the defeated South and they resisted the national government's dictates as stoutly and as long as any southern state. Abraham Lincoln's moderate program of Presidential Reconstruction was taken up by President Andrew Johnson after Lincoln's assassination in April 1865. Johnson, a former states' rights Democratic senator from Tennessee, followed Lincoln's inclination to "let the South up easy." Johnson issued a general amnesty to all southerners except high ranking political and military officials who were required to seek personal pardons. To regain full rights within the Union, including representation in Congress, southern state legislatures were required to ratify the Thirteenth Amendment abolishing slavery, repeal their secession acts, and repudiate debts incurred during the war. Texas was rankled even by these modest requirements and responded only grudgingly.

Though the war was lost and slavery was ended, southerners could not imagine simply treating the recently freed slaves as social, legal, and political equals, nor could they imagine investing in the educational and social services that would be required to close the gap between whites and blacks. Instead, southern legislatures passed laws barring blacks from suffrage and, through debtor and vagrancy laws, tying them to the land, often the land of their former owners. The plantation elite believed that they could not plant, tend, and pick the valuable cotton crop without black labor and blacks would not work without compulsion, which they meant to apply. The Republican U.S. Congress responded by seizing control of Reconstruction from President Johnson and instituting what came to be known in the South as Radical Reconstruction. Five military districts, including a district headquartered in Houston, were commanded by U.S. Army generals charged to oversee the construction and operation of loyal Republican state governments. Each state was required to grant suffrage to all adult men, black and white, except for legally excluded former rebels. Each state was also required to ratify the Fourteenth Amendment, granting citizenship and equality to blacks, prior to being readmitted to the Union. Only President Johnson's state of Tennessee ratified the Fourteenth Amendment. Every other southern state, including Texas, declined initially to do so.

By June 1868, six southern states—Alabama, Arkansas, Florida, Louisiana, North Carolina, and South Carolina—had reconsidered, ratified the Fourteenth Amendment, and regained admission to Congress. Not until 1870 did the final three states—Mississippi, Texas, and Virginia—ratify and regain their former status as fully enfranchised states. By this time, the Fifteenth Amendment, guaranteeing suffrage to black men, had to be ratified as well, which Texas did on February 18, 1870. President Ulysses S. Grant signed the Texas readmission bill in March 1870 and a newly elected civilian government took power in Texas on April 16, 1870.[52]

The Civil War and Reconstruction deepened the Texan sense that the national government short-changed it out of malice and perhaps hatred. Texans pushing the settlement line into Comanche territory in the 1870s believed the federal government provided an inadequate defense "out of anti-Texas prejudice, or hatred against the South."[53] To this day Texas politicians argue that national policies, especially during Democrat administrations, are designed to harm Texas with impunity and, perhaps, with secret glee. Former Republican U.S. Representative Henry Bonilla said that the Obama administration "just cannot stand that we're a successful red state." Republican Congressman Joe Barton, writing about Obama administration environmental programs, said "I think it offends the administration's sensibilities when ornery Texans go their own way and prosper by welcoming economic activity instead of chasing it away with federal style taxes and regulations."[54] Governor Rick Perry told a Republican women's group in Midland that, "This administration is interested in punishing Texas."[55]

Restoring the Traditional Order

Texans and other southerners knew that the federal government expended only modest and intermittent effort in restoring their security and economic vitality after the Civil War. Wrecks obstructed southern harbors and rivers for years and in some cases decades as an industrial boom drove population growth and wealth creation in the North. While the North grew wealthy, the energy of the southern elites was dedicated to a ruthless campaign to restore the traditional order of white supremacy. Between 1877 and 1950, almost 4,000 blacks were lynched across the South, 344 of them in Texas. The violence peaked in the 1880s and again in the 1920s and only began clearly to wane in the 1930s.[56]

The Anglo elites of the thickly populated areas of East and Central Texas struggled to turn back the social, political, and economic changes forced upon them by Reconstruction. Confederate Colonel William Stewart Simkins, a Ku Klux Klan leader in Florida after the war and later a prominent professor in the University of Texas Law School, spoke for many white Texans when he wrote that the Freedman's Bureau and Reconstruction more generally "were intended to humiliate the South, enforce the anticipated Civil Rights laws, the germ of which was social equality." Soldiers of the United States, he complained, obeyed the orders of the Bureau in order to "assist in crushing the pride of the South by the elevation of the Negro to political control."[57]

Anglo Texans treated the very idea of black equality as deeply humiliating. They could not conceive how blacks could rise if whites did not fall. How could the bottom rail be on top, in the phrase of the day, unless the top rail went to the bottom? In response, Simkins wrote, "arose the 'Invisible Empire' . . . composed of the best young men of the land, soldiers of the Southern army, . . . now as fearless in their duty as they had been in the war."[58] Klan violence was supplemented beginning in the late 1870s, following the end of Reconstruction, when public authority could be used, or misused, directly to limit black social, political, and economic activity. Cox and Phillips report that, "In 1896, forty [white] Democrats in Robertson County [just north of Bryan and College Station] held rifles while surrounding the courthouse to block entrance by black voters. The county judge later wrote, 'I went down to the polls and took my six-shooter. I stayed there until the polls closed. Not a negro voted.'"[59]

As the new century dawned, conservative Democrats moved to legally limit the electorate to its most dependable Anglo elements. In 1902 Texas voters instituted a poll tax aimed principally at blacks but impacting many Hispanics and poor whites as well. The Terrill election law required the poll tax to be paid six months before the primary and nine months before the general election, well before campaigns heated up and potential voters began to pay attention. The law also encouraged all-white primaries at the county level and put additional hurdles in the way of third parties seeking access to the ballot. Voter turnout fell by half to two-thirds from its highpoint in the mid-1890s.[60] Amy Bridges' classic study of municipal reform in the Southwest in the first half of the twentieth century concluded that, "In Texas, racial segregation was an organizing principle of social life and urban planning; disenfranchisement of African-Americans and Mexican-Americans the goal of much legislation limiting access to the ballot; the white primary the foundation of one-party politics."[61]

The poll tax and the white primary reduced black turnout to scattered urban precincts during the early decades of the twentieth century. Voting by what prominent mid-century political scientist V.O. Key called "unsponsored" Hispanics also was actively and effectively discouraged. Key noted "a markedly lower voter participation in the counties with large numbers of Mexican-Americans than in other comparable counties. . . . In many counties, unsponsored individual Mexican-Americans meet a barrier to the ballot similar in character if not in degree to that which discourages Negro voting in most of the South."[62]

The traditional social order was fully restored during the first quarter of the twentieth century. Jim Crow segregation was law, blacks were barred from the Democratic primary, and even progressive political reforms were progressive only for whites. The goal of progressive reform in Texas and the South was governance by educated and propertied elites. Texas was battered and beaten, military defeat and occupation still fresh in memory, but again securely under the management of its traditional Anglo elites.

But where exactly did Texas stand in relation to her sister states as the "Roaring 20s" gave way to the 1930s and what would become the Great Depression? Interestingly, 1930 saw one of the first systematic attempts to compare the states to each other on a wide range of economic, social, cultural, and political dimensions. H.L. Mencken, the leading political commentator and social critic of the day, and his colleague Charles Angoff at the *American Mercury* drew on the 1930 *Statistical Abstract of the United States* and dozens of other sources to compare the 48 states and the District of Columbia. They were assisted and advised by professors S.H. Hobbs of the University of North Carolina, Chapel Hill, and James M. Chalfont of Ohio State University. Mencken and Angoff presented 105 tables, 30 ranking all 48 states and D.C. and the remainder presenting the top ten and bottom ten states. The article, provocatively titled "The Worst American State," appeared in three parts in the September, October, and November 1931 issues of the *American Mercury*. Table 1.1 was the summary table, which appeared as Table 72 in the November issue on page 356, ranking the states on the broad dimensions of wealth, education, health, and public safety, plus an overall rank. Somewhat ominously, Texas and South Dakota did not present sufficient data on public safety to be ranked on that dimension. Texas's overall rank was 39. Texas ranked above most of the other southern states, but below the rest of the states. Keep this ranking in mind, because, as we shall see in subsequent chapters, it has not changed much in the more than eight decades since 1930.

The Great Depression: Liberal Action and Conservative Reaction

The state rankings presented in Table 1.1 should not come as a great shock. Throughout the 1930s, the years of the Great Depression, Texas remained a poor, rural, and agricultural state. No one knew this better than Texans themselves and they were searching for ways to bring change. On June 7, 1935, the *Austin American-Statesman* offered an editorial, entitled "Why Not Development of Manufactures?" explaining that "Texas is an agricultural state, . . . but the fact remains that the industrial states of America are the wealthy states, and powerful."[63]

Though the discovery of major new oil fields in East and West Texas softened the Depression's blows, regular Texans suffered greatly. Much of rural Texas still lacked basic services such as electricity, flood control, and decent roads. As Chandler Davidson has noted, "The great causes of the New Deal in Texas included rural electrification, which brought electricity to farm families; banking regulation; Social Security, . . . unemployment insurance; public works projects, . . . home mortgage guarantees; . . . and welfare measures."[64]

Texans in Washington were deeply involved in moving New Deal legislation through Congress, though some had misgivings. Uvalde's John Nance "Cactus Jack"

Table 1.1 The Relative Standing of the States in 1930

Rank	Wealth	Education	Health	Public Order	Aver. Rank
1	California	Massachusetts	Minnesota	Maine	Massachusetts
2	Connecticut	D.C.	Massachusetts	Vermont	Connecticut
3	New York	California	New York	New Hampshire	New York
4	D.C.	Connecticut	Connecticut	Massachusetts	New Jersey
5	Massachusetts	Michigan	Iowa	Rhode Island	California
6	Illinois	Colorado	Oregon	Connecticut	D.C.
7	Nevada	Utah	New Jersey	New Jersey	Minnesota
8	New Jersey	Illinois	Illinois	Wisconsin	Iowa
9	Rhode Island	New York	Nebraska	Minnesota	Illinois
10	Pennsylvania	Oregon	Washington	Iowa	Oregon
11	Ohio	Washington	New Hampshire	New York	Rhode Island
12	Michigan	Iowa	Pennsylvania	North Dakota	Michigan
13	Washington	Nevada	Wisconsin	Utah	Maine
14	Minnesota	Ohio	Rhode Island	Oregon	Washington
15	Delaware	Indiana	Wyoming	Michigan	Wisconsin
16	Colorado	Wisconsin	California	Pennsylvania	New Hampshire
17	Oregon	Minnesota	Michigan	D.C.	Ohio
18	Iowa	New Jersey	D.C.	Nebraska	Nebraska
19	Maryland	Rhode Island	Vermont	Ohio	Utah
20	Wisconsin	Missouri	Kansas	California	Kansas
21	Maine	Montana	Utah	Delaware	Pennsylvania
22	Nebraska	Maine	North Dakota	Washington	Vermont
23	Indiana	Nebraska	Ohio	Indiana	Colorado
24	New Hampshire	Kansas	Missouri	Kansas	Indiana
25	Kansas	Maryland	Idaho	Illinois	Nevada
26	Vermont	Pennsylvania	Maine	Idaho	Delaware
27	Missouri	New Hampshire	Indiana	Maryland	Missouri
28	Montana	Vermont	Colorado	Missouri	Maryland
29	Wyoming	Wyoming	Nevada	Colorado	North Dakota
30	Arizona	Delaware	Maryland	West Virginia	Wyoming
31	Utah	South Dakota	Montana	North Carolina	Montana
32	South Dakota	Oklahoma	Delaware	Virginia	Idaho
33	Florida	Idaho	West Virginia	Louisiana	South Dakota
34	North Dakota	Arizona	South Dakota	New Mexico	West Virginia
35	New Mexico	North Dakota	Oklahoma	Oklahoma	Arizona
36	Idaho	Florida	Florida	Montana	Oklahoma
37	West Virginia	**Texas**	Kentucky	Wyoming	Florida
38	Virginia	West Virginia	Arkansas	Arizona	Virginia
39	**Texas**	Virginia	**Texas**	Florida	**Texas**
40	Kentucky	Kentucky	Virginia	Kentucky	New Mexico
41	Oklahoma	Tennessee	Arizona	South Carolina	Kentucky
42	Tennessee	New Mexico	Louisiana	Arkansas	Louisiana
43	North Carolina	North Carolina	Georgia	Tennessee	North Carolina
44	Louisiana	Louisiana	Tennessee	Alabama	Tennessee
45	Georgia	South Carolina	New Mexico	Nevada	Arkansas
46	Alabama	Georgia	North Carolina	Georgia	Georgia
47	South Carolina	Arkansas	Alabama	Mississippi	South Carolina
48	Arkansas	Alabama	Mississippi		Alabama
49	Mississippi	Mississippi	South Carolina		Mississippi

Source: Charles Angoff and H.L. Mencken, "The Worst American State," *American Mercury*, vol. 24, no. 93, September–November, 1931, pp. 1–16, 175–188, 355–371.

Garner was the Democratic Minority Leader in the House in 1929 and Majority Leader after the Democrats took control in the 1930 midterm elections. Before Garner left Congress to serve as Roosevelt's vice president from 1933 to 1941, he groomed other Texans for leadership. Bonham's Sam Rayburn became the Democratic majority leader in 1937 and speaker of the house in 1940. Seven other Texas Democrats chaired House committees during some or all of the 1930s; Hatton Sumners of Dallas chaired the powerful Judiciary Committee from 1931 to 1947; Marvin Jones of Amarillo chaired the Agriculture Committee from 1931 to 1940; Joe Mansfield of Eagle Lake chaired the Rivers and Harbors Committee from 1931 to 1947; James Buchanan of Brenham served as chair of the critical Appropriations Committee from 1933 until his death in 1937; and a young Lyndon Johnson worked closely with Chairman Buchanan on rural electrification issues.

The modest resources of Texas state government were quickly overwhelmed by the Depression and state leaders had little choice but to look to Washington for help. As Randolph Campbell explains,

> Wanting relief and recovery for their state, they took federal aid but tended . . . to reject the underlying philosophy of big government and collective social responsibility. They spoke more and more often of threats to states' rights, disliked the increased spending necessitated by social welfare programs, objected to legislation that favored labor unions, and opposed even the discussion of civil rights and antilynching laws. . . . In the long run, the political and social conservatism of most leading Texans could not fully accommodate the New Deal.[65]

George Norris Green added that "New Deal legislation fostered liberalism, in fact, but in Texas and the rest of the South, it also generated a tremendous counterreaction among the monied interests."[66] Texas oilmen funded and led this reaction. Bryan Burrough has written that "conservative fury was fueled by a fear of what is known today as 'big government,' . . . Texas oilmen shared a deep loathing of taxes, labor organizers, and anyone who looked to change their ways."[67] Sam Rayburn described a broader anti-New Deal alignment in a December 4, 1933, letter to William P. Hobby, an old friend, former governor, and leading member of the Houston business community. Rayburn wrote, "Some of our people want everything static and always preach that any movement that goes forward is socialistic and destructive. The movement at this time seems to be led by the U.S. Chamber of Commerce and the large city bankers. . . . [T]heir selfish interests do not quite fit in with the interests of the average man."[68]

Even in the depths of the Depression, when the need across Texas was acknowledged to be great, conservative elected officials in Austin and Washington were wary. In January 1935, as the Texas Senate debated accepting federal aid, Senator T.J. Holbrook of Galveston, "bitterly assailed the proposals . . . Property rights and indeed personal liberty were at stake. . . . These are socialistic programs," he warned his colleagues. In Washington, Texas leaders voiced similar concerns and pointed to even more dire threats. In January 1936, Texas Senator Wilbert Lee "Pappy" O'Daniel opposed federal employment policy as "purely communistic," adding "and I should not be surprised to learn that it originally came from Moscow." The following year, Texas Congressman Martin Dies opposed FDR's minimum wage legislation as a threat to the southern social order, saying, "There is a racial question here, . . . And you cannot prescribe the same wage for the black man as for the white man."[69]

The New Deal strained the Texas Democratic Party to, and eventually beyond, breaking point. Though Rayburn and Johnson generally stuck with Roosevelt, the court packing debate of 1937 proved too much for Garner and Sumners. Upon returning from one White House meeting with Roosevelt on the court packing bill, Sumners famously said to his congressional colleagues, "Boys, this is where I cash in." The novelist Phillipp Meyer again captured the concern of Texas elites over the threat posed by federal overreach. The fictional Eli McCullough, patron of a South Texas ranch comparable to the vast King and Kenedy ranches, observed to his daughter in 1937; "It's this goddamn Roosevelt. . . . You mark my words, that was the last free election we will ever see in this country. We are on the verge of a dictatorship."[70]

Texas conservatives worked hard to maintain the old social and economic orders. That traditional order required cheap and willing labor. As late as 1943, amid race riots in the Galveston shipyards and a threat by the Mexican government to suspend the "Bracero program" over pervasive discrimination in South Texas, Governor Coke Stevenson was asked by the U.S. State Department to join in a Good Neighbor Commission designed to ease tensions. Stevenson agreed, observing that "Meskins is pretty good folks. If it was niggers, it'd be different."[71] To insure that white labor remained cheap too, Texas passed the Manford Act in 1943, the first state law to use the phrase "right to work." Several other southern and western states followed suit almost immediately and another set of anti-union laws were passed by the legislature and signed by Governor Beauford Jester in 1947. Right-to-work laws forbid the union closed shop, whereby a worker must join the union if hired into a union shop. Giving the worker a choice of whether to join or not is presented as an element of individual rights and personal freedom, but it weakens unions by giving workers the option of saving the union dues and free-riding on those who do pay dues.

Texas white workers, especially those in the rural areas, were just as tractable and easily managed as the establishment could have wished. In 1946, LBJ was campaigning in Brenham, east of Austin, and was introduced to the crowd by a local lumberman and cotton dealer. LBJ's speech was not as memorable as the local leader's description of the needs and expectations of Brenham's citizens. He explained that, "We are a lot of simple people here in Washington County. We don't ask much from our government. We really want to be let alone if we can be. We need a little money . . . not as much as some people, but we don't like a lot of giveaway programs. . . . All we ask is forty-cent cotton and ten-cent beer."[72] One suspects that this local leader might have underestimated the needs of the common people of Washington County, but it is also clear that he and they knew that their needs did not move the state's politics.

Governors Coke Stevenson, Beauford Jester, and Allan Shivers presided over the heyday of the restored conservative establishment in Texas. Former Governor W. Lee "Pappy" O'Daniel, then sitting in the U.S. Senate, led the conservative Texas Regulars to adopt their own platform for the 1944 elections. Their platform promised "a return to states' rights 'which have been destroyed by the Communist-controlled New Deal,' and 'a restoration of the supremacy of the white race.'"[73] Senator O'Daniel warned that wartime rationing was "a Communistic, totalitarian measure designed to beat the people of the US into submitting to the edicts of an autocratic, bureaucratic dictatorship."[74]

World War II brought the U.S. and Texas out of the Depression and changed both, but particularly Texas, forever. World War II made Texas an urban and industrial state. The war machine ran on oil and Texas had discovered massive new quantities of it in the 1920s and 1930s. During the war, "Dallas and Houston boomed. The demand for jet fuel and all manner of chemicals led to the building of dozens of new refineries and chemical plants along the coast south and east of Houston."[75] The military and aerospace industries, drawn by the dry climate, clear skies, and cheap land, moved to Texas in a big way, confirming San Antonio's history as a military town. And Texas companies, most notably Houston's Brown & Root, grew wealthy on military contracts. Brown & Root, a modest road building company in 1935, rose with Lyndon Johnson. "That Brown & Root could grow fat on a steady diet of cost-plus [meaning guaranteed profit margins] government contracts and at the same time defy organized labor as Socialistic" would surprise no one familiar with the Texas establishment.[76] Brown & Root later became Halliburton.

By mid-century, the Anglo elite, led by three-term Texas Governor Allan Shivers, was determined to battle the "trend to the left that is carrying us swiftly toward socialism in many forms and guises."[77] For many Texas conservatives, "the line between New Deal liberalism and socialism was thin, if it even existed at all, while the line between socialism and communism was only one of gradation."[78] The rest of the nation watched this Texas establishment rebellion against Washington and its liberal politics with amazement and not a little trepidation. John Gunther's tour of the post–World War II United States, entitled *Inside U.S.A.* (1947), was a generally light-hearted summary of the major figures, party divisions, and issues in each state. In Texas, Gunther was jolted by the intensity of the anti-Roosevelt sentiment, saying, "Nowhere in the United States, not even on Wall Street . . . did I find such a perfervid hatred for Mr. Roosevelt as in Texas. . . . I met with men who had been unfalteringly convinced that if FDR won again [in 1944], 'it would mean that the Mexicans and niggers would take us over.' This kind of passion makes for ruthlessness."[79] In fact, this reputation for passion fueling ruthlessness came to characterize the nation's view of Texas from the late 1930s through the Kennedy assassination and beyond.

Conclusion

"The Texas way," while by no means unchanging, has evinced a core set of principles since Anglo settlers first arrived in Texas. They remain recognizable today. The slave republic that Jared Groce, Stephen F. Austin, and Sam Houston founded reflected their social ideals. Plantation owners commanded all that they surveyed; they owned broad swaths of prime land and the people who worked it. They provided direction and discipline on their lands and were subject to few external checks. They commanded and were granted respect and deference. They were the leading men of the community and its governing class.

They only grudgingly recognized the need for government, to manage and distribute the public lands, secure order, protect property, facilitate commerce, and provide defense against external threats. Government should be strong enough to protect their interests and serve their needs, but not to dictate to them. To ensure that government fulfilled its proper role, it should be peopled by the intelligent tax-paying citizens of the community, its acknowledged elite. The clear interest of the elite was that government should protect their social primacy and their property at as little cost to them as possible. If others had needs, for education for their children, for example, let them buy as much of it as they desired and could afford. If taxes were to be levied to provide these services, then those who wanted the services should pay the taxes.

The Texas way has always highlighted individualism, small government, low taxes, and a states' rights interpretation of federalism. Individualism has always meant personal autonomy and responsibility for one's self and one's family. Initially, individualism was meant only for white men, but increasingly it has been applied to others, especially in the form of individual responsibility. The social and economic elites of Texas have always argued that small government and low taxes allow wealth to be enjoyed by those who created it, rather than taken from them by a too powerful government. While this is attractive to the poor who dream of becoming wealthy, it is really attractive to those who are already wealthy and eager to keep what they have.

History, culture, and tradition—most profoundly the Civil War and Reconstruction—continue to shape Texas, its people, and their responses to the political, social, and economic issues of the day. Most Texans, especially the elites, have long viewed American federalism as based on state sovereignty rather than national supremacy. Texas against federal intrusion has been an enduring theme of the state's politics. Texas independence, state boundaries, frontier defense, social spending during the Depression, civil rights, the recent economic stimulus and health care programs, were all cast as foreign or federal intrusions on the rights and prerogatives of the sovereign state of Texas.

In the next chapter, we ask how well or poorly the founding ideals and assumptions of Texas's first century have fared in recent decades. How does Texas compare to its sister states? Is Texas wealthier or poorer than most other states, better educated or less well educated, healthier or sicker, safer or more vulnerable? In later chapters, we look in some detail at the evolution of Texas public policy in regard to the economy, job creation, income, and wealth; public and higher education; social services such as welfare and health care; crime, punishment, and prisons; as well as transportation and the environment.

Notes

1 Noah Smithwick, *The Evolution of a State or Recollections of Old Texas Days*, Austin, TX: University of Texas Press, 1985, pp. 8–9, 48.

2 Gregg Cantrell, *Stephen F. Austin: Empresario of Texas*, New Haven, CT: Yale University Press, 1999, p. 178.

3 The Diary of William Fairfax Gray, from Virginia to Texas, 1835–1837, see http://sites.sme.edu/swcenter/FairfaxGray/wg_136.htm. See also p. 137.

4 Rutherford B. Hayes, *Diary and Letters of Rutherford B. Hayes, the Nineteenth President of the United States*, Columbus, OH: The Ohio State Archeological and Historical Society, 1922–1926, 1: 254.

5 Richard Parker, *Lone Star Nation: How Texas Will Transform America*, New York: Pegasus Books, 2014, pp. 24–25.

6 T.R. Fehrenbach, *Seven Keys to Texas*, El Paso, TX: Texas Western Press, 1983, p. 6.

7 D.W. Meinig, *Imperial Texas: An Interpretive Essay in Cultural Geography*, Austin, TX: University of Texas Press, 1969, p. 89. More recently, see David G. McComb, *Texas: A Modern History*, revised edition, Austin, TX: University of Texas Press, 2010, p. 149.

8 W.W. Newcomb Jr., *The Indians of Texas*, Austin, TX: University of Texas Press, 1961, p. 338.

9 Sean P. Cunningham, *Cowboy Conservatism: Texas and the Rise of the Modern Right*, Lexington, KY: University Press of Kentucky, 2010, p. 125; summarizing Leigh Clemons, *Branding Texas: Performing Culture in the Lone Star State*, Austin, TX: University of Texas Press, 2008.

10 N. Doran Maillard, *The History of the Republic of Texas*, London: Smith, Elder and Company, 1842, p. 205.

11 Billy D. Ledbetter, "White Over Black in Texas: Racial Attitudes in the Antebellum Period," *Phylon*, vol. 34, no. 4, 4th quarter, 1973, p. 406.

12 Wilbur Zelinsky, *The Cultural Geography of the United States*, Englewood Cliffs, NJ: Prentice-Hall, 1973, pp. 13–14. See also David McRaney, "How Your Address Changes Your Politics," *Politico*, August 2, 2015.

13 Randolph B. Campbell, "Statehood, Civil War, and Reconstruction, 1846–1876," pp. 174–175, in Walter L. Buenger and Robert A. Calvert, ed., *Texas Through Time: Evolving Interpretation*, College Station, TX: Texas A&M University Press, 1991.

14 Meinig, *Imperial Texas*, p. 47. Fehrenbach, *Seven Keys*, pp. 4–5. See also, Chad R. Trulson and James R. Marquardt, *First Available Cell: Desegregation of the Texas Prison System*, Austin, TX: University of Texas Press, 2009, p. 15.

15 Michael Lind, *Made in Texas: George W. Bush and the Takeover of American Politics*, New York: Basic Books, 2003, p. 26.

16 Carl H. Moneyhon, *Republicanism in Reconstruction Texas*, College Station, TX: Texas A&M University Press, 1980, p. 12.

17 David Montejano, *Anglos and Mexicans in the Making of Texas, 1836–1986*, Austin, TX: University of Texas Press, 1987, p. 5. See also, Ledbetter, "White Over Black in Texas," p. 406.

18 Gary Clinton Anderson, *The Conquest of Texas: Ethnic Cleansing in the Promised Land, 1820–1875*, Norman: University of Oklahoma Press, 2005, p. 41.

19 Meinig, *Imperial Texas*, pp. 48, 50.

20 Robert A. Calvert, Arnoldo De León, and Gregg Cantrell, *The History of Texas*, 4th ed., Wheeling, IN: Harlan Davidson and Co., 2007, p. 115.

21 Randolph B. Campbell, *An Empire for Slavery: The Peculiar Institution in Texas, 1821–1865*, Baton Rouge, LA: Louisiana State University Press, 1989, pp. 222–223. Italics added by the author.

22 James McEnteer, *Deep in the Heart: The Texas Tendency in American Politics*, Westport, CT: Praeger, 2004, p. 44.

23 McEnteer, *Deep in the Heart*, p. 5.

24 Calvert et al., *The History of Texas*, 4th ed., p. 175.

25 Robert Wuthnow, *Rough Country: How Texas Became America's Most Powerful Bible-Belt State*, Princeton, NJ: Princeton University Press, 2014, p. 8.

26 C. Vann Woodward, *The Burden of Southern History*, New York: Vintage Books, 1960, p. 105; Fred Arthur Bailey, "Free Speech and the 'Lost Cause' in Texas: A Study of Social Control in the New South," *Southwestern Historical Quarterly*, vol. 97, no. 3, January 1994, pp. 452–477, see page 454.

27 T.R. Fehrenbach, *Lone Star: A History of Texas and the Texans*, New York: Macmillan, 1968, p. 633.

28 Phillipp Meyer, *The Son: A Novel*, New York: Harper Collins, 2013, p. 499. See also, Campbell, "Statehood, Civil War, and Reconstruction," pp. 174–175.

29 Fehrenbach, *Lone Star*, p. 219.

30 James Conaway, *The Texans*, New York: Alfred A. Knopf, 1976, p. 241.

31 Fehrenbach, *Lone Star*, p. 132.

32 Milton Ezrati, "Just What Is It About Texas?" *Antioch Review*, vol. 62, no. 4, Autumn 2004, pp. 754–773, at 756.

33 Don Graham, "Remembering the Alamo: The Story of the Texas Revolution in Popular Culture," *Southwestern Historical Quarterly*, vol. 89, no. 1, July 1985, p. 48.

34 Fehrenbach, *Lone Star*, p. 198.

35 William Bollaert, *William Bollaert's Texas*, Norman, OK: University of Oklahoma Press, 1956, p. 109.

36 Jonathan Tilove, *Austin American-Statesman* blog, February 25, 2013.

37 Patrick Cox and Michael Phillips, *The House Will Come to Order*, Austin, TX: University of Texas Press, 2010, pp. 10–11.

38 Arica Grieder, *Big, Hot, Cheap, and Right*, New York: Public Affairs, 2013, p. 99.

39 George Pierce Garrison, *Texas: A Contest of Civilizations*, New York: Houghton-Mifflin, 1903, pp. 153–154, 156, 175.

40 Fehrenbach, *Lone Star*, p. 166; Meinig, *Imperial Texas*, p. 34.

41 Garrison, *Texas: A Contest of Civilizations*, p. 270.

42 Fehrenbach, *Lone Star*, p. 278.

43 Moneyhon, *Republicanism in Reconstruction Texas*, p. 8.

44 George Norris Green, *The Establishment in Texas Politics: The Primitive Years, 1938–1957*, Norman, OK: University of Oklahoma Press, 1979, p. 17.

45 Chandler Davidson, *Race and Class in Texas Politics*, Princeton, NJ: Princeton University Press, 1990, p. 188.

46 Sean Collins Walch, "State Lawmakers Face Likely Budget Cuts," *Austin American-Statesman*, January 9, 2017.

47 William C. Davis, *Lone Star Rising: The Revolutionary Birth of the Republic of Texas*, New York: Free Press, 2004, p. 125.

48 Chester Newell, *History of the Revolution in Texas*, New York: Wiley and Putnam, 1838, quoted in McLemore, *Inventing Texas*, p. 32.
49 Fehrenbach, *Lone Star*, p. 275.
50 James R. Arnold, *Jeff Davis's Own: Cavalry, Comanches, and the Battle for the Texas Frontier*, Edison, NJ: Castle Books, 2007, p. 63.
51 Michael Lind, *Land of Promise: An Economic History of the United States*, New York: Harper Collins, 2012, p. 131.
52 J. David Woodard, *The New Southern Politics*, Boulder, CO: Lynne Rienner Publishers, 2006, pp. 129–132.
53 Fehrenbach, *Lone Star*, p. 529.
54 Joe Barton, "Texas vs. Obama's Overreaching EPA," *Dallas Morning News*, June 21, 2010, p. A11.
55 Christy Hoppe, "Are Feds Punishing Our State?" *Dallas Morning News*, May 3, 2010, A1, A5. See also Christy Hoppe, "Texas Ties Up Feds in Court," *Dallas Morning News*, March 24, 2012, pp. A1, A13.
56 Equal Justice Institute, "Lynching in America: Confronting the Legacy of Racial Terror," 2nd ed. eji.org/sites/default/files/lynching-in-america-second-edition-summary.pdf.
57 Thomas D. Russell, "Keep the Negroes Out of Most Classes Where There Are a Large Number of Girls," https://papers.ssrn.com/sol3/papers.cfm?abstract_id=1583606.
58 Ibid., pp. 3–4.
59 Cox and Phillips, *The House Will Come to Order*, p. 18. See also, Campbell, *Gone to Texas*, p. 336. An early version of this story can be found in Martin, *The People's Party in Texas*, pp. 138–139.
60 Davidson, *Race and Class in Texas Politics*, pp. 20–21. See also, Jonathan Tilove, "How Should a 1910 East Texas Massacre be Remembered?" *Austin American-Statesman*, December 27, 2014.
61 Amy Bridges, *Morning Glories: Municipal Reform in the Southwest*, Princeton, NJ: Princeton University Press, 1997, p. 20. See also, Calvert, *History of Texas*, pp. 240–241.
62 V.O. Key, *Southern Politics*, New York: Alfred A. Knopf, 1949, pp. 272–273.
63 Anthony M. Orum, *Power, Money, and People: The Making of Modern Austin*, Eugene, OR: Resources Publications, 1987, pp. 44–45.
64 Davidson, *Race and Class in Texas Politics*, p. 28.
65 Randolph B. Campbell, *Gone to Texas: A History of the Lone Star State*, New York: Oxford University Press, 2003, p. 392.
66 Green, *The Establishment in Texas Politics*, p. 15.
67 Bryan Burrough, *The Big Rich: The Rise and Fall of the Greatest Texas Oil Fortunes*, New York: Penguin Press, 2009, pp. 126–127.
68 D.B. Hardeman and Donald C. Bacon, *Rayburn: A Biography*, New York: Madison Books, 1987, p. 161.
69 Ira Katznelson, *Fear Itself: The New Deal and the Origins of Our Time*, New York: W.W. Norton, 2013, pp. 189, 177.
70 Meyer, *The Son*, p. 145.
71 Green, *The Establishment in Texas Politics*, p. 81.
72 James Reston Jr., *The Lone Star: The Life of John Connally*, New York: Harper and Row, 1989, p. 120.
73 McEnteer, *Deep in the Heart*, p. 82.
74 Cunningham, *Cowboy Conservatism*, p. 28.
75 Lind, *Land of Promise*, pp. 317–318. See also, Burrough, *The Big Rich*, p. 154.
76 Conaway, *The Texans*, p. 92.
77 Morehead, *50 Years in Texas Politics*, p. 104.
78 Cunningham, *Cowboy Conservatism*, p. 43.
79 John Gunther, *Inside U.S.A.*, New York: Harper and Brothers, 1947, p. 844.

2 Texas: The Myth vs. the Reality

> Like most passionate nations, Texas has its own private history, based on, but not
> limited by, facts.
>
> (John Steinbeck, 1962)[1]

In Chapter 1, we drew on the best evidence from history and the social sciences to
describe the political culture, the basic or fundamental values, of Texas. The goal was to
show the consistency with which Anglo Texans have held to the values of small government, low taxes, light regulation, thin social services, personal responsibility, and elite
leadership from first settlement into the mid-twentieth century. Throughout the state's
history, Anglo leaders have argued that these commitments—which many have called
"the Texas way"—have made Texas a singularly open, vibrant, and dynamic place.
Some even argue that standing by these commitments, while others have flagged, has
made Texas the last refuge of freedom, opportunity, and the American dream. When
Texas Anglo leaders praised Texas as a model for her sister states and the nation, they
did not mean that Texas was the richest state, or the state with the best education or health
care systems. They meant that Texas was the most "business-friendly" state in the nation
because it was the state where independence, freedom, and opportunity still reigned.

Nor is the next generation of Texas conservatives likely to take a different tone.
In November 2014, George P. Bush, nephew of former President George W. Bush
and grandson of former President George H.W. Bush, easily won his first political
race to become Texas Land Commissioner. In his January 2015 inaugural remarks,
Bush declared that, "Texas isn't just some random place on the map . . . . It's an
idea—. . . That people can go as far and as fast as their dreams can take them, . . . that
government should work for us, not against us."[2]

In this and later chapters, we confront these claims not just with additional historical interpretation, but with the best objective data available. In this chapter, we begin
by showing in stark geographical and population density terms that Texas has been a
southern state throughout its history. Then we turn to a quick overview of how Texas
compares to the nation and to the other 49 states on standard measures of population and job growth, income, educational attainment, access to health care and social
services, crime and punishment, taxes and public spending, and much more. We confront the Texas myth, the story that Texas Anglo leaders love to tell, with the reality,
the results and outcomes, of Texas public policy. Our goal is to assess the costs and
benefits, historically and going forward, of "the Texas way." What are the pros and
cons—the trade-offs—of pursuing a small government vision that necessitates lower
spending on education and other social services than most other states?

The Cultural Foundations of the Lone Star Nation

Most analysts agree that the traditional political culture of the South is the foundation of the Texas political culture, but many see elements of Western individualism as well. Others see a changing Texas political culture driven by the state's dramatic twentieth-century transition from a poor, rural, agricultural past to a more prosperous, urban, industrial, high-tech, and service economy present. Perhaps, but if the Texas political culture has changed, we would expect to see Texas public policy change as well. In fact, Texas public policy has not responded to the evolution of the state. This suggests that the traditional political culture of Texas's rural past has shaped its urban present much more than most Texans realize or would like to admit.

Texas's southern roots were never in question during the nineteenth century. From the initial settlement of the Austin colony through the post–Civil War exodus of southern whites to Texas, the state's population stock and its political and social instincts were overwhelmingly southern. As we saw in Chapter 1, Wilbur Zelinsky's "Doctrine of First Settlement" contends that first settlers lay down the social, political, economic, and cultural matrices into which later arrivals must fit. Over the course of the nineteenth century, more than nine in ten Texans were born in the South or born in Texas of southern stock. Yet, as the nineteenth century turned into the twentieth, Texas elites grew increasingly concerned that the Civil War left that strong southern connection tainted with treason, defeat, and military occupation. This was, of course, true of all of the Confederate states, but, unlike the states of the deep South—South Carolina, Alabama, Mississippi, and others—Texas leaders came to think they had a way to blur if not blot out the state's history.

Beginning in the late nineteenth century, some Texas cultural leaders, abetted by generations of Texas historians, sought to expunge the memory of the Civil War, the Old South, and its failed defense of slavery by refocusing attention on the Texas Revolution as an iconic moment in the great westward advance of Anglo civilization and freedom. They believed that Texas could much more comfortably and profitably be defined in relation to Manifest Destiny, the winning of the West, and the fight for liberty and freedom at the Alamo and San Jacinto than with slavery, the Civil War, and memories of the Lost Cause. The desire to recast or redesign Texas history produced a long—even unending—debate over whether Texas was a southern, a western, or distinctively southwestern state.

The broad outlines of this debate were drawn in the new University of Texas Department of History (initially the Department of English and History). The University of Texas opened its doors in the fall of 1883 and the Georgia-born historian George P. Garrison joined the faculty in 1884. Garrison became chairman of the History Department when it separated from English in 1888 and he remained chairman until his death in 1910. Garrison's prominent book, *Westward Extension: 1841–1850* (1906), argued that Texas history was a major chapter in the winning of the West. Charles William Ramsdell joined the History Department in 1906 and published his *Reconstruction in Texas* in 1910. Ramsdell "argued that Texas had southern moorings, which made the state socially and culturally part of the South."[3]

Generations of Texas historians lined up behind Garrison or Ramsdell to battle over the best description of the state's cultural roots. Increasingly, the state's social and political leadership came to see Garrison's western view as the most congenial. Though modern historians are increasingly insistent on Ramsdell's view that "Texas had southern moorings," the Texas establishment was unmoved because "the Texas myth" required western roots. Myth has tremendous advantages in any fight between myth and history. For example, the journalist Erica Grieder's defense of the Texas way, *Big, Hot, Cheap, and Right: What America Can Learn from the Strange Genius of Texas* (2013), reported that most recent observers agree that "During the first half of the twentieth century, . . . Texas clearly was more affiliated with the South than with any other region." But she also reports that, "A hundred years after annexation . . . Like the rest of the former Confederate states, Texas was still working through the ruination of the Civil War and Reconstruction. The state's alternative regional identities were as yet inchoate."[4] Think about that last line, "The state's alternative regional identities were as yet inchoate," meaning, presumably, that a plausible story about how Texas was not really southern, had not yet come together. The historian Laura Lyons McLemore, author of *Inventing Texas: Early Historians of the Lone Star State*, was more blunt, saying that Ramsdell's view receded before "a desire to dilute, if not completely dissolve, the inglorious memory of the Civil War by reviving the glorious memory of the Texas Revolution."[5]

Despite a concerted effort by scholars across the humanities and social sciences, the myth of Texas's cowboy heritage continues to be quite pervasive. The prominent Texas folklorist and University of Texas English Professor Don Graham has resisted the quiet editing out of the southern roots of Texas history and culture. Graham recently wrote that the North Texas of his boyhood in the 1940s and 1950s "was scarcely distinguishable from the rest of Dixie." But as the mythic civility of the plantation culture morphed into school desegregation and civil rights fights of the 1960s and later, many sought to replace southern roots with western imagery. Graham notes that, "Just as knowledge of the Southern part of Texas history has faded away . . . the part of Texas that keeps being forgotten or erased—East Texas" fades with it.[6] Similarly, in 1989, Randolph B. Campbell, then a young historian at the University of North Texas, wrote a book entitled *An Empire for Slavery: The Peculiar Institution in Texas*. In 2011, Campbell explained his motivation for writing the book, saying "I wrote it because I believed that the historical record ought to be straight. . . . But it wasn't right for the people in Texas to allow themselves the luxury of saying that we didn't have slaves here or that we had only a handful."[7] As the place of East Texas, plantations, and slavery in the state's history has faded, the place of West Texas, cowboys, and cattle has assumed an importance that history simply cannot support. Glen Sample Ely, the state's most prominent historian of West Texas, author of *Where the West Begins: Debating Texas Identity*, wrote that "For far too long, Texas has cloaked itself in a Western identity to escape its southern legacy of racism, segregation, and lynching."[8] Ely presents West Texas as participating, though in distinctive and attenuated ways, in the state's history of racial and ethnic distinctions and exclusions.

Finally, before turning to the data that will resolve this issue, it is important to recall that Texas was settled mainly out of the South, was a slave state, joined the Confederacy, and mandated Jim Crow segregation into the 1970s. Texas is southern in fundamental respects, though, as Ely said, not uniformly so. Maybe the best that we can do within the historical literature is to listen to the prominent Texas historian Walter L. Buenger. Like Ely, Buenger wrote that, "All of Texas is connected—each region to the other and each region to the South."[9] Fortunately, there is an obvious and powerful way to measure the weight of East Texas, with its unambiguous southern roots, against that of West Texas, with its more western, but still notably southern, roots. When in doubt, recur to the facts.

Three geographical markers have been used to divide East and West Texas. Two are artificial, just intriguing lines on a map, while the third is strikingly physical. The first is the 98th meridian. "In 1905, Vernon Bailey, Chief Field Naturalist of the U.S. Department of Agriculture, conducted a biological survey of Texas. . . . 'the eastern part of Texas, west to approximately the 98th meridian, agrees very closely in climate . . . with the lower Mississippi Valley.' At the 98th meridian, he discerned a 'well-defined division' between East and West."[10] As Figure 2.1 shows, a little more than a third of Texas lies east of the 98th meridian. Others, including Glen Ely, point to the 100th meridian as the beginning of arid West Texas. Ely described the transition zone between the 98th and 100th meridian as the "shatterbelt region" where rough geography marks the transition from East to West. Wilbur Zelinsky also noted this transitional region in saying that "the South finally fades away as one approaches the famous 100th meridian and a critical decline in annual precipitation."[11] The 98th meridian runs north and south just west of Fort Worth and the 100th meridian runs 150 miles west of Fort Worth, near Abilene.

A more concrete way to identify the dividing line between East and West Texas is a geographical fault line called the Balcones Escarpment. The Balcones Escarpment was formed when two of the earth's plates came together and the western plate overrode the eastern plate. The faultline runs from Del Rio in the Big Bend area to just west of San Antonio before running north, passing just west of Austin and Fort Worth to the

Figure 2.1 The Disputed Division between East and West Texas

Red River. To the south, the hills associated with the escarpment rise nearly a thousand feet, while further north they rise about 300 feet. This rough country lies between the 98th and 100th meridians and is what Ely called the "shatterbelt region." The Balcones Escarpment divides well-watered East Texas from the much drier West Texas. As Figure 2.1 shows, the Balcones Escarpment divides Texas approximately in half.

Figure 2.2 shows quite clearly that the population of Texas has always been predominantly in East Texas, however defined, and only thinly scattered through West Texas. Moreover, East Texas was settled first and the weight of social and economic influence has always resided there. The 98th meridian divides Texas about one-third to the east and two-thirds to the west. Still, at no point in Texas history, including today, have more than one-third of Texans lived west of the 98th meridian, even though San Antonio, the second largest city in Texas and the nation's seventh largest city, lies west of the 98th meridian. No more than 15 percent of Texans have ever lived west of the 100th meridian. And if one takes the Balcones Escarpment as nature's best definition of the dividing line between East and West Texas, no more than one-quarter of Texans have ever lived in the west. Today, just 14 percent of Texans live west of the Balcones.

So unless we are to believe that the latest settled and most sparsely populated region of the state has driven the state's character and development; or unless we are to believe that reading western novels and watching cowboy movies erased generations worth of southern cultural instincts and assumptions from Texas minds—we must finally treat this debate about whether Texas is southern, western, or southwestern, as resolved. From its origins and to its core, Texas shares in the southern political culture only

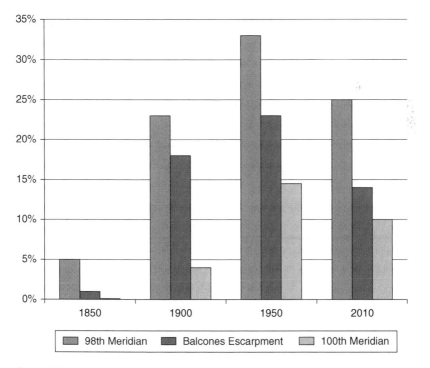

Figure 2.2 The Share of Texans Living West of the 98th Meridian, the 100th Meridian, and the Balcones Escarpment

slightly softened by a West Texas focus on different and marginally less threatening targets of discrimination.

The Stubborn Southernness of Texas in the Twentieth Century

During the first half of the twentieth century, the Texas political culture changed little, but its defenders became more strident as external pressures grew, beginning with the Great Depression and Franklin Roosevelt's New Deal. Texas leaders accepted federal aid because the need was great, but never without muttering about socialism under their breath. As the Depression waned in the late 1930s, resentment against federal intrusion in state affairs grew angrier and more overt. The increasing focus on civil rights in the middle decades of the twentieth century brought a deepening sense on the part of the governing elites that the Texas way was under assault.

In the middle of this Texas establishment rebellion against Washington and its liberal politics, Theodore White, a prominent journalist and future author of the *Making of the President* series of campaign accounts that ran from 1960 through 1976, wrote "Texas: Land of Wealth and Fear" for the May 1954 issue of *The Reporter*. White seemed puzzled, even stunned, that, "millions of Texans are convinced that their primary enemies are other Americans. . . . Ardent and devout states' righters at home bellowing and snorting that the 'sovereign' privileges of Texas must not be disturbed."[12] But disturbed they were, and soon.

By 1952, the state's conservative leaders had had enough. When the Democrats chose the liberal governor of Illinois, Adlai Stevenson as their standard-bearer, Texas Governor Allan Shivers led conservative Democrats to Dwight D. Eisenhower, the Republican candidate. General Eisenhower, the former Supreme Commander of allied forces in Europe during World War II, was the first Republican candidate for president to campaign actively in the South. Eisenhower, born in Denison, Texas, but raised in Abilene, Kansas, thrilled southern hearts by standing whenever "Dixie" was played— which was often. Shivers was joined in "Democrats for Eisenhower" by Governor Kennon of Louisiana and Governor Byrnes of South Carolina. Eisenhower carried five southern states in 1952 and did even better when he again faced Stevenson in 1956. Texas went for Eisenhower both times.

Soon, Texas conservatives were concerned that Eisenhower was not stout enough and they did not hesitate to let him know. On November 8, 1954, President Eisenhower responded to a letter from his older brother, Edgar Newton Eisenhower, a conservative lawyer. The elder Eisenhower touched a nerve with the president when he noted that many people he talked with were concerned about "centralization" and saw little difference between the previous Democrat administrations and his own on that score. President Eisenhower responded that he too was concerned about "centralization," but "[s]hould any political party attempt to abolish social security, unemployment insurance, and eliminate labor laws and farm programs, you would not hear of that party again in our political history." The president then focused his wrath directly on Texas, noting, "There is a tiny splinter group, of course, that believes you can do these things. Among them are H.L. Hunt (you possibly know his background), a few other Texas oil millionaires, and an occasional politician or businessman . . . Their number is negligible and they are stupid."[13]

While President Eisenhower's critique of his critics might have been broadly correct, the fact that his brother was forwarding him these Texas rumblings should have warned him that his critics might be more numerous and less stupid than he thought. As

Eisenhower's second term wound down and the 1960 presidential campaign loomed, the *Dallas Morning News* editorial page warned readers that, "On the one side will be those who want to carry the nation further along the road to socialism. They will advocate extended Social Security, federal health insurance and federal aid to schools, bringing with it federal control . . . . It is still uncertain that most voters will have the discernment to choose freedom over candy-covered socialism."[14] While conservative newspapers had reason to worry about the discernment of voters, they knew their politicians would stand firm for traditional Texas values. Democratic Governor Price Daniel rejected his party's presidential candidate, John F. Kennedy, and instead campaigned for the Republican Richard M. Nixon.[15] To no avail.

In 1960, Kennedy barely edged Nixon in one of the closest elections in American history. To help in Texas and the South, Kennedy chose LBJ as his running mate. Many Johnson insiders advised that he hold onto his spot as Democratic majority leader in the Senate, arguing that it was more influential and more secure, and Bobby Kennedy famously opposed LBJ on the ticket. John Kennedy knew that he needed LBJ. In fact, even with him, Kennedy carried Texas by just 45,000 votes out of 1.3 million cast. Nationally, Kennedy won 34.2 million votes to Nixon's 34.1 million for 49.72 percent to 49.55 percent. The political climate in Texas grew so fraught as the 1960 election approached that Bruce Alger, one of the first Republicans elected to Congress from Texas after Reconstruction, led a demonstration in Dallas in October in which he carried a sign declaring that "LBJ SOLD OUT TO YANKEE SOCIALISTS." The demonstration spun out of control and national coverage resulted when Lady Bird Johnson was spat upon.

Rising tensions within the Texas Democratic Party prior to the 1964 presidential election led Kennedy, despite the misgivings of Governor Connally and Vice President Johnson, to schedule a fund-raising and fence-mending trip to Texas in November 1963. On November 22, 1963, the day that the president and Jackie Kennedy were to be in Dallas, an ad appeared in the *Dallas Morning News*, outlined in thick black borders, paid for by Texas oilman H.L. Hunt and the local John Birch Society, declaring that "Kennedy was secretly in league with the American Communists." Venom dripped from the scornful greeting, "Welcome, Mr. Kennedy, to Dallas. . . . A CITY that will continue to grow and prosper despite efforts by you and your administration to penalize it for non-conformity to 'New Frontierism.'"[16] The New Frontier was the name given by the Kennedy administration to their mildly liberal domestic policy program and conservative Dallas wanted him to know that they would have none of it. As they prepared in Fort Worth for the brief flight to Dallas, the president is reported to have observed to Jackie Kennedy, "We're headed into nut country today."[17]

Kennedy's assassination in Dallas repulsed most Texans. Texas supported LBJ overwhelmingly in his 1964 run for election to a full term as president, defeated Bruce Alger for re-election, and swept all six Dallas Republicans out of the state legislature. John Connally, elected governor in 1962 and seriously wounded in the Kennedy assassination, had a slow recovery from his wounds but emerged politically invulnerable. A conservative Democrat, Connally increased state spending, especially for higher education, but he made few attempts to change the basic structure of Texas politics. James Reston wrote that "John Connally epitomized the big man of Texas. He stood in his elegant boots with the wealthy over the poor, the business executive over the working man, white over black and Hispanic, the glamorous over the commonplace. In short, he symbolized Texas royalty over Texas peasantry."[18] Moreover, the anti-government, especially anti-federal government, sentiment on display the day Kennedy was shot did not abate. George Norris Green noted in the late 1970s that, "Texans believe that there is a difference politically between their state and other states, and that the federal government is almost a foreign menace to Texas rights and privileges."[19]

Nonetheless, the electoral system that underpinned white supremacy and elite control in Texas and the South came under increasing federal pressure at mid-century. The key exclusionary devices of early registration, the white primary, and the poll tax were all tenaciously defended until Congress and the federal courts struck them down. The Supreme Court declared the white primary unconstitutional in *Smith v. Allwright* (1944); the Twenty-Fourth Amendment outlawed the poll tax in federal elections (1964); and the Supreme Court struck down the poll tax in state election in *U.S. v. Texas* (1966) and early registration in 1971. Texas fought each of these changes to the very end and, in fact, did not ratify the Twenty-Fourth Amendment until 2009. T.R. Fehrenbach stated the matter with characteristic bluntness, saying "Virtually all the political and social reforms of the twentieth century enacted by government have been forced down the Anglo-Texan throat."[20] It often fell to one federal judge, William Wayne Justice of the Eastern District of Texas, to do the forcing.

Judge Justice summed up the Texas record of suppression of minority voting in the case of *Seaman v. Upham* (1982). Judge Justice wrote that this history "stands as a disheartening testament to the perseverance and craft of the dominant political leaders, in their attempt to exclude minorities from participation in the process of self-government." He concluded that, "A century of neglect, sometimes benign, frequently malign, has created a climate of alienation and apathy, mixed with deep-seated resentment in many of the minority communities of Texas."[21] Judge Justice also was involved in a series of cases that challenged segregation in Texas schools, prisons, and asylums. Federal judges still regularly hold that Texas public officials work to suppress minority voter influence.

While the federal assault on segregation overwhelmed the Anglo elites' initial strategy of massive resistance, they soon settled on a new and ultimately more effective strategy. Progressive whites, blacks, Hispanics, and other minorities had long argued that discrimination in general and segregation in particular was a violation of the nation's fundamental commitment to equal treatment of citizens. After passage of the Civil Rights Act of 1964 and 1965, the Voting Rights Act of 1965, and the Fair Housing Act of 1968, Anglo conservatives simply said, OK, we agree, America should be a color-blind society. Support for a color-blind society, of course, requires that no group ask for special benefits, even to redress past grievances, because this would entail violation of others' rights to equal protection of the laws. If the Constitution is color-blind, and we believe that it is and must be, Anglo conservatives now said, laws that take account of race, let alone laws that distribute privileges and benefits based on race, even if intended to do some presumed good, are unconstitutional. Liberals sputtered and cursed, but conservatives smiled at having secured an unexpected ideological advantage.

Texas Mythology during the Boom Years

Texas grew rapidly during the 1960s and 1970s. These were the boom years during which oil revenues buoyed individual, corporate, and government bottom lines. Following the institution of a modest sales tax in 1961, burgeoning oil and gas severance taxes allowed Texas to increase expenditures without raising taxes. Citizens and leaders were confident in the future and so politics remained more about personalities than issues. John Connally dominated Texas politics during the 1960s. Connally biographer, James Reston Jr., wrote that,

> The major Texas papers doted upon him: "John Connally personifies confidence. Defeat is not in his make-up," the *Houston Chronicle* purred. "Retreat is not in his vocabulary. Skillfully, he directs this confidence where it belongs: in Texas and her people. In his mind, Texas has everything in her favor—charm, vigor, a reservoir of intelligence, a colorful history, courage for the present, a sense of destiny, abundant natural resources and proud people who are united to make this state the envy of the other 49." In short, John Connally was the personification of Texas, as establishment Texas wanted to see itself.[22]

A new image developed of the indomitable Texan pursuing his own success in a state destined to be the envy of the other 49. This is not the Alamo myth, heroism in the face of overwhelming odds, let alone myth of the Lost Cause masking the bitter taste of defeat, this is the myth of the Lone Star ascendant.

As a business-oriented conservative, Connally "spent a great deal of energy shaping Texas's image as a racially moderate and southwestern, rather than southern, state."[23] He spent far less time on trying to change Texas's standing on key social indicators of education, health care, and other social services. Reston noted that:

> The social ills of Texas were daunting in 1963. For all its fabulous oil wealth, it was thirty-third in the nation in per capita income . . . thirty-eighth in the country in education and thirty-sixth in public health . . . forty-fourth in adult literacy, and last in per capita expenditure for child welfare services. It had the largest pool of poor in the entire United States.
>
>   . . . In its racial attitudes, the state of Texas was only slightly more advanced than Alabama, Mississippi, and South Carolina. Only two percent of blacks actually attended school with whites.[24]

Texas conservatives remained resistant to new spending even when the money was in the till. In 1970, George Mahon, Lubbock's long-time conservative Democratic congressman, declared: "I am a firm believer in the old fashioned virtue of self-reliance, and I hold unwaveringly to the view that individual initiative, drive, and discipline need to be more encouraged in our country."[25]

As T.R. Fehrenbach wrote in 1983, even at the height of the oil boom, rising wealth made little difference to social spending. He observed that,

> Texas, especially in the 1980s, is relatively a rich state, and very rich in terms of resources. It stands at the very bottom of the tier of poorest states, however, in the sums it expends for public health and welfare. Teachers' salaries always hover near the lowest in the nation . . . Petroleum finances a third of all Texas public revenues, but the state gasoline tax in 1982 was the lowest in the nation.[26]

Fehrenbach is widely seen as the classic expositor of mythic Texas, but even he seems somewhat bemused by the fact that the flowing Texas wealth of the early 1980s barely moved the needle on state spending on health and welfare. Others thought that the explanation was quite clear. In 1984, Texas House Speaker Gib Lewis (D-Fort Worth) remarked that, "Most Texans are conservative. They look for a helping hand at the end of their arm."[27]

The Texas myth remained strong into the mid-1980s; largely unquestioned within the state and begrudged if hard to attack from outside the state. In 1987, when political scientist Gerry Riposa and his colleagues wrote *Texas Public Policy*, they reported that individualism was still central to the Anglo Texan self-image:

> Texans like to picture themselves as independent individuals handling their affairs without needing assistance from others. . . . The individualist thread in our culture considers the individual responsible for his or her own success or failure. Social forces, like poverty or racial discrimination, are used by individuals to excuse their own failures, but are not deterrents to those with true ability. Clearly, this theme is inconsistent with extensive government provision of social services.[28]

Similarly, political scientists Anthony Champagne and Edward Harpham noted in *Texas at the Crossroads*, that "Individualism continues to dominate the Texas psyche. Entrepreneurialism is still valued by a people who crave the opportunity to 'make it big.' But while such values survive, the people holding them and the actual opportunities available to them have changed enormously."[29] Champagne and Harpham also noted the smothering effect of Texas mythology. Harpham wrote that, "The mythos of the frontier, the idealization of the individual entrepreneur, and the idea that the government that governs least is the government that governs best all are well and alive in Texas in the 1980s. All have played a role in constraining a larger policy debate over the responsibility a society has to its poor."[30]

But challenges loomed on the horizon. Both Riposa's *Texas Public Policy* and Champagne and Harpham's *Texas at the Crossroads* appeared as the collapse in oil prices, followed by devastating collapses in property values and Texas banks, began to bite. Concern battled with confidence in these books and concern was beginning to get the upper hand. Champagne and Harpham tell the sobering story of the collapse in oil prices, though they could not know the depth of the problems that would follow:

> In January [1986], the price of oil had collapsed: it hovered around $12 and $15 per barrel for most of the spring. By July, the price of oil had dropped to a little over $11 per barrel. . . . By mid-summer, unemployment in Texas had topped 10%, among the highest in the nation, and the state that but a few years before had been holding itself up as a land of opportunity for the rest of the nation found itself in the midst of its largest recession since the Great Depression.[31]

Economic Collapse, Diversification, and "Never Again"

The late 1980s and early 1990s were hard on Texas. The old swagger of the boom years did not fully return until the mid-1990s—the Bush years—and then it was muted for a time by the bursting of the tech bubble in 2000 and 2001. While the return of prosperity brought increased state revenues, some went to tax cuts and some went to modest spending increases. Yet, increasingly, economic downturns brought tight budgets and severe budget cuts. Patrick Cox and Michael Phillips wrote that as the legislature faced deficits in 2003, "Despite the state ranking forty-third in per capita hospital, health, and welfare spending nationally in 2000, and forty-first in state aid per pupil in grades K-12, those budget items faced devastating reductions."[32]

Hard times returned with the global financial collapse of 2008 and 2009. Texas again cut to balance and slipped even further in national rankings on spending for education, health care, and social services. But to listen to state officials, you would never know that Texas had been hit at all. Texas Comptroller Susan Combs, interviewed in *Texas Monthly* in June 2009, was unrestrained in her boosterism. Combs explained that Texas was far better off than other states because it had learned the lessons of the late 1980s so well:

> The state has enjoyed tremendous growth—incredible sales tax growth of 12 percent three years ago, then 10-plus percent, then 6.6 percent. It has been rockin' and rollin'. In 2008 the state brought in about 71 percent of all new jobs in the country [an over estimate, but more about that in Chapter 4]. . . . We're not sleeping in our cars. We're still largely employed. We're actually fairly lucky. . . . So the state is so much better off than anyplace else. I really attribute that to how badly damaged we were in the mid-eighties. We lost 368 banks and 200,000 to 300,000 jobs, and we said, "Never again; let's diversify. Which we have done."[33]

Very similar themes were articulated by Governor Rick Perry in his 2011 Inaugural Address. In office since late 2000, Perry argued that Texas had survived the financial crisis of 2008–2009 better than most states and the nation because of its open, competitive, entrepreneurial culture. With another four-year term before him, Perry said:

> Given our state's economic success compared to that of other states and Washington's ongoing irresponsibility, I believe Texas will lead the way out of this turmoil. . . . Our state is the new, best hope for entrepreneurs and small businesses—the place where Americans can redeem their promise and fulfill their potential. . . . If I've said it once, I've said it a thousand times, and will say it a thousand times more: there is still a place where opportunity looms large in this country, and that place is called Texas.

What Anglo Texas leaders like Perry and Combs miss, of course, is that their triumphalist claims are made at the expense of other Americans. As Laura McLemore described in *Inventing Texas*, "Texans have tended to define themselves as against non-Texans generally."[34] And if Texas is "a whole other country" and the last refuge of opportunity, what of the American dream and American exceptionalism? American exceptionalism must have decayed, must have been lost, if it survives in its original vibrancy only in Texas. Naturally, other Americans, proud of American history, the American dream, and American exceptionalism, are, by turns, angry about and dismissive of Texan claims that their fellow citizens have lost faith with the American dream and will only find it again in "that place called Texas." So about those claims—is Texas a model for its 49 sister states or does she have much to learn from them? As we shall see, Texas is a model in some regards, but has much to learn in a good many others.

How Does Texas Compare?

The short answer to the question, "how does Texas compare," is not well. In Chapter 1, we presented a ranking of the states on four dimensions—wealth, education, culture, and public order—that appeared in the *American Mercury* in 1931. *American Mercury* was an ideas and opinion journal and the authors of the article, entitled "The Worst American State," were Charles Angoff and H.L. Mencken. Mencken in particular was a well-known iconoclast and political skeptic, so the ranking attributed to Texas, 39th among the then 48 states and D.C., should be taken with a grain of salt. Even if Texas did rank 39th in 1930, wouldn't rapid economic growth over the intervening decades have moved her up smartly in the rankings. Fortunately, the Federal Reserve Bank of Cleveland, as conservative and staid an organization as you are likely to find (no Menckens working there), attempted to answer just that question. The bank's 2005 Annual Report featured a study entitled, "Altered States: A Perspective on 75 Years of State Income Growth."[35] The study asked of the period from 1930 to 2005, "Why do residents of some states have higher incomes than residents of other states? Why have these income differences persisted for the past 75 years?"[36] Why, indeed!

The Cleveland Fed study pointed out that the dominant economic model of state income growth, the Solow model, named for the Nobel Prize-winning economist Robert Solow, predicts that if different regions, say the wealthier Northeast and poorer South, start out with different levels of wealth and capital investment, they should converge over time. Businesses stand to gain the most if they invest new capital in states with low wage rates. The study confirms that, "States that had lower incomes in 1930 have tended to grow at a faster pace than those whose incomes were greater at the time."[37] Convergence has occurred, but not enough, even after 80 years, to move the poor states up to the level of the wealthy. Texas lagged the average state income in 1939 by about 13 percent (ranking 31st) and continued to lag in 2004 by about 3 percent (ranking 25th). Two things happened in this data, the income differences between the states slowly closed but the states maintained their relative rankings. The rich states were generally still rich and the poor states poor, but less so. Finally, the Cleveland Fed study tried to assess the factors that most contributed to state income growth. They assessed education levels, taxes and public infrastructure, patents and technology. They found that higher taxes did not limit growth if the revenues were used wisely for infrastructure development. The factors that did effect income growth were patents, a measure of innovation, education, and industry specialization, measured as the share of the state economy in service and knowledge-intensive activities. Unfortunately, Texas lagged modestly on all three.[38]

To update the Cleveland Fed analysis, I have taken personal income per capita data by state for 1950 and 2015 (the latest available) to analyze convergence over those more than six decades. Dividing each state's personal income per capita by national personal income per capita shows how far each state is above or below the national average. Comparing the data for 1950 and 2015 will show how much convergence has occurred overall and which states have moved up (gotten comparatively richer) and down (gotten comparatively poorer) since 1950 (see Figure 2.3).

First, in both 1950 and 2015, there were fewer states above the national average for personal income per capita than below it. In 1950, 21 states were above and 27 below, and in 2015, 19 states were above and 31 were below. Second, just as the Solow model predicted, the range between the highest and lowest states closed between 1950 and 2015. In 1950, Delaware was the wealthiest state at 33 percent above the national average and Mississippi was the poorest at 51 percent below, for a range of 84 percent. In 2015, Connecticut was the wealthiest state at 40 percent above the national average while Mississippi remained the poorest state, but at just 25 percent below the national average, for a range of 65 percent. Third, convergence was not as simple as the wealthier states falling toward the national average and poorer states rising toward it. Poor states like Mississippi, Alabama, Arkansas, and South Carolina made impressive strides. Mississippi moved from −51 percent in 1950 to −25 percent in 2015; South Carolina from −42 to −20; Arkansas from −43 to −18; and Alabama from −42 to −18.

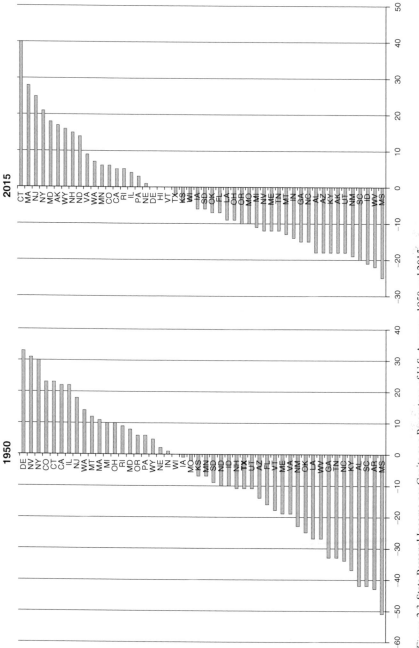

Figure 2.3 State Personal Income per Capita as a Percentage of U.S. Average, 1950 and 2015

Source: *Statistical Abstract of the United States*, 1952, Table 309, p. 258. *Statistical Abstract of the United States*, 2017, Table 705, p. 462. See also www.bea.gov/iTable/
iTable.cfm?ReqID=70&step=1.

However, some wealthy states in 1950 added to their lead. Connecticut moved from 23 percent above the national average in 1950 to 40 percent above in 2015; Massachusetts went from +11 to +28; Maryland from +8 to +18; and New Jersey from +18 to +25. In summary, there was a pattern of convergence overall, with the poorer states coming up nicely, but some of the wealthier states sprinted away to larger leads.

How has Texas done? The answer is, not bad, but not great. In 1950, Texas personal income per capita, at $1,278, was 11 percent below the national average of $1,436. In 2015, Texas personal income per capita, at $46,745, was 2 percent below the national average of $47,669. In 1950, Texas ranked 29th among the states and in 2012 Texas ranked 23rd. Texas has moved up, but just a bit and slowly. Progress is a good thing, but 9 percent over six and one-half decades is 1.5 percent per decade. This suggests that another decade or so will be required to reach the national average for personal income per capita. And what do we make of Connecticut and Massachusetts, two high tax states that Texas-elected officials love to revile, being wealthier than the national average in 1950 and improving by 17 percent from there?

As the Cleveland Fed study found, high taxes do not preclude growth and low taxes do not assure it. High taxes, well invested in infrastructure and education, can fuel growth. Low taxes, so long as they are not so low as to starve infrastructure and education, can spur growth by encouraging innovation and entrepreneurship. But one must say that it is highly unlikely that a revenue-starved state like Texas is going to overtake the breakaway winners in this century. To understand why, we take two looks at how Texas is doing on a wide range of measures dealing with population and job growth, education, crime, energy and the environment, and more. The first look draws on non-partisan historical data from the *Statistical Abstract of the United States* and the second draws from recent data prepared by the Texas Legislative Budget Board and Democrats in the Texas Legislature.

Measuring Texas More Broadly, 1950 to Present

Table 2.1 presents a broad comparison of Texas to its peers over the entire post–World War II era. Modern Texas emerged with remarkable speed during the 1930s and 1940s. As the grip of the Great Depression relaxed in the face of preparations for World War II, Texans streamed out of the rural areas and into the new industrial jobs in the cities.[39] For several decades after the war, Texas enjoyed the rapid growth of late-industrialization. Capital, technology, and skilled management flowed into Texas, fueling growth, adding jobs, and creating wealth at rates well beyond those of the more developed parts of the country. While similar growth rates were enjoyed by other late-industrializing states in the South, Southwest, and West, Texas alone stood at the center of the global oil industry. Oil revenues allowed expansion of government services in education, welfare, and transportation to keep up with population and urban growth. Strikingly, however, these were decades in which the national economy was growing strongly too, and while the nation did not grow as rapidly as Texas it spent a greater proportion of its increased wealth on social services, so Texas's ranking among the states barely budged. In fact, on key measures of income, education, and health care, Texas's ranking among the states actually fell and that fall has picked up speed in recent years. The reason that Texas makes little to no progress in national rankings on educational and social services is that every time state budgets tighten the conservative mantra is cut until the budget is balanced.

Texas pride has hinged on the twin facts that population growth and job growth have outstripped national averages and growth in most other states for many decades.

Table 2.1 A Troublesome Trajectory: Texas's Rank among the States, 1950–2015

| | *(1 = best, 51 = worst)* | | | | | | | |
	1950	*1960*	*1970*	*1980*	*1990*	*2000*	*2010*	*2015*
Population Growth	14	14	16	10	7	6	5	2
Job Growth		11	13	8	24	7	8	4
Median Family Income	30	35	35	27	36	34	30	27
Inequality (Gini Index)			38	41	41	45	43	43
Poverty Rate			38	39	39	44	40	39
Unemployment Recipiency			49	51	49	45	48	37
Av. Teacher Salaries	18	27	39	32	30	27	29	25
Av. Spending per Pupil	31	36	43	38	37	28	43	44
High School Completion	36	39	39	39	39	44	50	49
Teen Births as % Total	39	37	37	36	37	42	45	46
Overall Crime Rate	36	37	38	37	43	39	42	36
Incarceration Rate	14	35	45	45	35	47	46	44

The shorthand story is that Texas must be a highly desirable place because people keep coming, voting with their feet, to take up the jobs that they cannot find at home. Aspects of this story are clearly true. Texas has been at the heart of the post–World War II sunbelt expansion. Texas ranked about 15th among the states in population growth from the 1950s through the 1970s and then growth picked up. Texas was 10th in the 1980s and has been between 5th and 7th for the past couple of decades, and second between 2010 and 2015. Only a few states have matched Texas's population growth statistics. During the 1950s and 1960s, the densely populated Middle Atlantic states of Connecticut, New Jersey, Delaware, and Maryland, ran with Texas before falling back. California matched and exceeded Texas's growth rates from the 1950s through the 1980s and Florida kept up through the 1990s. In recent decades, only a few lightly populated states, Idaho, Utah, Nevada, and Arizona, have exceeded Texas population growth rates. Since 2010 only North Dakota, one thirty-fifth the population of Texas, grew more rapidly. In Chapter 3 we explore Texas population growth and, more importantly, demographic change in detail.

With the exception of the 1980s, job growth in Texas has exceeded the national average and those of three-fourths of the states. From the 1950s through the 1970s, a familiar group of southern, southwestern, and mountain states, including the Carolinas, Florida, Georgia, Colorado, New Mexico, Utah, and Nevada enjoyed job growth similar to that of Texas. Alaska and Hawaii did so as well once they achieved statehood. The Texas job growth engine sputtered in the 1980s, but roared through the 1990s and 2000s with just a handful of small southwestern and mountain states keeping pace. After 2010, only four states, California, Colorado, North Dakota, and Utah exceeded Texas job growth in percentage terms. So Texas does have much to brag about. Nonetheless, there are some stubborn facts.

Texas is not now and has never been a "wealthy" state. During the first several decades of the twentieth century, Texas and the South generally averaged about two-thirds of U.S. median family income. Because oil and agriculture cushioned the Depression's impact on Texas, median family income rose to three-quarters of the national average by 1940 and then skyrocketed to 87 percent by 1944. Texas came out of World War II with enough momentum in income growth that it was reasonable to think it would overtake and perhaps surpass national averages in a short time. It was not to be. In 1950, Texas ranked 30th among the 48 states and D.C., at 90 percent of median family income. Texas dropped back into the mid-30s during the 1960s and 1970s, before making an oil-fueled run at the national average, reaching 27th among the 50 states and D.C. in 1980. As the price of oil collapsed in the mid-1980s, Texas median family income fell back into the mid-30s. In 2010, Texas ranked 30th, just as it had in 1950. By 2015, Texas had climbed to 27th, where it had been in 1980.

The Gini Index is a statistic that measures the degree of income inequality between upper and lower income earners. The index ranges from zero to one, zero being complete equality and one being complete inequality. The higher the Gini Index, the greater the inequality. Over the past four decades, Texas's ranking among the states has ranged from .35 to .50. In 1970, a dozen states had higher Gini Index readings than Texas. In the 1980s and 1990s only an average of ten states had higher Gini Index readings and for the past 15 years only an average of six states have had higher ratings. In 2002, no state had a higher Gini Index rating than Texas, though D.C., which always ranks 51 (lots of well-paid government workers and poor people) did. In 2015, Texas ranked 43rd on the Gini Index. Compared to other states, Texas has the threatening combination of low family income and high inequality.

Not surprisingly then, as inequality in Texas has risen, so has poverty. Poverty has been a national focus since the Great Society era of the 1960s. State comparisons of the proportion of citizens in poverty have been available since 1970. From 1970 to 2000, Texas held steady at a ranking of 38 or 39, meaning only a dozen states, mostly in the South and Southwest, had a greater share of their citizens in poverty. Texas dropped precipitously into the 40s after 2000 and has remained there in recent readings. In 2007, only Mississippi (22.6 percent) and D.C. (18 percent), exceeded Texas's poverty rate of 16.5 percent. In 2008, the Texas poverty rate fell to 16 percent but in 2009, as the financial crisis took hold nationally and in Texas, the Texas poverty rate increased to 17.2 percent. In both years, Texas ranked 43rd among the 50 states and D.C. In 2015, Texas ranked 40th, near its historic norm. Moreover, when Texans lose their jobs they are less likely than workers in most other states to be eligible for unemployment insurance benefits. Texas usually ranks between 45th and 51st in the proportion of unemployed drawing on unemployment insurance benefits. Modest incomes, high poverty, and a thin social safety net have long made Texas a "business-friendly" state. Notice that no one claims Texas is "worker-friendly," though Anglo leaders do claim that Texas creates lots of jobs and that is good for workers. In the end, though, it is clear that personal responsibility rests lightly on the comfortable and heavily on the vulnerable.

Spending on Texas public schools has consistently limped along below the national average. Two measures are key: average teacher salaries and average spending per pupil. Texas has done somewhat better by teachers (they vote) than by students. Sadly though, compared to the national average and average teacher salaries in other states, Texas teacher salaries peaked in the early 1950s. Texas teachers ranked 18th among the 48 states and D.C. in 1950, before falling back into the high 20s and 30s thereafter. Texas teachers ranked 25th in 2015. Texas spending per student ranked 31st in the nation in 1950 and generally languished in the mid-30s to low 40s thereafter. Texas made a concerted run at the national average in the 1990s, reaching 28th in 2000, before falling back. Texas spending per pupil has ranked 43rd from 2010 and 44th in 2015.

Two sad statistics which track each other closely are high school completion rates and teen births as a percentage of total births. Teen pregnancy is only one of many reasons that students drop out of high school, but most drop outs face a bleak future. Texas ranked 36th among the states and D.C. in high school completion in 1950 and 39th from the 1960s through the 1990s, before dropping to 44th in 2000, 50th in 2010, and 49th in 2015. Similarly, Texas ranked between 36th and 39th from the 1950 through the 1990s in teen births as a percentage of total births before falling to 42nd in 2000, 45th in 2010, and 46th in 2015.

Finally, for more than half a century Texas ranked between 36th and 43rd among the states in its overall crime rate. Nonetheless, Texas's response to crime changed dramatically. In 1950, Texas's incarceration rate, the number of persons per 100,000 of population in prison, was modest, ranking just 14th in the nation. But as crime and civil unrest increased in the late 1950s and 1960s, Texas rapidly built one of the most extensive prison systems in the nation. The incarceration rate in Texas has risen dramatically. Texas ranked 35th in 1960, 45th in 1970 and 1980, before federal court decisions forced a slowdown in late 1980s, registered by a rank of 35th in 1990. Once shed of federal court supervision, Texas built more prisons and increased its incarceration rate to 47th in 2000, 46th in 2010, and 44th in 2015.

Ominously, while Texas has led the nation in population and job growth, it has lagged in family incomes and fallen in every other dimension reported in Table 2.1. Can Texas thrive if it is beaten by almost every other state on education, health care, and other public and social services? We will try to answer these questions in detail in subsequent chapters, but before we do, we must highlight the ongoing partisan squabble over Texas public policy and its results.

Partisan Perspectives: The *Texas Fact Book* vs. *Texas on the Brink*

Whether Texas is doing well or poorly has been debated for many decades and is, to some extent, a matter of perspective. Anglo elites tend to believe that Texas is doing wonderfully well and is a model for the rest of the nation, while others tend to see serious problems being left untended. In fact, an exchange in the classic 1952 novel, *Giant*, between the Anglo Texas ranching heiress, Vashti Snythe, and the Virginia-born Lacey Lynnton, Lady Karfrey after her marriage to a minor British nobleman, opposed the upper class Anglo view that Texas leads the nation to the view that Texas has left many economic and social problems to fester. After Vashti posted one more claim to Texas primacy, Lady Karfrey responded, "As you say, of all the states Texas is first in cotton—but last in pellagra [a crippling vitamin deficiency]. First in beef—and forty-fifth in infant mortality. First in wool—and thirty-eighth in its school system. First in mules—and forty-seventh in library service. . . . First in oil—and your hospitals are practically non-exis—."[40] Today, as we shall see below, Republicans tend to agree with Vashti and Democrats with Lady Karfrey.

Until recently, establishment Texas was so convinced that its low-tax, low-service, business-friendly model of state government was praiseworthy that it published a number of annual and biannual reports that, at first glance, seemed damning, the kind of information that would more likely be suppressed than touted. One of the most remarkable publications of Texas state government was the *Texas Fact Book (TFB)*, published biannually on the budget cycle by the Legislative Budget Bureau (LBB). The *TFB* for 2014, along with its predecessors back to 1996, showed where the revenues for state government came from, where they went, and how Texas ranked against the other 49 states and the 50-state average across a wide range of issue areas including taxes, income, education, health, welfare, transportation and the environment. Upon perusing the *TFB*, one wonders why it was published at all (the LBB ceased publishing *TFB* with the 2014 edition) since Texas compared embarrassingly on most of the substantive policy dimensions. As we saw in Table 2.1, Texas was occasionally last and often near last. But then one recognizes that Texas was last, dead last, on several measures of state taxing and spending. The *TFB*, while shocking to many, was a fine advertisement for Texas as a low-tax, low-service, business-friendly state.

On the other hand, since 2003, Democrats in the Texas Legislature have published similar data in a document entitled *Texas on the Brink (TOB)*. *TOB* was the brainchild of now former Texas State Senator Eliot Shapleigh (D-El Paso). Each edition of *TOB* opened with a variation on this claim, "In Texas today, the American dream is distant. Texas has the highest percentage of uninsured children in the nation. Texas is dead last in the percentage of residents with their high school diploma and near last in SAT scores. Texas has America's dirtiest air. If we do not change course, for the first time in our history, the Texas generation of tomorrow will be less prosperous than the generation of today."[41] While Republicans bet that Texas conservatives will appreciate and support the state's lowest of low tax ratings, Democrats bet that middle class, working class, and poorer Texans, especially minorities, will be offended by the evidence of thin, sometimes non-existent, public and social services. Republicans have won this bet regularly and there is little to suggest that this will change quickly.

First, let's look at Texas as a low-tax state. The 2014 *TFB* (reporting 2011 to 2014 data), reported that Texas ranked 43rd among the 50 states in per capita state government tax revenue and 45th on state tax revenue as a percentage of personal income. Texas ranked 46th among the 50 states in per capita state government expenditures. Governor Perry frequently said that Texas's simple formula for fiscal responsibility was "we don't spend all the money." More accurately, Texas takes in less revenue (ranked 43rd) than all but seven other states and spends less than all but four other states (ranked 46th).[42] The Democrat's *TOB* leads with the data on Texas's low ranking on taxing and spending. *TOB* (reporting 2010 data) ranks Texas 45th in tax revenue per capita and 48th in tax expenditures per capita.[43]

Few doubt that the most important expenditures that state and local governments make are those for public education. The quality of public education is an important input to the good business climate on which Texas prides itself. The *TFB* reported that Texas worked hard to keep elementary and secondary school class sizes low (22nd at 15.4 to 1) and to pay elementary and secondary school teachers decently (37th at $48,110). Even here the numbers are not stellar, but they are better than the numbers describing per pupil expenditures. In 2013, Texas ranked 48th in state aid per pupil and 50th in the percentage of the population graduated from high school.[44] *TOB* mentioned all of these and added one more: SAT scores, where Texas ranked 47th among the 50 states and D.C.[45]

Texas lagged just as badly in health and social services. Both the *TFB* and *TOB* reported that Texas ranked 51st in the nation on the percentage of its population without health insurance. It ranked 47th on the rate of cancer deaths per 100,000 of population and 41st on the percentage of fully immunized school children. Texas ranked 27th on the number of hospital beds and 43rd on number of physicians per 100,000 of population. Texas ranked 40th in the percentage of its population in poverty and 48th in the percentage of its population who were food insecure. To this litany of neglect the *TOB* added that Texas was 43rd on percentage of the population with employer-based health insurance, 46th on per capita spending on health care expenditures, 48th on percentage of the low-income population covered by Medicaid, and 50th on per capita state spending on mental health.[46]

TOB focused intently on what it described as Women's Issues, while *TFB* presented similar data, though it was scattered throughout the document. *TOB* reported that Texas ranked 48th in overall birth rate, 47th in teenage birth rate, and 50th in the percentage of pregnant women who received prenatal care in the first trimester. Similarly, Texas ranked 47th highest in percentage of women living in poverty and 51st in percentage of non-elderly women with health insurance. Texas ranked 47th in the percentage of women who have had a dental visit in the past year. And finally, Texas ranked 47th in women's voter registration and 51st in women's voter turnout. Not a pretty picture, lots of pregnancy but not much health insurance, prenatal care, or dental care. Not surprisingly, given Texas's traditional political culture, not much political participation or voting.

Understanding Texan

How to explain Texas braggadocio when the state has rarely, and never in the last 30 years, reached the national average on median family income and falls well below average on many measures of educational achievement and near the bottom on many measures of health and welfare? One attempt was made in an extensive piece in *Newsweek*. Evan Thomas and Arian Campo-Flores, in an article entitled "Don't Mess With Texas," began by quoting Rick Perry saying, "I'm willing to tell anyone that will listen that the land of opportunity still exists in America, and it's in Texas."

Thomas and Campo-Flores then touched upon several key elements of the Texas myth, sometimes without noting how far they have come to diverge from reality. They wrote that,

> not a few Texans wish the past could be their future . . . . As these people see it, America is turning into a multicultural hodgepodge, sapped of moral strength, run by government bureaucrats. But Texas they believe is different and always has been. "We don't want to become like them," says Shuck Donnell, General Manager of Coyote Lake Feedyard in Muleshoe, Texas. (By 'them' he means people living in the big metropolitan areas, especially on the East Coast.)

Forget for a moment that although Texas is one the most diverse and highly urbanized states in the nation, the *Newsweek* authors still managed to find 'Shuck' in Muleshoe—they make a very important point by tying the Anglo Texan's sense of independence to fear of social change, particularly if that change is being abetted by outside—read federal—forces.

Analysts viewing Texas from the outside have frequently pointed to insularity, anger, and suspicion. Thomas and Campo-Flores note that,

> The forces of suspicion and anger may be exaggerated in the Lone Star state. They're also compounded by a strong streak of Texas exceptionalism. It dates back to the War of Independence against Mexico and the founding of the Republic of Texas in 1836, says historian David McComb, professor emeritus at Colorado State University. Texans have a "kind of macho, frontier, independent attitude of 'I can do what I damn well please and nobody else can tell me.'"

Now, to read this description is to immediately recognize that it refers to Anglo Texans, not all Texans. Descriptions of a swaggering individualism, though often attributed to "Texans," does not refer to the 39 percent that are Hispanic, the 12 percent of Texans that are black, or the 5 percent that are Asian. In fact, as Thomas and Campo-Flores note,

> The independent strain has a racial dimension. . . . The less dominant whites become in Texas, the more some of them cling to a mythical past of the cowboy and oilman. "A lot of these conservatives don't want to change. The ground is moving underneath them, and they don't want to recognize that and don't know what to do about it. So they join a tea party group and strap on a six-gun and strut around," McComb says.[47]

For more than a decade, Anglo Texans looked to Governor Rick Perry to hold the line against undesirable change. Rick Perry was the longest serving governor in Texas history. He held statewide office in Texas from 1991 to 2015, winning twice for agriculture commissioner, once for lieutenant governor, and three times for governor. What made Rick Perry such a formidable Texas politician was that he channeled the Texas myth with confidence and ease. Anglo Texans, because the myths are so flattering to them, respond favorably, but blacks and Hispanics tend to be much more skeptical.

On April 15, 2009, Perry addressed a raucous crowd of nearly 1,000 tea party activists and sympathizers from the steps of Austin City Hall. Perry's speech drew national attention and won him some prime time attention on Fox News and other conservative outlets. Less noticed was that Perry was voicing deeply historic Texas themes which, while less resonant in recent decades, were common in the nineteenth century and from the late 1930s through the 1960s. Perry revved up the crowd by saying,

> I'm just not sure you're a bunch of right-wing extremists. But if you are, I'm with you! Cause you are a true patriot today in this country. And I might add, you are surrounded by fellow patriots—individuals who embrace concepts like lower taxes and smaller government and freedom for every individual. I'm talking about states' rights! States' rights! States' rights!

After the speech, in response to a reporter's question about whether he was threatening secession, Perry mused, "There's a lot of different scenarios. We've got a great union. There's absolutely no reason to destroy it. But if Washington continues to thumb their nose at the American people, you know, who knows what might come out of that?" Under additional questioning, Perry observed, "We are very proud of our Texas history; people discuss and debate the issues of 'Can we break ourselves into five states, can we secede'—a lot of interesting things that I'm sure Oklahoma and Pennsylvania would love to be able to say about their states, but the fact is, they can't, because they're not Texas."[48]

Perry made an unsuccessful run for the Republican presidential nomination in 2012, concluded his 15-year tenure as governor in 2014, and then briefly ran again for president in 2016 before being appointed U.S. Secretary of Energy by President Donald Trump. His boots have been filled, though not quite, by Governor Greg Abbott and Lieutenant Governor Dan Patrick. Patrick, a radio talk show host before being elected to the Texas Senate and then lieutenant governor, lacked the "aw shucks" presentation that made Perry's conservatism seem less threatening, even to opponents. Patrick's focus during the 2017 legislative session on SB6, the "bathroom bill," requiring transgender Texans to use the bathroom of their biological gender seemed mean-spirited even to many conservatives. Perry would probably have side-stepped the issue rather than fanning the flames unless, of course, there was an election looming.

Greg Abbott was a lawyer, judge, and attorney general before being elected governor in 2014. His first instincts are judicial, so, while his political instincts are well honed, he usually speaks carefully. Perry enjoyed the scuffle over Texas secession that followed his 2009 States' Rights comments, but Abbott was more cautious when the "Brexit" vote, in which British voters declared a desire to leave the European Union, brought calls for a "Texit," from the United States. Texas gadfly Larry Scott Kilgore, who legally changed his middle name to Secede, said, hopefully, "I think the people of Texas will look at this and say: 'Man, we can have freedom; we can make our own decisions. We don't have to have the U.S. empire tell us what to do.'" Governor Abbott was more careful than Kilgore and, more importantly, than Perry might have been, though he did touch the "Texas exceptionalism" base. When asked by Fox News's Sean Hannity whether "Texit" was in prospect, Governor Abbott demurred, saying, "What Texans believe in is that we need the United States to be more like Texas . . . . In fact, I believe America longs to be the way Texas is."[49] In subsequent chapters we explore "the way Texas is" in some detail.

But before we do that we need to explore in a little more detail how Abbott might think to make the U.S. more like Texas. While Abbott has not been as politically flashy as Perry, he has been more systematic, more judicial, and—just possibly—more radical. While Perry was happy to whip up a crowd by flirting with secession, no one really thought Texas was going to take another run at leaving the Union. Abbott has charted another course, a real constitutional, legal, and judicial course grounded in the U.S. Constitution's Article V. At Abbott's insistence, the 2017 Texas Legislature adopted Senate Joint Resolution 2 calling for a Convention of the States to amend the U.S. Constitution. Texas was the 12th state formally to call for such a convention and, in typical Texas fashion, Representative Rick Miller (R-Sugar Land) declared, "We know that there are many states that are lined up behind us just waiting to see what Texas is going to do."

Article V of the U.S. Constitution provides two ways to amend the document; one, and the only one so far used in U.S. history, is for Congress, by a two-thirds vote of both houses, to propose one or more amendments and for three-fourths of the states to approve. The second way, never employed to date, is for two-thirds of states (34 of 50) to call for a Convention of the States, which would meet, produce one or more amendments, and submit them to the states for ratification. If three-fourths of the states (38 of 50) ratified the proposed amendments, they would become part of the Constitution. While a Convention of the States is unlikely, it is an indisputably legitimate pathway to constitutional change. Secession talk is political horseplay, while an Article V Convention of the States is a real, if distant, prospect. Big difference.

Nonetheless, should a Convention of the States occur, Governor Abbott has prepared the "Texas Plan." Recall that in the Constitutional Convention of 1787, James Madison, George Washington, Governor Edmund Randolph, and others offered the "Virginia Plan" to guide the Convention's early deliberations—you see the hoped for comparison, right! Governor Abbott's Texas Plan has been described in a document entitled "Restoring the Rule of Law With States Leading the Way." Abbott's complaint is simple: the entire national government is out of control. The press release announcing the Texas Plan declared that, "Congress routinely violates its enumerated powers, ... The President exceeds his executive powers to impose heavy-handed regulations. And the Supreme Court imposes its policy views under the guise of judicial interpretation." In Abbott's view, the U.S. Constitution held its form throughout the nineteenth and early twentieth centuries, only to be eroded and then increasingly washed away by FDR's New Deal and later expansions of federal government authority—illegitimate and unconstitutional authority. To restore the "Rule of Law" in America, Abbott proposed nine amendments that would sum to a modern states' rights constitutional revolution.

At the center of Governor Abbott's constitutional reform efforts are several amendments that employ supermajorities to make federal action more difficult and state defensive action easier. He proposed to allow two-thirds of the states, meeting in convention as often as necessary, "to override a federal law or regulation" or "a U.S. Supreme Court decision." He also proposed requiring a "seven-justice supermajority vote for the U.S. Supreme Court" to "invalidate a democratically enacted law," federal or state. He proposed flatly prohibiting "administrative agencies—and the unelected bureaucrats that staff them—from creating federal law" or "preempting state law." Finally, Abbott proposed the old standby, a balanced budget amendment, strengthening the Tenth Amendment, a purported defense of states' rights frequently ignored by the federal courts, a standing right of the states to sue the federal government for overreach, and a return to the more limited nineteenth-century understanding of the commerce clause.

Of course, if a Convention of the States were to be held, Abbott's proposed amendments would be thrown into the hopper with amendments proposed by all of the other states attending, so what such a convention might produce is by no means certain. But say 34 states did approve a convention, and that convention did adopt a set of strong states' rights amendments, Abbott's or some others, 38 states would be required to ratify them before they could become part of the U.S. Constitution. So how likely is that? Would California go along? How about Hawaii, Oregon, Washington, Minnesota, Wisconsin, Illinois, Massachusetts, Connecticut, Maryland? Can you get to 13—a blocking coalition?

Conclusion

Texas has always been a southern state and, though it is often dangerous to take campaigning politicians too literally, one can find open declarations of that fact to this day. Texas Senator Ted Cruz, campaigning in South Carolina for the 2016 Republican presidential nomination, roused a crowd by reminding them that, "South Carolina and Texas: we have a lot in common. There are South Carolinians who came to the Alamo and bled and died so that Texas could be free . . . . We're southern states . . . . And we're fed up with the damage and the destruction coming from corrupt politicians in Washington."[50] The roots of Cruz's rhetoric run deep in Texas history.

Though less likely than their ancestors to connect it directly to the South, Anglo Texans are comfortable with, in fact they revel in, the mythology of their state. The myth is flattering to them and has advantaged them in obvious and important ways, both historically and in the present. But like all myths, the Texas myth points to a partial truth while ignoring and even masking much else. As we have seen above and will explore in greater detail in later chapters of this book, Texas is not a wealthy state, though it does have a substantial body of wealthy and privileged people within it. Unfortunately, for many Texans, modest wages, absence of fringe benefits such as employer managed health care, underfunded schools, hospitals, and social services, and environmental degradation are the norm. Texas's most prominent contemporary historian, UT's H.W. Brands, has drawn the obvious conclusion, saying "We have prided ourselves on our uniqueness and idiosyncrasies, but you only become a beacon state if people from the outside see something to emulate. And outside of Texas, not many people look at Texas and say, 'we want to be like that.'"[51]

In the mid-twentieth century, the prominent Texas-born political scientist V.O. Key thought that the dramatic economic changes of the 1930s and 1940s would drive political change in the direction of a competitive two-party politics that would allow the poor to better defend their interests against the organized rich. Instead, the fight over civil rights and desegregation drove whites together even as their majority moved from the Democratic to the Republican Party. In the early twenty-first century a business-oriented conservative establishment governs Texas as surely as it did when Key wrote. In fact, in many public policy areas, including the critical areas of education, health, and social services, Texas ranks lower among the 50 states than it did in 1950. Today, analysts frequently argue that demographic change, especially the burgeoning Hispanic population, will drive political change in Texas and nationally over the next half century. It might, but, with Key in mind, we should not expect it to happen quickly. Change is not impossible, even in Texas, though one is always wise to expect it to come grudgingly and only after a fight.

Nonetheless, as we shall see in detail in Chapter 3, demographic change in Texas has been dramatic over the past three decades and will continue through the twenty-first century. Texas was 39 percent Hispanic in 2015 and will be majority Hispanic in the late 2030s. Hispanics have tended, with occasional exceptions, to vote two-to-one Democrat, but have voted at only about two-thirds the rate of Texas blacks and Anglos. As a result, while Hispanic numbers are up, Hispanic political clout is not. In Chapter 3, we look in detail at demographic change in Texas.

Notes

1 John Steinbeck, *Travels with Charley: In Search of America*, New York: Viking, 1962, pp. 201–202.
2 Robert T. Garrett, "Bush Sworn in as State Land Chief," *Dallas Morning News*, January 3, 2015, 3A.
3 Walter L. Buenger and Robert A. Calvert, ed., *Texas through Time: Evolving Interpretations*, College Station, TX: Texas A&M University Press, 1991, p. xv.
4 Erica Grieder, *Big, Hot, Cheap, and Right*, New York: Public Affairs, 2013, pp. 136–137.
5 Laura Lyons McLemore, *Inventing Texas: Early Historians of the Lone Star State*, College Station, TX: Texas A&M University Press, 2004, p. 73. See also Gregg Cantrell, "The Bones of Stephen F. Austin: History and Memory of Progressive Era Texas," *Southwestern Historical Quarterly*, vol. 108, no. 2, October 2004, pp. 145–178; and Michael Phillips, "Why Is Big Tex Still a White Cowboy: Race, Gender, and the 'Other Texans,'" in Walter A. Buenger and Arnoldo de León, ed., *Beyond Texas Through Time: Breaking Away From Past Interpretations*, College Station, TX: Texas A&M University Press, 2011, p. 183.
6 Don Graham, *State of Minds: Texas Culture and Its Discontents*, Austin, TX: University of Texas Press, 2011, pp. 19, 32.
7 Brian D. Sweany, "Time Will Tell," *Texas Monthly*, March, 2011, pp. 10–14.
8 Glen Sample Ely, *Debating Texas Identity: Where the West Begins*, Lubbock, TX: Texas Tech University Press, 2011, p. 129.
9 Walter L. Buenger, "Texas and the South," *Southwestern Historical Review*, vol. 103, no. 3, January 2000, pp. 308–324, 310.
10 Ely, *Debating Texas Identity*, p. 8.

11 Wilbur Zelinsky, *The Cultural Geography of the United States*, Englewood Cliffs, NJ: Prentice-Hall, 1973, p. 124. See also the precipitation map in David G. McComb, *The City in Texas: A History*, Austin, TX: University of Texas Press, 2015, p. 12.

12 Bryan Burrough, *The Big Rich: The Rise and Fall of the Greatest Texas Oil Fortunes*, New York: Penguin Press, 2009, p. 233.

13 Michael Lind, *Land of Promise: An Economic History of the United States*, New York: Harper Collins, 2012, p. 360.

14 Bill Minutaglio and Stephen L. Davis, *Dallas 1963*, New York: Twelve, 2013, p. 20.

15 Benjamin Marquez, *Democratizing Texas Politics: Race, Identity, and Mexican-American Empowerment, 1945–2002*, Austin, TX: University of Texas Press, 2014, pp. 24–25, 62.

16 James McEnteer, *Deep in the Heart: The Texas Tendency in American Politics*, Westport, CT: Praeger, 2004, p. 112.

17 James Reston Jr., *Lone Star: The Life of John Connally*, New York: Harper and Row, 1989, p. 273; Robert Dallek, *An Unfinished Life: John F. Kennedy, 1917–1963*, Boston, MA: Little, Brown and Company, 2003, p. 693.

18 Reston, *Lone Star*, p. 213.

19 George Norris Green, *The Establishment in Texas Politics: The Primitive Years, 1938–1957*, Norman, OK: University of Oklahoma Press, 1979, p. 3.

20 T.R. Fehrenbach, *Seven Keys to Texas*, El Paso, TX: Texas Western Press, 1983, p. 117.

21 Frank R. Kemerer, *William Wayne Justice: A Judicial Biography*, Austin, TX: University of Texas Press, 1991 and 2008, pp. 230–231.

22 Reston, *Lone Star*, p. 296.

23 Sean P. Cunningham, *Cowboy Conservatism: Texas and the Rise of the Modern Right*, Lexington, KY: University of Kentucky Press, 2010, p. 104.

24 Reston, *Lone Star*, pp. 264, 289. See also McEnteer, *Deep in the Heart*, p. 136; and Patrick L. Cox and Michael Phillips, *The House Will Come to Order*, Austin, TX: University of Texas Press, 2010, p. 90.

25 Cunningham, *Cowboy Conservatism*, p. 121.

26 Fehrenbach, *Seven Keys to Texas*, pp. 112–113.

27 Chandler Davidson, *Race and Class in Texas Politics*, Princeton, NJ: Princeton University Press, 1990, p. 17.

28 Gerry Riposa, ed., *Texas Public Policy*, Dubuque, IA: Kendall Hunt, 1987, pp. 17–18.

29 Anthony Champagne and Edward J. Harpham, *Texas at the Crossroads: People, Politics, and Policy*, College Station, TX: Texas A&M University Press, 1987, p. 3.

30 Ibid., p. 270.

31 Ibid., p. 9.

32 Cox and Phillips, *The House Will Come to Order*, p. 182.

33 Evan Smith, "Rain, Rain, Go Away," *Texas Monthly*, June 2009, pp. 142–147, 189–190.

34 McLemore, *Inventing Texas*, p. 95.

35 www.clevelandfed.org/global%20search.aspx?q=annual+report+2005.

36 Ibid., p. 7.

37 Ibid., p. 9. See also, G. Andrew Bernat Jr., "Convergence in State per Capita Personal Income, 1950–1999," *Survey of Current Business*, June 2001, pp. 36–48.

38 Ibid., p. 17. See also, Brian Chappatta, "States Lacking Income Tax Get No Boost in Growth," BGOV Barometer, Bloomberg News, June 24, 2012.

39 David G. McComb, *Texas: A Modern History*, revised edition, Austin, TX: University of Texas Press, 2009, p. 145.

40 Edna Ferber, *Giant*, Garden City, NY: Doubleday & Company, 1952, p. 359.

41 *Texas on the Brink* (*TOB*), A Report from the Texas Legislative Study Group on the State of Our State, March 2013, p. 4.

42 *Texas Fact Book* (*TFB*), Texas Legislative Budget Board, 2014, pp. 21–22, www.lbb.state.tx.us/Documents/Publications/Policy_Report/Fact_Book_2014.pdf

43 *TOB*, 2013, p. 5.

44 *TFB*, 2012, pp. 18–19.

45 *TOB*, 2013, p. 5.

46 *TFB*, pp. 21–22; *TOB*, 2013, p. 6.

47 Evan Thomas and Arian Campo-Flores, "Don't Mess With Texas," *Newsweek*, April 26, 2010, pp. 28–32. See also Ezrati, "Just What Is It About Texas?" *Antioch Review*, p. 761.

48 Paul Burka, "The Secret of My Secession," *Texas Monthly*, June 2009, p. 8.

49 Manny Fernandez and Jonah Engel Bromwich, "Brits Vote Revives Calls for Secession," *Dallas Morning News*, July 4, 2016, 4B. See also Bobby Blanchard, "Governor: 'Texit' Is Not Happening," *Dallas Morning News*, June 28, 2016, 3B.
50 James Hohmann, "Will South Carolina Republicans Buy That Marco Rubio Is Just as Conservative as Ted Cruz?" *Washington Post*, "The Daily 202," February 19, 2016.
51 William McKenzie, "175 Years of Texas," a Q&A with H.W. Brands, *Dallas Morning News*, February 27, 2011, 5P.

3 Demographic Change and Its Implications

> One of the basic rules of politics is that demographic change produces political change.
> (Paul Burka, 2011)[1]

More than a century ago, Associate Justice John Marshall Harlan stood alone on behalf of racial equality in the infamous case of *Plessy v. Ferguson* (1896). Justice Harlan reminded his colleagues that "in view of the Constitution, in the eye of the law, there is in this county no superior, dominant, ruling class of citizens. There is no cast here. Our Constitution is color-blind, and neither knows nor tolerates classes among citizens." Tragically, Justice Harlan was on the wrong end of an eight to one majority that found in favor of Louisiana's right, and that of other states (i.e., states' rights), to separate blacks and whites in public places. Justice Harlan's claim that the Constitution was meant to be color-blind was rejected by his colleagues.

In *Parents Involved in Community Schools v. Seattle School District #1* (2007), United States Supreme Court Chief Justice John Roberts wrote that "The way to stop discrimination on the basis of race is to stop discriminating on the basis of race." American law, the Chief Justice declared, should be color-blind. This view strikes a positive cord with most Americans; every school-child knows that the most famous phrase in the Declaration of Independence is that "all men are created equal." Yet, race and ethnicity have been touchstones of American life throughout our history. White majority status has always commanded privilege, even if only in the absence of road blocks, while minority status has often meant limited opportunity. In a sense, Justice Harlan and Chief Justice Roberts were saying the same thing; that America should be a color-blind society. So why is Justice Harlan seen as a great hero of the court and Chief Justice Roberts not so seen—at least not yet?

Race and ethnicity have been profoundly important in American and Texas history. Distinctions of race and ethnicity were written into every U.S. immigration statute from the 1790s through the 1950s and remain central to our discussions of immigration today. Similarly, Texas used its constitutions and laws to define who was welcomed, who was excluded, and with what degree of force. As the Anglo majority that has governed Texas since its independence fades into history, what kinds of political change will follow? In this chapter, we describe the demographic changes that have brought Texas to its current majority minority status and to the verge of a Hispanic majority.

Bragging Rights: Population Growth in Texas

Texas has grown more rapidly than the U.S. since the 1830s, a fact in which Texans take pride each time new census figures are announced. The 2015 census update showed that

Texas had grown by 9 percent since 2010, adding almost 2.3 million people, while the U.S. had grown by just 4 percent. Many Texans assume that their burgeoning population numbers reflect the state's dynamic economy when compared with an over-taxed and regulated national economy. To some extent they do, but they reflect both the plusses and minuses of being a business-friendly, low-wage, state. A few of the plusses are rapid population and job growth, but a few of the minuses are modest wages and benefits. It has always been a trade-off. Still, Texas has been putting up big numbers for a long time.

During the first half of the nineteenth century, the U.S. grew at a very robust 35 percent per decade. During the second half of the century, U.S. growth moderated a bit, to the still very solid 25 percent per decade. By 1900, the frontier was closed, the processes of urbanization and industrialization were well under way, and by the mid-twentieth century the U.S. was an advanced industrial society. Though immigration was limited from the mid-1920s through the mid-1960s, population still grew at the rate of about 15 percent per decade.

Not surprisingly, late arrivals on the periphery—Texas, California, and Florida—grew more rapidly than the nation, especially in their early decades. Once independence was secured in 1836, Texas experienced a 187 percent population increase in the 1840s, rising from 78,000 to 223,592, and in the 1850s growing by 170 percent from 223,592 to 604,215. The 1849 discovery of gold at Sutter's Mill near Sacramento drove a 310 percent population increase in California during the 1850s. Figure 3.1 shows that growth rates for Texas, California, and Florida remained well above the national average after 1860. California grew by almost 50 percent per decade for the next hundred years. Florida grew by 39 percent per decade during the same period, while Texas grew at 33 percent per decade. In the past half century and more, since 1960, Florida has grown at 33 percent, Texas at 21.4 percent, and California at 19.2 percent. From 2000 to 2010, Florida grew at 25 percent, Texas grew at 21 percent, and California trailed off to just 10 percent, no better than the national average. Texans struggle not to celebrate the decline of California, but they also worry about what the future holds for them. There are reasons for concern.

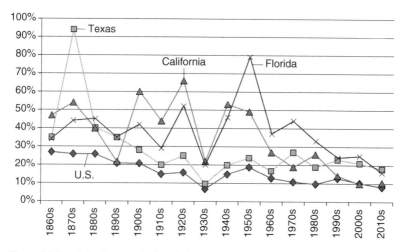

Figure 3.1 Population Increase by Decade in the U.S., Texas, California, and Florida

Source: U.S. Census data, see www.census.gov/population/www/censusdata/hiscendata.html. 2010s are author estimates based on actual data from 2010 through 2015.

Paul Burka's statement that "demographic change produces political change" was first and most colorfully stated by the nineteenth-century French philosopher Auguste Comte. Comte's declaration that "demography is destiny" has been much on Texans' minds lately. Demography is the statistical study of the size, structure, growth, and distribution of human populations. Other social sciences, including economics, sociology, and political science, draw on the findings of demography to study variations in income, wealth, education, health, and the like by race and ethnicity. Many Texans are aware that broad demographic changes have been under way in the state for decades. Some wonder whether ongoing demographic changes— a shrinking Anglo population and an expanding Hispanic population—foretell a certain "destiny" for Texas (Table 3.1).

Texas's rapid population growth has masked some internal dynamics of the growth that will repay detailed attention. In 1800, there were probably fewer than 30,000 inhabitants in Texas and more than 85 percent of them were Indians. The rest were Spanish and Mexicans with just a few black slaves. In 1850, when Texas was first included in

Table 3.1 Texas Population Growth by Decade, Race, and Ethnicity

Decade	Anglo	Black	Hispanic	Indian	Asian/Other	Total
1780		20	2,250	30,000		32,270
1790		40	3,169	27,500		30,709
1800		60	3,500	25,000		28,560
1810	250	80	4,000	22,500		26,830
1820	1,000	100	2,500	20,000		23,600
1830	20,000	2,000	4,000	17,000		43,000
1840	50,000	10,000	5,000	13,000		78,000
1850	145,537	58,555	8,500	11,000		223,595
1860	398,291	182,921	15,000	8,000		604,212
1870	534,004	253,475	24,975	6,100	25	818,579
1880	1,152,365	393,384	42,864	3,000	136	1,591,749
1890	1,685,356	488,171	59,287	2,000	713	2,235,527
1900	2,355,926	620,722	70,213	1,000	849	3,048,710
1910	3,080,722	690,049	124,634	702	435	3,896,542
1920	3,469,425	741,694	448,778	2,109	1,222	4,663,228
1930	4,285,069	854,964	682,459	1,001	1,222	5,824,715
1940	4,751,112	924,391	736,433	1,103	1,785	6,414,824
1950	5,727,045	977,458	1,000,000	2,736	3,955	7,711,194
1960	6,974,831	1,187,125	1,400,000	5,750	11,971	9,579,677
1970	7,950,575	1,399,092	1,840,648	17,231	62,640	11,196,730
1980	9,390,437	1,692,542	2,985,824	40,075	120,313	14,229,191
1990	10,284,909	1,976,360	4,339,905	65,877	319,459	16,986,510
2000	11,074,716	2,451,653	6,669,666	125,111	685,785	20,851,820
2010	11,397,345	2,886,825	9,460,921	220,000	1,180,470	25,145,561
2020	11,723,184	3,274,738	11,963,951	250,000	1,601,409	28,813,282
2030	11,792,588	3,616,745	14,900,906	295,000	2,074,978	32,680,217
2040	11,593,202	3,876,830	18,095,574	340,000	2,644,989	36,550,595
2050	11,265,371	4,065,757	21,516,362	410,000	3,245,259	40,502,749

Source: Tracing the racial and ethnic development of Texas is no easy task. Prior to 1850, we must depend on scattered Spanish, Mexican, and Texan enumerations and the educated guesswork of anthropologists and historians. Still, the numbers are small and there is a rough consensus. The U.S. Census of 1850 was the first to include Texas. Whites and blacks were carefully enumerated, but Hispanics were not separated from whites and one can reasonably assume that Hispanics were undercounted. Hispanic numbers have been estimated by historians and are subtracted from the census count of whites above. The data and projections for 2000 to 2050 are from the Texas State Data Center and Office of the State Demographer, 2014 Texas Population Projections.

the U.S. Census, there were fewer than a quarter million people in the state, but most now were whites and their black slaves. Population took off from there, breaking one million in the early 1870s and three million by 1900. In 1900, Texas was an over-whelmingly Anglo republic. Whites were almost 80 percent of all inhabitants, the black population was falling, and Hispanics, though probably undercounted, were reported to be less than 5 percent of the population. Total population grew steadily through the twentieth century, breaking 5 million in the 1920s, 10 million in the 1960s, 25 million by 2010, with projections of 40 million by 2050. Prior to the 1980s, there was little suspicion that Texas's Anglo republic was threatened.

Though Anglo Texans know that the demographic make-up of the state is chang-ing, most probably do not realize that the Anglo population of Texas has grown more slowly than the national population since 1980 (7.3 percent per decade compared to 11 percent). Moreover, the Texas State Demographer projects that the growth of the Anglo population over the next four decades will be slightly negative—that is, less than zero. While black population growth has outstripped Anglo growth since 1980, it is Hispanic growth that has been truly eye-popping. Over the past three decades, Hispanic popula-tion growth in Texas has averaged 45 percent per decade and is projected to grow at 20 to 25 percent per decade over the next four decades.

Between 1900 and 2000, the Hispanic share of the Texas population increased from less than 5 percent to 32 percent and by 2050 is expected to be 53 percent. Bluntly, the question now is—since Hispanic income and educational attainment are lower than Anglos—does this mean that an increasingly Hispanic Texas must be poorer, less edu-cated, and less productive? The answer, some assure, is no; especially if Hispanics, or Texas, or some combination of the two, act to improve Hispanic educational attain-ment. Then Hispanic productivity and income will grow and Texas will continue to prosper. Others worry that demographic change is outrunning improvement in edu-cational attainment. As Texas State Demographer Lloyd Potter said recently, "A [Hispanic] population that isn't making enough money to fuel our economy, or ends up being a burden on the state—that is not indicative of having a higher quality of life in the future."[2]

Texas has two choices: it can either try to change these numbers or it can try to change the social and economic attributes of the coming Hispanic majority. Over the first century and more of the state's history, Texans and their political leaders took the first path: they tried to shape the racial and ethnic make-up of the state. During the com-ing decades, Texans and their political leaders will either commit to the second path, changing Hispanic social and economic attributes, or pay an unsustainably heavy price.

Shaping the Anglo Republic

Few states have seen the sweeping demographic changes experienced by Texas. As the American Revolution raged on the Atlantic Coast, there were no Anglo-Americans and very few blacks in what was then northern Mexico, now Texas. There were fewer than 2,500 Spanish, Mexican, and Mestizo settlers north of the Rio Grande and perhaps 30,000 to 50,000 Indians. While the Indian population sank to between 20,000 and 30,000 by 1820, the Mexican population rose to about 3,500 by 1800, before falling back toward 2,500 during the Mexican war for independence from 1810 to 1821. The first Anglo settlers did not arrive in Texas until about 1815 and then only in small numbers.

Prior to the first Anglo settlers, a few white men, almost always looking for trouble, wandered into Texas. One of the first was a persistent pest named Philip Nolan. Nolan entered Texas several times during the 1790s from what was then Spanish Louisiana. Though he bore a trade license from the Spanish authorities in New Orleans when he entered Texas in 1791, his goods were seized by Spanish authorities in San Antonio and he was jailed. He returned to New Orleans two years later with nothing to show for his efforts but a couple dozen mustangs. Nolan made two more trips into Texas, but his last trip was fatal. After spending the winter of 1800–1801 catching and trading for mustangs in Central Texas, Nolan awoke on the morning of March 22, 1801, to find his camp surrounded by Mexican cavalry. When Nolan approached the soldiers to plead his case, they opened fire and he was killed almost immediately.[3]

Anthony Glass was another early trader into Texas. Glass was a Mississippi plantation owner and Louisiana Indian trader who entered Texas in 1808 to trade with the Caddo, Wichita, and Comanche on the Red River and the Middle Colorado. Glass and ten colleagues, bearing passports and licenses from U.S. agent for Indian Affairs John Sibley of Natchitoches, Louisiana, crossed into Texas in July 1808 with 16 horses packed with goods and three saddle horses per man. Glass's party successfully traded for mustangs over the fall and winter and returned to Louisiana in May 1809. The daily journal that Glass kept is one of the first Anglo reports of early nineteenth-century Texas. But traders were not the only Anglos in Texas during these years.

In the first two decades of the nineteenth century, especially once the Spanish and Mexicans were distracted by the Mexican war for independence (1810–1821), Anglo adventurers, called filibusterers, sought to seize some or all of Texas for themselves. The most famous Texas filibuster was Natchez doctor and businessman James Long. In 1819, Long led about 300 armed men into East Texas, easily capturing Nacogdoches. Long then proceeded to Galveston Island, hoping to strike an alliance with the pirate Jean Lafitte. In Long's absence, Spanish forces from San Antonio forced his men out of Nacogdoches and he escaped back to New Orleans. Long returned to Texas in 1820 with just 50 men and set up a camp called Fort Las Casas, at Point Bolivar on Galveston Bay. Long and several of the filibusterers were joined by their families. The leisurely pace of their planning meant that they did not select their target, La Bahia, and attack until September 1821. Again, Long's forces initially prevailed only to fall to a Spanish counterattack a few days later. Long was captured, sent to Mexico, jailed, and eventually killed. His wife, Jane, and daughter remained at Point Bolivar, eventually alone except for a slave girl, awaiting word on James Long's fate. Abandoned, her husband dead in Mexico, Jane Long delivered a baby she named Mary James Long on December 21, 1821, reported, incorrectly as it turned out, to be the first Anglo baby born in Texas. Though the baby died before she was two, Jane Long left Texas only briefly, returning as one of Stephen F. Austin's early settlers.[4]

Once Mexico secured its independence from Spain, Mexican authorities moved to rebuild their depopulated and dangerous northern frontier. They worried about both American expansion into the Mississippi Valley and Comanche raids out of Texas into northern Mexico. As early as 1818, Moses and Stephen Austin claimed land in Southwest Arkansas at Long Prairie on the Red River. On the other side of the Red River lay Mexican Texas. By late 1820, Moses Austin was in San Antonio seeking an empresario contract to bring settlers into Texas. By late June 1821, Moses was dead and Stephen was in Natchitoches, Louisiana, preparing to cross the Sabine into Texas to complete his father's plan. The Austin grant anticipated 300 families, willing to declare Catholicism and Mexican citizenship and to settle in South Central Texas between the Colorado and Brazos rivers. There were perhaps 1,000 Anglos in Texas when Stephen Austin arrived, 100 slaves, just about 2,500 Mexicans, and at least 20,000 Indians. Mexican trepidation about Anglo immigration is easy to understand. Just as Stephen

F. Austin was in San Antonio negotiating the details of his first empresario contract, James Long was attacking La Bahia, 90 miles to the southeast.

Mexican authorities always were skeptical of American immigrants to Texas. In 1828, General Manuel de Mier y Teran toured Texas to assess its stability and prospects. General Teran was a sophisticated man, an artillery officer trained in engineering, math, and science. He found much to be wanting in Texas among both its Mexican and Anglo populations; writing, "The Mexican is dissipated and consistently in town. . . . The North Americans are haughty; . . . They devote themselves . . . to the hardest labors—as well as the grossest vices—with exceptional ardour. They do not think they have relaxed from their gruelling tasks until drunkenness dulls their senses, and in that state they are fierce and scandalous."[5] Amen!

By 1836, when Texas secured its independence from Mexico, the Anglo population had grown to nearly 30,000, almost eight times the 4,000 residents of Mexican extraction, 5,000 slaves, and perhaps 15,000 Indians.[6] University of Texas geographer and demographer Terry G. Jordan, working in the tradition of Wilbur Zelinsky's "first settlement" thesis, reported in an article entitled "A Century and a Half of Ethnic Change in Texas, 1836–1986," that "In Texas, the host/dominant group . . . consisted of old-stock Anglo-Americans of colonial eastern-seaboard ancestry. More precisely, *southern* Anglos . . . ."[7] Billy D. Ledbetter's famous article, "White Over Black in Texas," used settlement patterns to explain the prevalence of southern racial attitudes in Texas, saying "Only four Northern states had contributed over 1,000 settlers to . . . [Texas], whereas all the Southern states that ultimately seceded from the Union, with the exception of Florida, were represented by over 9,000 settlers."[8]

Moreover, southerners in Texas thoroughly dominated the state's economy, society, and politics. Nearly three-quarters of Anglo heads of households in 1860 had southern roots as did fully 90 percent of slave-owners. Randolph B. Campbell's *An Empire for Slavery: The Peculiar Institution in Texas, 1821–1865*, concluded that "Antebellum Texas, . . . had all the characteristics of an advanced slaveholding society." Though only 27 percent of Anglo heads of household owned slaves as the Civil War approached in 1860, and just 3 percent held 20 or more slaves, they were the state's leadership elite. Campbell reports that slaveholders in 1860 owned 71 percent of the state's improved acreage, 73 percent of the state's wealth, and fully 91 percent of its cotton crop. Their economic dominance gave them social primacy and political control. In 1860, slave-owners held 68 percent of local, state, and federal offices.[9]

As we shall see below, though it will seem harsh in the viewing, "Anglo Texas racism against Mexicans, Indians, and Blacks defined and directed nineteenth-century Texas history."[10] Anglo Texans sought to remove both Indians and Mexicans from Texas. While slavery was legal, blacks were thought useful, even indispensable, but after slavery, that view changed.

Texas and the Indians

Scholars disagree about the number of Indians in North America generally and in Texas more specifically before Europeans arrived. David La Vere, author of *The Texas Indians* (2004), reviewed the scholarship and reported that estimates of the North American native population, once one to two million, had risen to seven to nine million, with some saying perhaps 18 million. Population estimates for Texas in 1500 range from 50,000 to several hundred thousand to perhaps a million. Adopting the middle range of seven to nine million Indians on the continent and perhaps half a million in

Texas in 1500 seems a reasonable guess, but it is only a guess. Still, La Vere reminds us that in 1500 "Indians lived in virtually every part of Texas . . . and a person could not travel far before they encountered Indians and often a considerable number of them."[11]

Precise numbers, even fairly general population estimates, are not possible for many reasons. First, some Indian tribes ranged in and out of Texas depending upon the seasons and the movement of the buffalo herds. Second, even the more fixed agricultural tribes, such as the Caddo, resided in more than one state. The Caddo spilled out of Northeast Texas into Louisiana and Arkansas. Third, and most importantly, Indians had no written languages and they took no surveys or census counts. Modern experts are dependent upon scattered reports from Spanish, French, and, later, American soldiers, traders, and travelers. Hence, David La Vere discussed the Caddo population from 1500 to 1700 and beyond as follows: "Much controversy exists over the size of the Caddo population at the beginning of the sixteenth century. Some scholars suggest . . . between 200,000 and 250,000 in 1500. Others say not nearly that many. In any event, by the late seventeenth century the Caddo population had dwindled to somewhere between 8,000 and 40,000 and was still falling." Similarly broad ranges are offered for the Coahuiltecan, the Wichita, and others.[12]

Whatever their numbers before the arrival of Europeans, Indians suffered steep population declines after contact. Contact occurred first in South and East Texas and only much later in West Texas, but once it occurred Indian numbers always fell quickly. The first Europeans in Texas were Alvar Nunez Cabeza de Vaca and about 90 of his shipmates. Initially shipwrecked in Florida, they built rafts and put back to sea, finally wrecking again on Galveston Island on November 6, 1528. Most soon died from their ordeal or were killed by Indians, but Cabeza de Vaca and a few colleagues were taken in by the Coco band of the Karankawa Indians. Soon "cholera hit the Indians and killed half of them."[13] Over the next three centuries, contacts between Europeans, Americans, and Texas Indians decimated the Indians. By the time that Anglo settlement of Texas began in earnest, around 1820, Indians in Texas numbered only 20,000 to 40,000. John Ewers translated a book by Jose Francisco Ruiz, entitled *Texas Indians in 1830*, that places the number near 40,000, but most historians, including T.R. Fehrenbach, place the number at 30,000 in 1820, while Randolph Campbell says 20,000.[14]

The precise number of Indians in Texas in the 1820s matters little, because in a few short decades they were virtually all gone and epidemics were not the only cause of their decline. Stephen F. Austin arrived in Texas convinced that "The Indians . . . may be called universal enemies of man. There will be no way of subduing them but extermination."[15] While Sam Houston, first president of the Republic of Texas, was sympathetic to the Indians and sought to treat with them, his successor, President Mirabeau B. Lamar, pursued a policy of removal or extermination.

Lamar's opening address to the Texas Congress in December 1838 made his intentions clear. He warned that, "If the wild cannibals of the woods will not desist from their massacres, if they will continue to war upon us with the ferocity of tigers and hyenas, it is time that we should retaliate their warfare." The goal, he said, was "their total extinction or total expulsion."[16]

In 1842, William Bollaert observed that, "Texas . . . is now fast becoming the grave of the tribes of Red Men."[17] Subsequent policies, equally brutal, had cleared North Texas by 1860. The final battles on the high plains against the once mighty Comanche occurred in the early and mid-1870s. The fundamental fact, however, is that by the time large numbers of Anglos arrived in Texas, the Indians were already broken, a shadow of their former selves, their numbers down 90 percent and falling. Despite the terror that a Comanche war party might still cause on the Texas plains in the early 1870s, these warriors represented the chips and shards of long lost Indian nations. Within half a century of the establishment of Austin's colony, Anglo Texans had cleared the state of its native population.

Two stories, one concerning treaty negotiation and one concerning the establishment of reservations in Texas, highlight the Anglo attitude toward the Indians. Sam Houston had long mourned that Indians were easy prey for dishonest white traders and settlers. He sought to negotiate fair treaties to free some Indian land for white settlement while securing some land for permanent Indian use. The Texas Congress ratified few of Houston's treaties because nearly all Anglo Texans saw Indian land as wasted. When Lamar succeeded Houston as president in late 1838, he charted a far more popular course on Indian policy. Lamar shared in the widely held Anglo view that Indians lacked integrity and so could not be negotiated with in any meaningful sense. Indians likely thought the same about whites.

In 1840, chiefs of the Penatekas band of the Comanche rode into San Antonio to meet Texas authorities to discuss suspension of hostilities and the return of white hostages. The Indians brought few hostages, but one they did bring, 16-year-old Matilda Lockhart, bore obvious signs of torture and abuse. Texans moved to take the chiefs hostage as leverage for the return of all white captives and fighting broke out, leaving seven Anglo Texans and 37 Indians, including 12 chiefs, dead and three dozen Indian women and children captive. The Comanche, with Kiowa and Mexican support, attacked Victoria, stealing 1,500 horses, and sacked Linnville. Texan volunteers intercepted the Indians at Plum Creek as they retreated north. A running battle left nearly 100 Comanche dead. In the fall, another battle near modern-day Ballinger saw Texans, supported by Lipan Apache and Tonkawa warriors and scouts, attack a Comanche village, kill 130 Indians, and retrieve much of the booty from Victoria and Linnville.

The story of Texas's short-lived Indian reservations is equally remarkable. Though most East Texas Indians had been pushed north of the Red River by 1840, conflict between advancing Anglos and Indian remnants, as well as raiding parties from the Oklahoma Indian Territory, continued into the early 1850s. Establishing an effective Indian policy after Texas accession to the U.S. was difficult because Indian policy was a federal government responsibility but Texas had retained control of all public lands within the state and most whites opposed leaving any of it to Indians. Houston famously said, "If I could build a wall from the Red River to the Rio Grande, so high that no Indian could scale it, the white people would go crazy trying to devise means to get beyond it."[18]

In what seemed a breakthrough, the Texas Legislature agreed in 1854 to provide land for two Indian reservations in North Texas.[19] One was called the Clear Fork Reserve, the other the Brazos Reserve. Anglo Texans never accepted the presence of the reservations and blamed any crime or mischief in their vicinity on the Indians. Anglo vigilantes, led by John R. Baylor, attacked the Brazos Reserve several times in 1859. Earlier Baylor had been an Indian agent to the Comanche at the Clear Fork Reserve. Baylor was fired by his supervisor, John Neighbors, when he accused the reserve Indians, perhaps correctly, of cooperating with non-reserve Indians in local raids. The final attack, in which Baylor led a ragged force of 250 Anglo residents of the area, convinced Neighbors to close the two Texas reserves and lead the Indians north into the Oklahoma Indian Territory. Historian David La Vere concluded that, "The removal of the Clear Fork and Brazos Reserve Indians was the culmination of the process begun by Mirabeau Lamar some twenty years earlier. By 1860 Texas found itself virtually denuded of Indian peoples."[20]

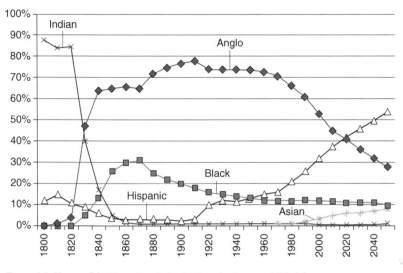

Figure 3.2 Shares of the Texas Population by Decade, Race, and Ethnicity

Source: Percentage population shares derived from the data in Table 3.1.

The respective fates of John Neighbors and John Baylor make the story even more poignant. When Neighbors returned to Texas after overseeing the Indians' removal, he was assassinated, killed by a shotgun blast to the back. John Baylor served, always controversially, as a Confederate army officer and congressman. He sought the Democratic Party nomination for governor of Texas in 1873 before settling into the life of a prominent rancher near Uvalde. He died peacefully in 1894. Baylor County, immediately north of the reserves, was named for Baylor's brother Henry. The demise of the Indian population in Texas was no cause for Anglo mourning. John Wesley Wilbarger spoke for many Texas Anglos in his 691-page book, *Indian Depredations in Texas* (1889), when he wrote that, "We are glad . . . that there are no Indians now in Texas except 'good ones,' who are as dead as Julius Caesar."[21] Wilbarger was wrong, there were a few Indians left in Texas as the nineteenth century closed, but just a few. The U.S. Census of 1900 counted fewer than 1,000 (see Figure 3.2).

Texas and the Mexicans

Texas Hispanics also suffered greatly in the wake of Texas independence. Stephen F. Austin described the Texas revolt as "a war of barbarism . . . waged by a mongrel Spanish-Indian and Negro race, against civilization and the Anglo-American race."[22] The Texian battle cry, "Remember the Alamo, Remember Goliad," was a blood reminder of Mexican savagery and Anglo bravery and sacrifice. As Leigh Clemons reminds us, "Tejanos living in the Republic of Texas after the Revolution were dispossessed of their property, harassed, and forced to flee or, in some cases, killed."[23]

Despite the fact that Tejanos fought for independence at the Alamo and San Jacinto, mistrust and greed put Anglos and Tejanos at odds. Lorenzo de Zavala was an accomplished Mexican diplomat and politician, appointed governor of the state of Mexico, who resigned his positions and fled to Texas after denouncing Santa Anna as a tyrant.

He signed the Texas Declaration of Independence and assisted in drafting the Republic of Texas Constitution before being elected *interim* vice president of Texas. He resigned due to ill-health and died in November 1836 before the tensions between Anglos and Tejanos grew ugly. Juan Seguin, perhaps the most famous Tejano participant in the Texas Revolution, was not so fortunate.

Juan Seguin came from a prominent Tejano family in San Antonio. Seguin fought at the Alamo before Travis sent him through the Mexican lines with letters and instructions to bring back reinforcements. Seguin delivered the letters but returned with reinforcements too late; the Alamo had already fallen. Seguin then led cavalry covering the retreat east of Houston's ragged army and of Anglo families trying to outrun Santa Anna's advance. Seguin's cavalry detachment rejoined Houston's army at San Jacinto. As with the Indians, Houston was sensitive to the ambiguous place of the Tejanos in the fight for independence. On the eve of the decisive battle, Houston ordered Seguin and 19 Tejanos to the rear with orders to guard the baggage train. Seguin protested and Houston relented, permitting the Tejanos to join the line only after they had placed distinctive markers on their hats so the Anglos could tell them from the enemy.

After independence was secured, Seguin retained his rank in the Texas army and in 1840 he was elected mayor of San Antonio. As Texas filled with aggressive Anglo adventurers ignorant of the Tejanos service in the revolution, two Mexican invasions of South Texas in 1842 caused a spike in Anglo/Tejano tensions that brought Seguin down. In the first invasion, Seguin was ordered by Texas military officials to burn San Antonio to prevent its capture and use by the Mexicans. Seguin refused, abandoned the city, and then counter attacked, chasing the Mexicans from Texas, but both Texas officials and San Antonio Anglos accused him of cowardice, if not treason. Fearing for his life, Seguin fled to Mexico, to "seek refuge among my enemies." In Mexico, Seguin was arrested and impressed into the Mexican army where he fought during the U.S./Mexican War. Though Seguin returned briefly to Texas after the war, there was no place for him. He spent most of the rest of his long life—he died in 1890—in Nuevo Laredo, Tamaulipas, Mexico.

Anglo Texans made little effort to distinguish between Mexicans and Tejanos. Quite the contrary, some Texas leaders sought to equate Indians and Mexicans and urge the expulsion or extermination of both. Branch T. Archer, Texas Secretary of War, argued for the removal of Mexicans as well as Indians from Texas. Archer argued that Mexicans were worse than Indians, saying "The merciless Indian savage is, if possible, eclipsed in cruelty by our semi-barbarian Mexican foe; who are at this time engaged in the work of plunder and rapine, desolating in their bloody career, the fairest portion of our western frontier."[24] Others, perhaps the moderates of their day, urged discrimination rather than expulsion. A delegate to the Texas Constitutional Convention of 1845 reminded his colleagues that, "In their taste and social instincts, they [the Mexicans] approximated the African. . . . Notice how [the peons] meet [the slave] on an equality. They do not intermarry with the white population; they form their connections among the slaves."[25] Whether the Mexicans were more like the Indians or more like the Africans might be debated in early Texas, but they were not to be mistaken for citizens.

The Texan attitude toward Mexicans, Indians, and Africans was nicely captured by Joseph Eve, United States Chargé d'Affaires in a May 10, 1842 letter to Richard Southgate. Eve is quoted by Texas historian William Ransom Hogan, saying "most Texans were contemptuous of Mexicans, 'feble, dastardly, superstitious priest ridden race of mongrels, composed of Spanish Indian and negro blood' and were 'always willing to fight them or the Indians five to one.'"[26] David Montejano, a prize-winning historian of Anglo–Mexican relations in Texas, noted that the "Anglos who settled in the Southwest brought with them a long history of dealing with Indians and blacks, while the experience of the Alamo and the Mexican War served to crystallize and affirm anti-Mexican prejudice. . . . Anglos and Mexicans stood as conquerors and conquered, as victors and vanquished."[27] By 1850, Hispanics and Indians each constituted about 5 percent of the population and both declined from there.

Moreover, Anglo Texans often resented Mexicans undercutting Anglo wages and sometimes used violence to stop it. In the famous "cart wars" of the late 1850s, Anglo haulers working the route between San Antonio and the coast killed 75 Mexicans because their rates were lower than the Anglos thought they needed to stay in business. The *Nueces Valley Weekly* spoke for moderate Anglo opinion. The paper editorialized that, "There is evidently a large amount of prejudice among our people against the greaser population, which often breaks out in acts of violence. . . . The fact of their being low in the scale of intelligence is no excuse for making them scapegoats."[28]

Mexicans fought back, but with no more than occasional and temporary success. Most famously, Juan Cortina was a borderlands legend from 1859 to 1875. After witnessing a Brownsville marshal pistol-whip a Mexican cowhand from his mother's ranch, Cortina intervened, shot the marshal in the shoulder, and carried the cowhand to safety. Anglo authorities pursued him; Cortina gathered Mexican supporters from both sides of the border and counterattacked, briefly capturing Brownsville in the fall of 1859. Cortina was eventually pushed south of the border but he continued to organize raids from Mexico. In the 1860s, he became a Mexican army general and later was governor of Tamaulipas.[29] As late as 1875, Mexican raiders identified with Cortina were stealing Texas cattle. The fact that Cortina harassed the Norte Americanos made him a Mexican hero, but Anglo Texans were not amused. Texas Rangers under the command of the famous Captain L.H. McNelly "caught a group of Mexican cattle banditos red-handed near the border and 'naturalized' thirteen of them."[30] Ranger violence in South Texas eventually made Mexicans a cowering and subservient population. As Montejano notes, "By 1900 the Mexican upper class would become nonexistent except in a few border enclaves."[31] But change was coming.

In 1898, Robert Kleberg, scion of the fantastic King Ranch, discovered that deep wells on his Santa Gartrudis ranch tapped a huge aquifer. In 1905, entrepreneurs opened the 160-mile-long St. Louis, Brownsville, and Mexico Railway between Brownsville and the Corpus Christi terminal of the Missouri–Pacific Railroad. By 1909, a spur had been run out into the Winter Garden counties of Dimmit, Zavala, Frio, and La Salle, linking the central valley to northern markets. As the economy of South Texas evolved from ranching to agriculture, the number of Mexicans grew rapidly and the relations between the Anglos and Mexicans changed. In the ranching society, the patron ruled over a relatively stable underclass of Mexican ranch-hands—vaqueros and rancheros—and their families. The farmers did not need permanent hands; they needed large numbers of transient, migratory, low-wage laborers at harvest time.

The Mexican Revolution of 1910 to 1920 brought great instability to the border region. During and after the revolution, violence and poverty in Mexico sent streams of refugees north. Texas Governors Oscar Colquitt, James Ferguson, and William Hobby each called for a greater federal presence on the border. The Mexican-American population in Texas rose from less than 5 percent in 1910 to 12 percent in 1930. However, the Great Depression of the 1930s brought widespread unemployment and a wave of anti-immigrant rhetoric and policy. In 1935, Texas's arch-conservative Congressman Martin Dies called for a "relentless war without quarter and without cessation" on foreigners illegally in America "until the last one is driven from our shores. Either we are for or against our country."[32]

From the perspective of Anglo Texans, Mexicans were a mixed race, sharing with blacks and Indians many characteristics that required a place outside Anglo society. In 1925, Edward Everett Davis, Dean of the North Texas Agricultural College, now the University of Texas, Arlington, declared that, "All that has been said about the Negro regarding his low economic productivity, poor standards of living, and large family, . . . apply with equal validity to the Mexicans."[33] Nor was Dean Davis alone in his negative evaluation of Mexicans and other Texas minorities. Walter Prescott Webb, a leading Texas historian and author of the classic *The Texas Rangers: A Century of Frontier Defense* (1935), wrote, "There is a cruel streak in the Mexican nature, or so the history of Texas would lead one to believe. This cruelty . . . may, and doubtless should, be attributed to their Indian blood."[34]

But Hispanic numbers continued to increase, so that by the late 1940s "persons of Hispanic ancestry surpassed blacks in number to become the largest ethnic minority in Texas." Terry G. Jordan argued persuasively that this seismic demographic shift, still ongoing today, allowed the Anglo host culture to shift its self-image from southern to western. "Indeed, the widely held self-image of Anglo Texans as westerners rather than southerners may be linked in part to the displacement of blacks by Mexicans as the largest ethnic minority."[35] We turn now to the evolving place of blacks in Texas history and society.

Black Texans in Slavery and Freedom

From Anglo first settlement through the end of the Civil War, Texas was an Anglo slave republic. Though Stephen F. Austin later claimed that he had resisted the idea of slavery in his colony, he early concluded that, "Texas must be a slave country. Circumstances and unavoidable necessity compel it. It is the wish of the people there, and it is my duty to do all I can, prudently, in favor of it."[36] Austin's first empresario contract, calling for 300 families, was complete by 1825. By the fall of 1825, "sixty-nine families in Austin's colony owned slaves and the 443 bondsmen were nearly 25 percent of the total population of 1,800."[37]

Not surprisingly, history takes only slight and always ambivalent note of blacks in the Texas revolt. Though only two men were known to have survived the Alamo—one was the Tejano Brigido Guerrero and the other was William B. Travis's slave Joe—neither is included in the pantheon of Texas heroes. While William Travis gained eternal fame as co-commander, with Jim Bowie, of the Alamo and author of the letter "To the People of Texas and All Americans in the World," promising "Victory or Death," Joe is dismissed. During the final assault, Travis ordered Joe to get his gun and join him on the wall. Both men fired, but Travis was soon hit and fell backward inside the wall. The PBS documentary, *Remember the Alamo*, reports that "Joe, seeing his master fall, and the Mexicans coming over the wall . . . ran, and ensconced himself in a house." Though wounded in the later fighting, Joe survived, and even more remarkably, was taken before Santa Anna and ordered returned to Travis's heirs. Two years later, Joe stole two horses and escaped to freedom. Texas history has seemed more interested in counting Joe a coward and a thief than noting his presence at the Alamo or his subsequent flight to freedom.

History is even less certain what to make of Emily Morgan, sometimes known as Emily West, though legend has it that she aided in the decisive Texan victory at San Jacinto. The legendary "Yellow Rose of Texas," Emily Morgan was reported to have been a mulatto slave who occupied or distracted Santa Anna in his tent on the afternoon of April 12, 1836. Houston and the Texans, attacking in the mid-afternoon, caught the Mexicans napping and destroyed them in just 20 minutes. Leigh Clemons reports that virtually all the details about Emily Morgan are in dispute: her name, her race, her status as slave or free, and how she came to be in Santa Anna's tent. Nonetheless, the legend renders her impure and, therefore, suspect. To have been in Santa Anna's tent, she must have been at least mulatto and a slave—no honor there.[38]

Section 9 of the Republic of Texas Constitution of 1836 "guaranteed that people held as slaves in Texas would remain in servitude and that future emigrants to the republic could bring slaves with them. Furthermore, no free black could live in Texas without the approval of Congress, and any slave freed without the approval of Congress had to leave the republic."[39] In every decade through the 1860s, the black slave population grew more rapidly in percentage terms than the Anglo population. The locus of the slave population in antebellum Texas was in the old Austin colony, along the lower Brazos and Colorado rivers, in East Texas centering on San Augustine, and near the Red River in far Northeast Texas. By 1850, six counties in East Central Texas and Northeast Texas had black majorities. By 1860, the number of black majority counties had risen to 13.[40]

In 1860, Texas was 66 percent Anglo, 30 percent black slave, less than 5 percent Hispanic, and about 1 percent Indian. As General Sherman and the Union armies swept through the South, some wealthy white southerners sent their families and slaves to the comparative safety of Texas. Estimates of the number of slaves sent to Texas range from under 50,000 to as many as 150,000.[41] Once the war was over and blacks were free, their presence, at least in Anglo eyes, became deeply problematic. The freedmen wanted real freedom; some whites wanted black labor under as close to the old terms as possible, while other whites simply wanted the blacks gone.[42]

In the wake of the Civil War, few Texas whites could envision a bi-racial society. The general assumption among Anglos was that blacks, unchecked by slavery, would run amuck, threatening white persons and property. Some turned immediately to violence to keep freedmen in their traditional roles, while others hoped for a black exodus from Texas. John H. Reagan, former Confederate Post-Master General and future congressman and U.S. senator from Texas, 1875–1891, predicted that, "The negroes will, it is hoped, gradually diffuse themselves, . . . many of them will probably go to Mexico, and other countries, in search of social equality, and few or none of their race will be added . . . by accession from other countries."[43] Anglo hopes were realized in that the state's population became increasingly Anglo and decreasingly black in the final decades of the nineteenth century, while Hispanic numbers remained under 5 percent and Indian numbers fell to a fraction of 1 percent. By 1900, Anglos were 77 percent and blacks were 20 percent and continuing to decline.

For most of American history, certainly well into the twentieth century, migration paths led west. The upper Midwest was settled out of New England, the Ohio Valley out of the Middle Atlantic region, and Texas out of the South. The westward course of migration makes understanding the impact of migration on post–Civil War Texas quite challenging. As the westernmost southern state, Texas received migrants, white and black, from the Old South, while losing native Texans, white and black, to other states. After the Civil War, southerners, white and black, but mostly white, drifted west in search of new cotton lands. The largest numbers came, as they had before the war, from Alabama, Tennessee, Mississippi, Georgia, and Arkansas. The economist Neil Fligstein has reported that, "The major difference between black and white patterns is the fact that the net outmigration rates were almost always higher for blacks than whites."[44]

Texas historians explain the decline in the black share of the total population as a function of post–Civil War interstate migration patterns. T.R. Fehrenbach explained that, "Thousands upon thousands of Southern poor whites, seeing the hopeless landscape around them, determined to move to Texas. . . . The Negro population rapidly fell, since the new arrivals brought no slaves."[45] Randolph Campbell similarly reports that, "Most of the [post–Civil War] immigrants came from the states of the Old South to escape the ruin and stagnation left by the war. . . . blacks declined from 32 percent of all Texans in 1870 to 22 percent by 1890."[46]

While the broad story of rapid growth of the white population, slower growth of the black population, and a declining black share of total population is correct, it was more a product of intention and policy among both whites and blacks than is commonly understood. White entrepreneurs advertised the virtues of Texas throughout the South to attract dispossessed whites. They came in droves during the 1870s. The Anglo population in Texas increased by 116 percent during the 1870s, more than twice as fast as black population growth. In fact, during the 1870s, 230,700 more whites immigrated to Texas than emigrated from Texas, while 10,300 more blacks emigrated from Texas than immigrated to it from other states. Similar patterns held for the 1880s and 1890s; whites moved to Texas while blacks left (Table 3.2).

Despite the numbers involved and the decades over which it occurred, black migration out of Texas was no simple matter. Most freed slaves had no property or money income, most were illiterate, and most knew little of the broader world. Some blacks, especially those recently brought to Texas, returned east to search for home and family. Some Texas freedmen chose to try life in the North or West.[47] Most famously, the "Great Exodus" of 1879 saw about 6,000 blacks leave Texas, Louisiana, and Mississippi for Kansas.[48] Texas experienced a net out-migration of 10,300 blacks during the 1870s, so, obviously, Kansas was not the only destination. In the 1880s, Texas experienced a net out-migration of 16,700 and another 12,800 left in the 1890s. Between 1870 and 1900,

Table 3.2 Post–Civil War Net Migration by Decade for Texas Whites and Blacks

Decade	Native Whites	Blacks
1870–80	230,700	−10,300
1880–90	63,700	−16,700
1890–00	23,800	−12,800
1900–10	−62,500	−54,000
1910–20	−79,200	−15,600
1920–30	−2,700	−39,700
1930–40	−146,000	16,300
1940–50	305,485	−77,630
1950–60	321,435	−102,926
1960–70	339,729	−97,264

Source: Everett S. Lee, Ann Ratner Miller, Carol P. Brainerd, and Richard A. Easterlin, prepared under the direction of Simon Kuznets and Dorothy Swaine Thomas, *Population Redistribution and Economic Growth, United States, 1870 1950*, Philadelphia: American Philosophical Society, 1964, vol. 1, pp. 74–77 and 87–90. State-of-Birth Methodology. 1950 Census, Special Reports, 4A–16, Table 9, 1960 Census, Vol. II, Special Reports, 2A, State-of-Birth, Table 13 and 14, 1970 Census, Vol. II, Series PC(2), Subject Reports, 2A, State-of-Birth, Tables 7, 8, and 9.

the Anglo population of Texas increased from 534,004 to 2,355,926, a total increase of 341 percent, while the black population increased from 253,475 to 620,722, a total increase of 149 percent. In 1870 blacks made up 31 percent of the Texas population; in 1900, just 20 percent.

Net migration numbers are a sum of in-migration minus out-migration. If in-migration is greater than out-migration, net migration is a positive number, if in-migration is less than out-migration, net migration is a negative number. Readers should keep in mind that net migration underreports total migration for many reasons. Two obvious reasons are that a single person moving several times from one state to another is counted just once and a person moving from one state to another and back is not counted at all.

Between 1900 and 1950, the Anglo population of Texas increased by an average of 20 percent per decade while the black population grew by less than 10 percent. During that period the black share of the total population of Texas fell from 20 percent to 13 percent. In the first decade of the twentieth century, 54,000 more blacks left Texas than arrived. In the second and third decades of the century, 55,300 more left and in the 1940s more than 77,000 left. Only in the 1930s, when Texas suffered less than many other states during the Depression, did more blacks, 16,300 more, come to Texas than left it. Nonetheless, once the economy began to rebound in the late 1930s, Texas blacks were on the move again.[49] During the three decades from 1940 to 1970, about 100,000 more blacks left Texas than arrived each decade.

The economist Gavin Wright provided the best study of the evolution of the southern economy in the twentieth century. Wright explained that, "blacks left the South at all ages and educational levels. Net out-migration became increasingly black over time, and the reason is evident; most new jobs in the South were reserved for whites." As the southern economic revival got under way in the 1940s, the black exodus gained momentum. Wright says that, "Between 1940 and 1960, the South thus presents us with an amazing economic spectacle. It was the most rapidly growing region in the country. . . . And yet all of this was occurring at the same time that job-hungry workers were leaving the region by the thousands."[50] Many blacks were simply in search of a less threatening social and economic environment.

In something of an understatement, the historian Numan Bartley observed that, "The sorry state of segregated black schools, the unavailability of on-the-job-training, and all the other hindrances that beset blacks left them at a disadvantage."[51] Hence, Wright concluded that despite the undeniable difficulties southern blacks faced in the North, they were better off than they would have been had they stayed in the South. He wrote that, "With all the suffering, the out-migration of blacks from the South after 1940 was the single greatest economic step forward in black history, and a major advance toward the integration of blacks into the mainstream of American life."[52] One hundred thousand blacks left Texas in the 1950s, many headed toward California.

The "Great Migration" continued through the 1960s even as early school desegregation and civil and voting rights victories convinced some blacks that change was actually coming. Over the course of the 1970s, a reverse migration began in which some blacks, facing deindustrialization in the North and a less threatening South, offering an expanding job market and the comfort of family ties, returned home. Nonetheless, the human costs of the "Great Migration" were high. Isabel Wilkerson, author of the Pulitzer prize-winning book *The Warmth of Other Suns: The Epic Story of America's Great Migration*, called it "Perhaps the single greatest act of family disruption and heartbreak among black Americans in the twentieth century."[53] When the Great Migration began, 90 percent of American blacks lived in the South. By 1970, only 53 percent lived in the South. That number has rebounded a bit as the 2010 census reported that 57 percent of

American blacks lived in the South.[54] While the return of some blacks to the South is an interesting sociological phenomenon, the numbers are small and are not expected to alter the more powerful demographic processes under way in Texas and the nation.[55]

In 2010, Anglos accounted for less than half, about 45 percent of Texans, Hispanics for about 38 percent, blacks for about 11 percent, Asians, barely present until the 1980s, for about 5 percent, and Indians far less than 1 percent. Texas state population projections, taking the median projection, say that by 2050 Anglos will have fallen to 28 percent, blacks to 10 percent, Hispanics will have risen to 53 percent—a simple majority—Asians will be about 7.8 percent, and Indians will still be less than 1 percent. Will Texas in 2050 be a better place, a worse place, or just a different place?

Asians in Texas

The number of Asians in Texas during the nineteenth century was quite small. No one can say definitively that there were no Asians in Texas prior to the 1860s, but credible scholarly estimates begin with 25 Asians in Texas in 1870. Initially, most were Chinese. After the Civil War, some plantation owners sought, without much success, to replace freed slaves with Chinese laborers and in the 1880s and 1890s other Chinese were brought to Texas as railroad workers. Virtually all were young single men, very few were women, and while some Chinese men found mates locally, most drifted out of Texas once their labor contracts were complete. In the white supremacist culture of the late nineteenth-century Texas, Asians ranked below whites and above blacks, but ambiguously in relation to more familiar Hispanics. By 1900, just about 850 Asians were submerged among 2.35 million Texas Anglos and a total population of a little over 3 million.

In the first half of the twentieth century, Japanese began to arrive in Texas, again in small numbers, usually amounting to about half of Chinese numbers. The Japanese, however, often arrived as families and usually with some financial resources in hand. Chinese immigration was forbidden by the exclusion acts of the 1880s and later, and all immigration was sharply curtailed by the National Origins Act of 1924, in force until the mid-1960s. Moreover, Japanese in Texas during World War II were confined in internment camps and the U.S. government encouraged Latin American nations to send their resident Japanese to Texas for internment. The biggest internment camp for Japanese was at Crystal City, but there were seven camps in all holding Japanese, Germans, and Italians.[56]

After World War II and especially after U.S. immigration laws were revised in 1965 to treat Asians the same as others seeking immigration, the Asian population in Texas began to grow more rapidly. In addition, beyond Chinese and Japanese, Filipinos, Koreans, and Vietnamese arrived in the 1950s, 1960s, and 1970s, and Indians, Pakistanis, Bangladeshis, and others thereafter. Most settled in urban and suburban areas, including Dallas, Harris, and Travis counties, and even more heavily in Collin County north of Dallas and Fort Bend County southwest of Houston. The Asian population was about 4 percent of all Texans in 2010 and is projected to be more than 7 percent by 2050.[57]

Meeting the Challenges of the Coming Hispanic Majority

Half of children born in the United States in 2015 were born to minority parents. Minorities comprise almost 40 percent of the U.S. population: Hispanics account for 18 percent, blacks for 13 percent, Asians for almost 6 percent, and Native-Americans for just under 1 percent. The Hispanic population is by far the fastest growing because it is young, fertile, and supplemented by larger immigration flows than other races and ethnicities. Of the Hispanic share of U.S. population increase in 2010–2015, three-fourths come from births and one-fourth from immigration. Strikingly, Hispanic births outstrip deaths by nine to one whereas white births and deaths balance at about one to one.[58] No wonder the sociologist Stewart Tolnay described fertility, mortality, and migration as "the traditional trinity of demographic processes."[59]

Several states, including California (2000) and Texas (2003), the nation's two most populous states, have already made the transition from majority Anglo to majority minority and the U.S. will follow sometime around 2040. The burgeoning minority population has triggered some Anglo trepidation. As early as 1978, California passed Proposition 13, limiting state property tax increases to no more than 2 percent per year and requiring a two-thirds vote in the state legislature to raise other taxes. Proposition 13 is blamed for having severely limited funding of public schools and other services. In the 1990s, California voters adopted propositions eliminating state affirmative action and bilingual education, as well as tightening laws against illegal immigration.[60] As the recipients of California's (once) generous public services and students in their (once) excellent public schools became increasingly minority, Anglo Californians tightened the purse strings. As we shall see below, political dynamics in Texas have been different because the purse strings in Texas were never loose to begin with.

Tight purse strings have generally made Texas Anglos more sanguine about the Hispanic presence than their California, or more recently Arizona, counterparts. If social services in Texas were more generous and, therefore, more expensive, Anglo Texans might share more of the Californians' skepticism. On the other hand, low wages and thin public services have left Texas Hispanics, both citizens and illegal aliens, poor, less educated, less competitive, and more vulnerable. As we shall see throughout this book, much will hinge on providing enough high-quality public services, especially in education and health care, to allow, even promote, Hispanic advancement.

The Hispanic Center of the Pew Research Center charts in detail the place and prospects of Hispanics in the U.S. and in each of the individual states. In 2015, Texas's 10.5 million Hispanic residents comprised 38.6 percent of the state's total population, behind only New Mexico (48 percent) and just barely behind California (38.6 percent). Nearly one in five U.S. Hispanics resides in Texas. Seventy percent of Texas Hispanics are native-born U.S. citizens, while 30 percent are foreign-born and generally not U.S. citizens. Nearly nine in ten Texas Hispanics trace their origins to Mexico.

Texas Hispanics have annual personal earnings of $22,000, compared to $25,400 for Texas blacks, and $39,000 for whites. For comparison, California Hispanics make $22,000, blacks make $30,000, and whites make $42,000. Texas Hispanics make 83 percent of what Texas blacks make and only 56 percent of what Texas whites make. Not surprisingly then, poverty rates are high among both adult and young Texas Hispanics. Among Texas adults, 20 percent of Hispanics, 18 percent of blacks, and just 8.7 percent of whites live in poverty. Among Texans aged 17 and younger, 34 percent of Hispanics, 33 percent of blacks, and 10 percent of whites live in poverty. For comparison, poverty rates for all groups in California are similar. Among California adults, 19 percent of Hispanics, 21 percent of blacks, and just 10 percent of whites live in poverty. Among California young people, 31 percent of Hispanics, 36 percent of blacks, and 11 percent of whites live in poverty. Similarly, Texans struggle to afford health care. Thirty-one percent of Hispanics in Texas and fully 53 percent of foreign-born Hispanics lack health insurance, compared to 17 percent of blacks and 11 percent of whites. For California, the comparable numbers show that 20 percent of Hispanics and 34 percent of foreign-born Hispanics lack health insurance, compared to 11 percent of blacks and 7 percent of whites.

Finally, age and fertility differences by ethnicity and race promise that Hispanic presence in the nation's population, as well as those of Texas and California, will continue to grow. The median age of the U.S. population is 37, while that of Hispanics is 28 and that of Hispanics of Mexican origin, just 25. In Texas, the median age of whites is 41, blacks 33, and Hispanics 28. Moreover, the median age of native-born Hispanics, two-thirds of all Hispanics in Texas, is just 20. For comparison, California whites are older, 45, and native-born Hispanics are younger, 19. The age profile of a population relates to family formation and fertility in ways both ominous and direct. In Texas, Hispanic women in this age range had 53 percent of all births. Though 70 percent of Texas Hispanics are native-born, they had only 64 percent of babies, while the 30 percent of foreign-born Hispanics had 36 percent of babies.

Figure 3.3 makes the now unremarkable point that Texas's past was heavily Anglo and that its future is heavily, though not quite so heavily, Hispanic. Looking at Texans 85 and older today is like looking at Texas in 1950. Seventy-five percent of Texans 85 and older are Anglo, fewer than 20 percent of older Texans are Hispanic, while 7 percent are black and 3 percent are Asian and other. Forty-five-year-old Texans are 43 percent Anglo, 38 percent Hispanic, 12 percent black, and 7 percent Asian and other—about the racial and ethnic make-up of Texas today. But just over half, 50.5 percent, of all five-year-old Texans are Hispanic, 31 percent are Anglo, 11 percent are black, and a little less than 8 percent are Asian and other. By mid-century, Texan will look like its pre-school and kindergarten population looks today.

For Hispanics in Texas to enjoy greater economic success, they must first improve their educational attainment. Better jobs and higher incomes follow higher educational achievement. Richard Fry of the Pew Hispanic Center explains that Texas Hispanics underperform their Anglo and black counterparts at all levels of the educational system. Texas has higher high school drop-out rates than the nation as a whole, with Texas Hispanics having higher rates than Anglos and blacks. Texas also has lower college attendance rates than the nation as a whole, with Texas Hispanics having lower college attendance rates than Anglos and blacks. The

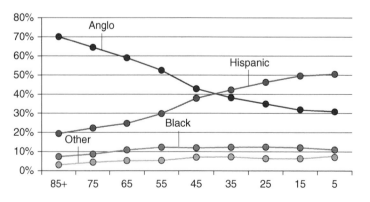

Figure 3.3 Population Shares by Race, Ethnicity, and Age

Source: Texas State Data Center, "Estimates of Population by Age, Sex, and Race/Ethnicity," July 1, 2015.

Federal Reserve Bank of Dallas reports that in 2010, "About 32 percent of Hispanic workers did not have a high school diploma or equivalent . . . versus only 5 percent of non-Hispanics. Nearly 16 percent of Hispanic workers were college graduates, compared with 38 percent for non-Hispanics."[61] In 2008, 54 percent of the nation's white high school graduates went on to college, as did 48 percent of black graduates, and 43 percent of Hispanics. In Texas, the numbers were lower: 52 percent of whites, 45 percent of blacks, and 41 percent of Hispanic high school graduates went on to college.[62]

Inadequate education leaves many Texas Hispanics with few economic options. Emily Kerr, Pia Orrenius, and Madeline Zavodny of the Dallas Federal Reserve Bank find that, "Latino workers in Texas are on the short end of two pay gaps. They earn substantially lower wages than the state's non-Hispanic white workers. They also earn less than Latinos working in other parts of the U.S." They further find that low educational attainment "explains more than half of the Latino pay gap vis-à-vis non-Hispanic whites in the state and 20 percent of the gap vis-à-vis Latinos outside Texas." The remainder of the in-state gap between Hispanics and Anglos is likely explained by the relatively low cost-of-living in Texas, "the state's proximity to Mexico, long history of discrimination and relatively low minimum wage." While Kerr and her colleagues do not make policy recommendations, they do note that, "targeting educational outcomes would likely pay off in reducing occupational inequality and increasing Latino wages."[63] They do not say what they think the likelihood of such "targeting" is given the "long history of discrimination" in Texas, but one assumes they realize that it is very low.

Clearly, both the Federal Reserve Bank of Dallas and the Office of the State Demographer of Texas are keenly aware that, "The key issue facing Texas" in the coming decades "will be to reduce the economic and educational disparities prevalent among the state's ethnic groups as the population continues to grow and evolve."[64] As official agencies of government, neither has been eager to say exactly how difficult that will be, especially as Texas state government seems convinced that limiting expenditures on education and health care is necessary to balance the state's budget. In fact, the economic and educational disparities between Hispanics, blacks, and Anglos in Texas will grow inexorably unless effective action is taken.

The population of Texas has grown rapidly since 1950, increasing from 7.7 million to more than 27.5 million in 2015. Moreover, the composition of Texas

Table 3.3 Components of Population Change in Texas, 1950–2015

Year	Population	Numerical Change	Natural Increase	Net Migration	% from Natural Increase	% from Net Migration
1950	7,711,194					
1960	9,579,677	1,868,483	1,754,652	113,831	93.91	6.09
1970	11,196,730	1,617,053	1,402,683	214,370	86.74	13.26
1980	14,229,191	3,032,461	1,260,794	1,771,667	41.58	58.42
1990	16,986,510	2,757,319	1,815,670	941,649	65.85	34.15
2000	20,851,820	3,865,310	1,919,281	1,946,029	49.65	50.35
2010	25,145,561	4,293,741	2,358,981	1,934,760	54.94	45.06
2015	27,469,302	2,323,009	1,107,434	1,199,941	47.66	51.64

Source: Derived from U.S. Bureau of the Census Estimates for dates indicated by the Texas State Data Center, University of Texas at San Antonio. All values for the decennial dates are for the indicated census year. Data for 2010–2015 in ProQuest, *Statistical Abstract of the United States, 2017*, Table 16, p. 19.

population growth since 1950 has changed dramatically and these changes will have a cumulative impact over the next several decades. Table 3.3, derived from U.S. Census data and employed by both the Dallas Federal Reserve Bank and the State Demographer, presents data on the contributions to the state's rapid population growth since 1950 from natural increase and net migration. Table 3.3 is updated from a February 2016 presentation by Lloyd B. Potter, Texas State Demographer, entitled, "Demographic Characteristics and Trends in Texas." The data show clearly that Texas population growth in the 1950s and 1960s was produced overwhelmingly, 94 percent and 87 percent, by natural increase—births to Texas residents. Since 1980, just slightly more than half of the state's population growth, 52 percent, has come from natural increase. The rest, 48 percent, has come from net migration, both from other U.S. states to Texas and from other nations to Texas. High net migration is neither good nor bad. Its impact depends on who comes, how well-educated, trained, and talented they are or how well they are educated or trained once they arrive.

Finally, population projections from the Office of the Texas State Demographer for 2010 to 2050 suggest that almost 80 percent of the population growth in Texas will be in the Hispanic population, 13 percent will be among Asians and others, 8 percent will be among blacks, and −1 percent will be in the Anglo population (Figure 3.4). The point, made several times already, is that unless Hispanic educational attainment and earning power improve, Texas will inevitably become a less productive and poorer state. Hence, in Chapter 4 we look at the Texas economy, especially the job market and income levels in Texas. In Chapter 5 we look at public education in Texas because education and income are so closely connected.

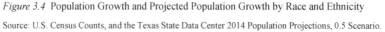

Figure 3.4 Population Growth and Projected Population Growth by Race and Ethnicity

Source: U.S. Census Counts, and the Texas State Data Center 2014 Population Projections, 0.5 Scenario.

A Concluding Exercise

Now, let's conclude with a simple, and to some extent implausible, but eye-opening, exercise. First, we analyze data on per capita income by race for Texas in 2015. Second, we analyze the same 2015 income data, but change the race and ethnicity data to those projected to be in place in 2040 to see what impact this change has on overall per capita income. We use per capita income figures, rather than median personal income, median household income, or median family income, because it accounts for differences in family size. Hispanics generally have larger families than Anglos, for example, and this means that income must be spread across more people. Nonetheless, all of these measures of income display the same general pattern that we see with per capita income.

In 2015, Anglos were 44.3 percent of the workforce and Anglo per capita income was $39,856 annually; blacks were 11.9 percent of the workforce making about $21,794 per capita annually; Hispanics were 35.6 percent of the workforce making about $16,909 per capita annually; and Asians were about 5.2 percent of the workforce making $33,754. As Table 3.4 shows, multiplying the percentage of the workforce in each racial and ethnic group by their average annual per capita income and adding the four resulting numbers gives a per capita income for Texas in 2015 of $28,021.

If we hold the average salary numbers at 2015 levels, but change the racial and ethnic make-up of the workforce to the composition projected for 2040, what happens to average per capita income in Texas? In 2040, the Anglo share of the workforce is projected to be 25.2 percent, the Hispanic share to be 58.7 percent, the black share to be 7.9 percent, and the Asian share to be 5 percent. If income by racial and ethnic groups does not change, average per capita income in Texas will be $23,380, down more than $4,600 and, shockingly, 20 percent.

These numbers, of course, are not set in stone, though some are firmer than others. The population projections are pretty firm and, if anything, have tended in past decades to underestimate the growth of the Hispanic population. The income numbers, on the other hand, could change if black and Hispanic earnings improve. We can hope that they will, but when we look for evidence suggesting that they will, we find little. Most analysts believe that improvements in Hispanic educational achievement, including better test scores, lower drop-out rates, and more attendance and success in college,

Table 3.4 Reason for Concern: Texas per Capita Income by Race in 2015 with Projections to 2040

	2015			2040		
	% Workforce	*Per Capita Income*	*Income Share*	*% Workforce*	*Per Capita Income*	*Income Share*
Anglo	44.3 ×	$39,856 =	$17,653	25.2 ×	$39,856 =	$10,044
Black	11.9 ×	$21,794 =	$2,593	7.9 ×	$21,794 =	$1,722
Hispanic	35.6 ×	$16,909 =	$6,020	58.7 ×	$16,909 =	$9,926
Asian	5.2 ×	$33,754 =	$1,755	5.0 ×	$33,754 =	$1,688
Statewide Per Capita Income			$28,021			$23,380

Source: Bureau of Labor Statistics, Table 14, Employment Status of the Population by State, Race, Ethnicity. http://www.bls.gov/lau/Table14afull15.pdf. ACS, B19301 series by race.

will have to precede significant increases in Hispanic per capita income. Pointedly, if the proportion of high earners in the workforce (Anglos) falls and the proportion of low income earners in the workforce (Hispanics) rises, per capita income in Texas must fall and the Texas economy will fall with it. Succeeding chapters ask what Texas is doing to secure the future.

Notes

1   Paul Burka, "Capitol Affair," *Texas Monthly*, July, 2011, pp. 12–14.
2   Mercedes Olivera, "Census Will Show Scope of Hispanic Growth," *Dallas Morning News*, January 1, 2011, p. 3B. See also Jill Cowan, "Texas Leads U.S. in New Residents," *Dallas Morning News*, December 23, 2016, pp. A1, A9.
3   Randolph B. Campbell, *Gone to Texas: A History of the Lone Star State*, New York: Oxford University Press, 2003, p. 85. See also Henderson K. Yoakum, *History of Texas*, New York: Redfield, 1856, pp. 111–115.
4   Ibid., pp. 95–96. See also Henry Stuart Foote, *Texas and the Texans*, Philadelphia: Thomas, Cowperthwaite and Co., 1841, pp. 201–217.
5   David G. McComb, *The City in Texas: A History*, Austin, TX: University of Texas Press, 2015, pp. 39–43.
6   Stanley Siegel, *A Political History of the Texas Republic, 1836–1845*, Austin, TX: University of Texas Press, 1956, p. 39.
7   Terry G. Jordan, "A Century and a Half of Ethnic Change in Texas, 1836–1986," *Southwestern Historical Quarterly*, vol. 89, no. 4, April 1986, p. 386.
8   Billy D. Ledbetter, "White Over Black in Texas: Racial Attitudes in the Antebellum Period," *Phylon*, vol. 34, no. 4, 4th quarter, 1973, p. 406. See also Gary Clayton Anderson, *The Conquest of Texas: Ethnic Cleansing in the Promised Land, 1824–1875*, Norman, OK: University of Oklahoma Press, 2015, pp. 38–39, 46, 60.
9   Randolph B. Campbell, *An Empire for Slavery: The Peculiar Institution in Texas, 1821–1865*, Baton Rouge, LA: Louisiana State University Press, 1989, pp. 209–210.
10 James McEnteer, *Deep in the Heart: The Texas Tendency in American Politics*, Westport, CT: Praeger, 2004, p. 31.
11 David La Vere, *The Texas Indians*, College Station, TX: Texas A&M University Press, 2004, p. 28.
12 Ibid., pp. 107, 64–65.
13 Ibid., p. 63.
14 T.R. Fehrenbach, *Lone Star: A History of Texas and the Texans*, New York: Macmillan, 1968, pp. 130–131; Campbell, *Gone to Texas*, p. 14.
15 Robert Perkinson, *Texas Tough: The Rise of America's Prison Empire*, New York: Metropolitan Books, 2010, p. 53.
16 Glenn Frankel, *The Searchers: The Making of an American Legend*, New York: Bloomsbury, 2013, p. 52. See also Anderson, *The Conquest of Texas*, pp. 174, 189. F. Todd Smith, *From Dominance to Disappearance: The Indians of Texas and the Southwest, 1786–1859*, Lincoln, NE: University of Nebraska Press, 2005, p. 168.
17 William Bollaert, *William Bollaert's Texas*, Norman, OK: University of Oklahoma Press, 1956, p. 73.
18 La Vere, *The Texas Indians*, p. 187.
19 W.W. Newcomb Jr., *The Indians of Texas: From Prehistoric to Modern Times*, Austin, TX: University of Texas Press, 1961/1989, p. 354.
20 La Vere, *The Texas Indians*, p. 201. Texas was by no means the only state to remove its Indian population. See Benjamin Madley, *An American Genocide: The United States and the California Indian Catastrophe, 1846–1873*, New Haven, CT: Yale University Press, 2016.
21 Frankel, *The Searchers*, p. 151.
22 McEnteer, *Deep in the Heart*, p. 26.
23 Leigh Clemens, *Branding Texas: Performing Culture in the Lone Star State*, Austin, TX: University of Texas Press, 2008, p. 61. See also Glen Sample Ely, *Where the West Begins: Debating Texas Identity*, Lubbock, TX: Texas Tech University Press, 2011, p. 76.
24 McEnteer, *Deep in the Heart*, p. 31.
25 Quintard Taylor, *In Search of the Racial Frontier: African Americans in the American West, 1528–1990*, New York: W.W. Norton, 1998, p. 43.

26 Joseph Eve to Richard Southgate, May 10, 1842, "A LetterBook of Joseph Eve, United States Chargé d'Affaires to Texas," *Southwestern Historical Quarterly*, XLIII, 4, April 1940, p. 494. Quoted in William Ransom Hogan, *The Texas Republic*, Norman, OK: University of Oklahoma Press, 1946, p. 14.

27 David Montejano, *Anglos and Mexicans in the Making of Texas, 1836–1986*, Austin, TX: University of Texas Press, 1987, p. 5. See also Arnoldo De León, *The Tejano Community 1836–1900*, Albuqerque: University of New Mexico Press, 1982.

28 McEnteer, *Deep in the Heart*, p. 43. See also Anderson, *The Conquest of Texas*, p. 80.

29 Robert A. Calvert, Arnoldo De León, and Gregg Cantrell, *The History of Texas*, 4th edn, Wheeling, IL: Harlan Davidson, Inc., 2007, p. 125. See also William D. Carrigan and Clive Webb, *Forgotten Dead: Mob Violence Against Mexicans in the United States, 1848–1928*, New York: Oxford University Press, 2013, pp. 45–48, 108–111.

30 James Reston Jr., *The Lone Star: The Life of John Connally*, New York: Harper & Row, 1989, p. 7; Fehrenbach, *Lone Star*, pp. 575–579.

31 Montejano, *Anglos and Mexicans*, pp. 50, 183. See also Terry G. Jordan, "The Forgotten Texas State Census of 1887," *Southwestern Historical Quarterly*, vol. 85, no. 4, April 1982, pp. 401–408.

32 McEnteer, *Deep in the Heart*, p. 80.

33 Gene B. Preuss, *To Get a Better School System*, College Station, TX: Texas A&M University Press, 2009, p. 45.

34 Water Prescott Webb, *The Texas Rangers: A Century of Frontier Defense*, Boston, MA: Houghton, Mifflin, 1935, p. 14.

35 Jordan, "A Century and a Half of Ethnic Change in Texas," pp. 392, 404.

36 Perkinson, *Texas Tough*, p. 51.

37 Campbell, *An Empire for Slavery*, p. 19.

38 Clemons, *Branding Texas*, pp. 55–57.

39 Campbell, *Gone to Texas*, p. 148.

40 Campbell, *An Empire for Slavery*, p. 57–58.

41 Calvert et al., *The History of Texas*, p. 148; David G. McComb, *Texas: A Modern History*, revised edition, Austin, TX: University of Texas Press, 2010, p. 72; Lawrence D. Rice, *The Negro in Texas, 1874–1900*, Baton Rouge, LA: Louisiana State University Press, 1971, p. 162. Charles William Ramsdell, *Reconstruction in Texas*, Austin, TX: University of Texas Press, 1910, pp. 23, 196.

42 Calvert et al., *The History of Texas*, p. 153.

43 Michael Phillips, *White Metropolis: Race, Ethnicity, and Religion in Dallas, 1841–2001*, Austin, TX: University of Texas Press, 2006, pp. 25–33, 37. See also Robert Wuthnow, *Rough Country*, Princeton, NJ: Princeton University Press, 2014, p. 25.

44 Neil Fligstein, *Going North: Migration of Black and Whites from the South, 1900–1950*, New York Academic Press, 1981, pp. 77. See also Stewart E. Tolnay and E.M. Beck, "Rethinking the Role of Racial Violence in the Great Migration," pp. 21–22, in Alferdteen Harrison, *Black Exodus: The Great Migration from the American South*, Jackson: University of Mississippi Press, 1991.

45 Fehrenbach, *Lone Star*, p. 603.

46 Campbell, *Gone to Texas*, pp. 290–291.

47 Rice, *The Negro in Texas, 1874–1900*, p. 202.

48 Nell Irvin Painter, *Exodusters: Black Migration to Kansas After Reconstruction*, Lawrence, KS: University of Kansas Press, 1976.

49 Alwyn Barr, *Black Texans: A History of African Americans in Texas, 1528–1995*, 2nd edn, Norman, OK: University of Oklahoma Press, 1996, p. 154. Wuthnow, *Rough Country*, p. 290.

50 Gavin Wright, *Old South, New South: Revolutions in the Southern Economy Since the Civil War*, New York: Basic Books, 1986, pp. 255–257.

51 Numan V. Bartley, *The New South, 1945–1980*, Baton Rouge, LA: Louisiana State University Press, 1995, p. 118; see also Calvert et al., *The History of Texas*, p. 260.

52 Wright, *Old South, New South*, p. 237.

53 Isabel Wilkerson, *The Warmth of Other Suns: The Epic History of America's Great Migration*, New York: Random House, 2010, p. 238.

54 J. David Woodard, *The New Southern Politics*, Boulder, CO: Lynne Rienner Publishers, 2006, pp. 45, 52. See also, Reniqua Allen, "Racism Is Everywhere: So Why Not Move South?, *New York Times*, July 8, 2017, SR1, 6-7.

55 James N. Gregory, *American Exodus: The Dust Bowl Migration and Okie Culture in California*, New York: Oxford University Press, 1989, pp. 1–19.

56   Bruce A. Glasrud, "Asians in Texas: An Overview, 1870–1990," *East Texas Historical Journal*, vol. 39, Issue 2, 2001, pp. 10–22.

57   "Asian Demographics in Texas: What We Do and Don't Know," Office of the State Demographer, November 20, 2015.

58   Renee Stepler, "Statistical Portrait of Hispanics in the United States," Pew Research Center, April 19, 2016, p. 5. See www.pewhispanic.org/2016/04/19/statistical-portrait-of-hispanics-in-the-United-States-key-charts.

59   Stewart E. Tolnay, "The African American 'Great Migration' and Beyond," *Annual Review of Sociology*, 29, 2003, pp. 209–232.

60   Gregory Rodriquez, "The White Anxiety Crisis," *Time*, March 22, 2010, pp. 52–54.

61   "A Conversation with Maria T. Mora: Hispanic Workforce Faces Smaller But Persistent Education, Wage Gaps," Federal Reserve Bank of Dallas, *First Quarter 2013, Southwest Economy*, p. 8.

62   On the Record, A Conversation With Richard Fry, "Why Hispanic Education Deficits Persist," Federal Reserve Bank of Dallas, *First Quarter 2010, Southwest Economy*, pp. 8–9.

63   Emily Kerr, Pia Orrenius, and Madeline Zavodny, "Texas's Latino Pay Gaps: Taking a Closer Look," Federal Reserve Bank of Dallas, *First Quarter 2010, Southwest Economy*, pp. 10–11, 13.

64   D'Ann Petersen and Laila Assanie, "The Changing Face of Texas: Population Projections and Implications," Federal Reserve Bank of Dallas, October 2005, p. 37. For 2015 data, see *Statistical Abstract of the United States, 2017*, Table 16, p. 19.

Part II

The Reality Thus Far

4   Jobs, Income, and Wealth in Texas

[T]he rankings of states by income have remained stable over the past century. . . . Thus, any discussion of rich and poor states is potentially as much about each state's history as peripheral and rural or as metropolitan and urban.

(Andrew Gelman, 2008)[1]

Texas frequently has been touted as the best job-producing state in the nation and as the most business-friendly state in the nation. For example, in April 2009, *Forbes*, one of the nation's top business magazines, ranked the job-producing prospects of 333 major metropolitan areas. *Forbes* reported that "the top five large metropolitan areas for job growth [are] all located in the Lone Star State. . . . Nine of the top twenty cities on Forbes' overall list are in Texas." In May 2016, *Chief Executive* reported a survey ranking the "Best and Worst States" for business. The best states for business were Texas, Florida, North Carolina, Tennessee, and Indiana, while the worst were California, New York, Illinois, New Jersey, Connecticut, and Massachusetts. Such reports have long been common. Texas has been ranked number one by *Chief Executive* every year since 2004. CNBC has conducted a similar ranking since 2007. Texas has finished either first or second every year.

Texas leaders treat such reports as unambiguously positive, declaring that they prove that Texas is a great place to work and do business. They rarely stop to ponder the fact that *Chief Executive*'s worst states for business are among the wealthiest states in the nation, with New York, New Jersey, Massachusetts, and Connecticut perennially among the five wealthiest. *Chief Executive*'s top five, including Texas, are all poorer states. Moreover, the reports are not new: similar reports have been a matter of course back into the 1950s. But as the quotation at the start of this chapter, as well as Table 1.1 and Figure 2.1 in previous chapters have shown, Texas has not been making a rapid transition from poor state to rich state, from low-wage state to high-wage state. In fact, it has held its own, perhaps moved up slowly, in fits and starts, but it has not sprinted ahead of the pack and there is little reason to believe that it soon will. To get a rounded picture of how well or poorly the Texas economy is performing, we examine not just job creation, but issues of productivity, income, unemployment, poverty, and inequality as well.[2]

Prior to World War II, the Texas economy was rarely described as booming. But since World War II, it frequently has been so described. Texas became urban and industrial in the 1940s and 1950s. Texas oil fueled the allied war machine, refineries and petrochemical plants sprang up along the Gulf Coast, and the aerospace industry and other major defense contractors clustered in the Dallas-Fort Worth Metroplex.[3] Texas cities continued to grow in the 1960s and in the 1970s and Exxon, Shell, and Gulf all moved their corporate headquarters to Texas. Migration to Texas and the broader sunbelt south and southwest from the rust belt of New England and the Midwest picked up speed. Population and job growth went hand in hand. Texas "became the nation's strongest state economy for much of the 1960s and 1970s."[4]

As we shall see below, Texas led the South and Southwest in its post–World War II build-out. The formula for attracting new businesses to the region was well known. Numan V. Bartley's *The New South: 1945–1980* reported that, "In a 1975 study of the 'business climate' of American states, that equated 'excellence' with 'low taxes, low levels of public assistance, restrictive labor legislation, and a low level of spending and debt'" Texas was placed number one.[5] Champagne and Harpham noted that by the mid-1980s, Texas had "repeatedly been identified as offering either the best or second best 'business climate' (behind Florida) in the nation."[6] Texas's selling points were: (1) a mild climate, in the sunbelt, centrally located in the U.S.; (2) a low cost-of-living, including cheap land and housing; (3) a growing labor pool, with low wages, limited benefits, and weak unions; (4) small government, low taxes, thin social services, and light regulation.

Texans have been showered for decades with assurances of how well their state is doing in terms of opportunity, jobs, and wealth creation. The Texas economy is often described as hitting on all cylinders, creating widespread opportunity and great wealth. But there have been headwinds and, as we shall see, the Texas economy has been more volatile, more given to booms and busts, than the economy of the nation or of most states. The Texas economic collapse of the mid-1980s and early 1990s halted and even reversed these developments and the bursting of the tech bubble in 2000, the recession that followed the 9/11 attacks, and the Great Recession of 2008–2009 hit Texas and the nation hard. As a result, while the boomer description of the Texas economy often is accurate, it is just as accurate to say that the Texas economy has performed little better than the national economy since 1950. The Texas economy has grown, jobs have been created, and some Texans have become wealthy. But growth since 1950 has occurred at about the national average, so Texas barely has advanced in the ranking of American states by income and wealth.

Moreover, Texas boosterism must always be held up to the mirror of demography.[7] The key question about the Texas economy is always—for whom is it great, for whom good, and for whom not so good? The answer today, as it has been throughout the state's history, is it is great for Anglo elites, good for Anglos in general, and not so good for most others.[8] Hence, Anglos praise the Texas economy because they generally do well, or at least better, in it, while others offer less praise because they do less well.

In this chapter, we systematically explore how Texas and Texans have fared economically in relation to the nation, to other states, and to each other. First, we confirm that Texas has been a prolific job-creation machine. Second, we demonstrate that as far back as good data go Texas workers have appeared to be more productive but less well paid than the average American worker. Unpacking that anomaly will be eye-opening. Third, we look at two general measures of economic well-being: per capita personal income and median family income. We find that Texas has lagged the national average since records have been kept and that the state's standing has not improved much since 1950. On key issues of wealth and poverty we look closely at differences by race and ethnicity. Fourth, we compare the unemployment rate and poverty rate in Texas to the national rates to see how poorer Texans are doing. We find that the unemployment rate in Texas is above the national rate about half the time and below about half the time while the poverty rate is always significantly above the national rate. Finally, we ask whether the gap between rich and poor in Texas is greater or smaller than the gap for the nation and the other states. We find that it is greater than the average for the nation and for about 40 of the 50 states and is increasing. The fundamental vulnerability for too many Texas workers has long been that they make less than other American workers and face a thinner social safety net when they stumble. That is—bluntly—what it means to be a "business-friendly" state.

Job Creation in Texas

In Chapter 3 we saw that the Texas population has been increasing faster than the national rate of population growth since the state's inception. Population growth means more customers and rising demand for the state's businesses and those businesses are then required to hire more workers. For example, looking back just to 1940, the U.S. has increased jobs at a rate of 20.8 percent per decade, while Texas has increased jobs at a rate of 35.2 percent per decade. As in Chapter 3, we can also compare Texas to other large, fast-growing sunbelt states over this same period. Since 1940, California has increased jobs at 31.8 percent per decade, a bit slower than Texas, while Florida has increased jobs at an astounding 46.5 percent per decade (Table 4.1).

If we look just at the last quarter century, 1990–2015, Texas outperformed the U.S. and both Florida and California in job growth. Clearly, Texas has been a prolific job-creation machine and Texas politicians have celebrated this fact endlessly. In this instance, Texas leaders are right to note that most states would love to have both the population growth and the job growth that Texas has enjoyed throughout its history. Still, it must be noted that the recent fall in the price of oil slowed Texas job growth and even allowed California to edge ahead.[9] Texans celebrate the Texas/California comparison when they are on the high side of it but they are sullen and quiet when they are not.

Californians have been, by turns, defensive and scornful in regard to the Texas economy. John Ellwood, a public policy professor at Berkeley (that would be the University of California, Berkeley), recently sniffed that the Texas "model is a low-wage economy with greater income inequality."[10] As we shall see, Professor Ellwood's characterization of the Texas economy is accurate, though perhaps incomplete. Evidence for the accuracy of the characterization comes from the Corporation for Enterprise

Table 4.1 Job Growth by Decade in the U.S., Texas, and Selected States, 1940–2015

	U.S.	*Texas*	*California*	*Florida*
1940–49	35.3	63.5	59.9	54.8
1950–59	17.9	31.0	48.8	80.7
1960–69	29.9	41.6	41.6	56.7
1970–79	26.7	54.5	39.1	57.1
1980–89	19.3	16.9	24.3	47.1
1990–99	17.8	29.0	12.0	26.8
2000–09	−1.0	9.6	−2.8	2.6
2010–15	9.4	14.5	15.5	12.8
Average	20.8	35.2	31.8	46.5

Source: Bureau of Labor Statistics, Current Employment Statistics Survey, "Employment, Hours, and Earnings." See also U.S. Census, Statistical Abstract of the United States, various years, Labor Force, Employment, and Earnings, "Employees in Nonfarm Establishments, by States."

Development, a Washington-based non-profit that has been compiling an "Assets and Opportunity Scorecard" for the 50 states since 1987. The scorecard compares the states on 69 measures and assigns rankings on each measure and an overall ranking—in Texas's case, 39th among the 50 states. The measure of most relevance here is the proportion of each state's jobs that are low-income jobs, defined as jobs that do not pay enough to keep a family of four above the federal poverty rate (about $23,624). Nationally, 25.6 percent of workers are low-wage, California ranked 18th at 22.2 percent, Florida ranked 44th at 33.5 percent, and Texas ranked 40th at 30.8 percent.[11] In addition, more Texans work for wages at or below the federal minimum wage than do low-wage workers in all but a few other states. In 2010, Texas tied with Mississippi for the state having the highest proportion of workers (9.5 percent) earning at or below the federal minimum of $7.25 an hour. In 2015, Texas had the sixth highest percentage of minimum wage workers and had more minimum wage workers, 550,000, than California and Florida combined.[12] So we need to look closely at the Texas job-creation story; is it mainly a story of prolific job creation, as Texas boosters claim, or is it mainly a story of low-wage jobs leaving too many Texans vulnerable? We turn to worker productivity to begin answering that question.

Worker Productivity in Texas

Worker productivity, usually thought of as the value created by a worker over some period of time, such as a year, is the basis of wealth creation and so a subject of consistent interest. Some early visitors and immigrants to Texas were scathing in their assessments of Texas workers, while others were highly laudatory. William Ransom Hogan's history of *The Texas Republic* presents an entertaining mix of both views. Not surprisingly, Europeans and New Englanders took a dim view of the work habits of early Texans. Hogan reports that, "In 1834 a young German, George Willich, Jr., wrote: 'So great is the indolence of the present inhabitants, that they hate everything that causes the least work like death, and they know no greater happiness than eating, drinking brandy, and sleeping.'" Similarly, "Francis L. Trask, a school teacher from Massachusetts, commented in a letter to her father written the following summer: 'The white people if ever so poor, consider it degrading to work, and would rather stay at home in their dirt, and rags, than to do the first days work for another—this is one of the evils of slavery.'"[13] Others, arriving from the South, took a more positive view of Texan energy, entrepreneurship, and general work habits:

> As one man wrote shortly after his arrival in 1839: "This country is full of enterprising and persevering people. The timid and lazy generally return to the States." In 1846 a visitor found an economic basis for Texas independence, and concluded that "the Texans are the most independent people under the whole canopy of heaven the wealthy of the old states not excepted."[14]

On one reading, slavery made whites, rich and poor, unwilling to work and certainly unwilling to work for wages, while on another reading this reluctance was simply an admirable Texan independence. In any event, modern Texas workers, though most do work for others, are generally praised as industrious, even if they are not quite paid that way.

For half a century, we have had good data comparing Texas workers to American workers in general. Worker productivity is calculated by dividing Gross Domestic

Product (GDP), the value of goods and services produced in a year, by the number of workers required to produce them. This gives the value created by the average worker annually and this can be done both for Texas workers and for U.S. workers. Then the value created by the average Texas worker is divided into the value created by the average U.S. worker and that gives the value created by Texas workers as a percentage of the value created by U.S. workers. The top line in Figure 4.1 shows quite clearly that, except for brief periods in the early 1970s and late 1990s, Texas workers created more value annually than U.S. workers in general. For example, by the late 1970s, Texas workers produced 10 percent more value than their counterparts nationally. In the early 1980s, Texas productivity peaked at 19 percent above the national average, and, after a steep decline in the mid- to late 1980s, stayed modestly above the national average until it experienced another sharp increase beginning in 2010. Texas workers produce great value, but, after all, averages are general measures. As we shall see below, a closer look brings into focus a more troubling picture.

The lower line in Figure 4.1 presents Texas worker pay as a percentage of U.S. worker pay. The calculation is similar to that for worker productivity, dividing personal income for the U.S. and Texas into the number of workers earning it and then dividing Texas pay into U.S. pay to produce the percentage seen in Figure 4.1. Obviously, the line for Texas worker pay as a percentage of U.S. worker pay has been much more stable than the productivity line, though in the wave-like ups and downs we can see a slow and steady improvement of Texas worker pay compared to the national average. In 1969, the first year for which we have appropriate data, Texas workers made 92 percent of what U.S. workers made and in 2014 they made 100 percent of what U.S. workers made. On the other hand, as early as 1979 Texas workers made 97 percent of what U.S. workers made before dropping back. While Texas

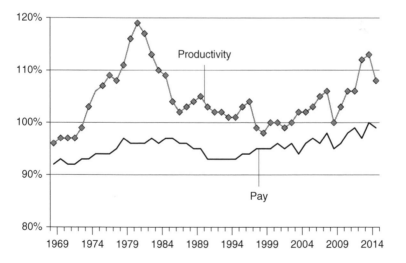

Figure 4.1 Worker Productivity and Worker Pay: Comparing the U.S. and Texas, 1969–2015

Source: Bureau of Economic Analysis: U.S. Table 6.4B, Full-Time and Part-Time Employees by Industry, line 10; Texas Table SA25, Total Full-Time and Part-Time Employees by SIC Industry, line 20; U.S. and Texas Gross Domestic Product (GDP) by State (millions of current dollars), line 1; U.S. and Texas, Tables SA5 and SA5N, Personal Income by SIC Industry, line 10.

workers reached 97 percent several more times after 1979, it was not until 2008 that Texas workers made 98 percent of what U.S. workers made. In 2014, Texas workers made 100 percent of what U.S. workers made before dropping back into 2015 and later as a steep drop in oil prices slowed the state's economy.[15]

Figure 4.1 paints an impressive picture of the productivity of Texas workers and the vibrancy of the Texas economy even as it leaves us puzzled over lackluster worker pay. It also demands that we explore the outsized impact that the energy industry historically has had on the broader state economy. A quick glance ahead at Figure 11.1 will show that the productivity line in Figure 4.1 and the price of oil in Figure 11.1 map onto one another very closely. While the Texas economy was generally strong in the 1960s and early 1970s, Texas workers were just as productive as U.S. workers, sometimes a bit more productive and sometimes a bit less. The spike in oil prices produced by the Arab oil boycott in the early 1970s and the fall of the Shah of Iran in the late 1970s brought great wealth to Texas. High oil prices expanded employment in the oil patch and beyond, though the value of Texas oil grew more rapidly than employment, so worker productivity (value created per worker) spiked to 119 percent of U.S. worker productivity in 1981 and held above 110 percent from 1979 through 1984. Even after the price of oil peaked and started down, Texas worker productivity stabilized and held above the national average for most of the next quarter century, averaging about 102 percent of the U.S. average, with a modest uptick in 2007 and 2008. The Great Recession of late 2008 and 2009 impacted Texas worker productivity because state GDP fell faster than employment, but the recovery after 2010 is clearly shown in Figure 4.1. The oil price collapse of 2015 again put downward pressure on productivity.

Historically, the energy sector bulked so large in the Texas economy that when oil and, to a lesser extent, natural gas prices declined the state often went into recession. In the mid-1980s, the recession was so deep that it took a decade and more to recover. Texas leaders brag that they have worked hard to diversify the Texas economy, making the state less dependent on the energy sector. This brag, like many others is both true and incomplete. Texas is less dependent on oil and gas extraction, but not on the energy sector understood more broadly, and this critical fact will focus our attention on a fundamental flaw in the Texas economy as most Texans experience it.

The data in Table 4.2 clearly show that despite the frequent claims that the Texas economy has diversified beyond the energy sector, the state is, in fact, more dependent on oil and gas extraction and refining than it has been in decades.[16] It is true that the energy sector provides proportionately fewer jobs than it once did; 6 to 7 percent of all non-farm jobs in the 1970s and 1980s, compared to about 5 percent since the 1990s. But the remaining jobs pay better than they ever have, so the share of wages going to energy sector workers has risen from an average of 6.5 percent between 1970 and 2010

Table 4.2 The Texas Energy Sector: Share of Workforce, Income, and GDP by Decade

Texas	1970s	1980s	1990s	2000s	2010s
% of Workforce	6.0	7.3	5.0	4.0	5.2
% of Income	6.5	7.6	5.5	6.5	8.4
% of GDP	15.9	17.6	11.0	13.1	18.7

Source: Bureau of Economic Analysis, SA25, Total Full-Time and Part-Time Employment by SIC Industry; Total Employment, Mining, and three categories of Non-Durable Goods; Petroleum and Coal Products; Chemicals and Allied Products; and Rubber and Miscellaneous Plastics Products. Same categories for share of personal income and state GDP.

to 8.4 percent in recent years. From the 1970s through the 1990s, energy jobs paid a premium of no more than 10 percent over other jobs, but since 2000 that premium has ballooned to 60 percent. Finally, the share of Texas GDP accounted for by the energy sector, extraction and refining, has been remarkably stable, despite a serious dip in the 1990s and early 2000s, averaging 16.8 percent in the 1970s and 1980s and 18.7 percent since 2010.

When the energy sector booms, it adds jobs, high paying jobs, and Texas boosters swell with pride.[17] In early 2017, Exxon Mobil announced plans to build 11 new refineries along the Texas and Louisiana Gulf Coast. Reflecting the obvious link between extraction and refining, Exxon Mobil CEO Darren Woods explained that the intention was to site new fuels, chemicals, and plastics plants close to the shale oil and natural gas fields of the region. Woods touted "45,000 jobs, many of which pay an average of $100,000 a year."[18]

Oil and gas, the energy industry from exploration, through extraction, to refining have an iconic role in the Texas economy.[19] Nonetheless, it is a role that needs to be unpacked. Since 2010, as we saw in Table 4.2, the energy industry in Texas has employed just 5.2 percent of the state's workforce. But these are well-paid and productive workers, drawing down 8.4 percent of the state's total payroll and producing fully 18.7 percent of GDP. What does it mean for the Texas economy that 5.2 percent of workers receive 8.4 percent of pay and produce 18.7 percent of GDP?[20] To answer that question we engage in a strikingly informative economic thought experiment. We ask what the Texas economy would look like without the energy industry?

We reproduce Figure 4.1, "Worker Productivity and Worker Pay: Comparing the U.S. and Texas," by simply subtracting the energy industry numbers for employment, income, and GDP from both the U.S. and Texas totals. Before we begin, we know that these calculations will impact the U.S. much less than Texas. In regard to 2015 employment, only 1.4 percent of U.S. workers were employed in energy extraction and refining, while in Texas it was 5.2 percent. In regard to 2015 personal income, energy extraction and refining accounted for 2.3 percent of U.S. personal income, while in Texas it was 8.4 percent. And just as tellingly, energy extraction and refining in 2014 accounted for 6.3 percent of U.S. GDP and fully 21 percent of Texas GDP.

Not surprisingly, the lines in Figure 4.2 describing Texas worker productivity and pay as a percentage of U.S. worker productivity and pay in the non-energy sectors of the economy drop, productivity drops substantially and pay drops a little. In the non-energy sectors of the economy, where 95 percent of Texans work, productivity has almost always been well below the national average. In fact, it has been nearly flat, ranging between 94 and 99 percent of the national average since 1986. While Texas worker pay as a percentage of U.S. worker pay tracks below productivity, as it did in Figure 4.1, the gap has usually been small, often just a couple of percentage points. In summary, the Texas energy industry, especially when oil and gas prices are high, inflate the apparent productivity and, to a lesser extent, pay of Texas workers. Outside the energy sector, where 95 percent of employed Texans work, Texas worker productivity and pay have languished below national averages.

These figures are striking, but as the rest of this chapter and later chapters will show, Texas has always been a low-wage state that invests more lightly than most in education and social services and that has a higher proportion of its workforce without a high school diploma than any other state. Moreover, half of Texas workers are black and Hispanic and they make less than 60 percent of what Anglo workers make—so

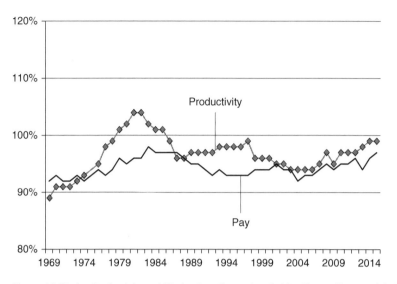

Figure 4.2 Worker Productivity and Worker Pay: Comparing the Non-Energy Sectors of the U.S.
and Texas Economies, 1969–2015

Source: Bureau of Economic Analysis: U.S. Table 6.4B, Full-Time and Part-Time Employees by Industry;
Texas Table SA25, Total Full-Time and Part-Time Employees by SIC Industry; U.S. and Texas Gross Domestic
Product (GDP) by State (millions of current dollars); U.S. and Texas, Tables SA% and SA5N, Personal Income
by SIC Industry. Removing the effects of the energy industry involved subtracting Oil and Gas Extraction and
three Non-Durable Goods refining categories, Chemicals and Allied Products, Petroleum and Coal Products, and
Rubber and Miscellaneous Plastics, from the employment, income, and GDP figures.

the modest productivity and low wages highlighted in Figure 4.2 should come as no
surprise. We now turn to personal income in Texas, including personal income by race
and ethnicity, to buttress and detail these findings.

Personal Income in Texas

The earliest reports on personal income in Texas suggest that money income was
uncommon. Pioneer Noah Smithwick reported that when he arrived in 1827, "Money
was as scarce as bread. . . . Pelts of any kind passed current and constituted the principal medium of exchange."[21] The Englishman William Bollaert reports that money
was so scarce in 1843 that barter, "Cotton for sugar and coffee, and bacon for boots—
corn for calomel quinine . . . beef for brandy" was the norm.[22] Within a few years a
money economy emerged and some Texans were able to take their leisure. Wilhelm
Steinert, writing in 1849, reported that, "Every American who can afford it keeps slaves
and does no work at all. The women likewise only work if they cannot afford a slave
woman. . . . As a rule, women then sit in their rocking chairs and smoke their pipes, or
at most embroider a bedspread." Most Texans, of course, did not have slaves and had
to work very hard, both men and women. Steinert reports that Texans who worked for
others received modest pay: "Wages for day laborers are 50 cents on the average. A
farmhand gets $10 to $15 per month plus board. . . . Girls get $4 to $8 per month."[23] The
journalist Frederick Law Olmsted generally confirmed Steinert's numbers, writing in
1854 that, "Journeymen (late emigrants and rough hands) informed me that they were

paid wages, $15 a month and upward, and found. Farm-laborers, $8 to $15, and found. Domestics (females), $5 to $8."[24]

By far the most thorough discussion of wealth-holding in antebellum Texas comes from Randolph B. Campbell and Richard G. Lowe and is entitled *Wealth and Power in Antebellum Texas*. They report that more than 75 percent of Texans in 1850 were directly involved in agriculture, of whom one-third were slave-owners and two-thirds were not and worked their own land. Slave-owners controlled between 60 percent and 70 percent of improved lands and produced about 90 percent of the valuable cotton crop. Finally, they report that slave-owners held ten times the net wealth of non-slave-owners.[25]

The outcome of the Civil War, obviously, brought great change. While Texas remained overwhelmingly agricultural, slavery was abolished and a new equilibrium in the labor market was slow in coming. Eventually, southern elites reestablished their control of agricultural wages, for both blacks and whites, and a new equilibrium emerged in which "the South was a low-wage region in a high-wage country." Gavin Wright explained in his classic *Old South, New South* that:

> Southern regional per capita income, though it stood at a level barely half of the U.S. average in 1880, nonetheless grew at about the national rate between 1880 and 1900, and faster than the national rate between 1900 and 1920. . . . But . . . the chaotic state of international trade stymied cotton demand . . . between 1920 and 1930. As a result, even before the Great Depression, the South lost virtually all of the relative income gains achieved by 1920.[26]

Texas was the wealthiest southern state, but in 1929 per capita income in Texas was only $474 annually, just 68 percent of the U.S. average.

From 1929 forward we have excellent annual data on Per Capita Personal Income (PCPI) for the United States and for the individual states. PCPI is a widely used general measure of comparative wealth and well-being which is derived by dividing total personal income by total population. PCPI includes all earned income including wages, self-employment income, interest, dividends, rent, social security, and other transfer payments.

The data in Figure 4.3 show that Texas has made real advances against U.S. PCPI, but they also show that most of those advances were made during the 1930s and 1940s. Texas survived the Great Depression of the 1930s better than most states, thanks to its dependence on agriculture and natural resources, as opposed to industry and finance, which were harder hit. Nonetheless, Texas agriculture and oil both suffered. The price of cotton, Texas's leading cash crop, dropped from 29 cents a pound to 6 cents from 1932 through mid-1933 before production limits produced a slow rebound in price. The oil industry, always boom and bust, gyrated wildly during the 1930s. "Dad" Joiner brought in the "Daisy Bradford 3" well in October 1930 to open up the great East Texas oil field. Within a matter of months the increased supply had driven the price from $1.30 to 10 cents a barrel in 1931 and, briefly, to 4 cents in 1933. Texas Governor Ross Sterling intervened, empowering the Texas Railroad Commission (TRC) to set production limits designed to bring supply back into balance with demand, and sending in the National Guard and Texas Rangers to shut down wells not abiding by the limits.[27] As agricultural and oil markets stabilized, Texas recovered somewhat faster than the rest of the nation.[28]

Texans are generally loath to admit that federal government programs and spending played a major role in the state's economic growth, but they certainly did in the 1930s and 1940s when Texas made most of its gains against the national per capita income

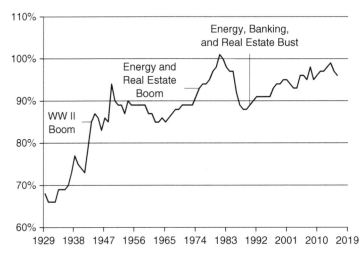

Figure 4.3 Texas per Capita Personal Income as a Percentage of U.S. per Capita Personal
Income, 1929–2016

Source: U.S. Bureau of Economic Analysis, SA1–3–Per Capita Personal Income by States, 1929–2016, www.
bea.gov/regional/docs/income/srius.cfm.

averages. Though the New Deal is most closely identified with President Franklin
Roosevelt, Texans were deeply involved, especially during the early and mid-1930s.
John Nance Garner of Uvalde was FDR's vice president, Sam Rayburn of Bonham
was House Majority Leader, and Jesse Jones, a prominent Houston banker, was named
by Roosevelt to head the powerful Reconstruction Finance Corporation (RFC). At
the depth of the Depression, the RFC acted as a government bank to capitalize and
resell bankrupt businesses, especially banks and railroads, fund relief programs such
as the Works Progress Administration, and loan money to states to use in battling the
Depression. Jones paid particular attention to Texas: "he turned on the spigot of federal funds from 1932 to 1945, and that infusion of capital transformed the state from a
rural agrarian to an urban industrial society."[29] Texans benefited not just from federal
relief projects but from dams and water projects, roads, and rural electrification.

In the 1940s, Texas was buoyed by war spending, which fueled both urbanization
and industrialization. The wartime boom transformed a rural economy based on agriculture, ranching, and oil into an urban economy based not only on oil and natural gas,
but also on energy services, petrochemicals, aerospace industries, and manufacturing
in general. Texas historian David McComb noted that, "By 1945 the federal government had built thirty-five air fields, twelve army training camps, five naval air stations,
and eight hospitals—more than any other state." Moreover, "During the conflict government and business invested $600 million in petrochemical plants in the Houston
area and added $300 million immediately thereafter. . . . What emerged in a 'golden
triangle' of Houston to Freeport to Port Arthur-Orange was one of the . . . major petrochemical complexes in the nation."[30] Texas benefited greatly from the move from
agriculture to the higher value-added activities of manufacturing. PCPI in Texas rose
from 66 percent of the national average in 1930 to 74 percent in 1940. In fact, in two
remarkable years, 1941 to 1943, Texas PCPI rose 12 points, from 73 percent of U.S.
PCPI to 85 percent, before peaking at 94 percent of U.S. PCPI in 1949.

Texas wanted federal funds and the economic advances that they fueled, but it wanted them on Texas terms. As a result, public policymaking during the Depression and war years was a tug-of-war between national and state officials. Federal policies in regard to race, wages, social security, unemployment compensation, poor relief, and social welfare were all designed to challenge the traditional low-wage economy of the South. Despite the obvious need of the South, the nation's poorest region, by 1937 southern elites, including those in Texas, were in revolt against the New Deal.[31] The South's representatives in Congress sought to limit the New Deal's impact on southern race relations by, for example, excluding farmers and domestics from social security and unemployment compensation. Southern congressmen battled, but ultimately failed to stop, the 1938 Fair Labor Standards Act setting minimum wages and hours and limiting child labor.

As the southern support that Roosevelt had enjoyed during the early New Deal faded, he made a major push to explain to the South the benefits of a higher wage structure for the region. In June 1938, President Roosevelt assembled an expert panel charged to produce a "Report on the Economic Conditions of the South." The report was delivered to the president in July, declaring that, "Ever since the War between the States the South has been the poorest section of the Nation. The richest state in the South ranks lower in per capita income than the poorest state outside the region." The report also said, quite explicitly, that, "Differences in cost-of-living . . . are not great enough to justify the differentials in wages that exist."[32]

President Roosevelt barn-stormed West Texas in July, 1938, to defend the report and to campaign for liberal candidates in the upcoming midterm elections. In Fort Worth, Roosevelt tried to convince Texas elites of the merits of the Fair Labor Standards Act or minimum wage bill, saying "You need more industries in Texas, but I know you know the importance of not trying to get industries by the route of cheap wages for industrial workers."[33] Texas political and economic leaders were, of course, unmoved as low wages were precisely how they intended to attract new jobs and industries.

"By the end of 1947 a majority of the southern states—seven of the thirteen—had passed open shop laws. . . . By prohibiting union shops, the right-to-work states of Arkansas, Florida, Georgia, North Carolina, Tennessee, Texas, and Virginia" sought to preserve the region's traditional low-wage economy.[34]

In 1950, as the nation recovered from the post–World War II economic slump, the South was on the move and Texas was the wealthiest of the southern states. Yet, for southern elites, the high wages required by the federal government remained a threat to the low-wage, small government, low-tax, thin social service model that had been the basis for their competitiveness. The rapid wage growth of the late 1930s and 1940s ended. For the next six decades and more, Texas averaged around 90 percent of U.S. PCPI, though it made two more runs at the national average, one in the early 1980s and another after 2005.[35]

The PCPI of Texans increased steadily after 1950, but so did income in the other states, so the ranking of Texas among the states did not change much. Texas was the highest-ranking southern state in per capita income in 1950, at 31st, while Florida ranked 34th and Virginia 37th. Louisiana, Georgia, Tennessee, North Carolina, and Kentucky followed at 41st through 45th, and the remaining southern states, Alabama, South Carolina, Arkansas, and Mississippi, held down the last four spots at 46th through 49th (D.C. was included but Alaska and Hawaii were not yet states). By 1962, both Florida and Virginia had surpassed Texas and would never fall behind again except very briefly in the oil boom of the early 1980s. Georgia surpassed Texas in 1987 and both North Carolina and Tennessee surpassed Texas in the mid-1990s before all three fell back in the late 1990s.

Between 1950 and 2016, Texas improved its ranking on per capita income, but three other southern states improved their rankings as much or more and Virginia improved considerably more. Texas moved up eight places to 23rd, Oklahoma moved up 11, to 28th, Louisiana moved up ten to 31st, and Virginia soared 25 places to 12th.[36] Alabama, South Carolina, Arkansas, and Mississippi continued to hold down spaces in the bottom ten as they had a half century earlier. Texas remained below the national average for per capita income throughout the twentieth century and into the twenty-first century, except briefly in the early 1980s.

Figure 4.4 provides a comparison of PCPI for the U.S. and Texas between 1970 and 2015. Here we compare PCPI for the U.S. with that for Texas and later for several other states to get a more nuanced view of how Texans fared compared to other Americans. The answer as we shall see, unfortunately, is not so well: "The myth of the wealthy Texan to the contrary, Texas traditionally has lagged behind the U.S. average in per capita income."[37] The data show that, with the exception of a very brief period in the early 1980s, Texas PCPI has always tracked below the national average. It also shows once again that the progress that Texas made from the 1950s through the early 1980s was lost in the devastating collapse of oil prices, property values, and the subsequent savings and loan debacle and banking crisis in the mid- to late 1980s.

During the 1970s and early 1980s, Texans regarded their economy as recession-proof. Agriculture and energy were thought to provide products with steadily rising markets. The oil boom began with the Arab oil embargo of 1973 and was fueled by shortages that followed the Shah of Iran's fall. These shortages drove oil prices from $3.50 a barrel to $35 by the early 1980s. The increase in oil and gas prices spurred domestic exploration and production and fueled a real-estate boom that made Texas one

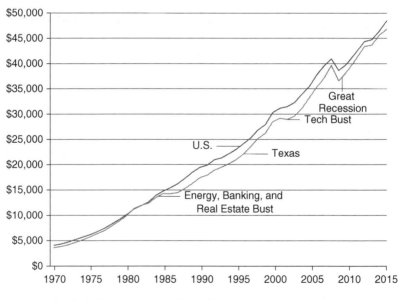

Figure 4.4 Per Capita Personal Income: Comparing the U.S. and Texas, 1970–2015

Source: U.S. Bureau of Economic Analysis, SA1–3–Per Capita Personal Income by States, 1929–2015.

of the most rapidly growing states in the nation. Texas hats and boots were increasingly visible in the nation's airports and money centers, while back home "Drive 80 mph, Freeze a Yankee" bumper stickers became common. More importantly, the impression grew that the interests of the oil patch and of the nation were in conflict and Texans were unconcerned.[38]

Interestingly, good times, especially when not enjoyed elsewhere in the country, trigger a deep sense of superiority in Anglo Texans that grates on other Americans. Two generations earlier, in the classic Texas novel and movie *Giant*, this theme of Texas interests in conflict with broader American interests is clear. Leslie Lynnton Benedict, played by Elizabeth Taylor in the movie, a Virginia socialite recently married to Texas rancher, Jordan "Bick" Benedict, played by Rock Hudson, had fled the dust and bluster of Texas for her Virginia family home. Bick had followed to win her back to the marriage and to Texas. As they tried to get comfortable with each other again, Leslie noted, "Texas is booming. The rest of the country is flat. Is that good?" Bick's response was classic Texas bombast. He said, "Only good enough to make us the richest state in the whole country. We're a country within a country." Leslie, subject to yet another bathe of Texas braggadocio, cried "Again!" To which Bick responded, "Oil and beef and cotton. You can't stop it and you can't top it."[39] Maybe not, but two points come to mind. First, Bick's claim that Texas was or was on its way to becoming the richest state in the nation is just wrong—though it might feel right to Anglo elites. Second, good times come and good times go and when they go Texas and Texans can fall hard. Though eager to claim credit for good times, Texans almost always see hard times as fathered elsewhere, usually in Washington.

As the 1980s opened, "projections called for Texas, California, and Florida to be the three fastest-growing states in the country over the next several decades."[40] While this broad projection generally held, the mid-1980s proved to be extremely challenging for Texas. Texas prosperity in the 1970s and early 1980s hinged on the Arab oil embargo and on Saudi Arabia's willingness to limit its production to prop up the world price. Oil prices rose from $3 a barrel in 1970 to $21 in 1980. After peaking at $37 in 1981 it fell to $27 a barrel in late 1985. In early 1986, Saudi Arabia flooded the world oil market, driving the price below $10, to highlight to other producers the cost of global oil surpluses.[41] Oil exploration, services, and distribution ground to a halt and unemployment in Texas spiked to 10.3 percent by mid-year. As the Texas economy reeled under the collapse of oil prices, Congress passed the Tax Reform Act of 1986, one provision of which removed key tax benefits to investing in real estate. Commercial property values in Texas dropped by 30 to 40 percent.

The Texas Legislature tried to respond to the pressure that the collapsing energy and real-estate markets placed on the Texas economy by lifting long-standing restrictions on Texas financial institutions. The Texas Constitution of 1876 mandated community banking, precluding both branch banking (where one bank could have multiple bank locations or branches) and interstate banking (where a bank could operate in multiple states). Though the prohibition on branch banking was loosened in 1956 and 1970 to permit bank holding companies, the constraints on Texas banks were still real. As the Texas economy buckled in 1986, the legislature hurriedly approved both branch banking and interstate banking in the hopes of attracting money into the state. It worked, after a fashion. Texas's weakened banks were forced, one by one, to seek outside buyers. By the end of the decade, nine of Texas's ten largest banks had failed or been bought by out-of-state banks. In fact, 506 banks and 225 savings and loans failed in Texas between 1983 and 1992, far more than failed in any other state.

Bankers, financial regulators, and the Texas business community understood the gravity of what had happened, though they differed as to why it had happened and whether Texans were in any way to blame. Ben Love of Houston's Texas Commerce Bank (TCB) and Jody Grant of Fort Worth's Texas American Bank (TAB) both admitted that Texas bankers were overextended and that wrongdoing had been common in the state's savings and loan institutions, but they ultimately blamed Texas politicians and U.S. financial regulators for not easing the banks through the crisis. Ben Love lobbied the Texas Legislature to pass both branch banking and interstate banking for more than a decade, 1974 to 1986, to no avail.[42] As the Texas banks came under increasing pressure in late 1986, Jody Grant dispatched TAB's Bayard H. Friedman to seek help from Governor Bill Clements. Friedman reported that "the governor said that the banks were broke, they deserved to be broke, and he wasn't going to do a damn thing to help them." Grant describes the governor's "attitude as shocking and appalling: it was incomprehensible that the Chief Executive of the state had so little understanding of the economic fallout that would result from the bank's crippled status."[43] The governor later changed his mind and agreed to work with Texas banks, but it was too late.

Texas bankers complained most bitterly that the Federal Reserve, the Federal Deposit Insurance Corporation (FDIC), and the Comptroller of the Currency were biased against Texas banks. Bankers pleaded for forbearance from federal regulators to give them time to recapitalize their banks. Regulators listened but concluded that undercapitalized banks simply needed to be liquidated, by seizure or sale, before incurring further losses. Texas bankers were devastated and blamed the regulators for being too harsh. Al Casey of Dallas's First Republic Bank thought the FDIC should have accepted management's recapitalization plan. When the FDIC refused and forced the sale of the bank, Casey declared in a later deposition that he felt "a sense at the time of betrayal toward the FDIC."[44] Love wrote that "In 1986, the Office of the Comptroller of the Currency regulators were transparently biased against Texas. In fact, the OCC examiners repeatedly demonstrated an anti-Texas bias, emphasizing that the Texas economy was faring worse than the major Texas banks believed."[45]

They were right, Bill Black of the Federal Home Loan Bank Board, which oversaw the savings and loan industry, said "Texas was at the top of the charts" in profitability in the early 1980s, "because more of its savings and loans engaged in accounting fraud than anywhere else. . . . Its state regulatory system was the worst in the nation and that's saying something."[46] Texas saw their small government, laissez-faire regulatory system as advancing growth and entrepreneurship. Federal regulators like Black saw it as inviting fraud.

Ben Love described the shock felt among Texans when the Texas myth crumbled along with the energy and property markets. Love described a conversation he had with Bill Taylor, then chief of staff of the Federal Reserve Bank in Washington. Love thought the Texas banks might have weathered the storm if the regulators had been more flexible. Once Love had made his case, he reported that Bill Taylor said, "Ben, you Texans always think what you have in Texas is worth one hell of a lot more than any of the rest of us do." Taylor then went on to restate Fed policy, which we came to know again after 2008 as "too big to fail." In the 1980s, the Texas banks were not too big to fail. Taylor told Love:

> The ten largest banks in this nation are not going to fail. As an element of federal government policy, the Federal Reserve will not let them fail. That's the way it is. But I will tell you one other thing: If we think it is proper, we *will* let any Texas bank fail because not one Texas bank is among the ten largest banks in the nation.[47]

Other bankers also looked somewhat askance at their Texas colleagues. Love reported a conversation with Bill Brown, head of the First National Bank of Boston, as Brown's bank fell under the gaze of the regulators. Brown said, "You know, Ben, I've heard you talk about how unfair the regulators were to Texas banks. I'm going to tell you, we're good friends, but I tended to dismiss what you were saying, thinking, Well, Ben's a Texan, and that's the way Texans are."[48] Love eventually brokered the sale of TCB to Chemical Bank of New York.

As the storm swept over Texas, financial analysts and observers recognized that the landscape would be different once it passed. The *Wall Street Journal* reported on December 17, 1986, that the demise of the Texas banks

> brought an end to the era in which Texas controlled its own capital and, ultimately, its own economic destiny. Francis Tuggle, dean of the graduate business school at Rice, agreed. "There is a strong symbolic message in this," he said. "The notion of the Republic of Texas and the idea that we can do everything all by ourselves have gone by the boards, . . . Given the economics in the state, it's inevitable that we just can't go it alone any longer."[49]

Floyd Norris, then a highly respected financial writer for the *New York Times*, saw the results of the Texas banking crash very differently from the Texas participants. Rather than adopting the local view—they hate us because we are Texans—Norris saw the federal government playing a positive role that enabled Texas to stabilize rather quickly. Norris confirmed that, "The United States let the Texas banking industry collapse, with out-of-state banks picking up the pieces. . . . At the time, there was handwringing about how Texas could function without banks. Just fine, it turned out." Though Texas pride was dented by the loss of its big banks, banking services never missed a beat and "the national deposit insurance fund suffered substantial losses" in cleaning up the balance sheets of Texas banks so they could be sold. Though few Texas bankers would agree, Norris concluded that, "Texas greatly benefited from the fact that the American economy was integrated, with a central government that could and would help out."[50] Robert Bryce, author of *Cronies*, reported that federal bail-out funds flowed to Texas totaling $4,775 per capita, while New Jersey citizens lost $1,047 per capita.[51] New Jersians apparently are not very entrepreneurial.

While the savings and loan scandal had a national impact, Texas was its epicenter and its impact in Texas was more severe than it was nationally. Notice that the upward arc of the U.S. line in Figure 4.4 was unbroken through the late 1980s while the Texas line went sideways between 1985 and 1987. During those lost years Texas went from a PCPI at 100 percent of the national average in 1982 to just 88 percent in 1988 and 1989. Notice also that the national recession of 2001–2002 slowed growth of PCPI for both Texas and the U.S., but Texas was harder hit than the nation. Texas PCPI actually dropped from 2001 to 2002, while national PCPI growth merely slowed. By 2014 Texas had clawed its way back to 99 percent of U.S. PCPI before being pushed back to 96 percent by the 2015 and 2016 travails of the global oil industry.

Median Family Income in Texas

Another way to compare the economic performance of Texas to that of the nation is in terms of median family income. Median family income, whether for the U.S. or for Texas, is the dollar income above which and below which are half of family incomes. Figure 4.5 compares U.S. and Texas median family income for 1959, 1969, 1979, 1989,

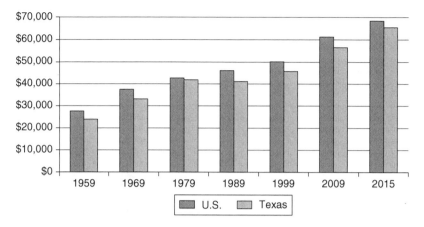

Figure 4.5 Median Family Income: Comparing the U.S. and Texas, 1959–2015

Source: U.S. Census Bureau, Table S2, Median Family Income by State: 1959, 1969, 1979, 1989, and 1999, www.census.gov/data/tables/time-series/dec/historical-income-states.html. 2009 and 2015 are from U.S. Census Bureau, American FactFinder, GCT1902, Median Family Income, http://factfinder.census.gov/servlet/ GCTTable?

1999, and 2009. Texas has lagged uniformly behind the U.S. median family income at every period, except 1979, which was near the peak of the go-go years just before the crash of the mid-1980s.[52] At every other measurement, Texas ranked between 34th and 36th among the 50 states and D.C. Essentially no improvement in Texas's standing among the states in median family income occurred in the half century between 1959 and 2009 (Texas ranked 34th in 2009). Texans got wealthier over this half century, but no faster than did their fellow Americans. Though Texas rose to 29th among the states on median family income in 2015, the economic slowdown caused by falling oil process likely will soon return Texas to its traditional ranking in the mid-30s.

We get an even more sobering view of the distribution of median family income in Texas by looking at race and ethnicity. In the previous chapter, we described Texas as an "Anglo republic" to highlight the fact that the state was founded and developed by Anglos for Anglos. To the extent that others, Native-Americans, blacks, and Hispanics, were present, they were tolerated only as they provided cheap and willing labor. Today's Texas leaders argue that these unfortunate truths are no longer relevant because all Texans enjoy equal opportunity and, hence, Anglos, blacks, and Hispanics are found throughout the state's social and economic structure—high and low. While it is true that there are wealthy blacks and Hispanics in Texas and that the black and Hispanic middle classes are growing, or were before the Great Recession, it is also true that there have long been stark and stable differences by race and ethnicity in median family income in Texas.[53]

As we see in Figure 4.6, median family income in Texas varies dramatically by race and ethnicity and the gaps are changing only very slowly. The 1960 census, reporting 1959 data, reported that non-white families made just less than half, 49.5 percent, of what white families made. In the 1970 and later censuses, non-whites were broken out into blacks and Hispanics, and in 1980 Asians were added (not reported in Figure 4.6 because the numbers were small). The 1970 census, reporting 1969 data, showed significant progress. Black families made 60 percent of what white families made and Hispanic

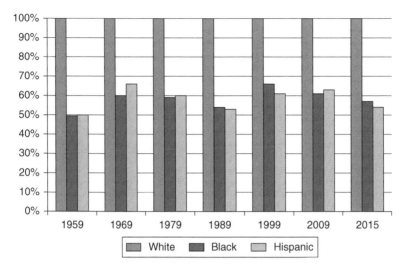

Figure 4.6 Texas Median Family Income by Race and Ethnicity, 1959–2015

Source: United States Census, 1960, Texas, vol. 45:345; 1970, 45:451; 1980, 45:160; 1990, 45:178; 2000, Texas State Data Center, median family income by race, 2009 and 2015, American Community Survey, median family income by race.

families made 66 percent. In 1980, blacks slipped back to 59 percent and Hispanics to 60 percent of white family income. In 1990, blacks and Hispanics slipped further back, to 54 and 53 percent, respectively, though in 2000, both rose with blacks making 66 percent of what white families made and Hispanics making 61 percent. The "Great Recession" of 2007–2009 knocked Texas minorities back yet again. The latest data, from the census's 2015 American Community Survey, reported that Texas black families made 57 percent of what white families did and Hispanic families made 54 percent.

While most Texans of all races and ethnicities are better off than they were a half century ago, it is also true that minorities have made little progress against Anglo median family income—they still make less than 60 percent of what whites make. Texas blacks and Hispanics have provided a low-wage labor force throughout Texas history and that is changing only very slowly if it is changing at all.

Unemployment and Unemployment Compensation in Texas

One often hears that jobs are plentiful in Texas and that anyone truly wanting to work will find a job. In fact, Texas has had an interesting and even erratic relationship to the U.S. unemployment rate (Figure 4.7). Again, the early 1980s marked an important turning point. From 1970 through 1985 the Texas unemployment rate tracked well below, often between 1 and 2 percent below, the national unemployment rate. The Texas financial crisis of the mid-1980s sent the state's unemployment rate one and a half to two points above the national rate from 1986 through 1989. By the early 1990s, the Texas unemployment rate came down to about one-third to two-thirds of a point above the national rate, where it remained through 2006. The national recession that began in 2008 initially hit the nation harder than it hit Texas. Between 2008 and 2015, Texas was a full point or more under the national unemployment rate; but in 2016 that margin declined to just one-third of a point.

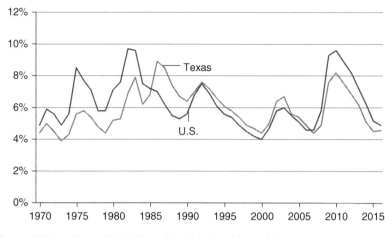

Figure 4.7 Unemployment Rate: Comparing the U.S. and Texas, 1970–2016

Source: U.S. Bureau of Labor Statistics, Household Data Annual Averages, Table 1, Employment Status of the Civilian Non-institutional Population, 1940—date. Texas data from http://www.bls.gov/lau/lastrk16.htm.

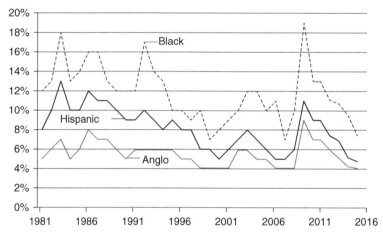

Figure 4.8 Texas Unemployment Rates by Race and Ethnicity, 1981–2015

Source: Bureau of Labor Statistics, "Employment Status of the Civilian Non-institutional Population in States, by Sex, Race, Hispanic Ethnicity," www.bls.gov/lau/#ex14.

Few events are as disruptive of individual and family life as the loss of a job and paycheck. Many people have enough savings to weather a job loss of modest duration, but few can manage longer-term unemployment. Unemployment Compensation (UC) is a set of programs designed to assist workers who lose jobs through no fault of their own until they find new employment. But how generous the benefits are and how long they last might influence how hard an unemployed person looks for new work and what job they are willing to accept. Not surprisingly, Texas is a hard place to be unemployed. Texas has one of the stingiest unemployment insurance systems in the nation and Texas politicians are absolutely determined to keep it that way.

Not surprisingly, blacks and Hispanics in Texas are substantially more likely to be unemployed than are Anglos. Over the last three plus decades, the period for which we have good data for unemployment by race and ethnicity, black unemployment rates are usually twice or more Anglo rates, while Hispanic rates usually fall between Anglo and black rates. As Figure 4.8 makes clear, unemployment in Texas goes up and it goes down, but the racial pecking order from earlier periods in Texas history remains fixed.

UC in the U.S. is a joint federal-state program with its origins in the New Deal. In fact, the Federal-State Unemployment Compensation Program was part of the Social Security Act of 1935. The federal government sets the general guidelines for UC and levies an unemployment tax through the Internal Revenue Service. The Federal Unemployment Tax Act of 1939 (FUTA) initiated the modern funding system. FUTA imposes a 6.2 percent tax on employers on the first $7,000 in salary paid to each covered worker. The states levy their own taxes and they determine eligibility requirements, weekly benefit amounts, and the number of weeks that those judged eligible may draw. If a state program is judged well-funded by the U.S. Secretary of Labor, state employers who are up to date on their state taxes get a 5.4 percent tax credit against their FUTA tax rate. The federal government keeps 0.8 of 1 percent to finance administration of the system, pay half of any extended benefits that might be approved, and to build up a loan fund from which states might borrow.

The Texas UC system came in for particular scrutiny as unemployment rose in 2009. President Obama's $787 billion stimulus program, passed by Congress in early 2009, offered states a piece of $7 billion in new money if they would expand eligibility for UC to cover various "part-time, low-income, and female workers." Texas's projected share of these monies was $556 million. Texas Governor Rick Perry responded, saying "If this money expands entitlements, we will not accept it. This is exactly how addicts get hooked on drugs."[54] Bill Hammond, then head of the powerful Texas Association of Business, echoed the same theme, saying "It's like a drug dealer. The dealer gives you your first hit for free to get you hooked, and then you are addicted and are paying the consequences for a long, long time."[55] Perry ultimately rejected the $556 million, just as he said he would.

Governor Perry's point was that government support, even in difficult times, was simply not part of the Texas model. "People living in Texas are a heck of a lot better off than the vast majority of the other ones. My instinct is they'd whole lot rather have a good-paying job than they would unemployment insurance."[56] Probably so, but what if unemployment is high, as it often is in Texas, good-paying jobs are hard to find, and UC is limited when it is available at all? "'This was pretty simple for us. Keep things going like they're going in Texas,' said the governor. . . . 'We can take care of ourselves. And we do not need any more strings from Washington attached to programs.'"[57]

What few appeared to realize during this debate was that Texas has always been very tight-fisted about access to UC. The U.S. Department of Labor has good data on the percentage of U.S. and Texas unemployed who draw on UC, commonly referred to as the recipiency rate, going back to 1976. Between 1976 and 2016, the average recipiency rate for unemployed U.S. workers was 35 percent, while for Texas workers it was 23 percent (see Figure 4.9). The coverage gap between the proportion of U.S. and Texas unemployed workers on UC was very steady over most of this 40-year period. Texas's average ranking among the states over this period—remember there are 51 programs— was 46th. However, in 2015 and then more markedly in 2016, Texas's unemployment recipiency rate—for the first and only time in 40 years—jumped up to the national average. These numbers, which might reflect the large job losses among the privileged workers in the energy sector, will bear watching in future years.[58]

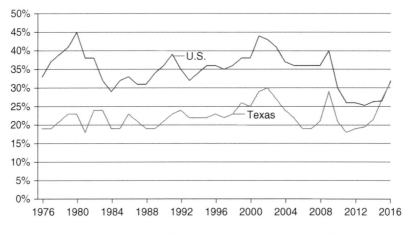

Figure 4.9 Unemployment Compensation Recipiency Rate: Comparing the U.S. and Texas,
        1976–2016

Source: U.S. Department of Labor, www.workforcesecurity.doleta.gov/unemploy/Chartbook.a13.asp.

Poverty in Texas

Poverty is another idea that fits uneasily with the Texas myth or the Texas model of
small government. Some 20 to 25 percent of Americans lived in poverty until President
Lyndon Johnson, following up on initiatives begun by John and Robert Kennedy, initiated a "War on Poverty" in the mid-1960s. By the early 1970s, poverty had dropped
to 11 or 12 percent. In the early 1980s, President Ronald Reagan initiated "welfare
reform" and poverty rates began to creep up, going to 15.2 percent in 1982 and holding
in the 14 to 15 percent range until the late 1990s. After falling to about 12 percent, the
Great Recession pushed it back to 15 percent.[59]

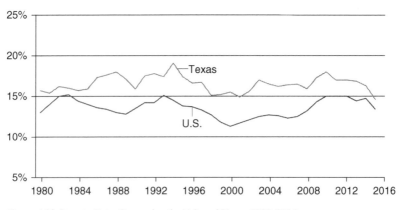

Figure 4.10 Poverty Rate: Comparing the U.S. and Texas, 1980–2015

Source: https://census.gov/dta/tables/time-series/demo/income-poverty/historical-poverty-people.html. For U.S.
see Table 2; for Texas see Table 21.

Texans experience poverty at a higher rate than do residents of most other states. Between 1980 and 2015, Texas had a higher poverty rate than the nation every year (Figure 4.10). The Texas poverty rate ran an average of one or two points above the national average between 1980 and 1985 before popping up to four or five points above national average through the end of the decade. Texas poverty rates ran consistently two to four points above the national average throughout the 1990s and the first decade of the twenty-first century. For example, in 2000 the national average was 11.3 percent while Texas was 15.5 percent, and in 2013 the U.S. rate was 15 percent while Texas was 17.6 percent. By 2015, the last year for which there is data, the U.S. poverty rate was 13.5 percent while the Texas rate was 14.7 percent.

In 2015, 4 million Texans, down from 4.3 million in 2009, lived in poverty. In percentage terms, Texans in poverty decreased from 17.3 percent in 2009 to 14.7 percent in 2015. Texas had the 12th highest poverty rate in the nation in 2015. Among Texans aged 18 and younger the poverty rates were even higher. In 2015, 24.7 percent of young Texans lived in poverty, down from 27 percent in 2010. Among young Texans, the state had the 15th highest poverty rate in the nation.

As with median family income and unemployment, poverty rates among Texas families shown in Figure 4.11 vary dramatically by race and ethnicity. For more than 40 years, as long as relevant data have been available, minority family poverty rates in Texas have been two and a half to nearly four times the Anglo rates. For example, in 1969, 12.4 percent of Anglo families in Texas lived in poverty, while more than 30 percent of black and Hispanic families did. In 1979, 1989, and 1999, minority family poverty rates were four times Anglo rates, while in 2009 and 2015, the latest data available, they fell back to about three and a half times Anglo rates. Again, not much progress there.

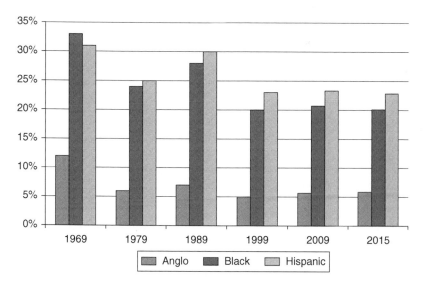

Figure 4.11 Texas Family Poverty Rates by Race and Ethnicity, 1969–2015

Source: U.S. Census, 1970, General Social and Economic Characteristics, Texas, 45:451; 1980, 45:160; 1990, 45:178; 2000, Texas State Data Center, Tables 28b, 28d, 28h, and 28i; 2012, American Community Survey, American FactFinder, Table S1702.

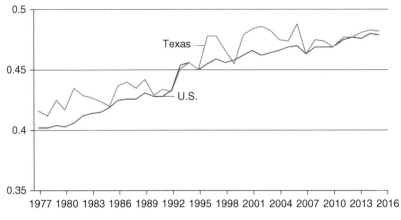

Figure 4.12 Gini Index of Household Income Inequality, 1977–2015

Source: U.S. Census Bureau, Historical Income Tables—Households, Table H-4, "Gini Ratios for Households," http://www.census.gov/hhes/www.income.histinc/h04.html. For Texas data see, U.S. Census Bureau, Current Population Survey, 1978 to 2015, Selected Measures of Household Income Distribution, Gini Index.

Measuring Income Inequality in Texas

The Gini Index is a widely used measure of income inequality. It is used to compare income inequality both between nations and between states within a nation such as the U.S. The Gini Index is a statistic that ranges between zero, when all households have the same income, and one, when a single household has all of the income and the others have none. Obviously, the tails of the range, near zero and near one, are unlikely distributions of income in the real world, so we expect actual measurements nearer the middle of the range. The Gini Index for nations rarely ranges above .65, usually for very poor African countries, like Lesotho and Swaziland, where just a few hold what little wealth there is, or .55 for Latin American countries such as Bolivia, Paraguay, and Guatemala, and .25 in quasi-socialist countries such as Sweden, Norway, Finland, and Germany.

The U.S., as a capitalist country in which competition for advantage is the rule, should have a Gini Index above Sweden but below Paraguay. In fact, that is exactly what we find, but that is not all we find (Figure 4.12). Over the past three decades, the Gini Index for the U.S. has steadily risen from .40 to .48 before falling a bit as the recession of 2007–2009 took hold.[60] The Gini Index for Texas is a bit more erratic but virtually always above the U.S. line. The Texas Gini Index was .42 in 1977 and had risen to .49 by 2002. Moreover, Texas's rank among the states has been high and quite steady. It has ranged between 35th and 50th with the overall average position of Texas among the states being 41st. In 2015 Texas ranked 42nd.[61]

Conclusion

In the finest tradition of the Texas way, reports that laud Texas are accepted unquestioningly. The Small Business and Entrepreneurship Council's Small Business Tax Index 2016 ranked Texas third, just behind South Dakota and Nevada and just ahead of Wyoming—Texans smile, South Dakota, Nevada, and Wyoming! These three states together do not have 15 percent of Texas's population or GDP—who's the big dog? The index measured "taxes, government spending, health care mandates, crime rates and regulatory and energy costs. The non-profit advocacy group noted that the top six states have no personal income tax."[62] First, there are only seven states that do not have an income tax, so that single measure seems to be driving the rankings. Second, the Small Business and Entrepreneurship's measures all anticipate low taxes, low spending, minimal public services, and light regulation. They are intensely present-oriented. They do not anticipate, in fact they punish, future planning and investment for education, health and welfare, transportation, and the environment. Good for business today perhaps, but not so good for the state's future.

Also in the finest tradition of the Texas way, ambivalent or negative reports are rejected out of hand, even when they point to problems that we know are quite real. For example, the Marion Kauffman Foundation's "2010 State New Economy Index" placed Texas at 16th on innovation and competitiveness. The study was meant to measure how well states are managing toward an economic future based on education, knowledge, innovation, and entrepreneurship. Scored on 26 indicators, Texas ranked in the top ten in manufacturing value-added, manufacturing and service exports, entrepreneurial activity, number of fast-growing firms, and number of initial public offerings. Texas ranked much lower, among the bottom ten, on educational preparation of the workforce and attraction of high-tech jobs. Rob Atkinson, who helped prepare the index for the Kauffman Foundation, said "The challenge for Texas is [to] make sure its strategy is driven toward a more knowledge- and innovation-based economy."[63] By 2014, Texas had slipped four spots to 20th.

Texans were either puzzled or offended by the findings. Brad Hancock, head of Texas Christian University's Neeley Enterprise Center, said "I would have thought we would have ranked higher," while others rejected the findings and criticisms outright. Jeremy Brandt, president of the Dallas chapter of the Entrepreneurs' Organization (EO), said "I don't see some of those negatives. Texas and the Dallas-Fort Worth area have a very educated and strong workforce. The Dallas EO chapter is one of the largest in the world."[64] Two points. First, it is almost certain that, as Brandt said, Dallas has one of the biggest EO chapters in the world and that it reflects the broader entrepreneurial culture of Texas. Second, the very dominance of the EO culture might explain the bias toward individualism and small government that leaves Texas schools, colleges, and universities underfunded and underperforming. As we shall see in the next chapter, Texas funding of public schools and resulting test scores rank in the bottom third and Texas has a smaller proportion of its population with a BA or better than all but a few other states.

Though Texans might resist, the telling point made by the Kauffman Foundation report is that the oil-fueled industrial and manufacturing growth that pulled Texas out of the economic backwater between the 1940s and 1980s is fading. It is being replaced by an education-fueled economy of knowledge, creativity, and experiment. Innovation and entrepreneurship will still be critically important, perhaps even more important than in the past, but Texas hustle, grit, and bluff will not be enough. The days of the Texas wildcatter with a sixth-grade education who struck it rich are gone.

We now turn to education in Texas and ask how we have been doing, both how much we have been investing in students and teachers, and, more importantly, how the students have been doing in comparison with students across the U.S.

Notes

1   Andrew Gelman, *Red State, Blue State, Rich State, Poor State: Why Americans Vote the Way They Do*, Princeton, NJ: Princeton University Press, 2008, pp. 62–63.

2   Joel Kotkin and Wendell Cox, "How Texas Is Reshaping Urbanism," *Dallas Morning News*, October 16, 2017, pp. 1P, 4P.

3   Michael Lind, *Land of Promise: An Economic History of the United States*, New York: Harper Collins, 2012, p. 317.

4   Sean P. Cunningham, *Cowboy Conservatism: Texas and the Rise of the Modern Right*, Lexington, KY: University of Kentucky Press, 2010, p. 240.

5   Numan V. Bartley, *The New South, 1945–1980*, Baton Rouge, LA: Louisiana State University Press, 1995, p. 403.

6   Anthony Champagne and Edward J. Harpham, *Texas at the Crossroads: People, Politics, and Policy*, College Station, TX: Texas A&M University Press, 1987, p. 46.

7   David Montejano, *Anglos and Mexicans in the Making of Texas, 1836–1986*, Austin, TX: University of Texas Press, 1987, p. 183.

8   Wilhelm Steinert, *North America, Particularly Texas in the Year 1849*, Dallas, TX: DeGolyer Library, 2003, p. 113.

9   Naureen S. Malik, Dan Murtaugh, and Lauren Etter, *Bloomberg News*, "Texas' Jobs Well Starts to Run Dry," *Dallas Morning News*, December 5, 2015, pp. 1D, 3D.

10   Evan Halper, "Texas' Finances Not as Rosy as They Seemed," *Los Angeles Times*, February 7, 2011.

11   http://scorecard.assetsandopportunity.org/2014/state/tx.

12   Bureau of Labor Statistics, Southwest Information Office, "Minimum Wage Workers in Texas, 2013," www.bls.gov/ro6/fax/minwage_tx.htm.

13   William Ransom Hogan, *The Texas Republic*, Norman, OK: University of Oklahoma Press, 1946, pp. 108–109.

14   Ibid., pp. 267–268.

15   Richard Parker, "Falling into Mediocrity," *Dallas Morning News*, April 2, 2017, P1, P5.

16   Michael D. Plante, "Lower Oil Prices Weaken Prospects for Job, Economic Growth in Texas," Federal Reserve Bank of Dallas, *Southwest Economy*, First Quarter 2015, p. 10.

17   Ibid., p. 11. See also Keith R. Phillips and Christopher Slijk, "Texas Economy Remains Resilient, but Lower Oil Prices Loom as Future Risk," Federal Reserve Bank of Dallas, *Southwest Economy*, First Quarter 2016, pp. 4–6.

18   Joe Carroll, Bloomberg News, "Exxon to Add Jobs in U.S.," *Dallas Morning News*, March 17, 2017, pp. 1D, 6D.

19   Michael D. Plante and Mine K. Yucel, "The Texas Energy Industry: From Boom to Gloom," Federal Reserve Bank of Dallas, Annual Report 2015, p. 3. See also Phillips and Slijk, "Texas Economy Remains Resilient," pp. 3–5.

20   Ibid., p. 4. See also Anthony Murphy, Michael Plante, and Mine Yucel, "Plunging Oil Prices: A Boost for the U.S. Economy, a Jolt for Texas," Federal Reserve Bank of Dallas, *Dallas Fed*, vol. 10, no. 3, April 2015, pp. 2–3. See also Stephen P.A. Brown and Mine K. Yucel, "Energy Brief: The Shale Gas and Tight Oil Boom: U.S. States' Economic Gains and Vulnerabilities," Council on Foreign Relations, October 2013, p. 4.

21   Noah Smithwick, *The Evolution of a State or Recollections of Old Texas Days*, Austin, TX: University of Texas Press, 1983, p. 8.

22   William Bollaert, *William Bollaert's Texas*, Norman, OK: University of Oklahoma Press, 1956, p. 183. See also Anthony M. Orum, *Power, Money, and People: The Making of Modern Austin*, Eugene, OR: Resource Publishers, 1987, p. 16.

23   Steinert, *North America, Particularly Texas in the Year 1849*, pp. 117, 120.

24   Frederick Law Olmsted, *A Journey through Texas*, Dallas, TX: DeGolyer Library, 2004, p. 116.

25   Randolph B. Campbell and Richard G. Lowe, *Wealth and Power in Antebellum Texas*, College Station, TX: Texas A&M University Press, 1977, pp. 29–30, 58, 63, 66–67, 88.

26   Gavin Wright, *Old South, New South: Revolutions in the Southern Economy Since the Civil War*, New York: Basic Books, 1986, pp. 12, 55–57. See also C. Vann Woodward, *The Burdens of Southern History*, New York: Vintage Books, 1940, p. 17; Michael Lind, *Land of Promise: An Economic History of the United States*, New York: Harper Collins, 2012, p. 344.

27   Bryan Burrough, *The Big Rich: The Rise and Fall of the Greatest Texas Oil Fortunes*, New York: Penguin Press, 2009, p. 77. See also Cunningham, *Cowboy Conservatism*, p. 19.

28 Randolph B. Campbell, *Gone to Texas: A History of the Lone Star State*, New York: Oxford University Press, 2003, p. 378.
29 James McEnteer, *Deep in the Heart: The Texas Tendency in American Politics*, Westport, CT: Praeger, 2004, p. 73.
30 David G. McComb, *Texas: A Modern History*, Austin, TX: University of Texas Press, p. 145.
31 Colin Woodard, *American Nations: A History of the Eleven Rival Regional Cultures of North America*, New York: Penguin Books, 2011, pp. 283, 302. See also Ira Katznelson, *Fear Itself: The New Deal and the Origins of Our Times*, New York, W.W. Norton, 2013.
32 Report on the Economic Conditions of the South, July 25, 1938, pp. 21, 38.
33 Lind, *Land of Promise*, p. 43.
34 Bartley, *The New South*, p. 49.
35 Ibid., pp. 145–146, 260, 430.
36 J. David Woodard, *The New Southern Politics*, Boulder, CO: Lynne Rienner Publishers, 2006, pp. 69–70.
37 Champagne and Harpham, *Texas at the Crossroads*, p. 267.
38 Michael Lind, *Made in Texas: George W. Bush and the Southern Takeover of American Politics*, New York: Basic Books, 2003, pp. 83–89.
39 Edna Ferber, *Giant*, Garden City, NY: Doubleday and Company, 1952, p. 351.
40 Jody M. Grant, *The Great Texas Banking Crash: An Insider's Account*, Austin, TX: University of Texas Press, 1996, p. 11.
41 McComb, *Texas: A Modern History*, pp. 165–166.
42 Ben F. Love, *Ben Love: My Life in Texas Commerce*, College Station, TX: Texas A&M University Press, 2005, pp. 226–227.
43 Grant, *The Great Texas Banking Crash*, pp. 101, 238.
44 Ibid., p. 256.
45 Love, *Ben Love: My Life in Texas Commerce*, p. 232.
46 Gail Collins, *As Texas Goes*, New York: W.W. Norton, 2012, p. 62.
47 Love, *Ben Love: My Life in Texas Commerce*, p. 236.
48 Ibid., p. 235.
49 Grant, *The Great Texas Banking Crash*, p. 73.
50 Floyd Norris, "The Texas Fix Is Unlikely for Ireland," *New York Times*, November 19, 2010, p. B1.
51 Collins, *As Texas Goes*, p. 65.
52 Champagne and Harpham, *Texas at the Crossroads*, p. 37.
53 Wuthnow, *Rough Country*, pp. 227, 291, 376.
54 Review & Outlook, "Governors v Congress: The Stimulus Sets a Long-Term Budget Trap for States," *Wall Street Journal*, February 23, 2009, p. A14.
55 Jason Embry, "Will Perry Reject Unemployment Piece of Stimulus Package?" in *First Reading* blog, February 24, 2009.
56 Todd Gillman, "Obama: Don't Put Politics before Job Creation," *Dallas Morning News*, February 24, 2009, p. A8.
57 Christy Hoppe and Robert T. Garrett, "Perry Rejects Part of Stimulus," *Dallas Morning News*, March 13, 2009, pp. A1, A14.
58 Jill Cowan, "U.S. Rate Falls; Texas Up, *Dallas Morning News*, March 1, 2017, p. D5.
59 Christine Nelson and John Lohmer, "An Old Battle Rejoined: States Are at the Front of a New Fight against Poverty," *State Legislatures*, January 2009, pp. 30–33.
60 Gelman, *Red State, Blue State, Rich State, Poor State*, pp. 48, 58.
61 Mark Frank, Department of Economics, Sam Houston State University, www.shsu.edu/eco_mwf/inequality.html.
62 www.sbecouncil.org/2013/04/17/business-tax-index-2013.
63 www.kauffman.org/what-we-do/research/2010/11/2010-state-new-economy-index.
64 Sheryl Jean, "Texas Improves Score on Economic Index," *Dallas Morning News*, November 18, 2010.

5   Public Education in Texas

It is admitted by all, that [a] cultivated mind is the guardian genius of democracy, and, while guided and controlled by virtue, is the noblest attribute of man.

(President Mirabeau B. Lamar, Republic of Texas, 1838)

In 2013, the U.S. Census reported that for the first time in U.S. history more than half of children under five were non-white. This transition to majority minority youth came to Texas more than a decade ago. In fact, the 2010 census reported that Hispanics accounted for 95 percent of child population growth in Texas since 2000 and that just 37.5 percent of children in Texas nursery, pre-school, and kindergarten programs were Anglo. In 2011, for the first time, half of all Texas public school students were Hispanic.[1] Only three states—Hawaii, New Mexico, and California—along with D.C., have smaller proportions of young Anglo students.[2]

What makes these numbers particularly intriguing is the near universal recognition that a good education, certainly a high school diploma and hopefully a college degree, is a prerequisite to a good job, a productive life, and a secure future. One cannot have a conversation about the future of the United States or Texas without the discussion turning quickly to education and the preparation of tomorrow's workforce. In today's Texas workforce, 40 percent of Hispanics lack a high school degree and, as we saw in the exercise that concluded Chapter 3, unless educational attainment among Texas Hispanics improves significantly in coming decades, Texas will be a less productive and poorer state.

Hence, we turn to an evaluation of Texas public schools. First, we provide a brief history of Texas public schools from their origins in the nineteenth century through the battle to desegregate them in the mid-twentieth century and to reform and adequately fund them in our own day. Second, we ask how well Texas has funded its public schools and paid its teachers since 1950. Finally, we evaluate the effectiveness of Texas public schools in terms of state and national exam results, high school completion, and college readiness. We will, of course, be interested to see whether the educational attainment of minority students in general and Hispanic students in particular has been improving as it must if Texas is to thrive in the coming decades.

A Brief History of Public Education in Texas

The Texas Declaration of Independence highlighted the failure of the Mexican government to establish public schools in Texas as one cause of the revolution. Prior to the revolution and after, Germans were quick to establish free public schools, but immigrants out of the American South were not. The planter class either left their younger children with relatives in the South to be educated or operated plantation schools for their children and those of neighboring plantation families. The older children of the wealthy, such as those of Stephen F. Austin's brother-in-law, the planter James F. Perry, were sent back to the U.S. for college. Perry's children went to Kenyon College in Ohio and Trinity College in Connecticut.[3] The children of the Anglo poor had few educational opportunities and other children had none.

Anglo Texans have always talked a better game on education than they have played. Texas's second president, Mirabeau B. Lamar (1838–1841), declared that "a cultivated mind is . . . the noblest attribute of man" and called upon the Congress of the Republic of Texas to set aside land in the public domain for the support of public education. He assured Congress that, "A suitable appropriation of lands to the purpose of general education, can be made at this time without inconvenience to the Government or the people."[4] In 1839 and 1841, Congress set aside four leagues of land (17,712 acres) in each county for public schools and 50 leagues (221,400 acres) for two state universities, but in what would become typical Texas fashion, they allocated no money. But having called for state-supported public schools was enough to earn President Lamar the sobriquet of "Father of Education in Texas." The classic history of Texas education, *The Story of Texas Schools* (1955), by C.E. Evans, explained that, "There was no sentiment in the Republic of Texas for school taxation. . . . Any attempt at this time to establish public free schools . . . would have been condemned as tyranny."[5]

The Texas statehood Constitution of 1845 renewed Lamar's call for public schools. Article 10, section 1 read: "A general diffusion of knowledge being essential to the preservation of the rights and liberties of the people, it shall be the duty of the legislature of this State to make suitable provisions for the support and maintenance of public schools." Article 10, section 2 called for a statewide property tax to fund free public schools, as well as an annual appropriation of 10 percent of state revenues to build a permanent fund to support the schools. Few schools were actually started because Texas "courts held that . . . the assessment of general taxes for education, was unconstitutional."[6] In the absence of public schools, Texans who could afford to do so depended on private academies and tutors.

Wilhelm Steinert visited New Braunfels, the principal German settlement in Central Texas, and wrote in 1849 that, "The schoolhouse was a small hut made of boards. . . . A group of some 15 students, boys and girls of different ages, sat in the small room. The open door let light into the room. Lessons consisted chiefly of reading, writing, and arithmetic." Steinert reported that, "people pay $2 per month per student" and many "would gladly have sent their children to school, but could not afford the tuition or lived too far from the school."[7]

The early 1850s brought an infusion of cash to Texas state government coffers and some of it was initially directed to education. Texas gave up claims to New Mexico in exchange for inclusion of El Paso and the Panhandle and $10 million in cash. After paying off war debts, Texas leaders had money remaining for transportation projects and another go at a public school system. Governor Elisha M. Peace signed a public schools bill on January 31, 1854, establishing a $2 million "Special School Fund," the annual interest from which was to pay operating expenses and teacher salaries. The fund generated $0.62 per student in 1854 and $1.50 in 1855, hardly enough to establish schools and pay teachers. Because state funding did not cover school expenses and teacher salaries, state law allowed tuition charges of up to 10 cents a day to cover the rest. Poor students would go to school during that portion of the year covered by state funds and drop out once tuition was required. Moreover, parents could take their pro rata share of state funds and enroll their children in a private academy or join with other parents to hire a teacher and start their own school. As Evans observed, "each parent claimed the right to give his children the kind and degree of education he thought wise, while the community insisted on the . . . right to manage its school in its own way."[8] The prominent Princeton University social scientist Robert Wuthnow reported that, "In 1860 only 42 percent of white children in Texas ages six through sixteen were in school, which was one of the lowest proportions anywhere in the country."[9]

After the Civil War, funding black education was a major political issue. In response to the hunger of former slaves for education, the Freedman's Bureau established 16 schools with more than 1,000 students in 1865. In early 1866, white conservatives met to draft a new state constitution in anticipation of being readmitted to the Union. The Texas Constitution of 1866 acknowledged the end of slavery, but refused civil rights to blacks, including the right to attend and send their children to public schools. Instead, the Constitution called for separate white and black schools, with the black schools supported by taxes raised from black parents. Black parents—slaves just the year before—had no property or income to support schools for their children.[10] The U.S. Congress rejected the proposed Constitution and instituted Congressional or Radical Reconstruction and military occupation to insure black rights. Though the Freedman's Bureau education program soon grew to 66 schools with more than 3,000 students, white violence was a constant threat.

Congressional Reconstruction forced a new constitution. The Constitution of 1869 was highly centralized, including a powerful executive, annual meetings of the state legislature, racially mixed state militia and state police, and state-funded public schools for all children between the ages of six and 18. State funding was to come from public land sales, property taxes, poll taxes, and general revenues.[11] Republican Governor Edmund J. Davis set about implementing the Constitution's mandate. The Freedman's Bureau schools discontinued operation in 1871. Soon 125,000 black and white students were enrolled in public schools, but white parents chaffed under the taxes, especially as part of the money was going to educate black children.[12] In September 1871, conservative white opponents of the Davis administration convened a "Tax Payers' Convention" in Galveston to protest "the taxes demanded of the people."[13] Despite the complaints about high taxes required for education, Texas officials reported that the number of schools, teachers, and students in 1872, "adjusted for total population, was still well below the national average. For schools, it was 51 percent of the national average; for teachers 40 percent; and for pupils, 45 percent."[14]

When the Democrats returned to power in 1873, Anglo elites began to dismantle even this limited system of free public schools. They immediately returned responsibility for the schools to parents and local governments and limited the power of local school boards to levy taxes.[15] When Reconstruction ended and a new state constitution was written in 1876, the job of dismantling the state's centralized school system was completed. The Constitution of 1876 provided in Article VII, section 1, that "A general diffusion of knowledge being essential to the preservation of the liberties and rights of the people, it shall be the duty of the Legislature . . . to establish and make suitable provision for . . . an efficient system of public free schools." Article I, section 3 provided that no more than one-quarter of state revenues shall be dedicated to education, but did not require that any money, beyond a $1 poll tax, be provided. The Constitution also mandated in Article VII, section 7, that, "Separate schools shall be provided for white and colored children, and impartial provision shall be made for both."

Fights over state funding of the schools began almost immediately. As cotton prices fell, state revenues tightened and Governor Oran M. Roberts vetoed the school appropriation for 1879. The legislature had appropriated the full constitutional amount, one-quarter of state revenues, but the governor thought the revenue estimates inflated and demanded a "pay as you go" policy of spending only money on hand. As a result, the school appropriation, spending per pupil, and state enrollments all fell even though Texas was in the middle of a population boom.[16]

Texas ended the nineteenth century with its public schools under heavy pressure. In 1890, Texas per pupil expenditures were 63 percent of the U.S. average. The sharp economic contraction of the 1890s led Texas to cut per pupil expenditures to 56 percent of the national average in 1900.[17] Gene Preuss, a prominent historian of Texas schools, noted that in 1901, "Despite the fact that Texas spent more per child per diem than other southern states, it still ranked thirty-eighth in the nation in the number of children enrolled in school, thirty-seventh in per capita expenditures for education, and thirty-fifth in literacy."[18] These rankings are essentially unchanged today.

Not only were Texas schools poorly funded in general, there were vast differences between urban and rural schools and white and black schools. In 1900, urban schools were in session an average of 162 days a year and spent an average of $8.35 per student. Rural schools met only 98 days a year and spent $3.34 per student. In 1910, school districts spent an average of $10 a year per white student and $5.74 per black student. Class sizes in black schools were about half again as large as they were in white schools.[19] UT professor Don Graham wrote that these schools, especially the rural schools, provided "functional literacy" and little more.[20]

Texas was slow to follow national educational advances during the first half of the twentieth century. Texas adopted compulsory school attendance in 1915, five years after neighboring Louisiana, and before only Georgia (1916) and Mississippi (1918).[21] In 1917, the U.S. Congress passed the Smith–Hughes Act, one of the first instances of federal funding of local schools, providing funds for the salaries of industrial arts and home economics teachers. Texas declined to come up with the matching funds required by the Act, so "only a small percent of the total funds available for Texas was used."[22] Sound familiar? The "Better Schools Campaign" of 1918–1920 did spur modest reforms. Free school text books were approved in 1918 and in 1919 voters considered a constitutional Amendment allowing local districts to raise taxes to supplement state education funds. A poster used by the pro-reform campaign posed this challenge: "First in Size. First in Agricultural Products. First in Production of Cotton. Third in Production of Oil. Seventh in Wealth. Thirty-Ninth in Education. Shall Texas Keep this Rank?"[23] Though the Amendment prevailed by a two-to-one margin, Texas per capita spending on education rose no faster than the national average. Texas spent 63 percent of the national average per student in 1930 just as it had four decades earlier in 1890.

Frederick Eby, a noted historian of early twentieth-century Texas education, blamed an inattentive public and scheming politicians for the failure to do better. In an analysis that could just as well be made today, Eby reported that in the 1920s, "Flattered by the boasts of office-seeking politicians . . . [Texans] were firmly persuaded that their schools were among the best in the entire nation." Advocates of school reform found that it was "necessary to convince the people that these notions which had been boastfully asserted by provincial politicians were wholly erroneous" before they would listen to calls for change.[24] Though spending on public schools in Texas held up better than some other states during the Depression years of the 1930s, reaching 73 percent of the national average by 1940, the overblown claims of the state's politicians were exposed embarrassingly during World War II:

> The National Education Association reported that Texas had one of the highest rejection rates for military service because of illiteracy. With the national rejection rate for poor schooling at 12 percent, the Texas rejection rate was . . . almost 23 percent. This placed Texas among the twelve states with high educational deficiency rates. The report noted that only South Carolina, Louisiana, Georgia, Mississippi, Alabama, Arkansas, Virginia, and North Carolina had higher rejection rates than Texas. . . . The NEA report connected the results to the amount of money the states spent on education—the more money the state spent on education, the fewer military rejections.[25]

Remarkably, from this low point, Texas would soon undertake major educational reforms, though the resistance would be stout.

The Depression and World War II drove changes in industrialization, urbanization, immigration, and migration. As the state's rural and agricultural economy became urban and industrial, attitudes toward education began to change as well. The 1947 regular session of the Texas Legislature debated the need for an interim committee to study public education and propose appropriate school reforms to the 1949 legislature. Some members, including Representative S.J. Isaacks (D-El Paso), supported the appointment of an interim committee but remained skeptical about what it would find. Isaacks declared, "'I have lost all patience with people who quote somebody from California or Chicago who say that Texas ranks thirty-seventh in education. I think Texas is among the first two or three states.' Yet, by almost every common yardstick, the status of education in Texas is far below par."[26] The interim committee was headed by Representative Claud Gilmer and Senator A.M. Aikin. The committee's work eventually convinced Representative Isaacks to support school reform.

In 1949, the Texas Legislature passed and Governor Buford Jester signed the Gilmer–Aikin Laws, which dramatically modernized both the organizational structure and the finances of Texas public schools. The package of three bills was introduced first in the Senate and passed by that body, as SB 115, 116, and 117, before being taken up in the House. The bills proposed to centralize the funding and administration of Texas public schools to a degree not seen since Reconstruction. SB 115 established "one Central Education Agency . . . [with] three main divisions: (1) a policy-forming State Board of Education elected by the people, (2) a professional Commissioner of Education appointed by the board to serve as its executive agent, and (3) a State Department of Education to serve as the professional and clerical staff of the commissioner and the board."[27] This structure remains in place today, except that in 1995 the legislature moved the power to appoint the Commissioner of Education from the State Board of Education to the governor. SB 116 created the Minimum Foundation Program to encourage consolidation and efficiency in school districts, set minimum standards for teacher pay, equalize school funding, and establish a nine-month school year and a 12-grade school system. SB 117 took school funding out of the annual budget debate by mandating sufficient funds to fulfill the new Minimum Foundation Program requirements.[28]

But make no mistake, progress such as that represented in the Gilmer–Aikin reforms comes hard in Texas. Education reform was labeled socialism and declared to be an intrusion on local and parental rights and responsibilities. Dolph Briscoe, a future two-term governor, was in his first term in the Texas House in 1949. In his

2008 autobiography, Briscoe noted that passage of the Gilmer–Aikin reforms was only achieved over strident opposition. "Opponents worked hard to prevent passage, even labeling the bills 'communistic.'"[29] Socialism and communism are terms that are frequently thrown around in Texas politics, especially in regard to "public" schools, which are, after all—public. Still, most parents were on-board this time. As we shall see below, 1950 was the highpoint for per pupil funding, teacher pay, and much more in Texas education.

During debate over the Gilmer–Aikin bills, proponents warned that failure to pass education reform might lead to federal intrusion in Texas public schools. Gilmer–Aikin passed but the federal intrusion came anyway. On December 1, 1953, one week before *Brown v. Board* came before the U.S. Supreme Court for re-argument, Governor Allen Shivers warned against accepting federal education money. With classic Texas bombast, Shivers declared, "We don't need [federal aid] and the federal money ought not to be taken into the school system because control follows the tax dollar."[30] On May 17, 1954, the Supreme Court declared in *Brown* that segregation of black and white students in public schools was an unconstitutional violation of the right of black students to the equal protection of the laws. Governor Shivers immediately trumpeted defiance, saying, "All my instincts, my political philosophy, my experiences and my common sense revolt against the Supreme Court decision. It is an unwarranted invasion of the constitutional rights of the states. . . . My administration has already told the local school districts that, as far as the state of Texas is concerned, there are no changes to be made."[31]

Two dynamics, a weak one toward compliance and a strong one toward resistance, competed in the two years after *Brown* was announced in May 1954 and implementation was mandated in May 1955. By 1956, 65 school districts, mostly in South and West Texas, where blacks were few, voluntarily moved toward integration, and, in 1957, 69 more followed suit. These included districts in Austin, Corpus Christi, El Paso, Harlingen, Kerrville, San Antonio, and San Angelo. Both Dallas and Houston resisted integration as did all of East Texas, where the vast majority of Texas blacks lived.[32] The battle that turned the tide in favor of Governor Shivers and the segregationists occurred in the Tarrant County town of Mansfield.

Mansfield, about 15 miles southeast of Fort Worth, "was a small town on the western edge of what was considered the 'Deep South.'"[33] In October 1955, a suit was filed in the federal district court in Fort Worth on behalf of three black students wishing to attend the all-white high school in their home-town of Mansfield. As the date for the federal court ruling neared, an editorial in the *Mansfield News* announced, "We are not against the Negro, but we are against social equality. We think the Negroes are making great strides in improving their race and commend them for it, as long as they stick to their race."[34] On August 27, 1956, the federal district court ordered that Mansfield High be desegregated immediately. On the evening of August 28 and August 30, effigies were hung over Main Street and from the high school flagpole. On the day that the black students were to register for school, several hundred white protesters massed on school grounds to block their access. When parents and lawyers of the black students called on Governor Shivers for help, he responded, in part, "It is not my intention to permit the use of state officers or troops to shoot down or intimidate Texas citizens who are making orderly protest against a situation instigated and agitated by the National Association for the Advancement of Colored People."[35] Unable to safely register, the black students withdrew, returned to their all-black high school in Fort Worth, and Mansfield High remained segregated until 1965.

Governor Shivers sought to strengthen segregation by forcing three referenda onto the July 1956 Democratic Party primary election ballot: one exempted any child from compulsory attendance at an integrated school, another strengthened state laws against interracial marriage, and the third advocated "interposition" in cases of federal overreach. All passed by greater than three-to-one margins.[36] The Texas State Democratic Executive Committee backed the referenda, declaring "that Mansfield had been selected by the NAACP to promote the 'destruction of the southern way of life and Texas traditions.'" To limit the damage that the NAACP might cause to "Texas traditions," Judge Otis Dunagan of the East Texas community of Tyler issued a permanent injunction against further legal or political action in Texas by the NAACP. Judge Dunagan cautioned local newspapers against misunderstanding his order, saying, "Don't think this is a suit against the nigger people. . . . Actually, it isn't. It's true it [the NAACP] is an organization for the nigger people, but after all, three fourths of its directors are white people. . . . I ain't got nothing against the nigger people." Given these officials' attitudes and actions, it is not surprising that "Between August 1957 and May 1962, only ten school districts integrated in Texas. None of these were in East Texas."[37] It took the Civil Rights Acts of 1964 and 1965 and the Elementary and Secondary Education Act of 1965 to break the back of segregation in Texas and the South. In 1963, only 4.3 percent of black children were attending school with whites; this rose to 7.3 percent in 1964 and 17.2 percent in 1965, before jumping to 44.9 percent in 1966.[38] By 1972, 92 percent of black children were attending school with white children. But the cost of the desegregation fight was high. During the fight, the legislature restricted state funding and many whites moved to the suburbs or placed their children in private schools.

By the late 1970s, issues of race began to recede and issues of educational quality began to come into focus. In the early 1980s, a "growing concern over deteriorating literacy among Texas's schoolchildren over two decades, reflected in students' scores on standardized tests," again prompted reform.[39] In 1983, Governor Mark White called upon Dallas businessman H. Ross Perot to head a "Select Committee on Public Education" to propose reforms intended to improve educational performance and quality. Other heavyweights on the committee were Lieutenant Governor Bill Hobby, Speaker of the Texas House Gib Lewis, and Comptroller Bob Bullock.[40] The Perot Committee's recommendations formed the basis of legislation passed in a special session of the legislature in the summer of 1984. Those reforms sought to make teacher competence and student learning the twin engines of enhanced academic performance.

Teachers received pay raises in exchange for tougher credentialing standards and competency testing. Students were held to more stringent attendance and promotion standards. The Perot Commission's student reforms "abolished social promotion; established an extensive program of testing and remediation for students in the first, third, fifth, seventh, ninth, and twelfth grades; [and] introduced an 'exit test' for high school graduation."[41] Still, most attention was paid to the new "no pass—no play" rule that barred students from participating in extracurricular activities, including varsity sports, unless they passed their classes.[42]

Even as the Perot Committee and state government moved to buttress academic quality, opposition to how Texas funded schools moved toward center stage. In addition to the state's Minimum Foundation Program, Texas schools depended on local property tax revenues and these varied dramatically by the wealth or poverty of different cities and districts. School funding issues came before state and federal courts regularly through the 1970s and 1980s. San Antonio's Edgewood ISD was usually among the plaintiffs. In *Edgewood ISD v. Kirby* (1989), lawyers pointed out that "Edgewood had

$38,854 in property wealth per student while Alamo Heights . . . had $570,109."[43] The trial court found for the plaintiffs, the appeals court overturned the ruling, and the Texas Supreme Court overturned the appeals court, finding that the school finance system was "neither financially efficient" nor did it provide "for a 'general diffusion of knowledge' statewide, and therefore it violates Article VII, section 1, of the Texas Constitution."[44] During the early 1990s the Texas Legislature sought twice to patch the old system by providing more equalization funds, but the Texas Supreme Court rejected both attempts as insufficient.

In 1993, much against its will, the legislature passed the "Robin Hood" school funding bill in which revenues were "recaptured" from high property tax districts and reallocated to low property tax districts. Administrators and parents in property-rich districts complained bitterly that their students were being denied enrichment opportunities in order to fund activities in property-poor districts. Tensions grew through the next decade as more and more school districts, 690 of about 1,020 districts by 2003, bumped up against state property tax limits and saw their budgets stagnate. School districts, knowing that Texas rarely spends money unless it is ordered to do so by state or federal courts, recurred to the lawyers. In 2004, 300 school districts went to court in a case called *West Orange-Cove CISD v. Neeley*. The districts claimed that an underfunded public education system limited their ability to fulfill their constitutional mandate to promote a general diffusion of knowledge within the state.[45]

The school districts prevailed up through the Texas Supreme Court and the legislature reluctantly returned to the drawing board. Governor Perry and the legislature responded to the Court's demand for funding reform by lowering local property taxes by one-third, enacting a broad new business tax, called the margins tax, increasing the state cigarette tax from $0.41 to $1.41 a pack, and drawing on the state surplus. With the new school funding plan in place, the state's share of funding, which had dropped from 80 percent in 1949 to 35 percent, rose to 50 percent, the localities' share dropped from 55 percent to 40 percent, and the federal share stayed at about 10 percent. State revenues from the margins tax came in lower than expected and school budgets again tightened. The 2009 state legislature increased school budgets by a minuscule $120 per student, but in 2011 tight budgets led legislators to cut $5.4 billion from school budgets. Both legislators and school superintendents assumed their traditional stances and the lawyers filed their briefs.

The problems facing Texas public schools are immense. Of five million public school students, nearly 3 million, or 60 percent, come from low-income households. Higher standards, less money, and a needy student body convinced two-thirds of Texas school districts, teaching three-quarters of the state's students, again to sue the state of Texas in District Judge John Dietz's court. Testimony before Judge Dietz showed that the top 10 percent of Texas school districts enjoyed $7,998 per student while the bottom 10 percent got $5,616 per student. After 12 weeks of testimony, Judge Dietz ruled that Texas was not providing enough money for schools to meet their constitutional responsibilities. The judge declared that, "there is no free lunch. We either want increased standards and are willing to pay the price, or we don't. However, there is a cost to acting, namely a tax increase. And there is a cost to not acting, namely the loss of our competitive position as a state."

Judge Dietz estimated that an additional $10 to 11 billion might be required to fund the schools at constitutionally acceptable levels. Since the legislature was in session when he ruled, Judge Dietz suspended the ruling to allow the legislature time to respond. The legislature responded in two ways: by reducing the number of high-stakes, end-of-course tests from 15 to 5 and by restoring part of the 2011 funding cuts. Judge Dietz again ruled against the state. The state appealed to the Texas Supreme Court and, unlike most previous school funding contests, the high court reluctantly sided with Texas over the schools. In doing so, the Texas Supreme Court declared that, "Our Byzantine school funding 'system' is undeniably imperfect, with immense room for improvement. But it satisfies minimum constitutional requirements."[46]

Average Spending per Pupil in the U.S. and Texas, 1950 to Present

Before taking a close look at Texas school funding, we must take note of a broader point. Two well-known Harvard economists, Claudia Goldin and Lawrence F. Katz, published a book in 2008, entitled *The Race between Education and Technology*. The thesis of this important book is that the U.S. led the world in technological innovation and wealth creation throughout most of its history because it also led the world in education. They also make a narrower point that is directly relevant to the history of education funding in Texas. They note that education funding is not just a question of economic means, but also of a sense of community and a willingness to spend money on the education of all of the community's children. Goldin and Katz note that "the wider the distribution of income . . . the less support there will be for public education, since the rich can opt out and the poor will have a lower demand."[47] Have high income inequality and long-standing racial and ethnic divisions limited school funding in Texas?

Texas school administrators have been in a 150-year-long tug-of-war with Texas politicians over school funding. Almost always the politicians have won and the school administrators and the students they serve have lost. So far, Texas parents have most often sided with the politicians, rising consistently to the promise of no new taxes, to the detriment of public education and their own children. As we shall see in detail below, the academic performance of Texas school children has reflected the state's limited willingness to invest in them.

Political observers and academics have long been aware that Texans are ambivalent about their schools. As Nelson Dometrius wrote in his chapter on education policy in Gerry Riposa's *Texas Public Policy* more than three decades ago, "Texans value education in the abstract. . . . At the same time, Texans manifest a cultural attitude that educators are incompetent, underworked and wasteful of public funds. These competing themes lead to a boom and bust cycle in education policy, years of ignoring educational needs, followed by a sudden realization that problems have developed requiring a massive infusion of funds."[48] This excellent description is correct right up to the closing phrase—"a massive infusion of funds"—though perhaps it merely means that any increase in school funding feels massive to tight-fisted Texas legislators and taxpayers.

In only one year, 1950, the year after the passage of the Gilmer–Aikin education reform and finance laws, did Texas spend more than the national average on its students. In 1950, Texas spent $208.88 per student compared to a national average of $208.83. Perhaps chagrined that they had wasted that nickel, Texas politicians tightened students' belts for most of the next seven decades. Though Texas never got back to the national average for expenditure per student, it did make a couple of runs. One was in response to the findings of the Perot Commission in the mid-1980s, and another was in response to the court mandates of the late 1990s. Yet, each funding surge was pitifully short-lived, reflecting the commitment of just one, or at most two, legislative sessions, before lethargy, charges of wasteful spending, or other pressing demands sapped or diverted attention.

Since 1950, Texas has spent an average of 84 percent of U.S. spending per pupil for elementary and secondary schools. Over that seven decade period, Texas has never been in the upper half, the top 25 states, in educational expenditures. Texas did briefly reach the 26th spot in 1998, but generally Texas has lagged in the thirties and forties, reaching 48th (meaning only two states spent less per pupil than Texas) in 1972 and 47th in 1976. Texas's average position among the states from 1950 to the present has been 38th.[49] Texas has slipped badly since 2000, falling from 28th in 2000 to 49th in 2012. In fact, between 2002 and 2012, state and local funding of public schools in Texas was flat after accounting for population growth and inflation. Modest gains have been posted in recent years, 2013 through 2015, with Texas spending 78 percent of the national average per student and rising back to its long-term average among the 50 states and D.C., at 38th in both 2014 and 2015.

Passions flow when discussion focuses on school funding: it is the largest expenditure of state government and it involves children, their future, and that of the state itself. As the 2011 Texas Legislature prepared to impose deep budget cuts, former Texas Lieutenant Governor Bill Hobby charged that, "A huge majority of public school students in Texas are . . . black and brown. . . . I think Republicans don't like public education because they are educating black children and brown children. That's the inevitable conclusion."[50] Governor Hobby's charge is not wrong, race has played a major role in school funding decisions, but it is way too narrow. While minority children have frequently been short-changed, it is also true that neither Republicans nor Democrats have shown much interest in the education of Texas public school children—whatever their color.

Figure 5.1 presents average annual spending per pupil for the U.S. and Texas and it shows the familiar picture of Texas tracking along below the national average.

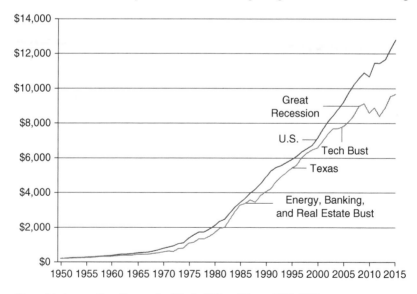

Figure 5.1 Average Spending per Pupil in the U.S. and Texas, 1950–2015

Source: U.S. Census Bureau, Statistical Abstract of the United States, each year from 1950 through 2017, www. census.gov/library/publications/time-series/statistical_abstracts.html. Various figure and table numbers, generally titled Average Current Expenditures per Pupil in Average Daily Attendance by States. See NEA, Ranking and Estimates, December 2015, Summary Table K, p. 96.

The pattern in the early years is indistinct because the numbers are small and the lines are compressed but the pattern becomes clear in the later years. For example, in 1965 Texas spent $449 per pupil, or 84 percent, of the U.S. average expenditure of $532, though this significant difference is hard to see on the graph. But we do again see the familiar pattern of Texas going sideways in the late 1980s as it is hard hit by the oil, property, banking, and S&L crises. Texas gathered itself to close on the national average again in the boom period of the late 1990s, only to fall back in the first decade of the new century and seriously so after 2009.

Figure 5.2 presents Texas's expenditures as a percentage of U.S. expenditures and the data present a stark picture. Passage of the Gilmer–Aikin laws in 1949 brought per capita education expenditures in Texas to 100 percent of the national average in the early 1950s. Commitment to education spending sputtered in the mid-1950s and then went into a steep decline, reaching just 65 percent of the national average by 1972. Texas resisted the demand of the U.S. Supreme Court in *Brown v. Board of Education* (1954) that schools be desegregated, and resisted the threat of the U.S. Congress in the Elementary and Secondary Education Act (1965) that federal funds would be withheld unless desegregation proceeded. By the early 1970s, Texas succumbed and desegregation of public schools did occur. However, between 1955 and 1972 one of the key ways that Texas resisted desegregation was to limit funding to its public schools. Once racial issues retreated from center stage, Texans began again to think about educational quality.

The broad arc of Texas school funding since 1950 shows three distinct peaks, highpoints identified with passage of the Gilmer–Aikin Laws in 1949, adoption of the Perot Committee's recommendations in the mid-1980s, and the adoption of the Robin Hood school funding program in the mid-1990s. But it shows more than that. To Texas's detriment it shows that each monumental effort, each historic success in dealing with school funding, was followed by a sense that the problem had been addressed, attention

Figure 5.2 Texas Spending per Pupil as a Percentage of U.S. Spending per Pupil, 1950–2015

Source: U.S. Census Bureau, Statistical Abstract of the United States, each year from 1950 through 2017, www.census.gov/library/publications/time-series/statistical_abstracts.html. Various figure and table numbers, generally titled Average Current Expenditures per Pupil in Average Daily Attendance by States. See also NEA Rankings and Estimates.

wandered, and the gains leaked away. On the other hand, and to Texas's credit, it shows that as the gains leaked away, attention returned, politicians tried and to some extent did respond, but those responses are only partial until the big push—Gilmer–Aikin, the Perot Committee, Robin Hood—put Texas schools back on track. Inevitably though, the low-tax, low-service model that has governed Texas politics from its earliest days has always reasserted itself and Texas students have suffered. Even more troubling, there has been an aggressive ignorance at work that has seen virtually all public spending as bad, even evil. The opponents of the Gilmer–Aikin reforms, it must be remembered, denounced those changes as communistic. In 2003, yes 2003, Republican state Representative Debbie Riddle (R-Houston) asked, "Where did this idea come from that everybody deserves free education, free medical care, free whatever?" In answer to her own question, she declared, "It comes from Moscow, from Russia. It comes straight out of the pit of hell."[51]

The current situation of school funding in Texas is dire. Texas historian David McComb noted that, "In 2005, after the state decreased funding, Texas ranked fortieth in the nation [on student funding] while its students placed forty-ninth in verbal skills and forty-sixth on the SAT."[52] Texas slipped to 42nd in 2006, 2007, and 2008, 44th in 2009, 49th in 2012, and slowly crawled back to 38th in 2015.

Still, the recent history of Texas school funding has been sobering. The 2011 Texas Legislature not only cut school funding by $5.4 billion, they changed the legal requirement to fund the Minimum Foundation Program, in place since the Gilmer–Aikin reforms of 1949, to a discretionary allocation set by the legislature each biennium. State Senator Dan Patrick (R-Houston) said, "I think it's a change we needed as we move forward. We have to have real cuts. . . . [This is] a true cut in an entitlement."[53] The 2011 cuts ultimately totaled more than $500 per student, or about 7 percent, from the preceding biennium.[54] Texans came late to seeing education as, yes, an entitlement, and now that commitment might be slipping away. Even more chillingly, in 2014 Senator Dan Patrick was elected lieutenant governor and presiding officer of the Texas Senate. Soon after his election, looking back on the 2011 cuts and talk of the need to restore those funds, Patrick said, "We just can't give them more money. . . . Our schools survived and we did fine."[55]

Teachers' Salaries in the U.S. and Texas, 1950 to Present

Not surprisingly, since school funding and teachers' salaries are set by the same people (the state's politicians), at the same time (in the biennial legislative session), very similar patterns pertain. Texas teachers in the immediate wake of Gilmer–Aikin's passage in 1949 were paid $3,122 in 1950, fully 104 percent of the national average teacher pay of $3,010. Texas teacher pay beat the national average only once more, in 1954. Texas teacher pay has trailed the national average in every year from 1955 to the present. During the boom years of the 1970s and early 1980s, the Briscoe and Clements administrations were able to increase teacher pay without raising taxes, of which they were quite proud. But these were high inflation years and other states were raising teacher pay too, so Texas teachers made only modest progress against national averages.[56] The Perot Committee reforms brought Texas teacher pay back near the national average in the mid-1980s ($22,600 compared to $23,500 in 1985, for example), but the gap quickly reopened as economic turmoil engulfed Texas in the late 1980s (Figure 5.3). Texas teacher pay ranked 18th in the nation in 1950 and 1954 and generally held in the

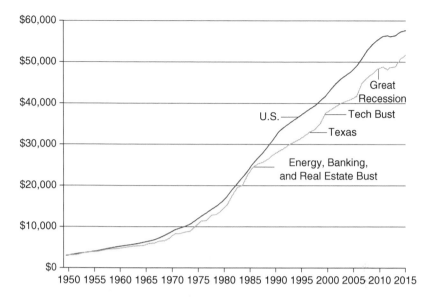

Figure 5.3 Average Teacher Pay in the U.S. and Texas, 1950–2015

Source: U.S. Census Bureau, Statistical Abstract of the United States, each year 1950 through 2015. Public Elementary and Secondary Schools—Numbers and Salaries of Teachers, by state, various figure and table numbers, www.census.gov/library/publications/time-series/statistical_abstracts.html. See NEA, Rankings and Estimates, December 2015, Summary Table G, p. 110.

twenties through the early 1960s and has bounced around in the twenties and thirties since. Texas's average ranking among the states since 1950 has been 29th.

As with per pupil funding, Figure 5.4 depicting Texas teacher pay as a percentage of U.S. teacher pay is very informative. Again, the high points following Gilmer–Aikin and the Perot Committee are obvious, but the impact of Robin Hood and the tax swap on teacher pay was more modest. Nonetheless, Texas teacher pay has held up more consistently over the decades than has per pupil funding. From 1950 to the present, Texas teacher pay has averaged 91 percent of U.S. teacher pay and has rarely fallen below 85 percent. It rests today at 89 percent.

Another way to think about the adequacy of teacher pay is to ask how it compares to private sector pay. A recent study by Professor Ed Fuller of the Department of Educational Administration at the University of Texas, Austin, reported that shortages of math and science teachers had grown. The reason was not far to seek as "secondary math and science teachers continue to earn substantially less than their peers in the private sector, even after adjusting for summers off. Teachers made, on average, between $23,000 and $40,000 less than individuals in nonteaching careers in math and science. The average salary in 2007 for math and science teachers was about $47,000." Texas Senator Florence Shapiro, chair of the Senate Education Committee, suggested that the way to deal with the teacher shortages might be to trim the math and science requirements for high school graduation, saying "There would still be math and science requirements, but we would not have as many students taking higher level courses such as calculus and physics."[57] Feel better now? Probably not, but lagging teacher salaries

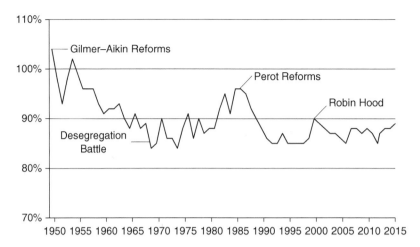

Figure 5.4 Texas Teacher Pay as a Percentage of U.S. Teacher Pay, 1950–2015

Source: U.S. Census Bureau, Statistical Abstract of the United States, each year 1950 through 2017. Public Elementary and Secondary Schools—Numbers and Salaries of Teachers, by state, various figure and table numbers, www.census.gov/library/publications/time-series/statistical_abstracts.html.

might help explain why half of new Texas teachers leave the profession in their first five years.[58] The 2015 State Teacher Policy Yearbook, produced by the National Center on Teacher Quality, still gave Texas a D+ on effective teacher retention.

Budget cuts imposed by the state legislature in 2011 cost 10,717 teacher jobs in the 2011–2012 school year. Class sizes increased and average teacher pay in the state fell by $263 to $48,110, 36th in the nation. To make ends meet, many teachers take second and third jobs. The Associated Press reported Department of Education National Center for Education Statistics data showing that teacher moonlighting nationally had increased from 10 percent in 1981 to 20 percent in 2011. In Texas, teacher moonlighting rose from 22 percent in 1980 to 41 percent in 2011, the highest in the nation.[59]

Accountability and Performance in Texas Public Schools

The Texas Legislature passed an extensive school accountability bill in 2009. It was lightly revised for the 2012–2013 school year. The accountability bill was a mixed bag at best. To start on the positive side of the ledger, the Texas Legislature maintained the basic 4 × 4 design of the core curriculum. As Table 5.1 shows, each Texas high school student must take four years of four basic subjects: English, math, science, and social studies. The requirement that students take two years of a foreign language also was maintained. Additional requirements that students take two semesters of computer technology and a semester of health education were eliminated and the PE requirement was reduced from three semesters to two. The reductions were intended to allow students to pursue their interests by taking almost twice as many elective courses as they could under the old system.

Soon after the school accountability bill was passed, State Education Commissioner Robert Scott declared that all high school students, not just freshmen, were eligible to proceed under the new curriculum requirements. Representative Rob Eissler (R-The

Table 5.1 The Texas Foundations, Plus Endorsements, High School Program, 2014

Subject	Previous Credit Requirements	New Credit Requirements
English	4	4
Math	4	4
Science	4	4
Social Studies	4	3
Foreign Language	2	2
Physical Education	1.5	1
Fine Arts	1	1
Health	.5	0
Speech	.5	0
Technology	1	0
Electives	3.5	7
Total	26	26

Source: Texas Education Agency. See also Terrence Stutz, "High School Graduation Changes are Approved," *Dallas Morning News*, February 1, 2014, p. A3.

Woodlands), chair of the House Education Committee, proudly explained that, "If a kid chooses a course, he or she is more likely to be interested in it and probably will do better in it. That was one of the goals of the legislation, to make our course requirements a little more market-friendly for students."[60] Within weeks it became evident that neither the legislators who drafted the bill nor Commissioner Scott understood exactly how student friendly were the new graduation requirements. Critics soon pointed out that students could load up on PE or PE substitutes such as football, band, and cheerleading for six and one-half credits, more than a quarter of what they needed to graduate.

Representative Eissler, of course, dismissed the prospect that students would try to game the graduation requirements by taking lots of PE and cheerleading. Eissler said, "I don't think it's going to happen. And if a bunch of kids tried to do that, local school officials could step in and adjust their course requirements. That's what we call local control." Maybe so, but others were less sanguine. Geraldine Miller (R-Dallas), a member of the State Board of Education, said "Kids are kids, and we know this could become an option for some. We need safeguards to prevent any abuses like this." State Board of Education staff were ordered to draft rules limiting how students could use their elective hours.[61] In late 2009, the State Board of Education closed the PE loophole by lowering the limit to four credits. The board arrived at the four-credit limit under heavy lobbying by the Texas High School Coaches Association. Board member Don McLeroy observed, absurdly, that, "The argument for counting four years of athletics toward graduation is pretty persuasive now that the state requires four years of math, science, English, and social studies to graduate."[62]

In the meanwhile, Texas has worked hard to maintain its own state assessment standards and avoid involvement in national assessment standards. Texas claims that this is so they can have strict standards, but critics are dismissive. For example, when Congress allocated $4.35 billion in stimulus funds to the Department of Education (DOE) for its "Race to the Top" educational reform program, Texas officials crowed that they had long been at work on educational reform and were well-positioned to win one of the grants and to serve as a model for others. Some of those others were skeptical. Bill Slotnik, executive director of Boston-based Community Training and Assistance Center, which consults nationally on education reform, said "Just being from Texas is not going to carry the weight that it did in the previous [Bush] administration." The Obama DOE will ask, "Are the things you are doing reaching the classroom in a way that is demonstrably benefiting students?" Arne Duncan, Secretary of the U.S. DOE, was just as blunt: "we want to reward those states that are willing to lead the country where we need to go and are willing to push this reform agenda very, very hard. And the states that don't have the stomach or the political will, unfortunately, they're going to lose out."[63]

Just weeks before applications were due, Governor Perry instructed Texas Commissioner of Education Robert Scott not to commit to adoption of national education standards, thereby compromising any Race to the Top application. Perry said:

> Texas is on the right path toward improved education, and we would be foolish and irresponsible to place our children's future in the hands of unelected bureaucrats and special interest groups thousands of miles away in Washington, virtually eliminating parents' participation in their children's education.[64]

Scott Hochberg, a Democrat from Houston and a leader of the Texas House Education Committee, observed that, "the governor is throwing up the white flag and admitting that they're not willing to compete."[65]

Texas does its own educational assessment, but its findings are suspect. One of the great problems with educational assessment in Texas is that it changes so often that it is difficult to establish and assess trends. Since 1979, Texas has had four major statewide testing regimes. Each took several years to develop, test, and implement and then each was in place for just a few years. The Texas Assessment of Basic Skills (TABS) was in place from 1979 to 1984, the Texas Educational Assessment of Minimum Skills (TEAMS) was in place from 1984 to 1990, the Texas Assessment of Academic Skills (TAAS) was in place from 1990 to 1999, and the Texas Assessment of Knowledge and Skills (TAKS) began development in 1999. TAKS was to be discontinued in 2011, but delays in launching its successor briefly extended its life. If you wanted to make accurate assessment next to impossible, the best way to do it, short of abandoning testing altogether, would be to frequently change the testing regime.

There are some data to analyze from the TAAS assessment regime of 1994 to 2002 and the TAKS regime of 2003 to 2012 (Table 5.2). Both exams test minimum standards for competency rather than complete command of the subjects tested. Both exams appear to register extraordinary educational achievement and steady progress year to year. But critics see an occasional thumb on the scale. In 2009 the state changed the criteria by which a school could earn the top exemplary rating. In 2009, the "Texas Projection Measure" was implemented which allowed schools to count a student as passing not just if they really did pass but if the new measure predicted that they would pass in a future year.[66] The proportion of Texas schools receiving an exemplary rating jumped from 13.3 percent in 2008, to 28.2 percent in 2009, and 33.9 percent in 2010. Uproarious laughter followed this maneuver and it subsequently was discontinued. In 2011, 15.5 percent of schools were labeled exemplary. The Texas Education Agency (TEA) reports that in 2011, 86 percent of rising seniors passed all four TAKS exams. Unfortunately, the failure rate on the TAKS test in 2012, even after retesting, was about 5 percent. That meant that almost 15,000 students completed their senior year in 2012 but did not receive a diploma. Moreover, black and Hispanic failure rates are about three times the failure rate for Anglo and Asian students.[67]

Beginning with the 2011–2012 school year, Texas introduced the new State of Texas Assessments of Academic Readiness, or STARR, exam. Like TAKS, STARR

Table 5.2 Texas Annual Academic Testing, TAAS and TAKS: Pass Rates, 1994–2015

TAAS	Total	White	Black	Hispanic
1994	56	69	33	41
1995	61	75	38	46
1996	67	80	47	54
1997	73	85	56	62
1998	78	88	63	68
1999	78	88	64	70
2000	80	89	68	72
2001	82	90	72	76
2002	85	93	77	80
TAKS				
2003	49	59	33	38
2004	72	83	58	61
2005	68	82	52	56
2006	64	79	45	52
2007	69	83	52	57
2008	71	83	55	61
2009	75	86	61	67
2010	82	91	73	76
2011	84	92	76	80
2012	86	92	78	83
2013	86	92	78	83
2014	84	85	77	84
2015	84	85	78	85

Source: tea.texas.gov/student.assessment/results/

tests students from third grade through high school, with high school students taking 12 end-of-course exams, three each in English, math, science, and social studies, beginning with 9th graders in 2011–2012. TEA officials claim that STARR will "again raise the bar for Texas education" and that the exams will be benchmarked to national and international standards to insure rigor.[68]

A rough roll-out of STARR was immediately followed by its roll-back. Signs of assessment fatigue were clear in early 2011 when Robert Scott, then Texas Education Agency Commissioner, told 4,000 school administrators that state testing had become a "perversion of its original intent." School testing had been accountability religion in Texas since 1993, especially after Governor George W. Bush took it national with his No Child Left Behind presidential initiative. Scott's comments fed into a debate within school districts about whether STARR could be implemented at all after the 2011 legislature cut $5.4 billion in school funding. Scott predicted, correctly, that the 2013 legislature would reassess and likely scale back testing in Texas.

Within weeks, key Texas state senators, led by the Senate education chair, Florence Shapiro (R-Plano), called for slowing down implementation of STARR. In June 2012, Texas 9th graders took end-of-course STARR exams for the first time. With passing standards set as low as 37 percent for Algebra I and biology and as high as 68 percent for reading, 87 percent passed biology, but only 55 percent passed English I reading. With passing standards set to rise in 2014 and again in 2016, students, parents, educators, and legislators expressed frustration with the number of end-of-course exams required—then 15—and the fact that the exams were mandated to comprise 15 percent of final course grades.

Commissioner Scott announced that he would step down in July 2012, but the fat was in the fire. Defenders of Texas's test-heavy school accountability regime, led by the Texas Association of Business's Bill Hammond, declared that, "What we are seeing today is a full-frontal assault on school accountability."[69] By November, both the State Board of Education and Governor Perry had called for suspending the requirement that end-of-course exams count for 15 percent of course grades. With the legislature scheduled to convene in January 2013, accountability advocates feared even more fundamental changes. In fact, new legislation resulted in a major roll-back of high-stakes testing in Texas. End-of-course exams were slashed from 15 to 5 and they no longer needed to be factored into final grades.

STARR test results for 2012–13 were reported on the day Governor Perry signed the new education law. Again, almost half of high school freshmen and sophomores failed the writing exams and historic differences by race and ethnicity were evident. Sixty-nine percent of Anglos passed the writing exams, but just 43 percent of black students and 45 percent of Hispanic students passed.[70] In classic Texas fashion, some political leaders blamed the test to avoid blaming the quality of education offered by the state. Senator Dan Patrick (R-Houston), chair of the Senate Education Committee, said, "I have great concerns about the validity of the tests. Either these tests are right, and we are in far worse shape than we imagine, or the tests just aren't testing what our kids are learning."[71]

By 2014, parent groups such as Texans Advocating for Meaningful Student Assessment, student assessment experts at UT and elsewhere, and politicians were in full retreat from the state's 30-year-old high-stakes testing regime. The new state election commissioner, Michael Williams, set low passing standards and then twice extended them but students still struggled. As the class of 2015 approached graduation, 16 percent or 48,000 students, had not yet passed all five exams required for graduation. The 2015 Texas Legislature responded by weakening testing requirements for graduation. Students needed only to pass three of the five exams, get a passing grade in all of their core courses, and be approved by a committee at their school. While some of the struggling students eventually passed all five exams, more than 23,000 did not, though almost 17,000 of those graduated with the blessing of school committees.[72]

Setting educational curricula in Texas has long been as much, and often more, about religious and ideological control of the curriculum than it has been about the integrity of academic standards.[73] A century ago, in 1913, the John Bell Hood chapter of the United Confederate Veterans mounted a campaign to remove anti-southern content, including a photo of Abraham Lincoln, from the state's history texts. The state textbook board sided with the veterans, but Governor Oscar Colquitt brought the scuffle to a halt by declaring, "I want the truth of history taught. . . . I had rather resign the Governor's office of Texas than to have my children studying a textbook in the public schools of Texas with Abe Lincoln's picture left out of it, and I am a son of a Confederate soldier."[74] Recent governors and state leaders have been less bold. Two decades ago the State Board of Education (SBOE) declared that Texas science teachers explore both the "strengths and weaknesses" of the theories they teach. The SBOE was particularly interested in assuring that evolution, Charles Darwin's theory of biological change, be presented as unproven, incomplete, and likely flawed. In 2009, a teacher advisory panel recommended that the "strengths and weaknesses" language be changed to instruct science teachers to "analyze and evaluate scientific explanations using empirical data." SBOE chairman Don McLeroy, who described himself as a "Darwin skeptic," led a seven-member minority of the 15-member board in a long and contentious fight to maintain the "strengths and weaknesses" language for another ten years. McLeroy failed but was able to get language approved advising teachers to inform their students "about aspects of the fossil record that do not neatly fit with the idea of species gradually changing over time."[75] Scientists were, of course, appalled. In 2013, new science textbooks were adopted following only minor skirmishes.

When the Texas Senate refused to renew Don McLeroy as chair of the SBOE, Governor Perry named Gail Lowe, another Christian social conservative to the position.[76] As Lowe took the helm of the SBOE, the board had just turned to reviewing the social studies standards. The board had already appointed a six-member expert panel to advise on the upcoming revision. Three of the six members were Texas educators and social studies experts, while the other three, named by the board's conservative members, were Christian fundamentalists and ideologues. State academic standards for history are almost as contested as those for biology, except where matters of race are concerned and then they rival biology. When new history texts for Texas schools arrived in 2015, the *Washington Post* announced that, "Five million public school students in Texas will begin using new social studies textbooks this fall based on state academic standards that barely address racial segregation . . . the Ku Klux Klan or Jim Crow."[77]

The role of ideology in Texas public schools is nowhere more evident than in sex education. While comprehensive sex education has become more and more common around the country, Texas doggedly adheres to an "abstinence only" program. Abstinence only makes the incontrovertible point that if young people abstain from sex before marriage, they will not get pregnant, while ignoring the equally incontrovertible fact that many do have sex and do get pregnant. A 2015 study by the Texas Freedom Network Education Fund found that 58 percent of Texas school districts taught abstinence only, 25 percent taught no sex ed., and about 17 percent taught a slightly more comprehensive program called abstinence plus, dealing with sexual health and safety in addition to abstinence.[78] The U.S. has a national teen pregnancy rate of 24.2 per 1,000 young women. The rate in Texas is 37.8 cases per 1,000; only Mississippi, Arkansas, Oklahoma, and New Mexico are higher. If facts mattered, changes would be made. They don't.[79]

High School Graduation Rates and College Readiness

Texas puts less money into its schools than do most American states. That fact is worrisome but not dispositive, what really matters is how well Texas students are educated. Two measures are available. Perhaps the best information we have on the educational attainment of the population over 25 comes from the U.S. Census. These data include students who graduate on time, return to school to graduate late, or get a General Educational Development (GED) degree later in life. These data also report educational attainment by race and ethnicity.

From the 1950s through the 1970s, Texas educational attainment trailed the U.S. rates by three or four percentage points; since the 1980s that gap has been more often in the six to eight point range. However, in both the U.S. and Texas, the gap between black and white educational attainment rates has closed while the gap between Hispanic and black and white rates has remained disturbingly large. Table 5.3 shows that U.S. educational attainment rates, measured as the share of adults over age 25 holding a high school diploma, have increased from 34 percent in 1950 to 87 percent in 2014, while Texas rates have increased from 30 percent in 1950 to 82 percent. White educational attainment rates remain about five points ahead of black rates and about 30 points ahead of Hispanic rates.

Table 5.3 Educational Attainment in the U.S. and Texas, Percentage of High School Graduates, 1950–2014

	U.S.				Texas			
	Total	White	Black	Hisp.	Total	White	Black	Hisp.
1950	34	36	14		30	33	12	
1960	41	43	20		40	42	21	
1970	55	57	36		47	50	39	
1980	69	72	51	45	64	68	55	
1990	78	81	66	51	75	76	66	45
2000	84	88	79	57	76	80	76	49
2010	87	88	84	63	80	91	84	57
2014	87	92	85	65	82	93	83	63

Source: U.S. Census Bureau, Statistical Abstract of the United States, each year 1950–2011, "Persons 25 and Over, Years of School Completed by States," www.census.gov/library/publications/time-series/statistical_abstracts.html and http://nces.ed.gov/programs/digest/d15/tables/dt15_104.85.asp. Texas in 1950 is Census, 43: 402; 1960 is Census, 45: 716.

Are those who graduate from high school in Texas ready for college? The Scholastic Aptitude Test (SAT) is the principal college placement exam taken by Texas high school seniors. About 60 percent of the class of 2016, nearly 196,028 students, took the SATs. We can compare the mean score achieved by Texas high school seniors with the mean score achieved by high school seniors nationally since 1987. Figure 5.5 shows that in every year from 1987 through 2016 Texas seniors trailed their peers nationally by anywhere from 14 to 38 points. Texas picked up some ground on the national average SAT scores in the early 1990s, closing the gap from 29 points in 1987 to just 14 points in 1995. But the gap widened to 34 points in both 2001 and 2004, and fully 38 points by 2016. Once again, year after year, Texas declined to invest in its students and feigned surprise when they fell further and further behind their peers nationally.

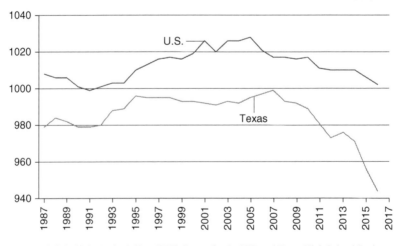

Figure 5.5 Scholastic Aptitude Test (SAT) Scores for the U.S. and Texas High School Seniors, 1987–2016

Source: Texas Education Agency, "Results of College Admissions Testing in Texas for 1997–98 Graduating Seniors," Table 1-A, p. 23; "College Admissions Testing of Graduating Seniors in Texas High Schools, Class of 2009," Table 22, p. 51. See tea.state.tx.us/index4.aspx?id=4112.

Table 5.4 allows us to look more closely at differences in performance on the SAT by racial and ethnic groups nationally and in Texas. Average SAT scores for the U.S. and Texas improved from 1987 through 2005 in the case of the U.S. and 2007 for Texas. In the past several years the bottom has fallen out of U.S. and Texas SAT scores, especially those of Texas. In the U.S. case they have slipped back to 1987 levels and in the Texas case they have slipped way below those levels. In the late 1980s, the average Texas SAT score trailed the national average by about 20 to 30 points and every major Texas ethnic group—whites, blacks, and Hispanics—trailed their respective national groups. Texas whites trailed national whites by about 20 points, Texas blacks trailed national blacks by about a dozen points, and Texas Hispanics trailed national Hispanics by single digits. By the late 1990s, all of these deficits had been cut to ten points or fewer though they increased in the early 2000s for blacks and Hispanics. By 2007 Texas Anglos and blacks passed their national peers, though Texas Hispanics still trail theirs narrowly. As late as 2013, Texas whites scored 1064

Table 5.4 Scholastic Aptitude Test (SAT) Scores for U.S. and Texas High School Seniors, 1987–2016

	U.S.				Texas			
	Total	*White*	*Black*	*Hisp.*	*Total*	*White*	*Black*	*Hisp.*
1987	1008	1038	839	908	979	1016	821	901
1988	1006	1036	847	910	984	1020	840	909
1989	1006	1038	849	919	982	1021	841	910
1990	1001	1034	847	911	979	1019	842	906
1991	999	1031	846	909	979	1022	842	904
1992	1001	1034	847	908	980	1025	835	902
1993	1003	1037	850	910	988	1034	845	911
1994	1003	1039	849	909	989	1038	843	913
1995	1010	1046	854	916	996	1043	853	917
1996	1013	1049	856	918	995	1044	852	912
1997	1016	1052	857	917	995	1046	848	911
1998	1017	1054	860	916	995	1048	850	910
1999	1016	1055	856	915	993	1047	847	906
2000	1019	1058	860	918	993	1051	850	904
2001	1026	1060	859	915	992	1051	846	900
2002	1020	1060	857	911	991	1052	840	896
2003	1026	1053	857	912	993	1054	841	894
2004	1026	1059	857	916	992	1050	843	897
2005	1028	1068	864	923	995	1061	853	905
2006	1021	1063	863	919	997	1063	861	907
2007	1017	1061	862	921	999	1062	868	916
2008	1017	1065	856	916	993	1065	861	910
2009	1016	1064	855	914	992	1069	862	908
2010	1017	1064	857	918	989	1068	861	910
2011	1011	1063	855	913	981	1062	861	902
2012	1010	1063	856	909	973	1062	857	897
2013	1010	1061	860	911	976	1064	859	899
2014	1010	1063	860	910	971	1063	860	891
2015	1006	1063	859	906	956	1057	848	880
2016	1002	1061	855	901	944	1054	841	871

Source: Texas Education Agency, Research and Evaluation Division, Academic Excellence Indicator System (AEIS). SAT, College Board, Total Group Profile Report and State Profile Report, Texas, various years. https://reports/collegeboard.org/pdf/total-group-2016.pdf. https://research/collegeboard.org/programs/SAT/data/archived.

on the SAT compared to 1061 for U.S. whites, Texas blacks very nearly matched U.S. blacks by 859 to 860, and Texas Hispanics trailed their peers nationally by 899 to 911. And then the bottom fell out.

Still, how can it be that when Texas's major racial and ethnic groups trail their national peers by 7 to 30 points, that the state's overall score trails the U.S overall score by 58 points? The answer is in the comparative ethnic make-up of the test groups nationally and in Texas. Nationally about 21 percent of SAT-takers are Hispanic and in Texas the number is about 43 percent. In 2016, Hispanic test-takers averaged about 165 points less than white test-takers in Texas, hence, with the Texas test group composed of fewer white test-takers and more Hispanic test-takers than the national test group, the Texas average is lower than the national average. 2013 was the first year that more Texas Hispanics than Anglos took the SAT. The American College Testing (ACT) exam was also taken by a large number of Texas high school students preparing for college, more than 142,877 in 2016. Texas ACT scores show the same pattern of trailing below the national average and slowly losing ground.

Conclusion

Texas was late to establish public schools, slow to make attendance mandatory, and unwilling for decades to fund minority schools at the level of Anglo schools. Though some important reforms were undertaken in the first half of the twentieth century, other states were reforming as well, so Texas's ranking among the states barely changed. Only after World War II, with the state rapidly urbanizing and industrializing, did Texas turn its attention to modernizing its school system. The Gilmer–Aikin reforms of 1949 actually did make Texas a model for educational reform in the other southern states. But like the other southern states, Texas's school system was segregated by race and many of the benefits of reform were lost to a 15-year struggle to maintain segregation.

Texas has consistently trailed national averages for per capita educational spending, teacher pay, high school graduation rates, and college preparation as measured by SAT and ACT scores. Over the past seven decades, Texas educational expenditures have averaged 84 percent of the national average for state expenditures. Texas has ranked 38th among the 50 states and D.C. since 1950, but has fallen far back in recent years—to 49th in 2012 before rebounding to its traditional 38th spot in both 2014 and 2015. Texas has done somewhat better on teacher pay, though we remain below 90 percent of the national average in the most recent data and our average rank among the states since 1950 has been 29th. There have been some improvements by Anglo and black students, but Hispanic students in Texas have continued to lag.

These facts highlight the importance of student effort and teacher effectiveness, but they also highlight the importance of effective public policy. To be perfectly clear, the future of Texas depends upon minority educational achievement. There were 5 million children in Texas public schools in 2015–2016 and two-thirds of them were minority students: 51.8 percent were Hispanic, 12.7 percent were black, 29.4 percent were Anglo, 3.7 percent were Asian, and about 2 percent were others. By 2040, Anglo children will be just 20 percent of Texas school children and the rest will be what historically have been called minority children. Anglo elites, who still control the state and likely will for decades to come, must fund high-quality public education for minority children. Funding equalization between wealthier and poorer schools, even channeling funding toward the poorer schools, seems imperative.

Notes

1 Kiah Collier and Alexa Ura, "The Changing Face of Texas Public Schools," *The Texas Tribune*, December 9, 2016.
2 William H. Frey, "A Demographic Tipping Point among America's Three-Year-Olds," Brookings Institution, February 7, 2011.
3 William Ransom Hogan, *The Texas Republic*, Norman, OK: University of Oklahoma Press, 1946, p. 146. See also Chris Tomlinson, *Tomlinson Hill*, New York: St. Martin's Press, 2014, pp. 128–129.
4 *Journal of the House of Representatives of the Republic of Texas*, Third Congress, pp. 168–170.
5 C.E. Evans, *The Story of Texas Schools*, Austin, TX: The Steck Company, 1955, p. 52. See Noah Smithwick, *The Evolution of a State*, Austin, TX: University of Texas Press, 1983, p. 169 for an unvarnished view of Texas education during the Republic.
6 T.R. Fehrenbach, *Lone Star: A History of Texas and the Texans*, New York: Macmillan, 1968, p. 303.
7 Wilhelm Steinert, *North America: Particularly Texas in the Year 1849*, Dallas, TX: DeGolyer Library, 2003, pp. 47, 72, 124.
8 Evans, *The Story of Texas Schools*, p. 68. See also George P. Garrison, *Texas: A Contest of Civilizations*, Boston, MA: Houghton-Mifflin, 1903, pp. 277–278.
9 Robert Wuthnow, *Rough Country: How Texas Became America's Most Powerful Bible-Belt State*, Princeton, NJ: Princeton University Press, 2014, p. 30. Randolph B. Campbell, *Gone to Texas: A History of the Lone Star State*, New York: Oxford University Press, 2003, pp. 228–230.
10 Alwyn Barr, *Black Texans: A History of African Americans in Texas, 1528–1995*, Norman, OK: University of Oklahoma Press, 1973/1996, p. 23.
11 Fehrenbach, *Lone Star*, pp. 411, 419; Gene B. Preuss, *To Get a Better School System*, College Station, TX: Texas A&M University Press, 2009, p. 10.
12 Carl H. Moneyhon, *Republicanism in Reconstruction Texas*, Austin, TX: University of Texas Press, 1980, pp. 172–174, 183–184.
13 Preuss, *To Get a Better School System*, pp. 11–12. See also Evans, *The Story of Texas Schools*, p. 87.
14 Wuthnow, *Rough Country*, p. 31.
15 Thad Sitton and Milam C. Rowold, *Ringing the Children In: Texas Country Schools*, College Station, TX: Texas A&M University Press, 1987, p. 7.
16 Preuss, *To Get a Better School System*, pp. 13–14. See also Evans, *The Story of Texas Schools*, pp. 99–100.
17 Gavin Wright, *Old South, New South: Revolutions in the Southern Economy Since the Civil War*, New York: Basic Books, 1986, p. 80.
18 Preuss, *To Get a Better School System*, p. 15.
19 Sitten and Rowold, *Ringing the Children In*, p. 206.
20 Don Graham, *State of Minds: Texas Culture and Its Discontents*, Austin, TX: University of Texas Press, 2011, p. 27.
21 Frederick Eby, *The Development of Education in Texas*, New York: Macmillan, 1925, p. 51.
22 Evans, *The Story of Texas Schools*, p. 122.
23 Preuss, *To Get a Better School System*, pp. 27–28.
24 Eby, *Development of Education in Texas*, p. 218.
25 Preuss, *To Get a Better School System*, p. 69.
26 Amarillo Daily News, April 11, 1947, p. 24. www.newspapers.com/newspage/15440608.
27 Rae Files Still, *The Gilmer-Aikin Bill: A Study in the Legislative Process*, Austin, TX: The Steck Company, 1950, p. 2.
28 Numan V. Bartley, *The New South, 1945–1980*, Baton Rouge, LA: Louisiana State University Press, 1995, pp. 149–151.
29 Dolph Briscoe, *Dolph Briscoe: My Life in Texas Ranching and Politics*, Austin, TX: University of Texas Press, 2008, p. 99.
30 Richard Morehead, *50 Years in Texas Politics*, Burnet, TX: Eakin Press, 1982, p. 110. See also Ricky F. Dobbs, *Yellow Dogs and Republicans: Allan Shivers and Texas Two-Party Politics*, College Station, TX: Texas A&M University, 2005, pp. 108–111; and Sam Kinch and Stuart Long, *Allen Shivers: The Pied Piper of Texas Politics*, Austin, TX: Shoal Creek Publishers, 1973, p. 157.
31 Robyn Duff Ladino, *Desegregating Texas Schools: Eisenhower, Shivers, and the Crisis at Mansfield High*, Austin, TX: University of Texas Press, 1996, pp. 37–38.

32 Sean P. Cunningham, *Cowboy Conservatism: Texas and the Rise of the Modern Right*, Lexington, KY: University of Kentucky Press, 2010, p. 101.
33 Ladino, *Desegregating Texas Schools*, p. 48.
34 Ibid., p. 5, editorial dated August 6, 1956.
35 Ibid., pp. 93–96, 102.
36 Cox and Phillips, *The House Will Come to Order*, Austin, TX: University of Texas Press, 2010, p. 75.
37 Ladino, *Desegregating Texas Schools*, pp. 130, 137, 140. See also Bill Minutaglio and Steven L. Davis, *Dallas 1963*, New York: Twelve, 2013, p. 93.
38 Southern Education Reporting Service, "A Statistical Summary, State-by-State, of Segregation-Desegregation in the Southern States," www.eric.ed.gov/fulltext/EDO19382.pdf.
39 *Texas Almanac, 2008–09*, published by *Dallas Morning News*, distributed by College Station, TX: Texas A&M University Press Consortium, 2008, p. 582.
40 Terrence Stutz, "'84 School Reform Law Reverberates," *Dallas Morning News*, July 7, 2014, pp. A1, A8.
41 Anthony Champagne and Edward J. Harpham, *Texas at the Crossroads: People, Politics, and Policy*, College Station, TX: Texas A&M University Press, 1987, p. 162.
42 Michael Lind, *Made in Texas: George W. Bush and the Southern Takeover of American Politics*, New York: Basic Books, 2003, p. 125.
43 Bill Hobby, *How Things Really Work: Lessons From a Life in Politics*, Austin, TX: University of Texas Press, 2010, p. 98.
44 J. Steven Farr and Mark Trachtenberg, "The Edgewood Drama: An Epic Quest for Education Equality," *Yale Law and Policy Review*, Vol. 17, No. 2, 1999, pp. 607–727.
45 E. Jane Irons and Sandra Harris, *The Challenge of No Child Left Behind*, New York: Rowman and Littlefield, 2007, p. 118.
46 Kiah Collier, "Texas Supreme Court Rules School Funding System is Constitutional," *The Texas Tribune*, May 13, 2016.
47 Claudia Goldin and Lawrence F. Katz, *The Race between Education and Technology*, Cambridge, MA: Harvard University Press, 2008, p. 208.
48 Nelson Dometrius, "Education Policy," in Gerry Riposa, ed., *Texas Public Policy*, Dubuque, IO: Kendall/Hunt, 1987, p. 45.
49 Goldin and Katz, *The Race between Education and Technology*, p. 345.
50 Robert T. Garrett and Christy Hoppe, "Political Veterans Dissect Budget," *Dallas Morning News*, January 23, 2011, p. A1.
51 Erica Grieder, *Big, Hot, Cheap, and Right*, New York: Public Affairs, 2013, p. 59.
52 David G. McComb, *Texas: A Modern History*, Austin, TX: University of Texas Press, 2010, p. 190.
53 Kate Alexander, "On School Funding, 'No Guarantee' Anymore," *Austin American-Statesman*, June 1, 2011; see also, Patti Kilday Hart, "Public Schools About to Take a Backseat," *Houston Chronicle*, June 4, 2011.
54 "The-Truth-O-Meter Says," *Austin American-Statesman*, March 24, 2012.
55 Terrence Stutz, "Schools Unlikely to Get Boost," *Dallas Morning News*, December 27, 2014, pp. A1, A2.
56 Briscoe, *Dolph Briscoe: My Life in Texas Ranching and Politics*, pp. 240, 249, 253.
57 Terrence Stutz, "Texas Teacher Shortage in Math, Science Worsens," *Dallas Morning News*, February 10, 2009, p. 4A.
58 National Center on Teacher Quality, "State Teacher Policy Yearbook: What States Can Do to Retain Effective New Teachers, Texas, 2008," pp. 1–2; Tony Wagner, *The Global Achievement Gap*, New York: Basic Books, 2008, p. 14.
59 Robert T. Garrett, "31 Percent of Teachers Hold a Second Job," *Dallas Morning News*, December, 27, 2014, pp. A1, A2.
60 Terrence Stutz, "Texas Adds Electives, Scales Back Required Classes in High School," *Dallas Morning News*, July 7, 2009, pp. A1, A6.
61 Terrence Stutz, "Education Board Seeks Limits on PE Classes," *Dallas Morning News*, August 15, 2009, p. 3A.
62 Terrence Stutz, "Board Changes Rules so Students Can't Load Up on PE Classes," *Dallas Morning News*, November 21, 2009, p. A1.
63 Kate Alexander, "How Will Texas Compete in Race to the Top?" *Austin American-Statesman*, June 29, 2009.
64 https://www.usnews.com/news/special-reports/a-guide-to-common-core/articles/2014/03/06/the-politics-of-common-core/.

65 Kate Alexander, "Texas Will Not Compete for Federal Education Grants," *Austin American-Statesman*, January 13, 2010.

66 Holly K. Hacker, "New Rule Boosts Schools to Top of the Ratings," *Dallas Morning News*, August 3, 2009, pp. 1B, 7B.

67 Terrence Stutz, "9th Graders Beat Lower STARR Expectations," *Dallas Morning News*, June 9, 2012, pp. A1, A2.

68 Terrence Stutz, "State's New Tests to Be Tougher, Longer," *Dallas Morning News*, December 2, 2010, p. A3.

69 Kate Alexander, "House Members Get Careful on STARR," *Austin American-Statesman*, June 19, 2012.

70 Terrence Stutz, "New Tests, Same Troubles," *Dallas Morning News*, June 11, 2013, pp. A1, A9.

71 Jeffrey Weiss, "After 3 Decades, a Rollback on Testing," *Dallas Morning News*, June 17, 2013, pp. A1, A6.

72 Robert T. Garrett, "Seniors Petition Their Way to Graduation," *Dallas Morning News*, November 20, 2015, pp. A1, A9.

73 George Norris Green, *The Establishment in Texas Politics: The Primitive Years, 1938–1957*, Norman, OK: University of Oklahoma Press, 1984, pp. 59, 64.

74 Gregg Cantrell, "The Bones of Stephen F. Austin: History and Memory in Progressive-Era Texas," *Southwestern Historical Quarterly*, vol. 65, no. 2, October, 2004, p. 176.

75 James C. McKinley Jr., "Split Outcome in Texas Battle on Teaching of Evolution," *New York Times*, January 24, 2009, p. A12.

76 Paul Burka, "Lowe and Behold," *Texas Monthly*, September 2009, pp. 8–10.

77 Emma Brown, "Texas Officials: Schools Should Teach That Slavery Was a 'Side Issue' to Civil War," *Washington Post*, July 5, 2015.

78 Texas Freedom Network Educational Fund, "Conspiracy of Silence: Sexuality Education in Texas Public Schools," www.tfn.org/sex-ed/tfn-sex-ed-report-2016-web.pdf.

79 Christy Hoppe and Danielle Abril, "Sex Ed Is Latest Culture Battle," *Dallas Morning News*, March 10, 2013, pp. A1, A4.

6   Higher Education in Texas

> We must ensure that Texas' four-year public universities claim five of the top 10 spots
> in future rankings of public universities by *U.S. News & World Report* magazine.
>
> (Greg Abbott, 2014)

Lofty goals are a signature of Texas politics, both endearing and amusing, but also a bit
sad. In the headnote immediately above, Republican Greg Abbott declared during his
successful 2014 gubernatorial campaign that "We," perhaps the royal "We" or maybe
just all of us Texans, must ensure that our public universities claim five of the top
ten spots in the prominent *U.S. News* annual ranking of public universities.[1] Governor
Abbott's laudable aspirations are, however, immediately confronted by the harsh fact
that no Texas public university has ever been anywhere near the *U.S. News* top ten. In
the magazine's most recent rankings of public universities (2017), the University of
Texas at Austin (UT) was 18, Texas A&M University (TAMU) was 27, University of
Texas at Dallas (UTD) was 74, Texas Tech (TT) was 93, and the University of Houston
(UH) was 103. Since the governor spoke, UTD has improved two spots, but UT has
fallen back one spot, Texas A&M has fallen back two spots, Texas Tech nine spots,
and Houston held steady at 103. Bold declarations, followed by tiny initiatives rendered
moot by budget cuts leading to no progress against competitors, have long characterized Texas higher education.

More pointedly, the ten-campus University of California (UC) system had six campuses: UC, Berkeley (1), UCLA (2), UC, Santa Barbara (8), UC, Irvine (9), and UC,
Davis and UC, San Diego (tied for 10), ranked above Texas's top public university, UT,
Austin (18). More remarkably still, the tenth campus in the UC system, UC, Merced,
established just over a decade ago in 2005, was ranked at 78. In addition to UT, only
two Texas public universities, Texas A&M (27) and UT, Dallas (74), ranked above
Merced. UC, Merced is so new that the grass has not fully taken root and already it is
ranked above all but a very few Texas public universities. The difference between talking about greatness and investing for greatness is palpable in these numbers.

As we shall see below, Texans have always been ambivalent about higher education
in general and their flagship institutions in particular, thinking them both expensive and
elitist challenges to the state's populist culture. So no one should have been surprised
that rather than planning a major push toward the top ranks of public universities, the
Texas Legislature in 2005 cut support to the state's colleges and universities and gave
up their historic control of tuition, allowing the institutions themselves to set tuition.
State appropriations to higher education have remained flat since 2005, while tuition on
many campuses has doubled. Attorney General Abbott, of course, knew all of that as
he campaigned for governor in 2014. Since winning the governorship, Abbott has made

no attempt to increase general state support of higher education or to restore legislative responsibility for setting tuition. Flat state appropriations and rising tuition, beyond limiting access to higher education for too many students, is simply not a plausible plan for building great national universities in Texas.

A Brief History of Higher Education in Texas

Most schools in early Texas, whether for basic instruction or for higher education, were private. Politicians talked from the start about the importance of public schools and colleges, but were unable consistently to deliver either until after the Civil War and Reconstruction. For example, only three years after independence, Republic of Texas President Mirabeau B. Lamar convinced the Texas Congress to set aside 221,000 acres for two public universities. These public universities would not arise for nearly four decades, so, in the meanwhile, wealthy Texans sent their children north and east to college, comfortable Texans had to depend upon a kaleidoscope of local academies, institutes, seminaries, and colleges, while poor Texans taught their children what they could at home.

Early travelers to Texas and historians have delighted in recounting one academic competition that led to gunplay in the streets of San Augustine in 1845. Two colleges, one sponsored by the Methodists and the other by the Presbyterians, operated under state charters in San Augustine. As they competed for a limited pool of potential students, the community took sides and passions escalated. Accounts of the demise of the Reverend James Russell, president of the Presbyterian institution, differ. Some point to academic competition, others to President Russell's adverse comments on a lady's character, objected to forcefully by her brother. In either case, the Reverend President Russell was left dead in the street. Even in Texas, such doings affected the reputations of both colleges and soon they were out of business.[2] By the 1850s dozens of private institutions of advanced learning were operating in Texas, but most offered a range of instruction that began with the rudiments and offered a slap-dash course of study thereafter. Some of these, much improved to be sure, still exist today: Baylor was established by Baptists in 1845, Austin College by Presbyterians in 1849, and St. Mary's in San Antonio by Catholics in 1852.[3]

As the Civil War loomed, Texas had few institutions that actually delivered college-level courses, but many that claimed to be working in that direction. In 1859, Texas had 8 universities, 37 colleges, 2 seminaries, a medical college, as well as 40 academies and 27 institutes. The academies and institutes offered college preparatory work and most of the colleges and universities also offered preparatory programs to ready their charges for more advanced offerings.[4] The destruction of the Civil War and Reconstruction both cut the number of higher education institutions in half and highlighted the need for state universities if Texas were to make good its recovery. But, as with so much else, populist suspicions and racial animus governed how state officials thought about higher education in the wake of the war.

The first public university in Texas, The Agricultural and Mechanical College of Texas, later Texas A&M University, was established in 1876 with support provided by the U.S. Congress under the Morrill Land-Grant College Act of 1862. In a gesture freighted with sad meaning, the presidency of the new university was offered to Jefferson Davis of Mississippi, the former president of the Confederate States of America. Mercifully, Davis declined.[5] Former State School Superintendent Thomas Gathright became the new institution's first president. Texas A&M opened its doors with 40 students and six faculty members. Gathright was almost immediately instructed by Governor Richard Coke to oversee the Alta Vista Agricultural College, soon to be renamed Prairie View A&M, for the state's black students. Until 1947, Prairie View was the only state-supported school to admit blacks.

In pursuit of the Texas Constitution's injunction to establish "a University of the first class," the legislature authorized the construction of the University of Texas at Austin in 1881. Construction began in 1882 and the first classes were held in a wing of the Old State Capitol in 1883. The University of Texas did not have a president during its first decade, but former Governor Oran M. Roberts, first head of the Law Department, was the most prominent figure among its nine-member faculty.[6] Once the University of Texas opened there was a strong move to close Texas A&M on the grounds that Texas did not need and could not afford two public universities. Texas A&M was saved by its president, Sul Ross, another former governor and Civil War general who reorganized and rejuvenated the university.

Texas expanded its system of public higher education slowly over the first two-thirds of the twentieth century. By 1900, there were 6 public colleges and universities in Texas; by 1920 there were 15, by 1950 there were 18, and there were 23 by the mid-1960s. In 1965, Texas created the Coordinating Board of the Texas College and University System to manage further expansion, limit program duplication, and insure access and quality. With Governor John Connally's energetic support, the Coordinating Board developed a plan, adopted in 1968, to stabilize enrollment at the state's senior colleges, authorize new institutions in underserved parts of the state, and initiate a major expansion of community colleges throughout the state.[7] As always, high aspirations and big plans were hobbled by flagging political commitment and recurring fiscal uncertainty.

Political Oversight of (or Is It Interference in) Texas Higher Education

Texas universities frequently have had strained relations with the state's politicians and public. While Texas college presidents are not shot in the street anymore, they are regularly harassed, hounded, and often run to ground. There are many great stories about titanic clashes between Texas governors and the leaders of the state's flagship universities, mostly UT since it is just down the street from the capitol, but Texas A&M more recently and others occasionally. Powering these clashes has always been the tension, not to say incompatibility, between the traditional, populist, political culture of the state and the dedication to inquiry and discovery in higher education and, especially, in major research universities. The fundamental ambivalence about higher education in Texas was nicely captured by John Gunther in his survey of the states in post–World War II America, entitled *Inside U.S.A.* Gunther wrote that, "Texas wanted, and wants, the greatest and richest university in the world. Yet it did not quite grasp the point that no university can be worthy of the name without being anchored on something that many conservative Texans feared, academic freedom."[8] That point still eludes many today.

What Gunther noticed was, by the time he wrote, an old story. When UT opened its doors in 1883, five of its nine founding faculty had served in the Confederate Army. But by the end of the century the university had expanded and some worried that it had hired men of more ambiguous principles. State leaders became restless. In 1897, the Texas Legislature demanded an investigation into whether UT faculty adhered to and taught Southern values and principles.[9] In a resolution passed on June 9, 1897, the legislature declared, "there has been employed and included in the faculty . . . those who are . . . not in sympathy with the traditions of the South, but hold our traditions and institutions in contempt and circulate and teach political heresies in place of the system of political economy that is cherished by our people." The resolution concluded by "requesting the regents of the University to exercise great care hereafter in selecting as members of the faculty only those who are known to be in sympathy with Southern political institutions, and further request them to cancel as soon as possible any existing contract with members of the faculty not so in sympathy."[10] To soothe legislative concern, UT recruited to its law faculty William Stewart Simkins. Simkins had been a leader of the Florida Ku Klux Klan after the Civil War and before moving to Texas to build a legal career. He served on the UT law faculty, actively defending the traditional Southern principles of the day, for three decades, 1899–1928.[11] While Professor Simkins still served on the faculty, another Texas governor, the redoubtable James E. "Farmer Jim" Ferguson (later known as "Pa" Ferguson once he had been impeached and successfully ran his wife, Miriam "Ma" Ferguson, for governor), found fault with UT faculty and administration. Governor Ferguson believed that there was "a political ring in the university" opposed to his policies. Ferguson demanded that UT President R. E. Vinson fire six faculty and staff members. When asked why, Ferguson initially replied, "I am the Governor of Texas, I don't have to give reasons," before offering that "a professor at this school . . . presided at a county convention with a crowd that refused to endorse this administration."[12] President Vinson and the Board of Regents refused to fire the offending faculty and staff, but Ferguson did not relent. After securing re-election in 1916, Governor Ferguson used his State of the State address opening the 1917 legislative session to warn that UT had become "aristocratic in its ways or customs and begins to arrogate to itself an unwarranted superiority over the great masses of the people." Following the end of the legislative session, Ferguson vetoed the university budget and announced to the regents that, "If the university cannot be maintained as a democratic University, then we ought to have no University."[13] UT alumni in the legislature and beyond pushed back. Governor Ferguson was impeached and removed from office in 1917. Ferguson's removal seemed to spare UT, but his successor, the widely respected Governor William Hobby, also felt entitled to intrude into university business. With anti-German emotions from World War I still running hot, Hobby vetoed the appropriation for the UT German Department in 1919.[14]

The most famous battle between the capital and the academy again came in wartime. In 1942, Governor Wilbert Lee "Pappy" O'Daniel and his lieutenant governor and successor Coke Stevenson, the UT Board of Regents, and Texas conservatives more generally, turned on UT President Homer Rainey. Once again, UT professors, economists this time, had attended a public meeting and spoken in favor of radical ideas such as a 40-hour work week and overtime pay. When the regents sought to remove the rebellious faculty, Rainey spoke out for academic freedom and in 1944 he was fired. When pressed for better reasons for the firings, the regents offered that Rainey "had allowed the school to become a 'nest of homosexuals.'"[15] The American Association of University Professors (AAUP) sanctioned UT and warned faculty that might consider taking a job there that the institution was subject to political interference. Unlike most university presidents, Rainey did not slink away; instead he declared for the Democratic Party nomination of governor in 1946 and ran second before losing to future Governor Buford Jester in the party primary runoff.

In the 1960s and 1970s, UT Regent Frank Erwin, a close political associate of Lyndon Johnson and John Connally, but not controllable even by them, dominated the board and the university. A larger-than-life figure, Erwin drove the UT campus in a Cadillac convertible painted burnt orange and white. Working through Johnson and Connally, Erwin directed new revenues to the university but expected to oversee their uses. He clashed frequently with campus demonstrators in the 1960s and personally led, bullhorn in hand, the removal of student protesters trying to defend a grove of live oaks against a planned stadium expansion. Any woolly headed academics who made themselves inconvenient, no matter the office they occupied, were summarily removed. Erwin personally fired John Silber, dean of the College of Arts and Sciences, to cries of political domination of and interference with the university.[16]

In 2009 it was Texas A&M's turn to be the plaything of the state's governing elite. In 2006, Perry successfully supported Mike McKinney, his former chief of staff, for the post of TAMU system chancellor. In 2009, Perry sent reinforcements. Still another Perry chief of staff, Jay Kimbrough, was hired as a special adviser to the TAMU system regents. Soon, TAMU president, Elsa Murano, just 17 months in office, was fired after a public split with TAMU system Chancellor Mike McKinney. In the TAMU system, the chancellor has oversight over all the campuses in the system, but, in the past, rarely intruded into the administration of individual campuses, let alone the flagship campus. Governor Rick Perry was thought to have been instrumental behind the scenes in hiring Murano, but he stood with McKinney when he clashed with her. John Haglar, a former chair of the A&M foundation, wrote in the *Bryan-College-Station Eagle* that "The Governor/Chancellor tandem, with the approval of the regents, is appointing and firing executives at Texas A&M, without consultation with its faculty. It is intervening in faculty compensation. And it tolerates no dissent."[17]

The history of political interference in Texas higher education is important because it is not just history—it is ongoing. In 2010, Rick Perry chose, to the surprise of many, to stand for a third full term as governor of Texas. The state's senior U.S. senator, Kay Bailey Hutchison, who thought she had received assurances from Perry in 2006 that he would not run again in 2010, had already declared for governor by the time Perry changed his mind. The conservative political class, many of whom held appointments from Perry but had long supported both Perry and Hutchison, had to choose sides. Most stuck with Perry, but some went with Hutchison and soon began to feel the heat. Several who supported Hutchison, including Earl Nye of the Texas A&M regents, Robert Rowling and John Barnhill of the UT regents, and Windy Sitton of the Texas Tech regents were not reappointed when their terms ended. More interestingly, Mark Griffin of the Texas Tech regents, with two years to go on his term, was pressured to resign. As Griffin told it, he was called by Brian Newby, Perry's former general counsel and chief of staff, who told him that the governor expected loyalty; "'I asked him if the governor wanted me to resign. He said he would accept it if you offered it up.'" Griffin offered it up and Perry accepted it. Feigning horror, the Hutchison campaign declared itself "shocked and dismayed to hear that Perry is yet again playing politics with Texas's universities."[18]

In 2010, a much bigger fight, brewing for at least five years, broke into the open and roiled capital–campus relations. For years Perry supported reforms designed to limit tuition increases, focus faculty efforts on students and teaching, and bring a leaner business-like efficiency to higher education in Texas. Texas universities, especially the flagship campuses of the UT and TAMU systems, and most especially UT, resisted, sometimes just passively, sometimes openly. The academic leadership of the universities sought to maintain the classic major research university model of good undergraduate teaching, but with a focus on graduate education, faculty research, and national reputation. Perry's response was to use his power of appointment and his broader political influence to reshape and make more responsive the leadership of the state's higher education community.

In 2008, Perry and the free-market Texas Public Policy Foundation (TPPF), with former UT business professor and TPPF board member Jeff Sandefer moderating, laid "Seven Breakthrough Solutions" before state higher education leaders. The Seven Breakthrough Solutions were higher education reform proposals designed, according to Sandefer, to increase efficiency, transparency, and a student-as-customer focus. Faculty would be judged for salary increases and tenure on teaching effectiveness and student evaluations. Students were to get learning contracts in their courses and state funding through scholarships that they could spend—free-market style—at the Texas public college or university of their choice.

In 2010, once the decks had been cleared, McKinney and Kimbrough oversaw the implementation of part of Perry's higher education reform program by developing a spreadsheet of all the faculty highlighting the revenue, a lot or a little, they generated through contracts, grants, and teaching large numbers of students. Texas A&M faculty, alumni, and national higher education groups warned that the narrow focus on teaching more students threatened research productivity and academic freedom. When Chancellor McKinney, despite his long ties to Perry, failed to push the reform agenda enthusiastically enough, he was forced out by Perry-appointed regents.[19] Live by the sword, die by the sword.

As always, despite the skirmishes in College Station, the decisive battles were fought in Austin between the capital and the UT campus. For the traditional major research university focus stood UT President Bill Powers, a confident, urbane, connected former dean of the UT Law School. With him stood most of the UT faculty and alumni. Some of those alumni, both of UT and its law school, were in the Texas Legislature. With Perry and Sandefer stood the powerful TPPF and Perry appointees on the UT Board of Regents. UT System Chancellor Francisco Cigarroa, a physician and former president of the UT Health Sciences Center in San Antonio, seemed caught in the middle, sometimes advocating the Perry/Sandefer reforms and sometimes voicing the university's concerns. Gene Powell, also of San Antonio, was selected by the regents as their chairman in February 2011.

One of Chairman Powell's first acts was, without a board discussion or vote, to hire Rick O'Donnell, a former Colorado higher education official and, more recently, a senior research fellow for higher education at TPPF, as a special adviser to the board. While at TPPF, O'Donnell wrote a paper entitled, "Is Academic Research a Good Investment for Texas?" His hiring set off alarm bells throughout UT and the legislative offices of the capital. Reactions to O'Donnell's hiring and the push for Sandefer's breakthrough solutions that it seemed to foretell were swift. Within a little more than two months O'Donnell was gone but the battle-lines in the fight over higher education, and the need to take sides, were clarified. Although it took years and many generals were lost in the battle, the universities and their supporters won, if only by hunkering down and absorbing the blows that the reformers rained down upon them.[20]

The battle raged into the summer of 2014 and, as the pressure built, UT academic leaders turned on each other. The UT regents were Perry appointees and most supported, more or less enthusiastically, the Sandefer reforms. Chancellor Cigarroa had to work with the board but did not directly run the campuses. UT President Bill Powers was determined to represent his faculty and what he and they took to be academic excellence. Finally, Cigarroa, about to retire as chancellor, concluded that Powers should go too—probably to clear the decks for the next leadership team. Cigarroa requested Powers' resignation in early July 2014. Powers responded by proposing that he stay one more academic year to finish various projects and then retire to the law school following the 2014–2015 academic year and the 2015 legislative session. By that time, Powers likely reasoned, Perry would be gone, his regents would serve out their terms, and the university would have lived—its principles intact—to fight another day as it would surely have to do.

Populist political intrusion has been a major factor limiting the academic improvement of Texas colleges and universities. Time and again Texas politicos have pushed back against unfamiliar opinions emanating from the state's campuses, whether those opinions dealt with science, politics, economics, or culture. As always, traditional opinions about race were tenaciously defended. The myriad ways in which race, both during and after slavery, shaped and limited the cultural, political, and economic options available to blacks, and to a somewhat lesser degree Hispanics, included all levels of education, especially higher education.

Race and Access to Higher Education in Texas

With the end of slavery came many questions regarding the place of freedmen in Texas public life. In slavery, education of any kind for blacks was scarce, sporadic, and elementary at best. As we saw in Chapter 5, Texas resisted spending on black public education well into the twentieth century. Not surprisingly, resistance to funding higher education for blacks in Texas was even stronger and, for three-quarters of a century, largely successful. Over that period, Texas established 17 public colleges and universities for whites and one for blacks. As noted above, soon after the Constitution of 1876 was adopted, the state purchased the Alta Vista plantation near Houston as a "State Agricultural and Mechanical College for Colored Youths." Alta Vista was later renamed Prairie View A&M and placed under the oversight of Texas A&M University. Prairie View developed as a hybrid high school, trade school, and normal school for the training of teachers for the state's black schools.[21] In the 1880s, when the University of Texas was founded in Austin, blacks pointed to the provision in the Constitution of 1876 mandating an associated campus for blacks. The state legislature declared it not "practicable" to create a black campus associated with UT.

Texas made no provision for black graduate education until 1937 and then only because the United States Supreme Court was moving to demand it of other states. The legislature and the Texas A&M Board approved Prairie View's proposal to open a division of graduate study. To refuse would have meant running the danger that the high court might order the state's white universities to open to black students. Just a little over a year later, the U.S. Supreme Court, in the landmark case called *Missouri ex rel. Gaines v. Canada, Registrar of the University of Missouri*, ordered that Lloyd Gaines, a black man, be admitted to the University of Missouri's white law school because there was no public law school for blacks in the state. Texas took notice, but rather than establish a black law school in Texas, the legislature in 1939 established a fund of $25,000 to assist black Texans wanting graduate education unavailable in Texas's black colleges to go out of state. White state officials found this less expensive than building graduate education programs for blacks in Texas and less socially disruptive than letting those students attend the state's white colleges and universities.

White state and university officials knew both that white Texans supported segregated schools, including colleges and universities, and that federal forces were bringing increasing pressure to bear against segregation. UT Regent Orville Bullington sought early in 1944 to reassure nervous constituents that there was not "the slightest danger of any negro attending the University of Texas, regardless of what Franklin D., Eleanor, or the Supreme Court says, so long as you have a Board of Regents with as much intestinal fortitude as the present one has."[22] Pressure to desegregate the state's white colleges and universities was soon personified for Texas by one black man, Heman Marion Sweatt. Heman Sweatt was from Houston. He graduated from one of the city's black high schools in 1930 before attending black Wiley College in Marshall, Texas, where he received a BA in 1934. Sweatt did graduate work in public health at the University of Michigan before returning to Texas in 1938.

Sweatt started a family, went to work for the post office, and joined the NAACP before volunteering to challenge the exclusion of blacks from the prestigious, all-white, University of Texas Law School. At the time, there were no black judges in Texas and fewer than two dozen of the state's nearly eight thousand lawyers were black—all the black lawyers had been trained out of state. On February 26, 1946, during a meeting at UT between NAACP officials and UT officials, including President Theophilus Painter and Registrar E.J. Matthews, Sweatt presented his Wiley College transcript and requested admission to the law school. President Painter took the application, noted that Texas law required segregation, but promised to seek guidance from Texas Attorney General Grover Sellers. Painter's letter to Sellers noted that Sweatt was "duly qualified for admission . . . save and except for the fact that he is a negro." Sellers advised the university that Sweatt should not be admitted and lauded "the wise and long-continued policy of segregation of races in educational institutions of this state."[23]

In response, Sweatt sued the university in state district court. Judge Roy C. Archer held that if the state created a black law school "substantially equivalent" to that at UT, he would dismiss Sweatt's suit. UT and Texas A&M cooperated in cobbling together a law school at Prairie View. This was just a holding action to allow the legislature to create a whole new institution—the Texas State University for Negroes (TSUN)—complete with a law school; actually a single classroom for law courses. State appellate courts upheld Judge Archer's decision, so the plaintiffs removed the case to the federal courts. As the case proceeded into and through the federal court system, Texas raced to build out its TSUN Law School, but in June 1950 the U.S. Supreme Court held that barring blacks from the far more established, prestigious, and networked UT Law School was a violation of Sweatt's Fourteenth Amendment right to "equal protection of the laws." When the fall semester of 1950 opened at UT, Heman Sweatt and 16 other blacks registered for graduate coursework at the university. That the legislature's interest in TSUN was merely tactical was made clear when Sweatt won; the legislature immediately cut TSUN's budget by almost 40 percent.[24] TSUN did survive, however, and today is Texas Southern University. Its law school now bears the name of NAACP litigator and Supreme Court Justice Thurgood Marshall. Sweatt never completed his law degree but he cleared the way for many who came later.

While newly elected state officials, including Governor Allen Shivers and Attorney General John Ben Shepperd, counseled resistance, UT and other higher education institutions around the state prepared for broader integration. The landmark U.S. Supreme Court decision in *Brown v. Board of Education*, handed down on May 17, 1954, set off more rapid change among colleges and universities than it did among the public elementary and secondary schools at which it was aimed. In the mid-1950s, a dozen public junior and senior colleges in Texas opened their doors to blacks, many under the threat of lawsuits, but it was UT, also under legal threat, that led the way. On July 8, 1955, the UT Board of Regents voted to desegregate Texas Wesleyan University for the fall 1955 semester and the rest of the UT system, including the main campus at Austin, for fall 1956.[25]

At the same time that UT was opened to blacks, the regents ended the long-standing policy of open admissions and replaced it with a standardized entrance exam. The new exam proved a hurdle too high for 80 percent of black students and nearly half of white students applying for fall 1956 admissions. Texas public colleges and universities had been forced open, 110 blacks were scattered among the 18,000 students registering for classes in the fall of 1956, but only the most naive assumed that the battle had been won. UT President Logan Wilson and the regents were subject to a stream of invective over desegregation. As a result, it was not until 1964 that UT hired its first African-American faculty member, Dr. Ervin S. Perry, as a Professor of Civil Engineering. Integration of campus facilities, especially dorms, took even longer.

In the 1960s and 1970s, the Johnson and Nixon administrations, along with many Americans, took the view that affirmative action programs would be required to bring the previously excluded into the social, economic, and academic mainstreams. In 1978, the U.S. Supreme Court said in *Regents of the University of California v. Bakke* that while universities could not set aside specific slots for minorities—no quotas—they could consider race and the educational value of racial diversity in the admissions process and decision. Texas universities, some more energetically than others, did act affirmatively and in 1983 the state initiated the first of several Equal Education Opportunity Programs to improve minority enrollment and degree completion.

The challenge was not long in coming and it came again in the courts. In 1992, Cheryl Hopwood, a white applicant to the UT Law School, sued when she was denied admission. She had better law school admission test scores (LSATs) than "36 of the 43 Hispanics and 16 of the 18 blacks admitted."[26] The race-conscious UT Law School admissions process was upheld by the federal district court, but the U.S. Fifth Circuit Court of Appeals overturned the district court and supported Hopwood's contention that race could not constitutionally be used as a factor in admissions. The Supreme Court refused to hear UT's appeal, leaving the Fifth Circuit Court's opinion in force in Texas, Louisiana, and Mississippi, though not nationally. UT's President Robert Berdahl worried that the Hopwood decision would lead to "the virtual resegregation of higher education" in Texas. Concern spread beyond the higher education community, leading the Texas Legislature to pass the 10 percent rule. The rule mandated that the top 10 percent of each high school graduating class in the state be granted admission to the state's public universities. Because so many Texas high schools are heavily one race—Anglo, black, or Hispanic—the top 10 percent rule fostered diversity in admissions without being overtly race conscious.

In 2003, Hopwood was overturned when the U.S. Supreme Court decided in *Grutter v. Bollinger*, often simply called the Michigan case, that universities across the country, including those within the jurisdiction of the Fifth Circuit, could use race as one among many factors in admissions. UT and other public colleges and universities proceeded to add race as a factor in admissions in addition to the top 10 percent cohort in order, they said, to assure a critical mass of minority students in the state's institutions of higher education. Over the years, the top 10 percent rule was reduced to the top 7 percent rule at UT to give administrators more flexibility in crafting the university's incoming class each year. Other Texas public colleges and universities continue under the 10 percent rule.

Finally, in 2008, Abigail Fisher, an unsuccessful white applicant to UT, sued on the argument that the top 10 percent rule had been so successful that the university should be barred from using race in its other admissions decisions. *Fisher v. Texas* got to the U.S. Supreme Court for the first time in 2012. Proponents of affirmative action saw it as a great threat. Lee Bollinger, president of Columbia University and former president of Michigan, hence a named party in the Michigan case, *Grutter v. Bollinger*, worried that *Fisher v. Texas* "threatened to undo several decades of effort within higher education to build a more integrated and just and educationally enriched environment."[27] UT narrowly prevailed when the high court announced its decision in 2013. But Abigail Fisher appealed and over the next three years she and UT fought another round. Finally, in 2016, the U.S. Supreme Court upheld the university's right to consider race in its admissions decisions, so long as race-neutral means had been exhausted and the use of race was "narrowly tailored" to achieve the university's educational objectives.

Both populist suspicion of government spending and the vestiges of past racial animus continue to affect higher education in Texas today. In the following sections we turn to data to compare Texas to national rates for state funding for higher education, tuition and fees, college attendance, and completion. We look at the admissions and degree completion data by race and ethnicity and we close with a discussion of whether the schools that Texas Anglos, blacks, Hispanics, and Asians attend vary by quality. What is your guess?

State Funding of Higher Education in Texas

Historically, public funding for Texas institutions of higher education has come from two sources; about 90 percent has come from General Fund appropriations, with the remainder coming from the Permanent University Fund (PUF). State appropriations, until very recently, always tracked well below the national average for state support of public higher education and, for most of that time, the PUF provided only modest additional support. Before saying more about the history of General Fund appropriations, we need to tell the story of PUF because it is distinctive nationally.

Texas declared its independence from Mexico in 1836 and in 1839 the Republic's second president, Mirabeau B. Lamar, advised the legislature to set aside, in addition to land for the campuses themselves, large swaths of West Texas land to support higher education. Eventually, a total of 2.1 million acres were set aside, the proceeds of which were to support what came to be the University of Texas at Austin. Throughout the nineteenth century, there was so much open land in Texas that it had little value. In 1900, Texas received just $40,000 in grazing fees on its 2.1 million acres, but in 1919 the PUF was opened to oil and, later, natural gas exploration. The Santa Rita #1 strike in 1923 began a flow of royalty payments that supplement General Fund appropriations to higher education in Texas.

Initially, the PUF was dedicated to the support of UT, but in 1930 it was decided to divide PUF funds, two-thirds to UT and one-third to TAMU. In 1984, voters ratified a constitutional amendment that gave other schools in the UT and TAMU systems access to PUF funds, though the bulk of those funds still go to the main campuses of those systems. Despite the romantic history and undeniable importance of PUF funds to the UT and TAMU systems, their life's blood still comes from the state's General Fund appropriation.[28]

Prior to the mid-1930s, state appropriations were made to each campus as need and politics seemed to dictate. However, in 1937, the SBOE set up a per student (really a per full-time equivalent or FTE) appropriation model that exists to this day. The initial

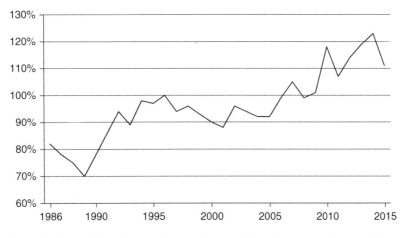

Figure 6.1 Texas Higher Education Appropriations per FTE as Percentage of Average State
Appropriations, 1986–2015

Source: U.S. Census, *Statistical Abstract of the United States*, "State and Local Financial Support for Post-Secondary Education by State," 1986–2015, various table numbers, www.census.gov/library/publications/time-series/statistical_abstracts.html.

appropriation was $225 per full-time upper level student and $175 per full-time lower level student. A decade later, the appropriation was raised to $306 for upper level students and $238 for lower level students.[29] By the mid-1950s, the average appropriation per FTE had risen to $400, almost $1,000 by 1970, and more than $2,500 by 1980.

Nationally comparable figures for higher education funding per FTE student by states became available in 1986 (see Figure 6.1). From 1986 through 2005, Texas state funding for higher education trailed the national average, initially by a lot, later by a little, until Texas broke above the national average in 2006, where it has remained since. Not surprisingly, the price of oil and gas has a great deal to do with the state's economic health, state government revenues, and the growth of the PUF. When prices are high, the PUF is growing and state appropriators are confident.[30] When prices are low, as they were from early 1986 through 2005, remaining below $40 a barrel for oil, Texas higher education suffers. But in 2005, prices broke above $60 a barrel, peaking in 2008 above $125, and remaining generally above $100 a barrel into mid-2014 when it began to drop like a rock, reaching $28 in early 2016 and ranging between $40 and $50 for the rest of the year.

The importance of PUF and related revenues was highlighted in a study by the LBB for the 2017 legislative session, entitled "Financing Higher Education in Texas: Legislative Primer." The study charted the growth of legislative General Fund appropriations and of "Other Funds," mostly made up of PUF funds, to higher education between 2000–01 and 2016–17. General Revenue funds were $9.3 billion in 2000–01 and $12.2 billion in 2016–17, an increase of 31 percent. Other Funds rose from $2.8 billion in 2000–01 to $8 billion in 2012–13, an increase of 186 percent. Other Funds accounted for 38 percent of higher education funding in 2012–13. But Texas's supercharged higher education funding slowed markedly with the collapse in the price of oil in the second half of 2014. In 2016–17, the General Fund appropriation remained flat at $12.2 billion, but Other Funds, mostly PUF, fell by 70 percent to $2.3 billion. The decline in PUF funds has just begun to show up in Figure 6.1, but there are good reasons to believe that state funding of higher education will continue to decline at least for the next several years. As the 2017 legislative session pondered cuts to higher education and especially to student financial aid, Texas Commissioner of Higher Education Raymund Paredes called for a reinvention of the state's higher education funding levels and formulaes.[31]

Tuition and Fees in Texas Higher Education

For most of the history of higher education in Texas, the "statutory" tuition rate was set by the state legislature, though the institutions were allowed to set additional "designated" tuition rates for high-cost programs, initially called "building use fees," of no more than the statutory rates. Hence, Texas tuition and fees were rarely as low as lore has suggested, but they were very low by national standards even into the early twenty-first century.[32] As the twentieth century opened, tuition at UT was free and room and board was just $13.50 a month. During the 1930s and 1940s, tuition at UT was $30 per semester and other four-year institutions in the state were near that, some a little higher and some a little lower.[33] In the mid-1950s, as the post-war enrollment boom began to ebb, tuition was raised to $4 per credit hour, $60 per semester for a 15-hour load, and held there until 1985. Even at this level, tuition accounted for just 16 percent of the cost of education at UT in the mid-1950s and by 1984 that had declined to 3 percent. State appropriations made up most of the rest.

In 1985, the 69th legislative session raised tuition from $4 to $12 per credit hour and subsequent legislatures raised it further, to $22 per credit hour in 1993 and $42 in 2001.[34] At $12 per credit hour, a full 15-hour semester load cost $180; at $22 it cost $330, and at $42 it cost $630. Even with fees added to the student bill, Texas college costs remained remarkably low and well below the national average into the early twenty-first century—but that was about to change.

In 2003, the Texas Legislature, always loath to bring bad news, such as tuition increases, to constituents, especially those who vote, passed control of tuition rates to the higher education governing boards. Almost immediately the politicians began decrying tuition increases and pushing back against the governing boards that authorized them. Even studies that showed clearly that tuition rose faster during the years the legislature set them than in the years the governing boards set them did not deter such as Lieutenant Governor Dan Patrick who noted, disingenuously, that Democrats had been in charge back then and Republicans were now.[35] Some have called for the legislature to take back tuition control but that is unlikely to happen because politicians immensely prefer criticizing tuition increases proposed by others to justifying and explaining tuition increases they have mandated.[36]

There are several good sources of data on tuition levels over time by state that allow Texas to be compared to other states and to the national average, but none go back much before the late 1960s (see Figure 6.2). All show the same pattern and trajectory; very low tuition rising toward the national average. The longest data trail we have comparing Texas tuition to the national average, though there are gaps to work through, comes from the Southern Regional Education Board (SREB). The SREB *Fact Book* and its predecessor publication on Southern Higher Education provide scattered data back to 1967–68 and complete data from 1992–93 to the present. In 1967–68, average annual tuition at four-year institutions in Texas was $171, or 57 percent of the $302 national average. By 1980, Texas tuition was $364, just 49 percent of the national average of $738. By 1984, Texas had dropped to 42 percent of the national average and the legislature decided to move. As noted above, the legislature increased tuition from $4 to $12 per credit hour, which brought Texas to 55 percent of the national average, and then left

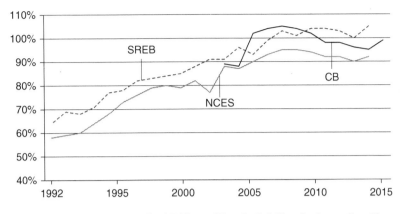

Figure 6.2 Texas Median Annualized Tuition and Fees for Full-Time Students at Four-Year Schools as a Percentage of the National Average, 1992–2015

Source: Southern Regional Education (SREB), *Fact Book on Higher Education 2015*, www.sreb.org/fact-book-higher-education-0. National Center for Education Statistics (NCES), *Digest of Education Statistics 2015*, https://nces.ed.gov/programs/digest/d13/tables/dt13_104.85.asp. College Board, Trends in College Pricing, https://trends.collegeboard.org/college-pricing/figures-tables/tuition-fees-sector-state-over-time.

it nearly alone into the early 1990s. Texas breached 70 percent of the national average in 1995–96, 80 percent in 1998–99, and 90 percent in 2003–04, the year that the legislature voted to turn tuition control over to the college and university boards.

The best national numbers come from the U.S. Department of Education's National Center for Education Statistics (NCES), but the state-by-state numbers go back only to 1990. The data show that Texas tuition rates for four-year public universities were 54 percent of the national average in 1990; $959 per semester compared to a U.S. average of $1,781. Texas tuition rates rose quickly against the national average, reaching 60 percent by 1995 and 80 percent by 2001. According to these data, the Texas tuition rate was about 82 percent of the national average when the legislature turned control over to the university boards and it rose into the mid-90s before falling back, under political pressure, to 92 percent in 2015, the last year of available data.

Finally, College Board, the organization that administers the SAT college entrance exams, agreed with SREB that tuition kept rising once the university system boards were in charge, reaching the national average in the mid-2000s. The SREB reports that Texas tuition and fees were above the national average in each year from 2008–09 through 2014–15 when they stood at 105 percent of the national average. College Board reports that Texas tuition and fees were above the national average from 2006–07 through 2010–11 and have remained in the high 90s since. In any event, the data make clear that as late as the mid-1980s Texas tuition was less than half the national average and for more than a decade it has been near, at, and sometimes above the national average. It rose both under the legislature and the boards, but it rose faster and further under the legislature, until, in a transparent blame-avoidance maneuver, they tossed the responsibility to the boards—the better to join parents in decrying tuition increases. The 2017 legislative session opened with calls from the Texas Senate for a four-year tuition freeze. So it goes. Nonetheless, whoever pays for higher education, the state legislature or students and their parents, what we really want to know is how much education is being bought and how good it is. We turn to those questions now.

Higher Education Enrollment in Texas

Texans have never been taken with the suspiciously abstract idea of academic excellence in their colleges and universities. More important has been that the state's institutions of higher education be inexpensive. Generations of Texans, as we saw above, attended college for a few hundred dollars a year and charges did not exceed one thousand dollars a year until the early 1990s. Yet, even when tuition and fees were low, fewer young Texans pursued a college education than did their peers in the rest of the nation. Even more sadly, during the 1960s and 1970s when Texas lore has it that Governors John Connally and Dolph Briscoe poured money into higher education, Texas enrollment fell steadily against the national average for college enrollment.[37]

In raw numbers, the growth in enrollment at Texas colleges and universities has been impressive. In 1900, Texas had just 5,302 students attending college in the state, by 1930 it was 40,646, and by 1950 it was just over 125,000. Today, more than 1.6 million students pursue higher education in Texas colleges and universities. However, when one looks at the proportion of students attending college in Texas compared to the proportion nationally, a different picture emerges. Figure 6.3 shows that except for a brief period around 1950, much as with Texas public elementary and secondary schools, a smaller proportion of Texas students than U.S. students were in college. Over the past six decades, college enrollment rates in Texas have averaged about 93 percent of national rates and there has been no appreciable improvement over time. Since 2000, only 90 Texans have been enrolled in college for every one hundred of their peers nationally.

Another way to demonstrate that Texas has long lagged in college attendance is to plot Texas's percentage of the total U.S. population and Texas's share of the total pool of U.S. college attendees. As we see again in Figure 6.4, during the 1950s Texas had a larger share of U.S. college students attending its universities than it had of the total

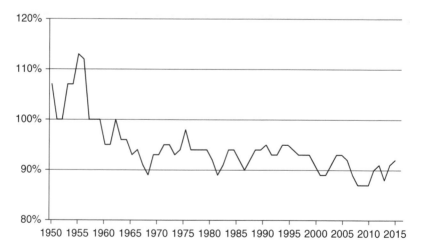

Figure 6.3 Texas Rate of College Attendance as a Percentage of U.S. College Attendance Rate, 1950–2015

Source: U.S. Census Bureau, *Statistical Abstract of the United States,* each year, 1951–2015, "Institutions of Higher Education, Total Enrollment by State," www.census.gov/library/publications/time-series/statistical_abstracts.html. See also NCES, "Total Fall Enrollment in Degree Granting Post-Secondary Institutions," Table 304.10. https://nces.ed.gov/programs/digest/d13/tables/dt13_304.10.asp.

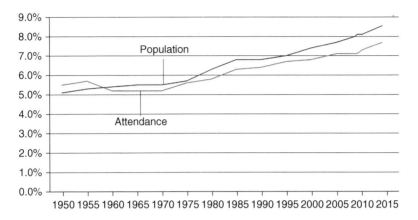

Figure 6.4 Texas Population and College Attendance as a Percentage of U.S. Population and College Attendance, 1950–2013

Source: U.S. Census Bureau, *Statistical Abstract of the United States,* each year, 1951–2015, "Resident Population—States," and "Institutions of Higher Education, Total Enrollment by State." www.census.gov/library/publications/time-series/statistical_abstracts.html. See also NCES, "Total Fall Enrollment in Degree Granting Post-Secondary Institutions," Table 304.10. https://nces.ed.gov/programs/digest/d13/tables/dt13_304.10.asp.

U.S. population. In the mid-1950s, just as *Brown v. Board of Education* led Texas legislators to reduce funding of public schools, Texas levels of college attendance began to fall against the national average and they have never recovered. By 1960, Texas had a larger share of the U.S. population than it did of U.S. college students and it has tracked below the national average ever since, never more so than in the years since 2000.

As Texas college enrollment rates lagged behind national averages and those of other large states, something like populist panic set in. Governor Rick Perry called in 2011 for "high quality, low cost" bachelor's degree programs costing no more than $10,000, books included, over four years. No public university in Texas offered a four-year degree for under $10,000 in tuition and fees, to say nothing of books, when Perry made his challenge—the closest was Texas A&M University at Texarkana at $18,584. Perry thought that web-based instruction, innovative teaching techniques, and "aggressive efficiency measures" made a cheap, high-quality, degree possible. Few beyond the circle of Perry appointees agreed, but not many higher education leaders scoffed publicly. A few smaller public four-year institutions, some teaming with local community colleges, proposed programs, but concern that quality would be sacrificed to price ran deep. One hears nothing of this initiative today.

Also in 2011, Gene Powell, then the chairman of the UT Board of Regents, circulated a memo suggesting that UT undergraduate enrollments be increased 10 percent a year for four years and tuition be slashed by 50 percent. Finally, he proposed the goal of making UT, Austin, the nation's number one public university.[38] University officials and legislators, including Senate Higher Education Committee chair Judith Zaffirini, responded with incredulity; Zaffirini said, "How in the world can we pursue a goal of making the University of Texas at Austin the No. 1 public university in the nation while funding is being slashed? And he wants to reduce tuition by half? And increase enrollment by 10 percent per year? It's ludicrous."[39]

Ludicrous seems such a harsh word. Better simply to say that Regent Powell's first attempt at pie-in-the-sky public policy pronouncements went somewhat awry. But readers might pause just briefly to ask themselves whether Regent Powell's proposals were really more pie-in-the-sky improbable, more ludicrous, than Governor Perry's call for a $10,000 bachelor's degree or Governor Abbott's campaign declaration that we "must" see that Texas public universities occupy five of the top ten spots among public universities nationally. Objectively, the Perry, Abbott, and Powell proposals seem similarly ludicrous; so why did Perry and Abbott draw admiration for their bold vision while Powell drew derision. It is all in knowing your audience. In elective politics, once it is clear that you will not raise taxes or more than marginally increase spending, you are free to make any promises you like; in fact, the bolder the better—why not, come to think of it, an $8,000 bachelor's degree or seven of the top ten public university spots. But when you are a UT regent, the public is not listening, just the humorless professionals are paying attention; the professors, administrators, and legislators, and they can be rude.

NCES data make clear that while overall attendance has continued to lag national numbers, the racial mix of Texas college students has changed dramatically over the past quarter century. As Table 6.1 so clearly shows, Anglo dominance of Texas public colleges and universities has markedly declined while minority presence has increased.

Table 6.1 Texas Higher Education Enrollment by Race and Ethnicity

	% White	% Black	% Hispanic
1988	70.5	8.9	14.8
1989	69.5	8.9	15.7
1990	68.5	8.9	16.5
1991	67.2	9.2	17.1
1992	65.7	9.5	18.0
1993	64.7	9.5	18.7
1994	63.1	9.8	19.5
1995	62.0	9.8	20.5
1996	60.9	9.9	21.2
1997	60.1	10.1	21.7
1998	59.0	10.4	22.2
1999	57.9	10.7	22.7
2000	56.5	10.9	23.6
2001	55.6	11.2	23.7
2002	54.6	11.7	24.1
2003	53.5	12.0	24.9
2004	52.5	12.3	25.7
2005	52.0	12.4	26.2
2006	50.9	12.5	26.9
2007	49.7	12.6	27.6
2008	48.8	12.8	28.4
2009	47.2	13.3	29.7
2010	45.1	13.6	30.7
2011	44.8	14.6	33.0
2012	43.4	14.3	34.4
2013	42.2	14.1	35.4
2014	41.1	14.2	36.0

Source: NCES, "Fall Enrollment . . . by Race/Ethnicity . . . and State," Table 306.70. https://nces.ed.gov/programs/digest/d16/tables/dt16_306.70.asp

In 1988, the first year for which we have good data from NCES, Anglos filled a little over 70 percent of the seats in Texas public higher education, blacks almost 9 percent and Hispanics almost 15 percent. Stunningly, in every year but one between 1988 and 2014, the percentage of seats filled by Anglos declined, falling below 60 percent in 1998, below 50 percent in 2007, and resting at 41 percent in 2014. Almost as consistently, the proportion of blacks attending Texas colleges and universities, just under 9 percent in 1988, held steady or rose in every year, reaching 14.6 in 2011, before falling back slightly to 14.2 percent in 2014. Even more remarkably, the Hispanic share of seats increased every single year between 1988 and 2014, rising from 14.8 in 1988 to 36 percent in 2014.

Part of this, of course, is baked in the demographic cake. For decades, the number of college age Anglos has been flat, while black numbers have risen a little and Hispanic numbers have risen a lot, so the minority share of college and university seats had to rise. But as they rose, state appropriations have decreased while tuition and fees have sharply increased, putting ever more intense pressure on families often unable to bear it. Not surprisingly, overall attendance numbers have languished.

Educational Attainment in Texas

Texas matched the nation in college completion, what the census and demographers generally call educational attainment, from the 1950s through the 1980s. However, for the past quarter century Texas has fallen steadily behind. The best data available for educational attainment for the U.S. by race and ethnicity come from the U.S. Census and from the Department of Education's NCES. Data for the U.S. go back to 1950 and is complete for 1985 through the present. Data for the states, including Texas, are not as complete. We have only six years of data between 1987 and 2005, but complete data from 2006 to the present. Fortunately, the data on educational attainment change slowly and in one direction, so we can get a pretty clear picture even with limited data (see Table 6.2).

Table 6.2 Educational Attainment: College Graduates as a Percentage of U.S. and Texas Adults over 25

	U.S.	%	%	%	Texas	%	%	%
	Total	White	Black	Hispanic	Total	White	Black	Hispanic
1950	6.2	6.6	2.2		6.0			
1960	7.7	8.1	3.5		8.0			
1970	11.0	11.6	6.1		11.0			
1975	13.9	14.9	6.4	6.6				
1980	17.0	18.4	7.9	7.6	16.0			
1985	19.4	20.8	11.1	8.5				
1986	19.4	20.9	10.9	8.4				
1987	19.9	21.4	10.8	8.6	20.0	20.0	11.0	7.5
1988	20.3	21.8	11.2	10.0	21.5	22.5	11.0	9.0
1989	21.1	22.8	11.7	9.9	22.0	23.0	11.0	8.0
1990	21.3	23.1	11.3	9.2	20.3	22.6	12.0	7.3
1991	21.4	23.3	11.5	9.7				
1992	21.4	23.2	11.9	9.3				

(continued)

Table 6.2 (continued)

	U.S.	%	%	%	Texas	%	%	%
	Total	White	Black	Hispanic	Total	White	Black	Hispanic
1993	21.9	23.8	12.2	9.0				
1994	22.2	24.3	12.9	9.1				
1995	23.0	25.4	13.3	9.3				
1996	23.6	25.9	13.8	9.3				
1997	23.9	26.2	13.3	10.3	22.0	22.5	16.9	9.0
1998	24.4	26.6	14.8	11.0				
1999	25.2	27.7	15.5	10.9				
2000	26.6	28.1	16.6	10.6	23.2	25.8	15.3	8.9
2001	26.1	28.6	16.1	11.2				
2002	26.7	29.4	17.2	11.1				
2003	27.2	30.0	17.4	11.4				
2004	27.7	30.6	17.7	12.1				
2005	27.7	30.6	17.6	12.0				
2006	28.0	31.0	18.6	12.4	24.7	32.4	18.0	10.3
2007	28.7	31.8	18.7	12.7	24.8	32.6	17.6	10.4
2008	29.4	32.6	19.7	13.3	25.1	33.0	18.2	10.7
2009	29.5	32.9	19.4	13.2	25.6	33.7	18.3	11.0
2010	29.9	33.2	20.0	13.9	25.8	33.7	19.2	11.4
2011	30.4	34.0	20.2	14.1	26.5	35.0	20.2	12.0
2012	30.9	34.5	21.4	14.5	26.9	35.6	20.9	12.1
2013	31.7	35.2	22.0	15.1	27.5	35.8	22.3	12.4
2014	32.0	35.6	22.8	15.2	27.9	36.4	21.9	13.0

Source: U.S. Census Bureau, Statistical Abstract of the United States, each year 1950 through 2015, "Persons 25 and Over, Years of School Completed by State," and NCES, "Educational Attainment," Table 104.85. See online at: www.census.gov/library/publications/time-series/statistical_abstracts.html and https://nces.ed.gov/programs/digest/d16/tables/dt16_104.85.asp.

In 1990, 21.3 percent of Americans and 20.3 percent of Texans over 25 years old held a bachelor's degree or better. White and black Texans were within a fraction of 1 percent of their national peers, whites trailed by half a point, blacks led by seven-tenths of a point, while Hispanics lagged by about two points. By 2000, 26.6 percent of Americans and 23.2 percent of Texans had BAs and all three racial and ethnic groups trailed their national peers; whites trailed by a little more than two points, blacks by 1.3 percent, and Hispanics by 1.7 percent. By 2006, Texas had fallen further behind the nation, 28 percent to 24.7 percent, but Anglo Texans had caught and passed their national peers. In every year since 2006, Texas Anglos have led whites nationally by about a point. Black Texans have been right with their national peers, trailing more often than not, but usually by no more than a point and occasionally nudging ahead. Texas Hispanics have uniformly trailed their national peers by two to two-and-one-half points.

Just as interestingly, the proportion of Texas Anglos, blacks, and Hispanics with four-year degrees have all increased. Anglos increased from 22.6 percent in 1990 to 36.4 percent in 2014, a total increase of 13.8 percent. The proportion of black Texans with four-year degrees increased from 12 percent to 21.9 percent, an increase of almost 10 percent. Hispanic Texans with BAs increased from 7.3 percent to 13 percent, an increase of 5.7 percent. Another way to say this is that for the past quarter century, the share of the black adult population with a BA has risen from 53 percent to about 60 percent of the white share and the Hispanic share has held steady at about 35 percent of the white share. Given the demographic changes taking place in Texas, the declining proportion of Anglos and the increasing proportion of Hispanics, the failure of Hispanics to thrive in regard to higher education is a major problem.

In 2014, Texas ranked 30th among the 50 states and D.C. on the proportion of residents with a bachelor's degree or better, at 27.9 percent compared to the national average of 32 percent. But not all Texans experience the same rates of success or failure in college. Race, ethnicity, and gender all make big differences in college completion. Just 56 percent of Texans attending public universities graduated in six years. While 65 percent of whites graduated in six years, only 45 percent of Hispanics and 36 percent of blacks did. Moreover, women graduated at higher rates than men in all racial and ethnic categories. Seventy-one percent of white women, compared to 61 percent of white men, graduated in six years. Fifty-one percent of Hispanic women and 42 percent of black women, compared to 41 percent of Hispanic men and 29 percent of black men, graduated in six years.[40]

Closing the Gaps: The Texas Higher Education Plan

In the face of languishing numbers, Texas higher education officials have been active, but largely on their own. In October 2000, the Texas Higher Education Coordinating Board (THECB) adopted *Closing the Gaps, 2000–2015: The Texas Higher Education Plan. Closing the Gaps* sheepishly admitted that "Although the Texas educational system is reasonably successful, there is room for improvement. In comparison to California, New York, Florida, and other large states, Texas falls short in higher education enrollment rates, degrees awarded, federal research funding and nationally recognized programs."[41] *Closing the Gaps* was a 15-year plan to improve "participation, success, excellence, and research" in Texas higher education. The plan's title highlighted the overarching goal of bringing minority participation and success up to Anglo levels and promoting progress from there for all Texans. The two goals of most concern were minority college attendance and degree completion. Improvements were made on both but targets were not always met.

Participation or attendance is easily measurable; NCES reported that 1,033,973 attended Texas colleges and universities in 2000 and THECB proposed to add 630,000 by 2015. They claimed to nearly meet their goal, adding 605,000, but NCES reported the somewhat lower number of 1,555,462, an increase of 50.4 percent. During that same 15-year period, the Texas population grew by 31 percent, from almost 21 million to nearly 27.5 million, so college attendance growth comfortably outstripped population growth. But *Closing the Gaps* envisioned more than simply increased attendance, it envisioned equalizing attendance across racial and ethnic groups in Texas. While black Texans increased college attendance numbers well beyond the targets projected in 2000 for 2015, Hispanic and Anglo Texans fell short of their targets. Hispanics, where much of the focus of increased attendance rested, increased from 244,492 in 2000 to about 550,000 in 2015, still nearly 109,000 short of the goal. More surprisingly, given Texas history and the state's class structure, Anglo attendance has languished since 2000. As the *Closing the Gaps: Final Progress Report* noted in June 2016, "White enrollment fell for the sixth straight year and the increase since fall 2000 of 31,468 students was far below the target of 101,248."[42] So, despite the generally upbeat tone of the final report, the hope in 2000 had been to grow college attendance among all racial and ethnic groups, especially Hispanics. To have fallen short of the goal among Hispanics and to have seen Anglo attendance lag over the course of a decade and a half was disappointing.

But digging below the top line numbers highlights many areas of worry and doubt. Two of these worries raise particular concerns; where minority students go to college and how many actually graduate. In 2016, though 14.2 percent of Texas college students were black, only 4 percent of students at UT and 3 percent at Texas A&M were black. Texas Tech and UT-Dallas were at 6 percent, UH at 11 percent, and UT-Arlington at 15 percent. Prairie View and Texas Southern, two historically black schools, remain 86 and 82 percent black, respectively. UT, Rio Grande and UT, Brownsville were 91 and 90 percent Hispanic and UT, El Paso and Texas A&M, Kingsville were 82 and 68 percent Hispanic. To have so many minority students clustered in some of the newest and weakest Texas colleges and universities is cause for worry, if not for surprise.

Texas higher education did meet the relatively modest goals set in 2000 for degree completion. In fact, the overall target of 221,000 Bachelor's, Associate's, or certificates was reached in 2011 and continued growing to 258,795 by 2015. By 2015, Hispanics had increased their share of BAs from 18.5 percent in 2000 to 30 percent in 2015. Blacks had increased their share from 7.4 percent to 10.7 percent. Nonetheless, six-year graduation rates in Texas colleges and universities continue to lag for Hispanics and blacks. Forty-one percent of African Americans, 51.1 percent of Hispanics, 67.7 percent of Anglos, and 73.6 percent of Asians who began their full-time higher education in 2009 had earned a degree or certificate by 2015.

Table 6.3 makes starkly clear that Anglo Texans go disproportionately to prestigious schools that cost more, but that have higher graduation rates and higher salaries for graduates ten years out. Among Texas private colleges and universities, the pattern is clear; Anglo and Asian students attend the best schools at rates well above their presence in the population and black and Hispanic students attend them at rates well below their presence in the population. St. Edwards, the only private on the list with a plurality Hispanic student body is the only school on the list with a six-year graduation rate under 70 percent, though it is still a very respectable 68 percent. But only 10 percent of Texas college students attend private institutions, so what about the publics?

The top Texas public universities also are expensive, if only because many of their students do not qualify for as much aid as do poorer students, though not as expensive as the privates. They have higher graduation rates, better post-graduation salaries, and they have mostly Anglo and Asian student bodies. Only the University of Houston has an Hispanic plurality and a broadly diverse student body. Middle-tier regional state universities such as Sam Houston, Tarleton State, and Stephen F. Austin, have lower graduation rates and lower post-graduation average incomes. But it is the newer regional universities in the Valley, as well as the historically black universities, that have the lowest graduation rates and post-graduation incomes and so suggest the modern face of limited opportunity, if not segregation. Think about Merced and ask why not in Texas!

Despite some gains, other significant problems, some grown worse in recent years, remain to be solved—reduced student aid and, not unrelated, increased student debt among them. The Texas Grant financial aid program was initiated in 1999 to help poor students afford college. To be eligible, students had to take a college prep curriculum and be from a family making less than $45,000 a year. High school grades and university admissions test scores were not taken into account. The Texas Grants were need-based rather than merit-based and awarded an average of $7,000 a year. The Great Recession of 2008–09 hit the Texas budget hard in 2011 and beyond.

Table 6.3 Cost, Quality, Race, and Ethnicity among Major Texas Universities

University	No. of Undergrad. Students	Average Annual Cost[a]	Grad. Rate (%)[b]	Salary after Grad.[c]	% White	% Black	% Hispanic	% Asian
Private Universities								
Rice	3,888	$16,466	91	$64,500	38	7	15	23
Trinity	2,223	$23,781	81	$54,000	56	4	18	6
SMU	6,340	$32,128	78	$54,600	66	5	12	7
TCU	8,600	$32,932	76	$50,000	74	5	11	3
Baylor	13,801	$32,741	73	$48,200	64	7	14	6
Austin Coll.	1,272	$21,498	74	$47,800	56	7	19	14
Southwestern	1,536	$23,633	72	$47,400	65	5	19	3
St. Edwards	3,991	$19,358	68	$44,200	38	4	40	3
Public Universities								
UT, Austin	38,914	$17,152	80	$53,000	46	4	22	19
Texas A&M	46,941	$11,315	79	$53,900	66	3	21	5
UT, Dallas	14,300	$12,050	67	$49,700	39	6	18	28
Texas Tech	28,278	$15,315	59	$47,500	61	6	22	3
Houston	31,643	$13,028	48	$48,900	27	11	31	22
Texas State, San Marcos	32,177	$13,363	56	$43,400	51	8	33	2
UTA	29,616	$13,790	41	$45,900	41	15	24	11
Texas Woman's	9,327	$8,855	43	$44,600	41	21	25	8
UTSA	23,815	$11,867	31	$43,100	26	9	51	5
UT, Permian	3,311	$6,900	30	$42,600	41	7	47	2
UNT	29,758	$10,856	50	$42,300	49	12	21	6
TAMU, Corpus	9,074	$14,165	39	$41,200	38	6	48	2
Sam Houston	16,819	$12,237	52	$41,100	54	19	19	1
Tarleton St.	10,214	$15,210	44	$40,600	71	8	16	1
UTEP	19,614	$6,984	39	$39,100	7	3	83	1
S.F. Austin	10,692	$19,556	43	$39,100	57	22	15	1
West TAMU	7,121	$12,028	40	$39,900	62	25	6	1
Lamar	9,043	$14,319	34	$39,500	49	28	13	4
UT, Tyler	5,550	$13,016	44	$42,200	59	9	16	3
UT, Rio Gr.	17,811	$2,840	41	$39,600	3	1	91	1
Prairie View	6,905	$9,583	37	$34,100	4	86	3	2
Angelo State	5,290	$12,717	30	$37,700	52	8	32	1
TAMU, Kingsville	8,815	$11,924	35	$38,800	20	7	68	1
TAMU, Commerce	7,358	$9,263	48	$36,900	51	21	16	2
TSU	6,880	$18,023	16	$30,500	2	82	6	2
UT, Brownsville	9,973	$6,425	27	$29,100	4	1	90	1

Source: U.S. Department of Education, "College Scorecard," Accessed January 2, 2017 from http://collegescorecard.ed.gov/

Notes:

a   Average Annual Cost: Average annual net price for federal financial aid recipients, after aid from the school, state, or federal government.

b   Graduation Rate: Proportion of first-time, full-time, students graduating within six years of starting.

c   Salary after Graduation: Median earnings of former students after ten years.

The 2011 Texas Legislature cut $17 billion out of state spending for 2012–13 and higher education was not spared. The legislature entertained proposals to reduce the total appropriation for Texas Grants by up to 43 percent and to make the awards merit-based rather than need-based. A late compromise cut total funding by 27 percent, reducing the award from $7,000 to $5,000, and cutting nearly 40,000 students from the program's rolls in 2012–13.[43]

The Great Recession of 2008–09 hit students in Texas and the nation hard: tuition kept rising, states cut student aid, and student debt and default rates rose. In 2003–04, 51 percent of graduates from Texas four-year colleges and universities had an average debt of $17,170. A little more than ten years later, in 2014–15, the proportion of students graduating with debt had risen to 56 percent and the average debt had risen to $27,324.[44] Even more worrisome is that the default rate on student debt payments by Texas students are among the highest in the country and have been in every year since 1993. Experts point to the fact that Texas has a higher proportion of poor students and a lower proportion receiving state financial aid, leaving Texas students more dependent on federal loans.

These financial pressures motivated many other policy changes, some unfortunate, some just sad. As early as 2009, UT declared that it would withdraw from the National Merit Scholarship Program to focus its funds on need-based financial aid. Each year about 8,000 of the nation's top high school graduates are designated National Merit Scholars and universities compete to attract them. UT provided them with $13,000 annually for four years and in 2010 had 281 in its entering class, second only to Harvard with 285. In 2012, UT attracted just 57 National Merit Scholars. Clearly, many very high-achieving students are not merit scholars, but it is sad when financial stringency leads a great institution like UT to give up the competition for these top students.

Texas Community Colleges

While we have focused on Texas's flagship and four-year universities, more than half of college students in the state attend two-year community colleges. In 1990, Texas community colleges enrolled about 370,000 students. Enrollment crested at about 732,000 in 2011 and has been relatively flat since. In fall 2016, the state's 50 community college districts enrolled 732,281 students compared to 636,750 at the four-year public universities. Some community college systems rival in enrollment the flagship UT and TAMU campuses. The community college system in Texas is big, important, and under pressure.

As Table 6.4 makes clear, the community college system serves a majority minority student body. Among the largest community college systems in the state, only the suburban system in Collin County, north of Dallas, serves a majority Anglo student body. The Dallas County Community College system is racially mixed, with 27 percent Anglos, 25 percent black, and 34 percent Hispanics, and 9 percent Asians. In South Texas, the student body populations are majority Hispanic, but most are highly diverse. Not surprisingly, about half of students arriving at Texas community colleges are not prepared for college-level work in one or more areas. Many require non-credit remedial work, many struggle, and about one-third do not return after the first year.

These problems have been aggravated by reductions in state funding, forcing community college leaders to raise tuition and fees, seek local property tax increases, or cut classes and other services. Deep cuts to state support for higher education in 2011 led most community college districts to an all-of-the-above strategy: tuition and tax increases and reductions in services. In 2011, Austin Community College raised its

Table 6.4 Cost, Quality, Race, and Ethnicity among Major Community College Systems

Community College System	No. of Undergrad. Students	Average Annual Cost	% Grad. Rate	Salary after Grad.	% White	% Black	% Hispanic	% Asian
Private Universities								
San Jacinto CC	23,881	$7,605	15	$36,600	28	10	50	5
Collin CCC	24,532	$16,526	11	$36,200	51	13	19	9
Austin CC	32,581	$8,404	7	$34,400	44	8	32	5
Tarrant CCC	42,189	$5,453	10	$33,600	41	20	29	6
Lone Star	59,920	$5,631	10	$32,900	32	19	35	6
Houston CC	58,048	$9,646	11	$32,500	14	32	32	9
San Antonio College	17,944	$6,904	9	$29,700	27	6	60	3
Dallas CCC	68,705	$4,903	9	$34,100	27	25	34	9
South Texas College	17,710	$1,158	19	$27,800	3	1	94	1

Source: U.S. Department of Education, "College Scorecard," Accessed January 2, 2017 from http://collegescorecard. ed.gov/

tuition by $15 for each three-credit course, from $174 to $189; in 2012, Collin and Tarrant counties raised tuition by $9 for each three-credit course; and Dallas County raised both tuition and local property taxes. Districts all over the state made similar decisions; some noting that the state provided two-thirds of their budgets in 1980 and less than one-third now.[45]

Degree completion is a challenge for four-year colleges and universities and a huge challenge for community colleges. Only about 30 percent of community college students earn a degree or certificate within six years of beginning study, while about twice that proportion graduate from four-year schools within six years. At least as troubling is the fact that students who take 60 hours of course work and then transfer to a four-year school take an average of two years longer to graduate than students that started at a four-year school. Despite these issues and difficulties, many Texas families cannot afford the state's premier colleges and universities and so are dependent on the community colleges. The state owes these families and students a better deal than it has been giving them recently.

Conclusion

In the Texas way, soon-to-be-Governor Greg Abbott, during his 2014 campaign, called for Texas universities to win five of the top ten positions in the *U.S. News* annual rankings of public universities. Unacceptably, from the governor's perspective, California had 6 of the top 11 spots (two California campuses tied for tenth) and he wished—wished is the key word here—that Texas held those prestigious spots. However, no Texas public university has even been anywhere near the *U.S. News* top 10 and in 2017 university leaders faced a legislature determined to trim university and college budgets, freeze tuition for up to five years, and further limit student aid.[46] Governor Abbott remained silent, wishing, one supposes, that Texas public universities might magically appear among the top ten in future *U.S. News* rankings. They will not.

Early institutions of higher learning in Texas were private and these institutions opened and closed their doors with dizzying frequency. Not until after the Civil War and Reconstruction did the state found and fund two state universities—Texas A&M in 1876 and UT in 1882. Almost immediately, concerns arose among the people of the state and their elected representatives that these institutions were both expensive and dangerously elitist. Politicians felt, and feel today, that these public institutions should, in fact must, reflect and even reinforce public mores and values. When the pursuit of knowledge within the universities seemed too directly to clash with the received wisdom of the community, epic battles between the capital and the campuses resulted. Some of these battles, say between Governor Wilbert Lee "Pappy" O'Daniel and UT President Homer Rainey, are Texas legend. However, a similar pitched battle between Governor Rick Perry and his appointees and UT President Bill Powers is of recent memory.

The uncertain place of public universities within the state's culture and politics has, not surprisingly, adversely affected the growth, development, and future of these critical institutions. So too has the racial animus that characterized Texas society, politics, and policymaking for much of the state's history. Texas A&M was established in 1876 as a school for whites. Almost simultaneously, what became Prairie View A&M was established, under Texas A&M's administrative control, as a school for blacks. Prairie View remained the only public university in Texas open to blacks into the middle of the twentieth century. The mid-1940s battle by Heman Sweatt, backed by the NAACP, to open UT to blacks is both a noble and a dispiriting saga. Though Texas opened its universities to all races in the 1950s and 1960s, racial segregation remains evident in Texas higher education today.

Ambivalence toward its public universities has produced a familiar pattern. Texas state appropriations for higher education have traditionally been lower than those of other states, a smaller proportion of students have sought higher education than in most states, and fewer have earned degrees. While these deficiencies are more disturbing than surprising, more disturbing still has been the evasion of responsibility by state-elected officials for responsible management of university tuition and fees. Until 2003, the state legislature set tuition and fees. In 2003, they turned tuition-setting responsibilities over to the university governing boards, not because the boards had better information, but so that legislators could avoid the wrath of parents when tuition and fees were increased. Immediately, legislators became the biggest critics of tuition increases and positioned themselves as advocates of students and parents against the university boards and administrators. It is very difficult to see how Texas public universities can improve against their national peers, let alone how they can capture five of the top ten spots in the *U.S. News* rankings, without steady, long-term, thoughtful support—which they are not now getting.

Notes

1   Ralph K.M. Haurwitz, "Politics, Lack of Funding Hobble Texas Universities' Climb to Top Tier," *Austin American-Statesman*, January 24, 2015.
2   Frederick Law Olmstead, *A Journey through Texas*, originally published by New York: Dix, Edwards, 1857, DeGolyer Library and William P. Clements Center for Southwestern Studies, Dallas, TX: Southern Methodist University, 2004, p. 61. See also, William Ransom Hogan, *The Texas Republic: A Social and Economic History*, Norman, OK: University of Oklahoma Press, 1946, p. 152.
3   Randolph B. Campbell, *Gone to Texas: A History of the Lone Star State*, New York: Oxford University Press, 2003, pp. 229–230.
4   T.R. Fehrenbach, *Lone Star: A History of Texas and the Texans*, New York: Macmillan Publishing Company, 1968, p. 304. See also *The Handbook of Texas Online*, "Higher Education," www.tshaonline.org/handbook/online/articles/khhsr.

5   C.E. Evans, *The Story of Texas Schools*, Austin, TX: The Steck Company, 1955, p. 258.

6   Gary M. Lavergne, *Before Brown: Heman Marion Sweatt, Thurgood Marshall, and the Long Road to Justice*, Austin, TX: University of Texas Press, 2010, pp. 68–69. See also, James Reston, Jr., *The Lone Star: The Life of John Connally*, New York: Harper & Row, 1989, p. 14.

7   Anthony Champagne and Edward J. Harpham, eds., *Texas at the Crossroads: People, Politics, and Policy*, College Station, TX: Texas A&M University Press, 1987, p. 180. See also, Gerry Riposa, ed., *Texas Public Policy*, Dubuque, IO: Kendall/Hunt, 1987, p. 48.

8   John Gunther, *Inside U.S.A.*, New York: Harper & Brothers, 1947, p. 816.

9   Dwonna Goldstone, *Integrating the Forty Acres: The Fifty-Year Struggle for Racial Equality at the University of Texas*, Athens, GA: University of Georgia Press, 2012, p. 6; Laura Lyons McLemore, *Inventing Texas: Early Historians of the Lone Star State*, College Station, TX: Texas A&M University Press, 2004, p. 90.

10 Thomas D. Russell, "Keep the Negroes Out of Most Classes Where There Are a Large Number of Girls," pp. 6–7, https://papers.ssrn.com/sol3/papers.cfm?abstract_id=1583606.

11 In 2010, after a long and public dispute, UT removed Professor Simkins' name from one of its dorms. Ralph K.M. Haurwitz, "UT Weighs Renaming Dorm with KKK Tie," *Austin American-Statesman*, May 19, 2010. See also, Alfred L. Brophy, "The Law and Morality of Building Renaming," *South Texas Law Review*, vol. 52, pp. 37–67.

12 Goldstone, *Integrating the Forty Acres*, pp. 6–7. See also James L. Haley, *Passionate Nation: The Epic History of Texas*, New York: Free Press, 2006, pp. 467–468.

13 Campbell, *Gone to Texas*, pp. 350–351.

14 Patrick L. Cox and Michael Phillips, *The House Will Come to Order*, Austin, TX: University of Texas Press, 2010, p. 31.

15 Haley, *Passionate Nation*, p. 530.

16 Ralph K.M. Haurwitz, "UT Controversy Echoes Tradition of Hardball Politics," *Austin American-Statesman*, April 6, 2013. See also, Ronnie Duggar, *Our Invaded Universities: Form, Reform, and New Status*, New York: Norton, 1974; and Kenneth Ashworth, *Horns of a Dilemma: Coping with Politics at the University of Texas*, Austin, TX: University of Texas Press, 2011.

17 Paul Burka, "Hullabaloo," *Texas Monthly*, August 2009, pp. 12–16. See also Jordan Rudner, "Ex-A&M Chief on List for Ag Post," *Dallas Morning News*, December 23, 2016, p 6A.

18 Christy Hoppe, "Ex-Regent Tells of Push to Quit," *Dallas Morning News*, September 5, 2009, p. 3A.

19 Reeve Hamilton, "Push for Higher Education Plan Comes to Shove for a University Chancellor," *Texas Tribune* for the *New York Times*, May 13, 2011, p. A23.

20 Paul Burka, "Storming the Ivory Tower," *Texas Monthly*, October 2012, pp. 108–113, 290–302.

21 Goldstone, *Integrating the 40 Acres*, p. 4. See also, Amilcar Shabazz, *Advancing Democracy: African-Americans and the Struggle for Access and Equity in Higher Education in Texas*, Chapel Hill, NC: University of North Carolina Press, 2004, p. 18; and Lavergne, *Before Brown*, p. 9.

22 Shabazz, *Advancing Democracy*, p. 38.

23 Goldstone, *Integrating the 40 Acres*, p. 21. See also, Thomas D. Russell, "Keep the Negroes Out of Most Classes Where There Are a Large Number of Girls," https://papers.ssrn.com/sol3/papers.cfm?abstract_id=1583606.

24 Lavergne, *Before Brown*, p. 266.

25 Goldstone, *Integrating the 40 Acres*, p. 41; Shabazz, *Advancing Democracy*, p. 158.

26 Paul Burka, "General Admission," *Texas Monthly*, April 2012, pp. 12–18.

27 Adam Liptak, "Justices Take Up Race as a Factor in College Entry," *New York Times*, February 22, 2012, pp. A1, A13.

28 David G. McComb, *Texas: A Modern History*, Austin, TX: University of Texas Press, 2010, p. 123. See also, Robert A. Calvert, Arnoldo de León, and Gregg Cantrell, *The History of Texas*, 5th ed., Malden, MA: Wiley Blackwell, 2015, p. 431.

29 Evans, *The Story of Texas Schools*, p. 254.

30 James Osborne, "Oil Funds Gush into UT," *Dallas Morning* News, June 1, 2014, pp. A1, A20.

31 Lauren McGaughy, "Chief: Higher Ed Funds Need Reinvention," *Dallas Morning News*, March 15, 2017, p. B3.

32 Jeongeun Kim and Kevin Stange, "Pricing and University Autonomy: Tuition Deregulation in Texas," RSF: The Russell Sage Foundation, *Journal of the Social Sciences*, 2016, vol. 2, no. 1, pp. 112–146.

33   Anthony M. Orum, *Power, Money, and the People: The Making of Modern Austin*, Eugene, OR: Resource Publications, 2002, pp. 30, 150.

34   Anthony Champagne and Edward J. Harpham, *Texas at the Crossroads*, p. 192. See also Calvert et al., *The History of Texas*, 5th ed., p. 431.

35   Ryan McCrimmon and Bobby Blanchard, "Deregulating Tuition Slowed Increase, Universities Say," *The Texas Tribune*, March 17, 2015.

36   Matthew Watkins, "Hopes Fading for New Rules to Limit Tuition Growth," *The Texas Tribune*, May 27, 2015.

37   John Connally, *In History's Shadow: An American Odyssey*, New York: Hyperion, 1993, pp. 224–225.

38   Ralph K.M. Haurwitz, "Regents' Chairman Suggests Boosting UT Enrollment, Halving Tuition," *Austin American-Statesman*, May 2, 2011.

39   Ralph K.M. Haurwitz, "Key Lawmaker Calls UT Regent Chairman's Plan 'Ludicrous,'" *Austin American-Statesman*, May 3, 2011.

40   Holly K. Hacker, "Graduation Lags Many Other States," *Dallas Morning News*, October 3, 2011, pp. A1, A12; and Hacker, "Graduation Edge Goes to Women," *Dallas Morning News*, December 11, 2011, pp. A1, A29.

41   Texas Higher Education Coordinating Board, *Closing the Gaps: The Texas Higher Education Plan*, p. 6.

42   Texas Higher Education Coordinating Board, "Closing the Gaps: Final Progress Report," June 2016.

43   Robert T. Garrett, "Deal Cuts Aid for College Students," *Dallas Morning News*, May 24, 2011, pp. A1, A2.

44   U.S. Department of Education, "Project on Student Debt," ticas.org/posd/map-state-data-2015#.

45   Jeffrey Weiss, "Tuition and Taxes to Rise in DCCCD," *Dallas Morning News*, September 9, 2012, pp. 1B, 4B.

46   Matthew Watkins, "Will Texas Universities Face Perfect Storm of Cuts?" *Texas Tribune*, March 28, 2017.

7 Health and Human Services in Texas

> As Texans, we always take care of the least among us. . . . We will protect them, . . . but cannot risk the future of millions of taxpayers in the process. We must cut spending to keep our economic engine on track.
>
> (Rick Perry, Inaugural Address, 2011)

The Texas political culture highlights independence and individualism and so has little patience with dependency. As with Governor Perry in the quotation above, Texas leaders claim to care about the needy and the afflicted, but they adopt constitutions, pass laws, and allocate funds in a manner that limits actual support for them to a minimum. The tragic consequences of the Texas way regularly come to light, sometimes as a result of official inquiry and action, but more commonly as a result of all too predictable tragedy. To live in Texas is to be subject to a numbing barrage of media reports on underfunded and poorly managed state institutions and programs supposedly designed to serve the poor and the disabled. Texas rarely responds to the needs of the poor and disabled without the intervention of the federal courts and some of these cases go on for decades.

Though Texas officials are deeply resistant to spending on social services, the 2016–2017 biennial budget allocated $33.4 billion of state general funds to health and human services—a lot of money. But the federal government put up even more: $43.2 billion or nearly 60 percent of total health and human services spending in Texas. To control spending, Texas restricts access to health and social welfare programs and leaves federal money on the table when taking it would require matching funds or commitments to increase future state spending. Texas is ever wary of the entangling "strings" that come attached to federal monies.

Minimal public service is a key component of a "business-friendly" policy model in Texas. Persons with access to public support for income, health care, and retirement services might be less willing to work for low pay, while persons without such access will have no choice. Social services raise the cost of doing business by increasing wages and, more importantly, benefits and taxes. Texas's conservative elite even resist spending federal money because they fear it could make the workforce more secure and, therefore, less compliant.

A Brief History of Health Care and Social Services in Texas

Texas has always ranked among the most reluctant states when it comes to social service provision. This has been so since the Republic and remains so today. Every travel account of early Texas is replete with complaints of the "ague," chills, fever, and days lost to slow recovery. East Texas and the Gulf Coast were southern lowlands, to which white labor was thought unfitted and only black labor, held to the task by the whip, could profitably be employed. Still, we know less than one might think about the diseases of early Texas. As the Texas historian T.R. Fehrenbach noted, "The actual incidence of dread diseases, cholera, typhus, and yellow fever, is hard to determine, because Texas newspapers vigorously suppressed such news."[1] Texans did not want to scare away potential immigrants, customers, buyers, or clients, with unfortunate reports about illness and disease.

But we do know that Texans dealt with the incidence of disease and its treatment in the Texas way. Wealthy Texans sought out the best health care available, oftentimes traveling to the United States, while most Texans had to depend upon the little health care available locally. Stanley Siegel's *The Political History of the Texas Republic* explained that in late 1840, "President [Mirabeau B.] Lamar, completely worn down by the cares of state and suffering from an intestinal disorder, asked Congress for a leave of absence to journey to the United States for treatment." President Lamar returned to Austin two months later, "his health restored."[2] The president's decision to seek medical treatment outside Texas was well-made, but not an option open to most of his fellow citizens. Chapter 9 in William Ransom Hogan's *The Texas Republic*, entitled "These Racking Fever Chills," described the medical and political uncertainties of health care in early Texas. Hogan observed that,

> The existence of a few crude hospitals did little to relieve human suffering. . . . For several years the small tax on incoming passengers from foreign ports was the source of support for the Galveston hospital, described by an Englishman as "that shell of misery, that great coffin of the unburied dead." In the summer of 1843 a court ruled that there was no provision for the tax in the city charter and that consequently it was illegal. In commenting on the finding of the court a local editor wrote: "The burden must now fall upon the charity of the people."[3]

Outside the Anglo culture of individualism and personal responsibility, in which the wealthy turned to the U.S. and the poor turned to prayer, lay the domain of slavery. Most slave-owner wealth was bound up in their human property, not land, and so slave-owners protected their investment by providing medical care, as they thought appropriate, to their slaves.[4] They cared for their own family and others dependent upon them, again, as they thought appropriate, but they had no incentive to participate in providing care to others. Robert Perkinson has noted that, "Out of the cauldron of slavery, with the endemic violence and dehumanization, emerged a political culture [in which] . . . leading southerners fought vigorously against intrusive government and all types of humanitarian initiatives, which they feared led inexorably to abolitionism."[5]

After slavery, Anglo Texas elites had few incentives to provide special services to the poor, whatever their color. Little changed until the early decades of the twentieth century, especially the 1930s and later, and again only in the Texas way. During the first three decades of the century, governors such as Tom Campbell, the Fergusons, Pat Neff, and Dan Moody campaigned on a more active state government, but every time the legislature considered new appropriations or the people considered referenda to provide new revenues, they pulled back. As Fehrenbach noted, "Public services of all kinds in Texas . . . were calculated to a grudging minimum in almost every case."[6]

When the Great Depression hit, the Hoover administration argued, and most Texans agreed, that poor relief was the responsibility of local communities, churches, civic groups, and state government where needed. These state and local resources were soon overwhelmed and when the Roosevelt administration came into office in March 1933, they moved to supplement state efforts. Texas did so little in poor relief that the federal government threatened to stop aid unless the state did more. In response, the Texas Legislature, with Governor Jim Ferguson's strong backing, submitted a proposal to the voters for $20 million in "bread bonds" to provide welfare benefits to poor Texans. Though the bonds were approved in August 1933, as late as November 1937 the average state welfare benefit was just $15 a month paid to about 140,000 recipients.[7]

Franklin Roosevelt's aggressive action to confront the Great Depression had many Texas supporters, including Vice President John Nance "Cactus Jack" Garner, Majority Leader and then Speaker Sam Rayburn, and a young Lyndon Johnson. But by 1940, Vice President Garner's distaste for the big, powerful, and expensive government of the New Deal provoked him to stand against FDR for the presidency. Rayburn supported Garner, but LBJ stuck with the president. Texans divided over the contest and great bitterness followed Roosevelt's easy defeat of Garner.[8] The Texas Democratic Party split into squabbling liberal and conservative factions even as the Republican Party began its slow rise.[9]

The Texas way early found a dominant political strategy in regard to social services—keep taxes low, depend on federal money where possible, but do not threaten the traditional compliance of Texas workers. A 1962 study by the non-partisan Texas Research League caught part of this, saying, "Texas has traditionally followed a policy of appropriating the minimum amount of state money necessary to get the maximum amount of federal money available."[10] As we shall see throughout this chapter, the modest but sensible strategy described by the Texas Research League has changed over the past half century. For decades now it has been quite common for Texas to leave large amounts of federal money on the table because it is unwilling to raise and spend the required matching funds.

No one disputes that Texas has long been one of the most tight-fisted states when it comes to public assistance broadly defined. There is, however, lively debate over why this is so and whether it is good or bad. Texas has long touted individualism and personal responsibility and disdained big, expensive, and intrusive government. Texas-elected officials frequently argue that overly generous government programs, whether administered from the national or state levels or jointly, might sap a person's willingness to work. They have moved forcefully to see that that does not happen. Of most direct relevance to the substance of this chapter, Article III, section 51a, of the Texas Constitution, an amendment approved in 1945, declared that, "The maximum amount paid out of state funds for assistance grants to or on behalf of needy dependent children and their caretakers shall not exceed one percent of the state budget." The Great Recession of 2008 and 2009 laid bare the need in Texas but did little to shake the commitment of the state's political elite to small government.

The *New York Times* highlighted the state's tight-fistedness on social spending. In a front-page story on May 10, 2009, the *Times*'s economic writer, Jason DeParle, surveyed the 50 states and D.C. on six social welfare programs: cash assistance, unemployment compensation, housing assistance, food stamps, and assistance with health care for both poor children and poor adults.[11] On each of the six measures, states were ranked by what proportion of the needy population was being served and then a general ranking was done across all six measures. Texas ranked 50 out of 51, only Colorado ranked lower, and Texas ranked in the bottom ten on four of the six measures and in the top ten on none. Even more strikingly, in 2012 the federal Agency for Health Care Research and Quality rated Texas worst in the nation, dead last, in health care services and delivery. Texas rated low in 9 of 12 major areas of comparison, including quality of home health care services, about which more below, preventive acute and chronic care, limited Medicaid services, and access to health insurance.[12] So was Governor Perry right in the headnote to this chapter to say that Texas protects its most vulnerable citizens even while keeping taxes very low? Or does the priority on low taxes preclude the possibility of protecting the poor in Texas?

Does Texas Care for Its Most Vulnerable?

We answer with a long sad tale about Texas and its most dependent citizens, the mentally challenged. Throughout 2009 the *Dallas Morning News*, one of the state's leading conservative papers, ran a series entitled "State of Neglect," referring both to the state of Texas and to the poor social services that it provides. One focus of this series was the condition of state institutions and programs to serve the mentally challenged. Stories such as these have run regularly in Texas newspapers for decades.

During the middle of the twentieth century, Texas consistently ranked near the bottom on state funding for care of those then called the mentally retarded. When Governor Buford Jester died unexpectedly on July 11, 1949, the sad state of Texas's mental hospitals had already been on the agenda for a decade. Allan Shivers, the state's new governor, toured the state facilities and in early 1950 called a special session of the legislature to deal with what he found. Shivers was a staunch conservative, wealthy businessman, and, through his wife, owner of the famous Sharyland ranching properties in South Texas. Nonetheless, Shivers decried the fact that, "Texas—the proud Lone Star State—first in oil—forty eighth in mental hospitals. First in cotton—worst in tuberculosis. First in raising goats—last in caring for state wards."[13] Just as it had three decades earlier with education, challenging the state's pride by mocking its low ranking on services carried the day, at least temporarily. Shivers got increased appropriations for the state's mental institutions, improvements were made, but soon other emergencies arose, attention drifted away, and the old status quo re-emerged. Despite a series of scandals, all centering on inadequate provision for the mentally challenged, the rankings that Shivers decried 70 years ago are largely unchanged today.

In late 1974, a quarter century after the Shivers reforms, the Dallas Legal Services Foundation sued the Texas Department of Mental Health and Mental Retardation (TDMHMR), in a case called *Lelsz v. Kavanaugh*, charging that "the state institutions were little more than barren and dreary warehouses for mentally retarded persons where, rather than receiving treatment, the residents were being subjected to chronic abuse and neglect amid deplorable conditions."[14] The suit dragged on for nearly a decade until in 1983 Texas Attorney General Jim Maddox pressured TDMHMR to agree to a settlement guaranteeing the mentally challenged the right to individualized care, often in community settings instead of large state institutions. Part of the settlement involved hiring an expert consultant, Linda R. O'Neall, to oversee implementation. O'Neall worried that "What you have in Texas is a great propensity to institutionalize people," and that once institutions are built, they become part of the political resistance to change.[15]

Yet, another quarter century on, though Texas spends less on assistance to the mentally challenged than virtually any other state and houses more people in large state institutions, politicians preen at their still modest accomplishments. The most recent data (2013) show that Texas ranks 50th among the 50 states and D.C. on state mental health spending. The national average for state spending on per capita mental health services is $120 while Texas spends just $41.[16] Before passing on too quickly, let your mind dwell on those numbers and then consider the following. By 2010, more than a quarter century after the state agreed to provide community care for the mentally challenged, 40,000 Texans with mental disabilities remained on waiting lists for home and community-based treatment.

Under new pressure from a four-year investigation by the federal Department of Justice, which found civil rights violations across the 13 state institutions for the mentally challenged, Governor Perry declared these institutions a legislative emergency in early 2009. Texas Senator Steve Ogden (R-Bryan), chair of the Senate budget committee said, as if echoing Linda O'Neall's comments from 25 years earlier, "My view is that it is politically impossible to close a state school, but we can manage the size of the state schools. There's always a constituency out there in support of each individual state school, and they can usually muster enough political firepower to prevent us from closing any state school." One of the state's major newspapers then noted, rather laconically, that "Nationally, there's a trend for states to move away from institutionalizing people with mental retardation, but Texas hasn't kept pace: The Lone Star State has a higher institutionalization rate than the nation as a whole and has more people living in state schools than any other state."[17]

Then in March 2009, as legislators debated, video surfaced of state mental health facility employees organizing late-night "fight clubs" by pairing off patients and forcing them to fight. As the footage aired on national and international news outlets, Texas officials had no choice but to move. By mid-May, Texas reached an agreement with the Justice Department requiring that the state spend $112 million over five years to hire 1,000 workers to improve staffing ratios, increase monitoring and oversight, and enhance care. State Senator Jane Nelson (R-Flower Mound), chair of the committee that oversaw the state's health and human services agencies, declared that "We are all ready for a new beginning in our efforts to take care of and protect Texans with disabilities."[18] Skepticism hung heavy in the air as the legislature initially did more than required by the Justice Department agreement. They allocated an additional $200 million (for a grand total of new and old money of $507 million) to provide community-based care to 8,000 people on waiting lists. But long-standing patterns held, good intentions (and embarrassment) faded, new crises arose in other underfunded programs, and the mentally disabled again faded from view. In 2016, during yet another spate of media stories focusing on the shortcomings of Texas mental health care, one headline stood out: "Mental Hospitals Crumbling Away."[19]

Texas politicians, mental health professionals, and citizens know that the next morning's paper might bring reports of another tragedy. Despite the most recent settlement with the federal government, many go unserved until it is too late. In July 2009, Otty Sanchez, a schizophrenic institutionalized for two weeks in 2008, suffering from post-partum psychosis, sought admission to Houston's Metropolitan Methodist Hospital's psychiatric unit. She was denied admission as neither suicidal nor homicidal. Less than a week later, she decapitated her infant son.[20] Just as tragically, in the summer of 2014, Jason Harrison, a 38-year-old man suffering from bipolar disorder and schizophrenia, upset his mother and family members with "disturbing remarks." She called "911" and the police responded. Jason came out of the home with a screwdriver. Police testified that he menaced them with the screwdriver and they shot him dead. Internet video of the encounter was ambiguous at best.[21]

Inadequate mental health treatment facilities produce tragedies of various kinds. One tragedy is that adults with mental health problems that might be treated instead end up in prisons and jails ill-equipped to handle them. It is common knowledge that Houston's Harris County Jail is the state's largest mental health facility. "Of the 9,000 or so inmates . . . , more than a quarter take medication for mental illness." Not to quibble, but Harris County Sheriff Adrian Garcia put the proportion of his 9,000 prisoners on psychotropic medication at one-third.[22] Just as sadly, Texas youth with mental health conditions must, by law, be released from Texas Youth Commission facilities that are not equipped to treat them. One such youth, unnamed because of his age, killed Todd Henry, his special education teacher at John Tyler High School in Tyler, with a butcher's knife.[23] The deep budget cuts enacted for the 2012–2013 biennium made Texas state mental health services even less available, with predictable consequences.

The 2015 legislative session added $87 million to state mental health funding. New money is good to be sure, but in a state that has ranked 49th or 50th for a decade, all the time touting its renewed commitment to addressing the needs of the most vulnerable, it is pitifully little. When the next set of comparative state figures come out, Texas will still rank near the very bottom.

Texas Health Care Practitioners and Expenditures

Texas has always had fewer doctors per 100,000 of population than most other states and the nation in general. Excellent data on doctors per 100,000 of population go back more than half a century and show that Texas had just 75 percent of the national average of doctors per 100,000 of population between 1955 and 1970 and about 80 percent since. Though the number of doctors per 100,000 of population has nearly doubled in both the U.S. and Texas in the past half century, from 133 to 253 for the U.S. and from 102 to 205 in Texas, Texas has lagged behind the entire time and has made up little ground over time. Today, Texas ranks 43rd among the 50 states (Figure 7.1). The doctor

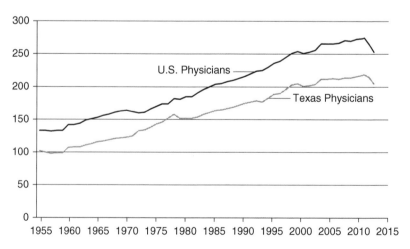

Figure 7.1 Number of U.S. and Texas Physicians per 100,000 of Population, 1955–2013

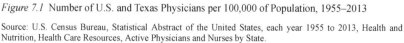

Source: U.S. Census Bureau, Statistical Abstract of the United States, each year 1955 to 2013, Health and Nutrition, Health Care Resources, Active Physicians and Nurses by State.

shortage is particularly acute in rural Texas. In 2012, more than half of Texas's 254 counties were designated by the federal government as primary-care (regular family doctors) shortage areas. Twenty-six counties had no doctors at all. Nonetheless, not until 2017 did Texas allow "telemedicine," whereby a doctor consults with, diagnoses, and prescribes for patients over the internet. Texas was the last of the 50 states to approve telemedicine. It should help alleviate the doctor shortage, especially in rural areas.[24]

Data on nurses actively working in health care are sketchier, showing a similar but even lower trajectory. Through the 1960s, Texas has less than 60 percent of the national average of nurses per 100,000 and has generally been in the 70 percent range since, reaching 80 percent only in the mid-1990s and since 2006. Moreover, Texas's physician and nursing force is aging. More than 40 percent of doctors and 35 percent of nurses are over 50 years of age and, hence, approaching retirement over the next decade or two.[25]

One might assume, rightly, as it turns out, that a tight supply of doctors and nurses would drive up the price of health care in Texas. Texas hospitals are more expensive than U.S. hospitals in general, and so Texans respond by spending less time in them. In 1970, the average daily cost of a hospital stay in Texas was 90 percent of the average U.S. cost, $73 compared to $81, while the average cost of a multiday stay was just 79 percent, $525 compared to $664 nationally. A decade later, in 1980, the cost per day was still just 90 percent of the national average, $252 compared to $281, while the average cost of a multiday hospital stay was still 78 percent, $1,661 compared to $2,126 nationally. By 1985, the average per day cost in Texas had eclipsed the national average, though the per stay cost remained at just 86 percent of the national average. By 1990, the average per day cost ballooned to 109 percent of the national average, $752 compared to $687, while the per stay cost had also risen, but just to 94 percent of the national average, $4,463 compared to $4,947. This pattern continues to hold today. The data in Figure 7.2 show Texans paying more for each day's hospital stay but staying fewer days in the hospital than do their fellow citizens nationally.

Another factor driving up the cost of care in Texas has been the number of persons without health insurance. Persons without health insurance tend not to seek care until

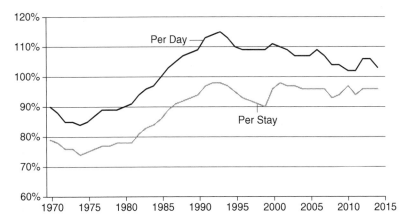

Figure 7.2 Average Cost per Day and per Stay of Texas Community Hospitals as a Percentage of U.S. Costs, 1970–2014

Source: U.S. Census Bureau, Statistical Abstract of the United States, Health and Nutrition, Health Care Resources, Average Cost of Community Hospitals by State. See also Kaiser State Health Facts.

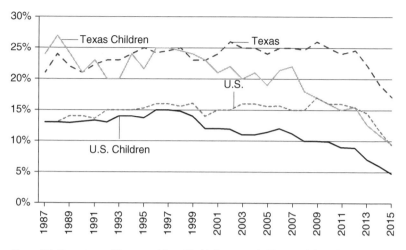

Figure 7.3 Percentage of Persons without Health Insurance in Texas and the U.S., 1987–2015

Source: U.S. Census Bureau, Historical Health Insurance Tables, Table H1–4 and Table H1–5, www.census. gov/data/tables/time-series/demo/health-insurance/historical-series/hib.html. See also *Statistical Abstract of the United States*, various years, Health and Nutrition, Table "Persons With and Without Health Insurance by State."

they are truly ill and then to seek it in the most expensive venue—the emergency room. Texas has for many years had among the highest proportion of uninsured residents in the country, and in recent years, Texas never ranked better than 48th. Over the past two decades, about 15 percent of U.S. residents and 25 percent of Texas residents have not had health insurance. Obamacare lowered the national uninsured rate to 9.4 percent and the Texas rate to 17.1 percent. Among children the numbers of uninsured are slightly lower, but Texas still has 5 percent more uninsured children than the U.S. in general. About 4.6 million Texas residents did not have health insurance in 2015 (Figure 7.3).

The large number of uninsured in Texas drives up insurance premiums and health care costs for those who do have insurance. The Center for American Progress reported that "cost-shifting" from the uninsured to the insured added $1,800 or 13 percent in premiums to every insured family plan. Finally, more of the uninsured in Texas are employed than is the case nationally. Texas is a low-wage economy that depends heavily on small businesses for jobs. Only 53 percent of the state's residents were covered by employer-sponsored insurance in 2015, compared to 56 percent nationally, the Census Bureau reported. The low rate for Texas reflects the fact that 75 percent of companies are small businesses, with under 50 employees, and just over one-quarter of them offer insurance. Fully 82 percent of uninsured Texans are in working families.[26]

Conservatives, especially Texas conservatives, argue that medical malpractice reform, often referred to simply as tort reform, is a critical element of reducing or at least slowing the rise of health care costs. Thirty states have enacted some version of medical malpractice reform, with Texas being among the most comprehensive. In 2003, Texas capped medical malpractice non-economic damages, for what is often described as pain and suffering, at $250,000. Doctors are still liable for loss of earnings and medical expenses, but the prospect of being on the hook for additional millions has been removed. As a result, medical malpractice suits fell by 70 percent, doctors' medical malpractice premiums fell by nearly half, but medical costs in Texas continued to rise at rates faster than the national average. Advocates of the reform claim that the number of doctors in Texas, and particularly the number of emergency room physicians, has increased, though, as we saw above, the overall numbers have not budged. In 2003, Texas had 80 percent of the physicians the U.S. had per 100,000 of population (212 vs. 266) and, in 2013, Texas had 81 percent (205 vs. 253).

A study by Northwestern University's Kellogg School of Management involving 10 million Americans covered by employer-sponsored health plans found that nationwide tort reform might lower health care costs by up to 2.3 percent. A 2004 study by the Congressional Budget Office reported that less than 2 percent of medical expenses could be attributed to malpractice awards and defensive medicine.[27] Studies of Texas Medicare spending between 2002 and 2009, led by UT law professor Charles Silver, found no reduction in doctors' fees and no influx of doctors into the state following tort reform.[28] Therefore, one must ask, if medical malpractice reform does not affect the cost of health care to the consumer, then what is the justification for limiting consumers' rights to legal redress for medical injury? Better than malpractice reform alone would be reforms that tackled both medical negligence and the uncertainty and expense doctors incur in insuring against it.

Medicare, Medicaid, and CHIP in the U.S. and Texas

Social Security was passed in 1935, during the Great Depression, to cushion the elderly from the loss of income when they were no longer able to work. Medicare and Medicaid were passed in 1965 to add pre-paid health care for the elderly and other eligible groups (Medicare) and free health care for the poor (Medicaid). Medicare was established as an adjunct to Social Security, organized and funded similarly, through payroll taxes paid by workers and their employers. Like Social Security, Medicare is administered and funded by the federal government. Medicaid is a joint federal/state program wherein the federal government establishes the broad design and provides base funding for the program and each state defines eligibility criteria and provides additional funding to reach the benefit levels that they have set. Some states add generously to the base federal funding for Medicaid and some states do not. Medicare and Medicaid, one run on federal money and one run on base federal funding and state matching funds, provide insight into Texas's attitude toward public services and their financial support.

Medicare is essentially a bottomless pool of federal money. Medicare negotiates reimbursement rates for health care services provided by doctors, hospitals, medical laboratories, medical equipment providers, home health care providers, and others and then reimburses providers at those rates for services delivered to eligible Medicare patients. Rates vary somewhat by region according to the historic and traditional costs of service delivery in that region. Once a provider is in the Medicare system as an eligible provider, there is little oversight of the millions of individual health care transactions, from office visits, to medical tests, hospital and out-patient procedures, and prescriptions.

Texans, both patients and service providers, have been among the nation's most enthusiastic users of Medicare services. Moreover, Texas's use of the Medicare system and the costs of that usage have increased dramatically in recent decades and especially in recent years. Medicare was established in 1965 and we have very good data on national and state usage beginning in 1967 (Figure 7.4). Between 1967 and 1981, Medicare costs per enrollee in Texas averaged about 95 percent of costs nationally. In the early 1980s,

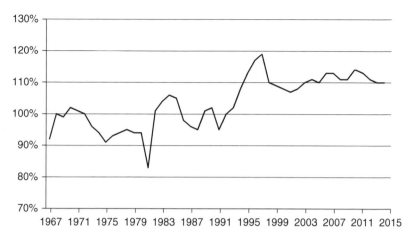

Figure 7.4 Texas Medicare Payments per Enrollee as a Percentage of U.S. Payments, 1967–2014

Source: U.S. Census Bureau, Statistical Abstract of the United States, each year, Health and Nutrition section, Table entitled Medicare—Summary, by State."

costs rose as high as 106 percent in 1984, before moderating later in the decade. By the mid-1990s, Texas Medicare costs jumped from 95 percent of the national average to 119 percent and have run between 110 and 115 percent since. As late as 1991, 20 states had average per enrollee Medicare costs greater than Texas. By 1995 only three states (Massachusetts, Florida, and Louisiana) had higher costs per enrollee, by 1996 only two states (Massachusetts and Louisiana) did, and by 1997 only Louisiana had higher rates. Though per enrollee costs moderated a little after 1997, from 1995 through 2014, Texas averaged 112 percent of the national average for expenditures per Medicare enrollee, placing Texas 5th highest among the 50 states during that period. In 2014, the latest year for which we have complete data, the average cost per Medicare enrollee in the U.S. was $9,423 while in Texas it was $10,340 per enrollee.

Explanations for the dramatic increase in Medicare spending in Texas over the last 20 years vary. Some point to the fact that Texas provides little health care to its nonelderly poor and so they arrive at Medicare eligible age with more problems than do their counterparts in other states. This is undoubtedly true, but there is more to it than that. A major study by the Dartmouth Institute for Health Policy and Clinical Practice, released in February 2009 and based on intensive analysis of two decades of data, declared that "Medicare beneficiaries in high-spending regions do not receive more 'effective care.' . . . Patients in high-spending regions are hospitalized more frequently, spend more time in the ICU, see physicians more frequently, and get more diagnostic tests than identical patients in lower-spending regions."[29] The Dartmouth study confirmed what many health professionals and experts already knew, that high cost, absent improved health outcomes, suggested substantial inefficiency and waste.

Medical studies, even on critical topics, rarely become the topic of national conversation. The Dartmouth study did when a provocative article, "The Cost Conundrum: What a Texas Town Can Teach Us about Health Care," appeared in the June 1, 2009, issue of *The New Yorker*. The author of the *New Yorker* piece, a medical doctor named Atul Gawande, particularized the issue of regional disparities in Medicare costs by asking how McAllen, Texas, hard on the Mexican border in Hidalgo County, one of the poorest counties in the nation, became one of the most expensive health care markets in the nation. Plausible reasons exist to believe that health care might be expensive in McAllen—poverty, lack of health insurance, the prevalence of heavy drinking, and high obesity rates obviously produce health consequences. But as Gawande noted, El Paso, Texas, 800 miles up the Rio Grande and also on the Mexican border, had a very similar social, economic, and demographic profile. Medicare expenses per enrollee in McAllen in 2006 were $15,000 while they were half that, about $7,500, in El Paso. In 2014, McAllen Medicare enrollees were still costing 124 percent of the national average per enrollee.

McAllen did not have more doctors, more specialists, or better equipment and facilities. Gawande concluded that overutilization of medical services, driven by and for the benefit of local doctors, hospitals, and other medical service providers, was the distinguishing driver of soaring costs: "Compared with patients in El Paso and nationwide, patients in McAllen got more of pretty much everything—more diagnostic testing, more hospital treatment, more surgery, more home care."[30] Gawande noted that "In 1992, in the McAllen market, the average cost per Medicare enrollee was $4,891, almost exactly the national average. But since then, year after year, McAllen's health costs have grown faster than any other market in the country, ultimately soaring by more than 10,000 dollars per person."[31] But McAllen is by no means alone in Texas. The Medicare market in Texas generally began to heat up in the early 1990s and has made Texas among the most expensive Medicare states. McAllen is just a particularly egregious example and was called out for it nationally.

Not surprisingly, the Dartmouth Study and the Gawande article have not gone unchallenged. Urban hospitals in particular have made the strong case that they serve patients that are sicker and poorer.[32] Despite the criticism, two points—that costs have risen much more rapidly in some areas than others and that higher costs do not necessarily mean better health care results—are now entrenched. For example, in late 2009, the Medicare Payments Advisory Commission released a study, entitled "Measuring Regional Variations in Service Use," in which five Texas metropolitan areas, including Houston and Dallas-Fort Worth, were among the 15 most expensive areas of 404 studied.[33] Dartmouth and the Medicare Payments Advisory Commission both highlight comparisons such as that between Sacramento and Dallas between 1994 and 2006. In 1994, Sacramento and Dallas were both near the national average for Medicare expenditures per patient at about $4,500. By 2006, Sacramento had risen to $7,324, the national average had risen to $8,304, and Dallas had soared to $10,103.[34] Sacramento held down costs by coordinating and integrating care, bringing together doctors, nurses, and hospitals and other caregivers around patient service and quality.

Increasingly, discussions of the high cost of health care in Texas cite the state's "entrepreneurial tradition." This is not a compliment; rather, it suggests a health care community built around provider profit more than around patient care. A glaring example of Texas entrepreneurialism that has drawn recent attention is Medicare-funded home health care. Home health care is an important service as the frail elderly often have difficulty getting to the doctor's office or the hospital. But even important services can be abused: "Texas has more home health agencies billing Medicare and more Medicare home health patients than any other state. It also ranks near the bottom in Medicare home health quality ratings and near the top in suspected waste and fraud." This is obviously problematic, but it gets much worse. In a near feeding frenzy between 2002 and 2006, Texas saw a 102 percent increase in the number of home health agencies billing Medicare and a 144 percent increase in home health care spending. In 2007, each Texan served by home health care cost Medicare $7,761, the highest cost in the nation, 41 percent per patient higher than California and 53 percent higher than the national average of $5,064.[35]

In 2010, according to AARP, Texas had more Medicare recipients receiving home health care than the national average (12.3 percent, compared to 7.4 percent), being visited more frequently (60 times a year compared to 37), by more home health care providers. Remarkably, by 2010 more than 20 percent of Medicare certified home health care agencies in the U.S. were in Texas, fully 2,114 of 10,135 nationally.[36] By 2013, the number of home health care agencies in Texas was up to 2,949. And in 2014, Texas Medicare patients receiving home health care still were receiving 50 visits a year compared to a national average of 32. It seems that Texans discovered that the honey pot was essentially unguarded and that you could dip into it with a bucket as easily as you could with a cup.

In early 2012, federal investigators moved against "a massive health care fraud scheme" in which Dallas area Dr. Jacques Roy, working with several dozen home health care companies, recruited clients, including in homeless shelters, and then billed Medicare and Medicaid for nearly $374 million in services. Roy's practice became the largest in the nation between 2006 and 2011 as he and others "certi-fied 11,000 Medicare beneficiaries for more than 500 home health services."[37] Investigators found and froze $4 million of an estimated $19 million of Dr. Roy's illicit charges and 78 Dallas area home health companies were suspended as approved Medicare and Medicaid providers.

In August 2012, the nation's top health care inspector called for a moratorium on new home health care agencies. He found that 80 percent of suspicious billing cases came from just four states—Texas, Florida, Michigan, and California—and 40 percent came from Texas alone. One reason that Texas had so many home health care agencies filing so many claims was that, unlike many states, Texas did not require new home health care businesses to file a "statement of need" for their services—entrepreneurship and limited regulation you see! But the Feds were closing in. In late 2014, Dr. Joseph Megwa was sentenced to 10 years in prison and ordered to repay $5.5 million for health care fraud. Between 2006 and 2012, 230 home health care agencies sent patients to Dr. Magwa and billed Medicare $100 million.[38] In 2016, Dr. Roy was convicted on 12 felony counts of health care and related fraud and subsequently was sentenced to 35 years in prison.[39] Drs. Roy and Megwa were caught, but they were by no means alone.

Finally, a 2016 study by the Commonwealth Fund, entitled "Rising to the Challenge," ranked 306 hospital referral regions around the nation. High costs and large numbers of uninsured placed Dallas 236th, Houston 252nd, and Beaumont 275th of 306. Even more strikingly, on health insurance coverage, fully 16 of the bottom 30 cities were Texas cities. Newspaper reports noted that these "findings were in line with other scorecards done by Washington's Brookings Institution and the Dartmouth Institute for Health Policy and Clinical Practice."[40]

One reason that the lid is off the honey pot in Texas is that state government has outsourced much of its health and human services claims processing and ser-vice delivery to private contractors. Privatization allows the pass through of federal funds to contractors with few state employees required for service delivery or over-sight of programs. Newspaper reports in early 2009 explained that, "Government outsourcing in Texas expanded dramatically with 2003 legislation that crunched twelve health and human service agencies into five . . . and replaced state workers with private contractors. . . . This year's [2009] health and human services budget is $29.3 billion. . . . nearly $25 billion was for contracts, including payments to doctors, pharmacies, hospitals and private companies."[41] If state government is undermanned, as it surely is in Texas, who is watching the private interests of both contractors and service providers?

Unlike Medicare, which is a federal program generally serving the retired elderly, Medicaid is a joint federal/state program serving poor children. Although the federal government establishes the general guidelines for the program, states set the eligibility rules and payment levels. When the program was passed by Congress in 1965, it was designed to be the insurer of last resort for the society's most needy. States were initially required to serve families who qualified for Aid to Families with Dependent Children (AFDC, about which more below) and elderly and disabled who qualified for Supplemental Security Income. In the 1980s, Congress began to require states to broaden and deepen eligibility, adding children of low-income families, pregnant women with children aged under 6 whose family income was below 133 percent of the poverty rate, children aged 6 to 19 whose family income was up to 100 percent of the poverty rate, and several other groups. States were encouraged to make still other categories of people eligible, such as poor adults without children, and to raise the income levels below which persons become eligible. Texas's response to the expansion of Medicaid, beginning in the mid-1980s, was to cut to a bare bones program. Unfortunately, good data on the Texas Medicaid program goes back just to 1979.

From 1979 through 1982, Texas limited the number of persons eligible for Medicaid services but built on federal Medicaid contributions. Texas Medicaid expenses per enrollee averaged 123 percent of the national average. But as the Texas economy began to stall in the mid-1980s, Texas held the number of Medicaid recipients steady while cutting back on state contributions to Medicaid. Medicaid expenses per enrollee in Texas did not increase between 1983 and 1990, they were $1,935 per enrollee in 1983 and $1,929 in 1990. By 1990 Texas was spending just 72 percent of the national average, $2,695 vs. $1,929, per Medicaid enrollee. Texas spending per enrollee averaged 75 percent until the late 1990s, before rising back to 90 percent in 2000 and 2001. It has declined to 85 percent in the most recent data (Figure 7.5).

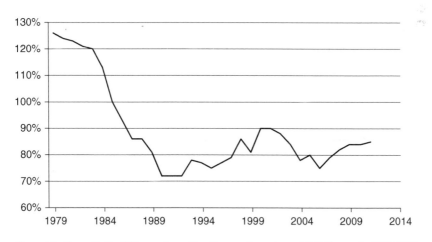

Figure 7.5 Texas Medicaid Payments per Enrollee as a Percentage of U.S. Payments, 1979–2011

Source: U.S. Census Bureau, Statistical Abstract of the United States, Health and Nutrition section, "Medicaid—Summary by State."

Texas will spend $61 billion, more than one-quarter of its $210 billion biennial budget, on Medicaid during the 2016–2017 biennium. Of this, $25 billion, about 42 percent, will be Texas funds and the remainder, $36 billion, will come from the federal government. Again, Texas limits its Medicaid expenses by setting tight eligibility and reimbursement limits, rather than by close monitoring and regulation of the program. The average state's Medicaid spending is 40 percent on mandatory services and 60 percent on optional and expanded services. In Texas, it is the other way around, 60 percent of funds go to mandatory services and 40 percent go to optional and expanded services.[42] To limit expenses, Texas Medicaid rules bar able-bodied adults who make more than $188 a month (26 percent of the federal poverty rate) and are not pregnant from coverage. Seventy-eight percent of Texas's 3.7 million Medicaid enrollees are children and younger adults and the remaining 24 percent are elderly and disabled. Sixty percent of Medicaid expenditures go to care of the elderly and disabled because they need more and more intensive health care than children. Even services to the 56,000 frail elderly in Texas nursing homes are tightly limited. The Texas Medicaid program reimburses nursing homes $125.68 per enrollee per day, 30 percent below the national average of $177.55 per enrollee per day. Texas ranks 49th, less than a dollar a day ahead of last place Illinois.[43]

Despite the fact that 42 percent of Medicaid funding is Texas dollars, oversight is remarkably lax. A report from the *Houston Chronicle* said that between 2006 and 2011 Texas dental and orthodontic charges to Medicaid increased from $67 million to $229 million. Subsequent investigation found that Texas dentists billed Medicaid more for braces in 2010 than all of the other 49 states combined. Clearly, more oversight is warranted.[44]

Not surprisingly, Texas has been deeply concerned about proposals to expand Medicaid as part of Obamacare. Despite the fact that Texas has more uninsured citizens than any other state, 23 of 34 Texas members of the U.S. House and Senate voted against the Democrats' health reform bill in 2010. Texas authorities immediately assaulted the bill, claiming that it would cost Texas an extra $27 billion over the next decade and that the state might be forced to pull out of Medicaid entirely, managing its own indigent health care system, to avoid the extra cost. When it became clear that withdrawing from Medicaid would halt nearly $15 billion a year in federal Medicaid funds to Texas, talk of withdrawing ceased but grumbling did not.

In 2012, though the Supreme Court found Obamacare constitutional, they declared that states could not be compelled to expand their Medicaid programs. Texas officials were immensely relieved and quickly declined to expand the state's Medicaid program despite the prospect of $100 billion in federal money over ten years in exchange for a $15 billion match from Texas. Obamacare encouraged states to expand their Medicaid programs to healthy adults making up to 133 percent of the federal poverty line, $14,856 for a childless adult and $30,657 for a family of four, by promising to pay 100 percent of the cost for 2014–16, sliding down to 90 percent in 2020 and beyond. Governor Perry and other conservatives argued that "Medicaid is broken" so it was unconscionable to add so many new beneficiaries, and, they claimed, it was a bait-and-switch scheme in which federal deficits would lead Congress to cut its promised support, leaving states holding the financial bag. But Texas leaders have never supported expansive public services, even with federal money—because, they claimed, it sapped individualism, personal responsibility, and the willingness, in fact, the need, to work.

In 2012 and 2013, another battle between Texas conservatives and progressives played out over the state's management of the Women's Health Program within Medicaid. Texas conservatives, or at least Texas conservative elected officials, abhor

Planned Parenthood, the progressive women's health care advocacy and services group. Texas received $35.4 million in federal money, for a $3.9 million state match, to deliver contraceptives and cancer screenings to poor women. Planned Parenthood provided 44 percent of these services to 130,000 Texas women. Conservatives moved in 2011 and then more successfully in 2013 to bar Planned Parenthood from the program on the argument that dollars are fungible and some Planned Parenthood affiliates provided abortion services.

The federal government required that women be able to select their health care providers, while Texas officials claimed that Medicaid rules allow them to define qualified, and unqualified, providers. When Texas would not relent, the federal government suspended its funding. Governor Perry promised that the state would run the program, sans Planned Parenthood, with its own money, though it struggled to do so. Once again, Texas demonstrated a willingness to leave federal money on the table, even in the case of a nine-to-one match, to both adhere to its values and limit services to the poor.

The Children's Health Insurance Program (CHIP) was enacted in 1997 to cover children in working families that earn too much to qualify for Medicaid but not enough to afford private health insurance. Although the federal government pays most of the costs, states set the eligibility rules and must decide how much of their own money they are willing to put up to attract the federal match. In general, the federal government pays 65 percent of the cost of state CHIP programs, but because Texas is a relatively poor state with high levels of uninsured, the federal government pays 71 percent. This means that Texas puts up only 29 cents of every dollar spent on CHIP in Texas, or, described another way, Texas gets $2.50 in federal dollars for every dollar it puts up. This is one of the truly good deals in U.S. federal relations, but Texas has long been skeptical. In fact, Texas has been more than ready to cut its own funding to CHIP, thereby sacrificing $2.50 for every dollar it cuts, when its budget gets tight.

Texas historian Robert Calvert noted that, "Between 2000 and 2005, the state lost some $832 million in federal funding for CHIP because it refused to appropriate the required matching funds."[45] In 2003, facing a $10 billion deficit, Texas trimmed CHIP and cut completely its dental, vision, and mental health benefits. It also reduced the assets that a family could have and still be eligible for CHIP, changed the continuous enrollment period from one year to six months, and trimmed provider payment rates. As a result, CHIP enrollment dropped from 726,000 to under 526,000. As budgets loosened, many of these changes were reversed—dental and vision benefits were restored in 2005 and eligibility rules were relaxed in 2007—but the number of children in the program did not return to 2003 levels until 2008. Nonetheless, Texas remained tight-fisted. In early 2009, President Obama signed a five-year extension of CHIP that included substantial increases in funding and raised the cap below which families were eligible for CHIP from 250 percent of the federal poverty rate to 300 percent.[46] Texas kept its eligibility cap at 200 percent of the poverty rate.[47] Nonetheless, the Great Recession of 2008 to 2010 drove CHIP rolls in Texas over 900,000 in 2010 and over 1 million in 2012 and later years.

Assistance to the Poor: TANF and Food Stamps

Prior to the Great Depression most social welfare policy was made by state and local government and most charity was administered by churches and civic groups. In 1933, four years into the Depression, "only 20 of 254 Texas counties offered mothers' aid, and the number dropped as the Depression deepened—to 8 by 1935 . . . and the average monthly grant of $12.07 was only half the national average and below even the average ($14.06) of the southern states." Texas politicians were worried about the socialist elements of public aid undermining the state's traditional commitment to personal responsibility. After the Social Security Act was passed in 1935, with AFDC one of its major components, Texas "limited its contribution to not more than $8 for one child or $12 per family and set the cut-off age at fourteen. The federal government, which contributed one-third of ADC grants, permitted a maximum of $18 for the first child and $12 for each additional child under sixteen."[48]

Still today, Texas participates, if only barely, in federal government programs designed to assist the poor through cash grants and food aid. From the Great Depression through the welfare reform of the mid-1990s, AFDC provided cash grants to poor families as a matter of right, usually where the adults were unemployed. AFDC grew rapidly in the Great Society years of the 1960s, doubling its number of recipients from five to ten million between 1967 and 1971, before it came under the downward pressure of more conservative administrations in the 1970s and 1980s. As with other federal/state social programs, the federal government provides about 60 percent of the funding and lays out broad rules. The states set more specific eligibility rules and payment levels. Writing more than three decades ago, Champagne and Harpham noted that, "Texas officials have used this power to make the AFDC program in Texas one of the most miserly in terms of payments and one of the most difficult for which to become and remain eligible."[49] Texas AFDC payment levels ranked 46th among the 50 states and D.C. in 1986.

In 1996, President Bill Clinton and the Republican Congress led by House Speaker Newt Gingrich passed a major welfare reform program. A key element of this reform was to change the focus of AFDC from provision of cash assistance to the non-working poor to work support through a revised program named Temporary Assistance to Needy Families (TANF). TANF still provides cash assistance to poor families, but the aid is limited to five years and adults must actively prepare for self-support through work. As a result, the number of beneficiaries drawing on AFDC/TANF has declined sharply since 1996 and, of course, more sharply in Texas than nationally. Robert Calvert noted, "These results were largely the product of the state's unwillingness to allocate matching funds in order to receive federal money."[50] In 1996, 624,000 Texans drew TANF support; by 2010 that number had declined to 100,000, most of them children. Texas has held down participation in the program by setting very low limits on assets one can have and still be eligible for the program and on earnings one can have while in the program. Only two states, Georgia and Delaware, have a lower asset limit than Texas ($1,000 and an auto worth no more than $4,650) and only five, Alabama, Arkansas, Florida, Indiana, and Louisiana, have lower earnings limits than Texas's $401 a month. Thirteen states allow more than $1,000 a month.

AFDC/TANF payments have always been modest, especially in Texas (Figure 7.6). Average monthly payments nationally did not break $100 until 1957, $200 until 1974, $300 until 1984, and $400 until 2007. In Texas, AFDC/TANF payments never broke $175 and have been flat since 1985. In fact, only the Connally administration in the 1960s and the White administration in the early to mid-1980s made meaningful commitments to AFDC. Texas cash assistance payments were about 75 percent of the national average in the mid-1950s but have been on a steady downward trajectory, steeply since the early 1970s, and are just 41 percent in the latest figures. This is among the very lowest rates in the nation. In 2015, the average monthly TANF payment for a family with two children nationally was $418, while the maximum monthly benefit in Texas was $173. Only Mississippi paid less.

Strikingly, Texas allows fewer people into its TANF program than most other states and then pays these fortunate few less than all but a few other states pay their

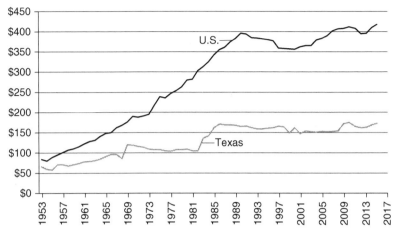

Figure 7.6 AFDC/TANF Average Monthly Benefits per Family, U.S. and Texas, 1953–2015

Source: United States Census Bureau, Statistical Abstract of the United States, Social Insurance and Human Services section, AFDC table prior to 1996, TANF tables thereafter, various years. See also Department of Health and Human Services, Administration for Children and Families, www.acf.hhs.gov/sites/default/files/ofa/characteristics_and_financial_circumstances_of_tanf_recipients.pdf Table 41, Families with two children.

beneficiaries (Figure 7.7). As Champagne and Harpham noted in the mid-1980s, and it is even truer today, "Welfare is an issue that is not popular in Texas. Poverty. The dole. Dependency. All appear to fly in the face of the reality and the myth which is Texas."[51] Texas has made the policy judgment that assistance to its many poor should be exceedingly meager.

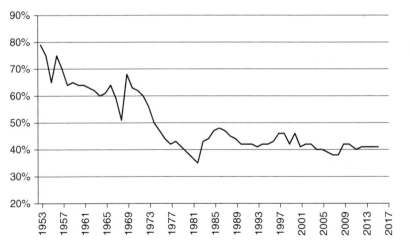

Figure 7.7 AFDC/TANF Average Monthly Benefits in Texas as a Percentage of U.S. Monthly Benefits, 1953–2015

Source: United States Census Bureau, Statistical Abstract of the United States, Social Insurance and Human Services section, AFDC table prior to 1996, TANF tables thereafter, various years. See also Department of Health and Human Services, Administration for Children and Families, www.acf.hhs.gov/sites/default/files/ofa/characteristics_and_financial_circumstances_of_tanf_recipients.pdf Table 41, Families with two children.

The Food Stamp program, whose name was changed in 2008 to the Supplemental Nutrition Assistance Program (SNAP), has for decades provided poor families with food stamps, now a benefit card, to supplement their food budget. The $5.3 billion annual cost of the program in Texas is borne by the federal government while the program is run by the state and administrative costs of $250 million are split 50/50 by the federal and state governments. So how do you suppose Texas approaches such a program? The benefit amount is capped, so no feeding frenzy, but Texas, as a poor state, does draw on the program at rates higher than the national average, 9.5 percent of households as opposed to 8.6 percent nationally. It also has a higher monthly average payment than the nation. In 2015, the Texas monthly household average was $282 compared to a national average of $258. Moreover, the high unemployment of 2009 and 2012 pushed recipients from 2.3 million in 2009, to 3.6 million in 2010, and 4 million in 2011 and 2012, a 75 percent increase over just three years. As unemployment abated, the SNAP rolls fell to 3.7 million in 2015.

Not surprisingly, program administration has been a problem. The Food Stamp program in Texas, like all of its social service programs, is understaffed even when things are going smoothly. When demand for services build, as they inevitably do during bad times, the staff are quickly overwhelmed. Federal rules require that Food Stamp applications be processed within 30 days. In 2009, Texas failed to meet that deadline on one-third of applications and ranked 52nd among the 50 states, D.C., Guam, and the Virgin Islands.[52] Texas finished just behind Guam. A big part of the problem in this and other Texas social service programs is low pay, high pressure, and the resulting staff turnover. In 2004, only 8.4 percent of staff had less than two years' experience, while in 2009 more than half of state Food Stamp workers had less than two years' experience. As a result, the error rate on handling applications, as measured by the state itself, rose from 2.8 percent in 2004 to 21.4 percent in 2008.[53]

In August 2009 Texas was sued in federal court by the Texas Legal Services Center and the National Center for Law and Economic Justice to try to force compliance with federal requirements on processing applications. In 2000, Texas had 10,400 state workers processing eligibility applications, a decade later they had 7,400. In the interim, the state undertook a major outsourcing effort involving private call centers to handle the initial screening of applicants. These call centers had major problems, but they were not the sole source of problems. In late 2009, the federal agency that oversees the Food Stamp program suggested that to save time and money Texas eliminate an asset test and stop fingerprinting applicants. Texas was one of only three states that required fingerprinting, which Texas officials claimed discouraged fraud. In 2010, after being assessed a $4 million fine for slow and inaccurate handling of applications and renewals, Texas added 850 new caseworkers and cleared out the backlogged applications. Moreover, error rates declined to, and have remained well below, the national average.[54]

Beyond the specific issue of food stamps is the broader issue of what the U.S. Department of Agriculture calls "food insecurity." During 2013–2015, 13.7 percent of U.S. households and nearly a quarter of minority households had difficulty keeping adequate food on the table. Among the states, Texas ranked 11th worst, with 15.4 percent of its families food insecure.[55] In the face of serious food insecurity, what does Texas do? Texas Agriculture Commissioner Todd Staples in 2010 drew attention to the fact that only 15 percent of children eligible for summer food programs actually take part. By 2016, the participation rate had fallen below 10 percent and $56 million in federal funds were left on the table because Texas drew too few students to encumber the entire allocation. Needless to say, Texas spent none of its own money to buttress this program.[56]

The Costs of Negligence: Teen Pregnancy, Obesity, and Diabetes

Texas legislators have not always been concerned about teen (and even pre-teen) pregnancy. In 1893, forward looking Texas leaders raised the legal age of consent for girls from 10 to 12 and in 1895 they raised it again to 15. Today in Texas it is illegal in most instances to have sex with a person under 18. [Google "age of consent in Texas" to see why we have to use the word "most" in the previous sentence.] These laws have not been particularly effective as teen pregnancy in Texas has long been, and remains, high. It is also a matter of some concern that almost 40,000 girls under 18 were married in Texas between 2000 and 2014. Only in 2017 did Texas pass a law prohibiting anyone under 16 from getting married and anyone under 18 from getting married without the approval of a judge.[57]

Teen pregnancy and child bearing is costly in many ways, not only to both the teenage mother and child, but also to the state and community. Not surprisingly, Texas has been well above the national average for teen pregnancy, often by three or four percentage points, for as long as records have been kept. Since the mid-1980s, Texas has risen from the mid-thirties to the mid-forties among the states in the teen pregnancy lists. In 1998 and 1999, Texas ranked 50th, surpassed only by Utah. From 2007 through 2014, Texas ranked between 44th and 46th.

Though teen pregnancy and birth rates nationally and in Texas have fallen by nearly half since the early 1990s, Texas teen pregnancy rates remain 30 percent above the national average. An analysis by the National Campaign to Prevent Teen Pregnancy reports that more than a million teen births occurred in Texas from 1991 to 2010, costing $24.3 billion over that period, mostly in social services such as Medicaid and CHIP.[58] In 2014, Texas had the sixth highest teen birth rate in the nation, an improvement on its third highest in the nation finish in 2008 and highest in the nation finish in 2007 (Figure 7.8).

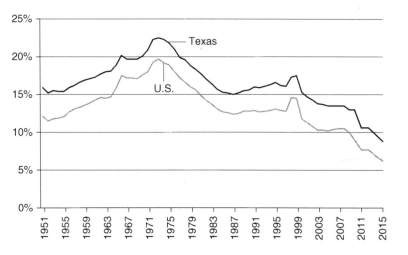

Figure 7.8 Teen Births as a Percentage of Total Live Births in the U.S. and Texas, 1951–2014

Source: United States Census Bureau, Statistical Abstract of the United States, "Low Weight and Births to Teenage Mothers and to Unmarried Women, by States, present to 1985"; prior to 1985, United States Department of Health and Human Services, National Center for Health Statistics, *Vital Statistics of the United States*, vol. 1, Table 1–62.

Texas's approach to the problem of teen pregnancy is more ideological than medical. As noted in Chapter 5, Texas is one of the few states in the nation to depend upon an "abstinence only" sex education program in its public schools.[59] In addition, Texas and Utah were the only two states in 2013 that barred unmarried teenage girls from accessing contraceptives without their parents' permission and one of four states that prohibits CHIP from providing contraceptives. In 2013, Senator Ken Paxton (R-McKinney) offered SB521, a bill to ban Planned Parenthood speakers and materials from Texas public schools.

Another key health problem facing Texans is the increasing rate of obesity. Just 20 years ago, the rate of adult obesity in the U.S. and Texas, while worrisome, was identical at 15.9 percent of the population. Texas moved slightly ahead of the U.S. average in 1996 and never looked back. The latest figures, for 2015, show that the rate of obesity in the U.S. has increased to 28.9 percent while the rate in Texas has increased to 32.4 percent. Colorado was best, with just 20.2 percent obese, Mississippi was worst at 35.6 percent, while Texas's 32.4 percent ranked tenth most obese. But before we celebrate one more time at Mississippi's expense, Texas State Demographer Lloyd Potter and the Texas Health Institute estimate that the obesity rate in Texas will be 42.6 percent by 2040 unless major changes in personal habits and public policy are undertaken.[60]

One of the most dangerous medical conditions related to obesity is diabetes. According to a recent report, about two million Texans are currently diagnosed as diabetic, with another half a million likely diabetic but undiagnosed. The report, by the Texas Health Institute, the State Demographer's Office, and the Methodist Health Care Ministries of South Texas, predicts that the number with diabetes will nearly quadruple to nine million over the next quarter century. Moreover, the burgeoning Hispanic population in Texas is particularly given to obesity and diabetes. The population of diabetic Hispanics is expected to rise from 855,000 in 2010 to 4.7 million by 2040. One in ten health care dollars now goes to manage diabetes and that share of health spending is bound to rise.[61]

Conclusion

The Texas way envisions small government, low taxes, deregulation, and personal responsibility. This model works very well to protect the assets, opportunities, and choices of the well-off. It does less well for those who have little to protect and many needs to fulfill. Some of those needs include access to adequate health care for themselves and their children as well as income and nutritional support during particularly difficult times. Texas elites have always understood that need, even the fear of need, makes the working and lower classes more tractable, more willing to work, even for modest pay and benefits, and more fearful of losing work.

Hence, we see distinctive patterns in the provision of health care and other social service support in Texas. In Medicare, where only federal money is involved, particularly in discretionary aspects of the program such as home health care, usage will be high tending toward abusive. For the last two decades, Medicare costs in Texas per recipient have been about 110 percent of the national average. Patterns of usage and abuse in Texas cities such as McAllen and Dallas have drawn scrutiny and new approaches to uncovering Medicare abuse have been piloted in Texas. The specialized home health care program within Medicare cost 53 percent more than the national average per recipient in 2007 and fully 20 percent of the nation's home health care providers were in Texas. The lid was off the honey pot. Amusingly, Texas denied all responsibility for the fraud but claimed credit for joining, under federal pressure, an initiative to stem it. One newspaper headline parroted the state's preferred interpretation, reading, "Texas to Help Detect Fraud."[62]

Where federal and state money are involved, as with Medicaid and CHIP health care programs, usage is restricted and payments are low. Even though the federal government pays more than 60 percent of the cost, Texas officials complain endlessly about the expense and inflexibility of Medicaid. Texas limits access to Medicaid mainly to poor children and the elderly and disabled. Treatment of elderly Texans under Medicare, including the lavish spending on home health care, provides a good comparison to the meager care afforded elderly Texans in nursing homes under Medicaid. Texas nursing homes housing elderly Medicaid recipients receive $125.68 a day compared to a national average reimbursement of $177.55 a day. Texas ranks 49th. For elderly Texans, if it is federal money, nothing is too good, if it is state money, too good is a dream and barely good enough is the norm.

If possible, Texas is even more tight-fisted with the remnants of what used to be called welfare programs. In the AFDC/TANF program, which provides income support to needy families with children, the national average monthly stipend is $418, compared to Texas's $173, 41 percent of the national average. The Food Stamp program distributes federal dollars, but states are required to share administrative expenses 50/50. Texas responds to these incentives by shortchanging the administrative elements of the program. As a result, during hard times when usage rates are high, Texas has among the highest proportion of applications handled late or erroneously.

Notes

1   T.R. Fehrenbach, *Lone Star: A History of Texas and the Texans*, New York: Macmillan, 1968, p. 598. See also Grieder, *Big, Hot, Cheap, and Right*, New York: Public Affairs, 2013, p. 99.
2   Stanley Siegel, *A Political History of the Texas Republic, 1836–1845*, Austin, TX: University of Texas Press, 1956, pp. 147–148, 151.
3   William Ransom Hogan, *The Texas Republic*, Norman, OK: University of Oklahoma Press, 1946, p. 241. See also Robert Wuthnow, *Rough Country*, Princeton, NJ: Princeton University Press, 2014, pp. 20–22. Roy Appleton, "Long Road to Care of Poor," *Dallas Morning News*, August 17, 2015, pp. A1, A14.
4   Randolph B. Campbell, *An Empire for Slavery: The Peculiar Institution in Texas, 1821–1865*, Baton Rouge, LA: Louisiana State University Press, 1989, pp. 141–142. See also Chris Tomlinson, *Tomlinson Hill*, New York: St. Martin's Press, 2014, p. 27.
5   Robert Perkinson, *Texas Tough: The Rise of America's Prison Empire*, New York: Metropolitan Books, 2010, p. 71.
6   Fehrenbach, *Lone Star*, pp. 649, 651.
7   Richard Morehead, *50 Years in Texas Politics*, Burnet, TX: Eakin Press, 1984, pp. 15, 23.
8   James Reston Jr., *The Lone Star: The Life of John Connally*, New York: Harper and Row, 1989, pp. 39–41, 92–93; D.B. Hardeman and Donald C. Bacon, *Rayburn: A Biography*, New York: Madison Books, 1987, pp. 232–233.
9   Ricky F. Dobbs, *Yellow Dogs and Republicans: Allan Shivers and Texas Two-Party Politics*, College Station, TX: Texas A&M University Press, 2005.
10 Anthony Champagne and Edward J. Harpham, *Texas at the Crossroads: People, Politics, and Policy*, College Station, TX: Texas A&M University Press, 1987, p. 275.
11 Jason DeParle, "For Recession Victims, Patchwork State Aid," *New York Times*, May 10, 2009, pp. A1, A18.
12 See https://nhqrnet.ahrq.gov/inhqrdr/state/select.
13 Dobbs, *Yellow Dogs and Republicans*, p. 54.
14 Frank R. Kemerer, *William Wayne Justice: A Judicial Biography*, Austin, TX: University of Texas Press, 1991/2008, p. 316.
15 Ibid., p. 325.

16 Kaiser State Health Facts, www.kff.org/other/state-indicator/smha-expenditures-per-capita/? state=tx.

17 Corrie MacLaggan, "Lawmakers Poised to Write New Chapter in State School Saga," *Austin American-Statesman*, February 6, 2009.

18 Emily Ramshaw, "Agency to Boost Staff, Conditions," *Dallas Morning News*, May 23, 2009, p. A4.

19 Brittany Martin, "Mental Hospitals Crumbling Away," *Dallas Morning News*, May 31, 2016, pp. A1, A2. See also Edgar Walters, "State Spending More on Mental Health Care, but Wait List for Beds Grows," *The Texas Tribune*, May 1, 2016.

20 Dave Mann, "Gone, Baby, Gone," *Texas Observer*, January 8, 2010, pp. 13–17.

21 Matthew Watkins, "Police Kill a Man at His Home," *Dallas Morning News*, June 15, 2014, A2. www.cnn.com/2015/03/18/us/dallas-police-fatal-shooting-mentally-ill-man-video/.

22 Emily DePrang, "Barred Care: Want Treatment for Mental Health in Houston? Go to Jail," *The Texas Observer*, January 2014, pp. 22–27. See also Ross Ransey, "Analysis: Pay for Mental Health Care or Pay the Jailer," *The Texas Tribune*, June 20, 2014.

23 AP, "Repeat Offenses in Texas Raise Questions over Release of Mentally Ill Juveniles," *New York Times*, December 21, 2009, p. A16.

24 Gromer Jeffers, Jr., "Telemedicine on the Way for Texas," *Dallas Morning News*, May 26, 2017, p. 5D.

25 Steve Jacob, editorial, "Texans Need More Doctors and Nurses," *Dallas Morning News*, July 15, 2010, p. A19.

26 Mitchell Schnurman, "Texans Need Obama's Backstop," *Dallas Morning News,* February 15, 2015, p. D1.

27 Catharine Arnst, "A Second Opinion on Malpractice," *Businessweek*, September 28, 2009, p. 30.

28 Mary Ann Roser, "New Study: Tort Reform Has Not Reduced Health Care Costs in Texas," *Austin American-Statesman*, June 20, 2012.

29 Elliott Fisher, MD, MPH, David Goodman, MD, MS, Jonathan Skinner, PhD, and Kristen Bronner, MA, "Health Care Spending, Quality, and Outcomes: More Isn't Always Better," The Dartmouth Institute, February 27, 2009, p. 2.

30 Atul Gawande, "The Cost Conundrum: What a Texas Town Can Teach Us about Health Care," *The New Yorker*, June 1, 2009, p. 38.

31 Ibid., pp. 37–38.

32 Reed Abelson and Gardiner Harris, "Study Cited for Health-Care Cuts Overstated Its Upside, Critics Say," *New York Times*, June 3, 2010, pp. A1, A8.

33 Jim Landers, "Texas, Take Heed if Medicare Commission Gains Muscle," *Dallas Morning News*, December 8, 2009, pp. D1, D5.

34 Jim Landers, "Getting in Sync, Saving Money," *Dallas Morning News*, December 27, 2009, pp. A1, A29.

35 Gregg Jones, "A Critical Component or Avenue for Fraud," *Dallas Morning News*, September 23, 2009, pp. A1, A12.

36 AARP, Quick Health Facts 2010, Texas, http://aarp.org/research/ppi.

37 Nomaan Merchant, "7 Accused of Bilking $375M from Medicare, Medicaid," *Austin American-Statesman*, February 28, 2012.

38 Jim Landers, "Dr. Gets 10 Years in Fraud," *Dallas Morning News*, December 18, 2014, pp. D1, D5.

39 Kevin Krause, "Doctor Gets 35 Years for Fraud," *Dallas Morning News*, April 10, 2017, pp. A1, A9.

40 Datacenter.commonwealthfund.org/scorecard/state/45/texas.

41 Gregg Jones, "Health Care Law Had Revolving Door Spinning," *Dallas Morning News*, January 5, 2009, pp. A1, A14; see also Daniel L. Hatcher, "Poverty Revenue: The Subversion of Fiscal Federalism," *Arizona Law Review*, vol. 52, 2010, pp. 675–726.

42 The Kaiser Commission on Medicaid and the Uninsured, Table 4a, p. 22.

43 Bob Moos, "Nursing Homes in a Tight Fix," *Dallas Morning News*, March 4, 2009, pp. 1D, 12D.

44 Brian M. Rosenthal, "State Drops Effort to Recover Millions from Alleged Dental Fraud," *Houston Chronicle*, September 22, 2015.

45 Robert A. Calvert, Arnoldo De León, and Gregg Cantrell, *The History of Texas*, 4th ed., Wheeling, IL: Harlan Davidson, Inc., 2007, p. 419.

46 Kevin Sack, "Defying Slump, 13 States Insure More Children," *New York Times*, July 19, 2009, pp. A1, A20.

47 Kaiser Family Foundation, State Health Facts, "Federal Matching Rate for CHIP," www.kff.org/medicaid/state-indicator/total-chip-spending/?dataView.

48 Judith N. McArthur and Harold L. Smith, *Texas through Women's Eyes*, Austin, TX: University of Texas Press, 2010, p. 90. See also Wuthnow, *Rough Country*, pp. 215, 376.

49 Champagne and Harpham, *Texas at the Crossroads*, p. 264.

50 Robert A. Calvert, Arnoldo DeLeon, and Gregg Cantrell, *The History of Texas*, 5th ed., Malden, MA: Wiley Blackwell, 2014, p. 461.

51 Champagne and Harpham, *Texas at the Crossroads*, p. 262. See also Grieder, *Big, Hot*, pp. 121–122.

52 www.fns.usda.gov/snap/government/program-improvement.htm.

53 Corrie MacLaggan, "Backlog, Processing Errors Bedevil Food Stamp Program," *Austin American-Statesman*, September 24, 2009.

54 Robert T. Garrett, "State Praised for Better Handling of Food-Stamp Cases," *Dallas Morning News*, June 17, 2011, p. 3A.

55 U.S. Department of Agriculture, Economic Research Service, *Food Security in the U.S.*

56 Aliyya Swaby, "Texas Has More Kids Eligible for Free Summer Meals. Why Is the State Feeding Fewer," *The Texas Tribune*, August 2, 2017.

57 McComb, *The City in Texas*, p. 193. See also Alex Samuels, "Former Child Bride Lobbies for Bill to Save Others from Her Nightmare," *Texas Tribune*, May 25, 2017.

58 The National Campaign to Prevent Teen Pregnancy, "By the Numbers: The Public Costs of Teen Childbearing," www.teenpregnancy.org/costs.

59 O. Ricardo Pimentel, "Urgency Lacking on Teen Pregnancy," *San Antonio Express-News*, June 2, 2011.

60 For the Eschbach study, see www.texashealthinstitute.org/files/Key_findings_obesity_Eschbach.pdf.

61 Susan Combs, Comptroller of Texas, "Gaining Costs Losing Time: The Obesity Crisis in Texas," 2011 Special Report.

62 Sabriya Rice, "Texas to Help Detect Fraud," *Dallas Morning News*, June 18, 2016, pp. A1, A2.

8 Crime and Punishment in Texas

> In your dealings with Texans of the American extraction you must take care not to provoke them. The consequence might be a bullet in your head, and nobody would take any notice of it.
>
> (Wilhelm Steinert, 1849)[1]

To the modern mind, society's response to crime involves police, courts, and prisons. It was not always so. In early Texas, government was a wispy presence at best. Individual citizens assumed responsibility for their own defense. Those with much to defend used government and law to authorize action at discretion and those who could not defend their own autonomy were dealt with summarily. Local jails held most offenders for brief periods, serious criminals were generally warned away with a pistol butt to the skull or hanged, while only the most fortunate white criminals saw the inside of a prison. For rebellious slaves, it was shackles and the whip.

Interpersonal conflicts tended to be settled directly. The Texas pioneer Noah Smithwick, remembering San Felipe de Austin in the late 1820s, wrote,

> There was a certain doctor who, when under the "influence," was always belligerent. He had a falling out with Colonel DeWitt and challenged him. "You can have your choice of weapons," said the doctor. "All right," said the colonel, "I accept your challenge, and this is my weapon." And with that, he raised his cane and gave the bellicose medico a drubbing that cured him of dueling.[2]

The colonel did not think to call upon the authorities for assistance. Yankees and foreigners found this sort of swift dispute resolution to be disconcerting.

Douglas A. Blackmon, winner of the Pulitzer Prize for his masterful 2008 study, *Slavery by Another Name*, reminds us that, "Prior to the Civil War, all of government in the region, at every level, was unimaginably sparse by modern standards. . . . Incarceration was an expensive and impractical outcome in a society where cash rarely changed hands."[3] Francis C. Sheridan, visiting Texas in 1839, made the same point to his journal, noting "that laws may be said to be received only on sufferance by the people, for the government have not the power or means to enforce them."[4]

Wilhelm Steinert, a 30-year-old German school teacher sent to Texas in 1849 to scout it out for potential immigrants, advised his countrymen to mind their tongues as Texans of American extraction were dangerous when provoked. Probably not coincidentally, 1849 was the year that the Texas state prison at Huntsville, soon known as "the Walls," opened its doors. The Huntsville prison had 225 cells at a spacious $7 \times 5 \times 7$ feet, but just three prisoners on opening day. In 1850, when the prison population had reached 16, the legislature held their first hearings into how to defer the costs of incarceration. Inmate labor seemed the obvious answer. From the beginning, inmates grew their food and performed all of the carpentry, brickwork, and smithing required by the prison and its staff. In 1854, a cotton mill was constructed on prison grounds where inmates produced cloth for their own clothing and for local sale. The cotton mill was the prison's first profit-making enterprise. For the first century and more of their history, Texas prisons were expected to hold inmates at as little cost to the public as possible.[5]

The Texas political culture shaped the state's criminal law and penal system. The dominant traditionalism of the older and more thickly populated sections of the state used law and prisons to protect and serve the interests of the state's propertied Anglo elite. Texas sociologists and criminologists Chad R. Trulson and James M. Marquart wrote that, "In the antebellum Texas prison system . . . Only the most serious white criminals . . . were confined in the . . . penitentiary."[6] Often the formal apparatus of law and courts, much less prisons, were not thought necessary to doing justice, even to white outlaws. Steinert noted in the late summer of 1849 that, "thieves had made the vicinity of Mill Creek [near LaGrange] unsafe. Then 300 citizens caught and hanged 18 of the accused thieves." For his European readers, Steinert explained, "This is called 'lynch law.'"[7] Texans, of course, knew about lynch law and generally approved the efficiency.

Black slaves who ran afoul of white social expectations might be managed in a number of ways. Formally, Texas law gave slaves the right to a jury trial for all major crimes, but as Randolph Campbell noted, "many slaves were punished by their masters without regard to the law."[8] And in some cases, the law had to be forcefully pushed aside before the master's justice could be applied.

> Francis C. Sheridan told of a Negro who had run away from his master and later stolen a stranger's horse. After being apprehended by the horse's owner, the Negro was tried and sentenced to hang. His master heard about the affair and, unwilling to lose valuable property to the gallows, rode with a friend to the town where the Negro was held. "At night, they very easily extracted him from the jail, mounted him on a spare horse, and galloped away."[9]

After slavery, both law and lawlessness were directed at controlling the place and role of blacks in Texas society. Trulson and Marquart point to both phenomena. They note that, "From 1865 to 1883, the Texas prisoner population grew from 165 to 2,301 prisoners, more than half of which were freed slaves." And many black men coming to the adverse notice of whites never made it to prison. Extra-legal racial violence from the petty to the deadly was common. "Between 1885 and 1942, there were 468 lynching victims in Texas, and of these 339 were African-American, 77 were white, 53 were Hispanic, and 1 was Native American . . . Lynchings . . . [were] regarded by many whites at the time as a necessary form of social control."[10] As Robert Perkinson noted in *Texas Tough*, "The strong arm of the law has regularly been deployed not only to protect public safety but to preserve privilege, bolster political fortunes, and, most of all, to discipline those on the social margins, especially African-Americans."[11]

Studies of crime and prisons in Texas highlight the traditional political culture that we have discussed throughout this book. As argued in earlier chapters, Texas was established as an "Anglo republic," Indians and Mexicans were excluded and blacks were enslaved. Texas criminologists James Marquart, Sheldon Ekland-Olson, and Jonathan R. Sorenson apply this broad logic to criminal justice by describing "a cultural tradition of exclusion."[12] People of color were "excluded" from the Anglo understanding of society except as they were useful in subservient roles. After slavery and as the Hispanic population began to increase in the early decades of the twentieth century, segregation maintained racial and ethnic exclusion. Exclusion from social, political, and economic opportunity left Texas minorities with unattractive options and results. Anglo political control allowed use of the state's criminal justice and penal systems to secure Anglo persons, property, and social control against outsiders, whether those outsiders lived among them or not.

As we shall see throughout this chapter, the focus of Texas law, courts, and prisons on minorities, especially blacks, is long-standing. The 3.5 times overrepresentation of blacks at the end of late nineteenth- and early twentieth-century lynch mob ropes and the 2.5 times overrepresentation of blacks in early twentieth-century Texas prisons is present in today's criminal justice statistics. Texas's historic use of law, courts, and prisons as tools of social order and control still stands, as do the effects of the Texas way on the state's poor and minority populations.[13] In Texas prisons today, 34 percent of inmates are black, three times their presence in the population, while 33 percent are Hispanic, and 32 percent are white.

A Brief History of Crime and Punishment in Texas

Nineteenth-century Texas was such a breathtakingly violent place that "Can you top this?" stories became commonplace. The Englishman William Bollaert's diary entry for September 20, 1842, explained that, "[if] a *friend* tells you he will shoot you, or it is intimated by another friend that s^d *friend* intends to have a *difficulty* with you—if you wish to save your own life you must kill s^d *friend* as soon as you can—a jury will find a verdict of not guilty."[14] New York journalist and landscape architect Frederick Law Olmsted, after touring Texas in 1854, confirmed Bollaert's shoot on first frown advice. Olmsted described the regular course taken by personal disputes in Texas; "More often than otherwise, the parties meet upon the plaza by chance, and each, on catching sight of his enemy, draws a revolver, and fires away. As the actors are under more or less excitement, their aim is not apt to be of the most careful and sure, consequently it is, not seldom, the passers-by who suffer."[15]

In fact, as Bollaert and Olmsted well understood, the willingness of offended parties to shoot on sight, even on a public plaza, was dependent upon the understanding nature of Texas juries. Juries were often willing to overlook the unintended injury to persons in the wrong place at the wrong time as, well, unintended. Even military men found the violence of early Texas disconcerting. Albert Sidney Johnston, a West Point graduate and regular U.S. Army officer before moving to Texas in 1834, rose from private to major during the Texas Revolution and, by 1838, was Secretary of War in President Sam Houston's cabinet. Johnston rejoined the U.S. Army during the Mexican War and by 1855 he was in command, with Robert E. Lee as his second in command, of the U.S. Second Cavalry fighting Indians on the Texas frontier. Johnston was responsible for preparing his non-Texan officers for what they might face not just from the Indians in front of them but from the Texans to the rear. Johnston's *Reminiscences* relate, "a story in which a man, after due deliberation, decided to kill his neighbor. He went to his door, rang the bell, and plunged his Bowie knife into his breast. . . . Subsequently he realized that he had killed the wrong man. The coroner's jury acquitted him on the grounds that the man had died by an accident."[16] In mid-nineteenth-century Texas, a jury of one's peers was a true blessing as everyone went armed and knew the danger of recognizing an enemy too late.

Yet, when the army is warned to be careful of the civilians, you can be pretty sure you are in a violent place.

With juries as understanding and lenient as these, Texas judges could assume that those actually convicted of serious crimes were really dangerous. The following story, based on a composite of the real-life misfortunes of John Quick and David Jones, executed for murder in Houston in 1838, is probably apocryphal but was told and retold in Texas and beyond for decades. The *Mississippi Free Trader and Natchez Gazette* rendered the story this way in January 1843:

> A very learned and compassionate judge in Texas, on passing sentence on one John Jones, who had been convicted of murder, concluded his remarks as follows:—The fact is, Jones, that the court did not intend to order you to be executed before next spring, but the weather is very cold—our jail, unfortunately, is in a very bad condition—much of the glass in the windows is broken . . .; besides, owing to the great number of prisoners, not more than one blanket can be allowed to each; to sleep soundly and comfortably, therefore, will be out of the question. In consideration of these circumstances, and wishing to lessen your suffering as much as possible, the Court, in the exercise of its humanity and compassion, do hereby order you to be executed tomorrow morning, as soon after breakfast as may be convenient to the Sheriff and agreeable to you.[17]

Since not everyone could be hanged in the morning, other ways to limit the number of prisoners and the cost of holding them had to be found. The prison population at Huntsville grew in the 1850s but declined during the Civil War—authorities undoubtedly figuring, if these men want to fight, let's send them to the war—from 211 in 1861, to 157 in 1863, and 134 in 1866. In the wake of the Civil War, the Thirteenth Amendment to the U.S. Constitution freed the slaves, presenting white Texans with the critical issue of how to hold free black labor to its traditional agricultural tasks. Share cropping was the general solution, but prisons provided a source of "enslaved" labor. In 1866, the legislature created the Board of Public Labor and charged it to contract with private interests, mostly plantations, to employ the convict labor.[18] In an 1875 report to the governor, the superintendent of prisons explained that "The greater number of persons who have incurred Penitentiary punishment for lesser offenses, since liberty was bestowed upon our uneducated population, are unfitted for other than agricultural employment. . . . Many of these convicts are now at work on plantations."[19]

The initial prisoner lease system was so brutal because, unlike the antebellum slaveowners, the leasors into whose hands the prisoners were placed had no economic reason to concern themselves with their life or health. Initial reforms put prison officials in charge of leased prisoners at their work sites. Still, between 1876 and 1899, fully 2,142 prisoners died and 3,075 escaped. In 1876 alone, 16 percent of all convicts escaped. Over the first two decades of the twentieth century, Texas slowly abandoned convict leasing in favor of prison farms.[20] These new prison farms not only were located in the old East Texas plantation belt, they were organized and run like plantations, principally with black field labor.

The prison at Huntsville housed 503 in 1870, just under 1,700 in 1876, and 2,301 in 1883. There were about 4,000 prisoners in 1909 and 4,800 in 1929. Prison population grew during the Great Depression decade of the 1930s, reaching 7,000 by 1939, before falling during World War II to just 3,000 in 1946. Blacks initially formed a majority of prisoners, falling from about 60 percent in the late nineteenth century to 40 percent in the 1930s. Whites accounted for 30 to 40 percent and Hispanics for about 10 percent.[21] Racial segregation was a mainstay of the Texas prison system. Anglo, black, and Hispanic prisoners were segregated on separate farm units into the mid-twentieth century.

During the third quarter of the twentieth century, the Texas prison system grew slowly under incredibly stable leadership. That leadership was given a free hand so long as it kept scandals out of the press and costs low. H.H. Coffield was chair of the prison board from 1948 to 1977 and only three men served as director of Texas prisons between 1947 and 1983. They were O.B. Ellis (1947–1961), George Beto (1961–1972), and W.J. Estelle (1972–1983). This was the heyday of the Texas prison system; Ellis commonly gets credit for successfully reforming the Texas prison system, Beto gets credit for refining the classic "corrections model" of hold them securely and cheaply, while Estelle gets the blame for the fact that he stood unblinking as it all came apart. Mid-twentieth-century Texas prisons were run by no nonsense characters such as Warden Carl L. "Beartrack" McAdams of the Wynne unit and Warden James V. "Wildcat" Anderson of the Ramsey I unit.

Even as Texas Department of Corrections (TDC) officials boasted that their system was "one of the best in the nation," the nation's corrections community was entering a period of dramatic change. Beginning in the 1960s, the U.S. Department of Justice and the federal courts reflected an evolving national consensus concerning the civil and individual rights of prisoners in which Texas and much of the South did not share. In 1968, the federal courts held in *Lee v. Washington* that Alabama's segregation of its jails and prisons was a violation of the Fourteenth Amendment guarantee of "equal protection." In the early 1970s, the Arkansas and Mississippi prison systems, both organized around prison farms and featuring both official and prisoner violence to maintain order, were found by federal courts to be in violation of Eighth Amendment guarantees against "cruel and unusual punishment." Texas officials girded for a fight.

On October 17, 1972, Allen L. Lamar, a black TDC inmate, filed a lawsuit claiming that segregation in Texas prisons constituted a denial of his and other prisoners' civil rights. In May 1973, the U.S. Department of Justice intervened on behalf of Lamar and against the state of Texas and its TDC. Once consolidated with related cases, *Allen L. Lamar v. H.H. Coffield* became one of the most important civil rights cases in the history of the Texas prison system. *Lamar v. Coffield*, and the even more prominent *Ruiz v. Estelle*, discussed in more detail below, moved in tandem through the federal court system over the course of two decades, from the early 1970s through the early 1990s. Their results transformed the Texas prison system in many ways, some good, some bad.

Lamar challenged segregation by race in Texas prisons from intake and prisoner classification, to assignment to particular prisons and work details, to segregation in social settings such as prison barber shops, day rooms, and mess halls, to cell block and single cell assignments. Texas lost and by October 1978 had signed a consent decree to desegregate, though full compliance took another decade. With the consent decree in *Lamar* signed, attention shifted to the *Ruiz* case where no consent decree could be reached.

On June 29, 1972, David Ruiz, a Hispanic inmate in the maximum security Eastham Unit, filed a broad prisoner rights case, which became *David Ruiz v. W.J. Estelle. Ruiz v. Estelle* was filed in Judge William Wayne Justice's federal courtroom in Tyler,

Texas. Once consolidated with several similar cases, *Ruiz* went to trial in 1979. "Ruiz quickly developed into the most comprehensive prison reform case in legal history."[22] Judge Justice ruled in December 1980 that underfunding and overcrowding produced constitutional deficiencies in the TDC. Justice wrote that "Over crowding at TDC exercises a malignant effect on all aspects of prison life." He also found that underfunding compromised prison security and led to an over-reliance on force. "TDC compensated for its chronic shortages of civilian security personnel by using inmates to perform security functions." "Staff brutality, Justice wrote, was 'widespread' and 'nothing short of routine.'"[23] Texas resisted doggedly. Finally, in 1987 Judge Justice held Texas in contempt of court because its progress had been so slow. Only then did Texas begin to comply with the court's orders. Judge Justice did not release the Texas prison system from federal oversight until 2002, almost 30 years after *Ruiz v. Estelle* was initiated. Needless to say, over this period of time, the great characters among Texas prison wardens disappeared. When you are being hauled into federal court for prisoner abuse, it does not help to be nicknamed "beartrack" or "wildcat."

This remarkable battle between the State of Texas and Judge Justice, and behind him the U.S. Department of Justice and the U.S. Constitution, turned on different and incompatible models of criminal justice and penology. Texas held consistently to a correctional model in which "Their primary responsibility was to the public, and as they saw it, the public in Texas asked only that offenders be held securely and that they work to defray the cost of their incarceration." Hence, as the case played out and Judge Justice found guard brutality and abuse of the system of building tenders, Governor Bill Clements declared that "our department of corrections is one of the finest in the country and I am confident that we will prevail in the higher courts."[24] The State of Texas opened its 1981 appeal of Justice's ruling before the Fifth Circuit Court of Appeals by declaring, in fine Texas fashion, that the TDC administers "the largest prison system in the U.S." and that "the eighteen separate prison units operated by the TDC [are] among the best penal facilities in the country."[25]

Texas Attorney General Mark White (1979–1983), later Governor Mark White (1983–1987), a Democrat, was steadfastly supportive of TDC. As attorney general, even after the Fifth Circuit affirmed Justice's finding that the Texas prison system was unconstitutional and that his court could oversee remedies through a Special Master, "White claimed that the ruling gave 'the state of Texas a sweep on the issues that were before the court. . . . It gives us a much stronger negotiating point. We have the hold cards and they don't.'" Unfortunately for White and for Texas, more and more information supporting Justice's findings on the pervasiveness of the prison tender system and of excessive violence by guards continued to pour out. Finally, White was forced to observe that "It does very little good to try to . . . punish a prisoner, if members of the officials appointed there are violating the law. I hope they weren't. I trust they weren't. If they were, they're going to be dealt with harshly." Yet, as White was leaving the governorship in early 1987, he went out of his way to visit a TDC prison to declare his view that Texas operated "constitutional prisons."

White's successor, Governor Bill Clements, a Republican, used his State of the State address to the opening of the 70th legislative session to declare that the battle over Texas prisons was lost. Clements said, "Let me state clearly the facts of the Ruiz case. The lawsuit is over. . . . We must get in compliance as quickly as possible. We have no choice." Still, the chairman of the TDC Board wondered "how we are ever going to get the judge to believe us, after we lied to him for ten years."[26] Fortunately, by 1990,

Judge Justice was almost as eager as Governor Clements and the recently renamed Texas Department of Criminal Justice (TDCJ) for the case to be concluded. "Judge Justice issued an order in 1990 phasing out the Office of Special Master and ordering the parties to negotiate a comprehensive settlement. In 1992, he approved the settlement in a final judgment consent decree that returned day-to-day control of the system to the Texas Department of Criminal Justice."[27] Judge Justice died in 2009 at age 89.[28]

In 1972, when the Ruiz case was filed, the Texas prison population was just under 17,000. In 1988, as Texas began to move seriously to comply with the court's orders in Ruiz, the Texas prison population was still under 40,000.[29] Over the next two decades, even as crime rates nationwide and in Texas peaked and began a long decline, Texas spent billions of dollars improving and expanding its prison system. The population of Texas prisons more than tripled between 1990 and 1999, rising from 50,042 to 163,190. At its peak in 2008, Texas had 172,000 prisoners distributed among 52 state prisons, 7 contract prisons, and 60 state jails, transfer facilities, boot camps, and hospital facilities. Moreover, unlike most of the policy areas that we have surveyed in previous chapters, the cost of prisons is paid in Texas tax dollars; less than 6 percent comes from the federal government.[30]

The Fiscal Year 2015 Statistical Report of the TDCJ reports that of the 148,146 state prisoners (Texas federal prisoners are not included in the report), 50,191 are black (34 percent), 47,740 are white (32 percent), and 49,427 are Hispanic (33 percent). Recall that the population of Texas in 2015 was 43 percent white, 39 percent Hispanic, and 12.5 percent black, so blacks are overrepresented in Texas prisons by a factor of three, while whites and Hispanics are underrepresented. Texas prisons are no longer segregated, but they are still used for social control.

Crime and Crime Rates in the U.S. and Texas

Texas has often had more crime than the domesticated parts of the country, but reliable numbers go back only to 1960. The FBI collects data on violent crime, which include murder, rape, robbery, and aggravated assault, and property crime, which include burglary, larceny, and auto theft. Both violent crime and property crime increased dramatically in the U.S. and Texas from 1960 into the early 1990s before beginning a steady decline. Annual crime rates are generally reported as the number of crimes per 100,000 of population.

Figure 8.1 shows violent crime in the U.S. and Texas from 1960 to 2015. The levels of violent crime in the U.S. and Texas were identical in 1960 at 161 violent crimes per 100,000 of population. For the next quarter century, violent crime rates nearly quadrupled, to 557 in the U.S. and 550 in Texas in 1985, with Texas numbers at or often trailing U.S. numbers. But since 1986 it has been a different story. Violent crime rates in Texas surpassed those in the U.S. in 1986, peaking in 1991 at 840 in Texas and 758 in the U.S. Since the early 1990s, violent crime rates in Texas and the U.S. have fallen, to 383 in the U.S. and 412 in Texas in 2015, but Texas rates have run ahead of the national average in 22 of the 25 years between 1991 and 2015. In summary, violent crime rates in Texas ran ahead of the U.S. rates in 29 of the 56 years between 1960 and 2015.

Property crime rates in Texas run consistently ahead of U.S. rates and often well ahead (Figure 8.2). During the 1960s and the first half of the 1970s, property crime in the U.S. and Texas rose steadily with Texas usually just marginally ahead of the U.S. That changed in the mid-1970s as U.S. property crime slowed, plateaued from the late

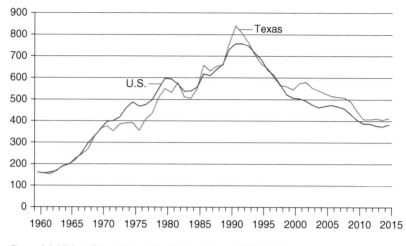

Figure 8.1 Violent Crime Rates in the U.S. and Texas, 1960–2015

Source: U.S. Department of Justice, Office of Justice Programs, Bureau of Justice Statistics, Reported crime in the U.S. and for Texas, violent crime, www.bjs.gov/ucrdata/Search/Crime/State/RunCrimeStatebyState.cfm.

1970s to the early 1990s, and then began a steady decline. The property crime rate continued to rise in Texas through the early 1980s, then saw a dramatic rise from the early 1980s through the early 1990s, before it began its decline, but from much higher levels. For example, in 1980, property crime in Texas registered 5,593 per 100,000, while the national rate was 5,353, lower, but not appreciably. By 1988, the national rate had fallen to 5,027 while the Texas rate had surged to 7,365. The Texas numbers came down in the 1990s, but since 2000 they have remained 15 to 30 percent above the national average.

Figure 8.2 Property Crime Rates in the U.S. and Texas, 1960–2015

Source: U.S. Department of Justice, Office of Justice Programs, Bureau of Justice Statistics, Reported crime in the U.S. and for Texas, property crime, www.bjs.gov/ucrdata/Search/Crime/State/RunCrimeStatebyState.cfm.

We can get another view of how Texas violent and property crime rates compare to those in the U.S. by showing Texas as a percentage of the U.S. rates since 1960 (Figure 8.3). Prior to 1985, Texas usually trailed the U.S. in violent crime but surpassed it in property crime. Since 1985, Texas has generally been above the national average in both violent crime and property crime though it has led in property crime by much more. Still, the most striking aspect of this figure is the dramatic surge in property crime in Texas during the 1980s and early 1990s. As we shall see below, the nation's war on drugs, fought with special gusto in Texas, swelled the prisons. In 2015, Texas violent crime was 108 percent of the U.S. average while property crime was 114 percent of the U.S. average.

Figure 8.1 and Figure 8.2 show that crime rates have been falling in the U.S. and Texas since the early 1990s. Falling crime rates are obviously a good thing, though criminologists and other experts have a hard time explaining why the rates are falling. Some cite new police methods, including the "broken window" theory and CompStat system introduced in New York City in the early 1990s, while others cite the burgeoning prison population. The broken window theory of fighting minor crimes, such as graffiti and vandalism, so that a permissive environment conducive to more serious crime does not develop is undoubtedly part of it. So is CompStat which is a system for tracking crime rates block-by-block so pockets of crime can be flooded with police assets as soon as they arise. But crime rates began to fall in New York City a few years before police methods changed and crime rates fell both in cities that followed the New York model and in cities that did not. Moreover, larger prison populations might reduce crime rates by taking more criminals off the street, but Canada experienced falling crime rates without a rise in prison populations.[31]

Again, falling crime rates are obviously a good thing, even when you are not entirely clear on why they are falling. But Robert Perkinson points out with particular relevance to Texas that crime rates and prison populations "correlate only weakly." As we have seen, crime rates in Texas have been falling since the early 1990s, but as we shall see next,

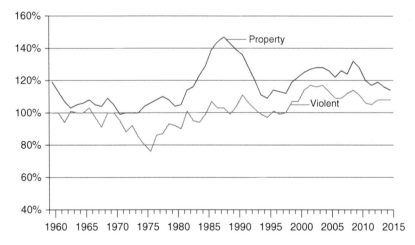

Figure 8.3 Texas Crime Rates as a Percentage of U.S. Rates, 1960–2015

Source: U.S. Department of Justice, Office of Justice Programs, Bureau of Justice Statistics, Reported crime in the U.S. and for Texas, violent crime, www.bjs.gov/ucrdata/Search/Crime/State/RunCrimeStatebyState.cfm.

Texas prison populations grew, in fact skyrocketed, during these same years. Perhaps there are reasons other than rising crime rates for rising prison populations in the U.S. and, more specifically, Texas. Perkinson points out that, "the rise of imprisonment since the seventies has been concentrated overwhelmingly among young African American men, a trend unexplainable by criminal offense data."[32]

Prisons and Incarceration in the U.S. and Texas

The prison population in the U.S. and in the states is generally discussed both in raw numbers (how many people are in prison) and in incarceration rates (the number of prisoners per 100,000 of population). First, the number of persons imprisoned in the U.S. from 1950 to 2009 increased more than ten-fold—from 148,362 in 1950 to 1,615,487 in 2009. A five-year decline, beginning in 2010, left the U.S. prison population at 1,526,800 in 2015. In Texas, the rise in imprisonment has been even steeper, soaring from 6,424 in 1950 to 172,224 in 2011, a nearly 27-fold increase. Texas saw a decline to 163,909 prisoners in 2015, though this is still by far the largest prison population among the states and is falling late and slowly. Strikingly, the U.S. prison population grew moderately from 1950 into the mid-1970s and then much faster through the late 1990s before leveling off. In Texas, the growth was faster from 1950 into the mid-1970s than it was in the U.S. in general, but not dramatically so, before it absolutely exploded through the rest of the century, slowing thereafter.

The social instability of the 1960s convinced many Americans that "law and order" was in danger. President Nixon advocated adoption of mandatory sentencing provisions for drug crimes at both federal and state levels. In 1973, New York's Governor Nelson Rockefeller pushed through a set of stiff mandatory sentences for drug crimes. Many states followed suit and the nation's prison population began to grow. California and Texas were eager participants. Texas Governor Dolph Briscoe used the 1973 and 1977 legislative sessions to enhance the state's anti-drug laws and penalties. In 1973, he supported stiffer penalties for drugs from speed to heroin, and in 1977, he supported stricter rules on probation and parole. Republican Governor Bill Clements, first elected in 1978, continued the anti-drug, tough on crime campaign. Long-time Texas Lieutenant Governor Bill Hobby (1973–1991) has written that, "The Texas war on drugs . . . created new crimes, set higher penalties for old ones, and made it harder to get parole." As a result, "Texas has the largest prison system in the United States."[33]

The U.S. Justice Department's Bureau of Justice Statistics, which collects and organizes most of our national justice statistics, described the general pattern in a study entitled "The Prevalence of Imprisonment." The bureau wrote that "In the 1960s, while crime soared, prison populations declined. What followed in the 1970s was a marked shift in national opinion: increasingly, the public began to demand that the justice system get tough with criminals. The response of the justice system seemed immediate."[34] The U.S. prison population grew by 25 percent in the 1950s, dropped by 7 percent in the 1960s, grew again by 58 percent in the 1970s, 115 percent in the 1980s, 99 percent in the 1990s, before slowing to 21 between 2000 and 2009 (Figure 8.4). Over the entire 59-year period, the U.S. prison population grew 870 percent while the total population merely doubled. A slow decline in the nation's prison population began in 2010.

Texas's contribution to prison growth in the U.S. has been Herculean. As we discussed above, the Texas prison case of *Ruiz v. Estelle* was filed in 1972, went to trial in 1978, was decided against Texas in 1983, and the federal courts did not release Texas prisons from direct supervision until 1992. Texas's response to the intervention of the federal courts

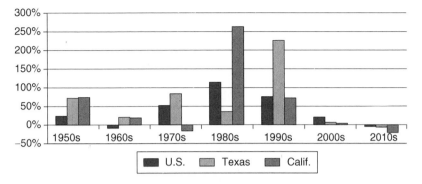

Figure 8.4 Percentage Growth in Prison Population by Decade, 1950–Present

Source: U.S. Census Bureau, Statistical Abstract of the United States, Law Enforcement, Courts, and Prisons, Prisoners under Jurisdiction of State or Federal Correctional Authorities, Summary by State, various years, www.census.gov/library/publications/time-series/statistical_abstracts.html.

was to build more prisons. In 1950, Texas held just 6,424 prisoners in Huntsville and a handful of smaller facilities. By the end of the 1970s, the Texas prison system comprised 18 prisons holding about 25,000 inmates. During the 1980s, Texas struggled to hold down the prison population, comply with Judge Justice's ruling, and build prisons for the day when they no longer answered to the judge: "In the late 1980s and early 1990s, the state built eighty-nine more prisons that could house 140,000 more inmates."[35]

As the U.S. prison population burgeoned in the last quarter of the twentieth century, not all states grew at the same rate or began their growth at the same time. Figure 8.4 and Figure 8.5 show this clearly. In the 1950s, Texas expanded its prison population by 73 percent while California expanded by 75 percent; in the 1960s, Texas grew by 21 percent, California by 20; in the 1970s, Texas grew by 85 percent while California shrank by 15 percent. But California was just taking a breather to build more prisons. In the 1980s, Texas's prison population grew by just 36 percent while California's skyrocketed by 263 percent. Not to be outdone, Texas expanded by 226 percent in the 1990s, compared to California's 76 percent. Both slowed between 2000 and 2009, to 8 percent for Texas and 5 percent for California. The federal courts have demanded reductions in California's prison population while Texas's has declined more slowly due to financial pressures. Between 2010 and 2015, the California prison population fell by 21 percent while the Texas prison population declined by 6 percent.

Figure 8.5 shows that the prison population of some states, California and Texas, grew dramatically, Florida and New York grew steadily but moderately, while Virginia and Georgia obviously worked to hold down growth. New York is particularly interesting. New York in 1950 had the nation's largest prison population, though it had fallen behind California in terms of population. But New York held its prison population steady for the next quarter century, until the Rockefeller drug laws more than quadrupled it between 1973 and 1999. California surpassed New York by the late 1950s and, except for a brief period in the late 1970s, has held twice as many prisoners as New York. Figure 8.5 clearly shows, as the bar chart did, that the California prison population took off nearly a full decade before Texas's truly began to soar. Under federal court mandate, California's prison population began a steep decline in 2010. Florida's

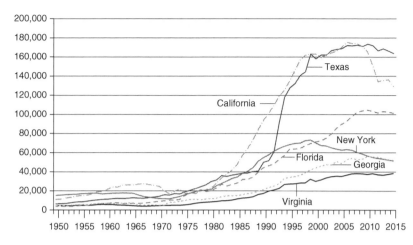

Figure 8.5 Prisoners Held in Texas and Other Large States, 1950–2015

Source: U.S. Census Bureau, Statistical Abstract of the United States, Law Enforcement, Courts, and Prisons, Prisoners under Jurisdiction of State or Federal Correctional Authorities, Summary by State, various years, www.census.gov/library/publications/time-series/statistical_abstracts.html

prison population grew steadily beginning around 1980, but never as dramatically as California and Texas. New York tracked Florida's steady rise through the 1980s and 1990s, but its numbers declined over 36 percent between 2000 and 2015. Georgia and Virginia have held their prison populations down throughout.

Another way to look at imprisonment in the U.S., Texas, and other states is to move from the raw number of prisoners to incarceration rates. Incarceration rates control for population growth by measuring imprisonment as the number of prisoners per 100,000 of population. Incarceration rates paint a remarkable picture, especially in regard to Texas. Interestingly, in 1950 Texas had a lower incarceration rate (at 83) than the U.S. (109) or any of the states, California (104), New York (103), Virginia (134), Florida (143), and Georgia (132), that we have been using to put Texas in context.

Looking more closely at the pattern of growth in the U.S. incarceration rate, we see that it rose modestly between 1950 and 1961, from 109 to 119, before falling slowly through the 1960s to a low of 93 in 1972. A slow rise through the 1970s put the incarceration rate at 133 in 1979. Looking across the period 1950 to 1979, we see a modest rise of just 22 percent, or less than 1 percent per year. Growth rates increased dramatically during the 1980s, almost exactly doubling from 139 in 1980 to 276 in 1989. Incarceration rates increased another 60 percent during the 1990s, rising from 297 in 1990 to 476 in 1999, before slowing to 5 percent for the period 2000 to 2009. Incarceration rates have declined modestly since 2009.

Glancing briefly back at Figure 8.5, which depicts prison population by state, the figure suggests that both California and Texas expanded dramatically in the 1980s and 1990s. Figure 8.6 tells a different and more accurate story. California's incarceration rate was 104 per 100,000 of population in 1950, rose to the 140s for most of the 1960s, before falling to a low of 80 by 1977. In fact, California's incarceration rate dropped by 11 percent, from 104 to 93, well below the national average, during the three decades from 1950 to 1979. California's incarceration rate increased by 196 percent, effectively tripling, during the 1980s. In 1980, California's incarceration rate stood at 98 per 100,000

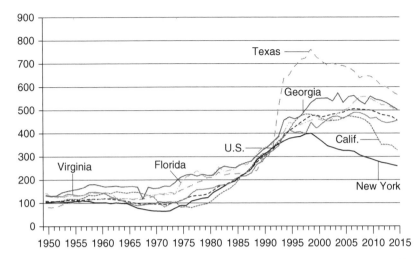

Figure 8.6 Federal and State Incarceration Rates, 1950–2015

Source: The U.S. incarceration rates come from the U.S. Census Bureau, Statistical Abstract of the United States, Mini-Historical Statistics, No. HS-24, Federal and State Prisoners, 1925–2001. U.S. Census, *Statistical Abstract of the United States*, various years, section "Law Enforcement, Courts, and Prisons." U.S. Department of Justice, Office of Justice Programs, Bureau of Justice Statistics, "Prisoners in 2015" and various years; www.bjs.gov/content/pub/pdf/p15.pdf

of population and in 1989 it stood at 290. Nonetheless, because California's population was so large and growing so fast, its incarceration rate never went much above the national average. During the 1990s it increased to 481 before dropping slightly thereafter. A court-enforced reduction in the state's prison population sent its incarceration rate from 458 in 2009 to 329 in 2015.

The pattern for Texas in Figure 8.6 is much more striking. In 1950, Texas had an incarceration rate, at 83 per 100,000 of population, that was just 76 percent of the national rate (109). The Texas rate rose faster than the national rate during the 1950s until Texas tied with the U.S. in 1959 and 1960 at 117. The 1960s saw very moderate growth, just 4 percent, in Texas. The 1970s and 1980s saw somewhat faster, but still fairly moderate growth, 87.5 percent over two decades, from 128 to 240 per 100,000 of population, compared to 187.5 for the nation. In fact, as late as 1987 Texas and the U.S. were tied at 231 and from 1988 through 1991, the incarceration rate in Texas was below the national rate. The years 1993–1994 changed everything as the incarceration rate in Texas jumped from 385 per 100,000 in 1993 to 636 in 1994 and then kept going through the remainder of the decade, peaking at 762 in 1999. It has since fallen to 568, seventh highest in the nation behind Louisiana (at an astonishing 776), Oklahoma (715), Mississippi (689), Alabama (611), Arizona (596), and Arkansas (591).

Figure 8.6 highlights the impact of *Ruiz v. Estelle* on incarceration rates in Texas. Prior to Ruiz, rates increased a bit in the 1950s and fell a bit in the 1960s, but they remained in a fairly narrow band. Incarceration rates picked up in the 1970s, growing by 39 percent nationally and 53 percent in Texas, but Texas remained in the middle of the pack. Briefly, in the late 1980s, as the court orders issued by Judge Justice in *Ruiz v. Estelle* took effect, Texas fell behind the national average and behind all of our comparison states. However, as dramatically increased expenditures brought new capacity online, Texas incarceration rates leapt. In 1992, the U.S. and all six states in our chart had nearly identical incarceration rates, ranging from Virginia's low of 327 to Georgia's high of 365, with the U.S. average at 332 and Texas at 344. Over the next two years, Texas jumped to 511 and then to 636, a jump highlighted in the chart.

Figure 8.7 provides the clearest perspective yet on Texas's evolving proclivity to imprison. Figure 8.7 compares Texas's share of the total U.S. population with Texas's share of the total U.S. prison population. In 1950, Texas accounted for 5.1 percent of the total U.S. population and 4.3 percent of its prison population. By 1959 the population and prison number had met at 5.3 percent of both population and prisoners. Over the next two decades, the tumultuous 1960s and the more conservative 1970s, Texas sought social order in an expanded prison system. In 1980, Texas accounted for 6.3 percent of the U.S. population and 9.5 percent of its prisoners. However, as Judge Justice pushed toward a final resolution of the *Ruiz v. Estelle* lawsuit, overcrowding of Texas prisons was a major point of contention. In early 1982, 4,000 Texas prisoners were housed in tents. In spring 1982, the corrections board ordered the prison system not to accept any more prisoners. Before long 30,000 state prisoners were backlogged in county jails. Texas's response was a prison-building program. Texas added 108,000 beds after 1983 at a cost of $2.3 billion, but in the short term it was forced to bring its inmate population down. By 1989, Texas had 6.8 percent of population and just 6 percent of prisoners. But just as soon as Judge Justice relinquished day-to-day control of the prisons and new prison capacity came online, the Texas prison population shot to unprecedented heights. By 1999, Texas accounted for 7.4 percent of the total U.S. population and 12.5 percent of prison inmates. In 2015, Texas accounted for 8.5 percent of the U.S. population and 10.7 percent of inmates.

Figure 8.7 suggests that, absent Judge Justice's control of the Texas prison system in the late 1970s and 1980s, its response to the cultural revolution of the 1960s would have been a rapid build out from the 1960s through the 1990s. The cultural panic spawned in Texas by the civil rights revolution, the anti-war movement, the women's movement,

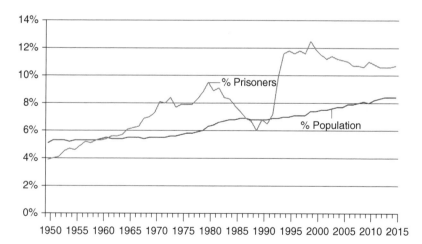

Figure 8.7 Texas Population and Prisoners as a Percentage of U.S. Population and Prisoners, 1950–2015

Source: U.S. Census Bureau, Statistical Abstract of the United States, various years, Population section and Law Enforcement, Courts, and Prisons section.

and rising crime rates produced the state's gargantuan prison system. Issues of race and gender are still with us, but crime rates began abating more than a quarter century ago. Nonetheless, the Texas prison population did not stop growing until 2011 and now the state is saddled with a bloated prison system and unsustainable prison costs. A few Texas politicians have begun to think about new directions.

In 2007, led by Senator John Whitmire, chair of the Senate Criminal Justice Committee, and Representative Jerry Madden, chair of the House Corrections Committee, the Texas Legislature decided it could afford no more new prisons. Texas prisons were near capacity and the state was looking at another $503 million in additional construction costs over the next five years. Instead, working with the U.S. Department of Justice and the Pew Charitable Trusts' Center on the States, the 2007 legislative session diverted about half of those funds from new prison construction to programs for prison diversion, more effective use of probation and parole, and community residential and addiction treatment facilities.[36]

By 2009, growth of the Texas prison system had slowed markedly. Officials claimed that they had 2,000 empty prison beds and that no new prisons would be needed for at least five years. Representative Madden noted that, "the research showed that our prisons were being overwhelmed by those who could receive alternative treatment to incarceration and therefore preserve our resources for the dangerous violent offender." Madden neglected to say that these insights had come to other state prison authorities a decade or more earlier. Instead, he simply noted that Texans are, "a proud people who don't like to change. But now being tough and smart on crime is a better utilization of the taxpayer dollar."[37] Despite the official crowing, inmates in Texas numbered 172,116 in 2006 and 172,224 in 2011, though the number did drop to 163,909 in 2015.

Correctional Employment and Expenditures in the U.S. and Texas

Looking at correctional employment in Texas and the U.S. provides another interesting insight into the effect on the Texas prison system of Judge Justice's handling of *Ruiz v. Estelle*. In his testimony at the Ruiz trial, Director W.J. Estelle (1972–1983) reported that staff-to-inmate ratios in Texas were among the lowest in the nation during his tenure. At the time of trial, October 1978 through June 1979, the average guard-to-prisoner ratio nationwide was 1 to 5, while in Texas it was 1 to 12.45. Estelle also testified that turnover ratios among lower level staff ran at 60 to 70 percent annually.[38] Judge Justice found that overcrowding and insufficient staffing led to an unconstitutional denial of prisoner rights. When Judge Justice issued his final decree in April 1981, he ordered that the staff-to-prisoner ratio be reduced from 1-to-12 to 1-to-6. Texas appealed the overcrowding and staffing findings, which were modified by the Fifth Circuit Court of Appeals in June 1982, but not before the TDC Board closed Texas prisons to new admissions in May. In a June Special Session, the legislature authorized $58 million in new expenditures for prison construction and additional staffing. Nonetheless, as we have seen above, the Texas prison population went sideways during the 1980s, awaiting new prisons and more staff. Between 1979 and 1985, corrections staff expanded from 2,500 to 9,000.[39]

Still, Texas responded only as it had to and only in its traditional fashion. Texas increased prison spending and hiring, but continued to spend less per capita on prisoners and guards than the rest of the nation. State appropriations for prisons rose from $50 million in 1975, to $300 million in 1980, $1 billion in 1985, $1.7 billion in 1996, $2.3 billion in 2001, and $4 billion in 2015. Texas also increased its corrections staff.

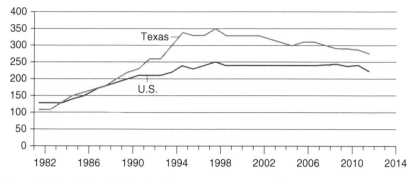

Figure 8.8 Correctional Staff in the U.S. and Texas per 100,000 of Population, 1982–2012

Source: Bureau of Justice Statistics, Criminal Justice Expenditure and Employment Extracts, Table 8, www.bjs. gov/index.cfm?ty=pbdetail&iid=5239.

In 1982, Texas had 110 corrections staff per 100,000 of population compared to 130 nationally. By 1985, Texas had surpassed the U.S. average by 150 to 140 and by 1995 Texas had 340 correctional staff for every 100,000 of population while the U.S. averaged 240. As Figure 8.8 shows, the U.S. has dropped to about 220 while Texas has just fallen below 270.

Despite decades of increased prison funding, Texas continued to lag on expenditures per prisoner and on pay for corrections officers. Data on annual cost per prisoner in the U.S. and Texas are scattered but quite consistent. In 1974, Texas spent just under $1,100 annually per prisoner. As *Ruiz v. Estelle* was about to be decided in 1980, Texas spent $2,679 annually, in 1983 it spent $6,951, in 1985 it spent $10,950, and in 1988 it spent $12,500. By comparison, California spent $22,597 per prisoner in 1988 and in 1990 the U.S. average per prisoner was $18,400.[40]

In 1996 and 2001, the Bureau of Justice Statistics' "State Prison Expenditures," the only systematic federal comparisons of state prisoner expenditures per year, showed Texas lagging far behind. In 1996, Texas spent $12,215 per prisoner, compared to the U.S. average of $20,142 and California's $21,385. Texas ranked 47th among the states, trailing only Alabama, Mississippi, and Oklahoma. In 2001, Texas spent $13,808, compared to the U.S. average of $22,650 and California's $25,053. Texas ranked 46th among the states, trailing only Alabama, Louisiana, Mississippi, and Missouri. A recent study by the highly respected Pew Charitable Trust, "One in 31: The Long Reach of American Corrections," using 2008 data, shows a national cost per prisoner of $28,817 to Texas's $15,527. Finally, the Vera Institute of Justice did a study, using 2015 data from 45 states, that included incarceration costs outside the traditional corrections budget. The Vera study reported an average cost per prisoner of $33,274, compared to Texas's annual cost of $22,012—66 percent of the national average.[41]

Perhaps even more telling is the comparison between the annual salary of corrections officers in the U.S. and in Texas. Recall that Director Estelle testified in the Ruiz trial that he had a turnover ratio of 60 to 70 percent annually among his lower level guards. Even today, we can immediately see why that would be so. We have good data only for 1993 through 2012, but it is telling. In 1993, Texas prison guards made 82 percent as much as their peers nationally, $24,252 vs. $29,556. In 2012, Texas prison guards made just 70 percent as much as their national peers, \$35,448 vs. \$50,436 and—surprise—turnover remained high. By 2013, guards were leaving in droves to take jobs in the oil and gas fields and guard pay had slipped to 43rd in the nation.[42] Texas did legislate an 8 percent raise for corrections officers during the 2016–17 biennium, which will help, but officers in other states will be getting raises too. Texas will only make real progress in stabilizing its guard population if it sticks with pay and benefits improvements over a number of years and the state has not shown the ability to do that in the past.

The Death Penalty in the U.S. and Texas

One of the more puzzling aspects of Texas's approach to crime and punishment has been its relatively recent but fervid commitment to the death penalty. For most of the state's history, the death penalty was used regularly, at somewhat higher rates than the nation as a whole, but not at rates disproportionate to the South as a region. Like the rest of the South, Texas used the death penalty predominantly against minorities until the U.S. Supreme Court stepped in to demand change. First, we will look at the broad sweep of Texas history to show that the death penalty was, in fact, used largely against minorities. Second, we will compare use of the death penalty in Texas to that in other major states and the nation from 1950 to the present. Finally, we will look at the exoneration movement nationally and in Texas.

First, from 1819 to 1974, 62 percent of the persons executed in Texas were black, 28 percent were white, 10 percent were Hispanic, and a small number were unidentified by race.[43] Simple inconsistency in how the death penalty was applied in the U.S. led the Supreme Court, in a series of decisions beginning with *Robinson v. California* (1962) and culminating in *Furman v. Georgia* and *Branch v. Texas*, both in 1972, to find the death penalty as then applied unconstitutional in light of the Eighth and Fourteenth Amendments provisions regarding "cruel and unusual punishment" and "equal protection of the laws." The court noted racial disparities in the application of the death penalty but did not cite them as the basis for unconstitutionality.

Interestingly, when the death penalty came under judicial scrutiny in the Robinson case, Texas, though not directly involved, suspended its use of the death penalty in 1965. The U.S. Supreme Court suspended the death penalty nationally in 1972 and after a four-year moratorium, states that had reformed their death penalty statutes and standards to insure that they were employed consistently were permitted to reinstate the death penalty. Even states that did reinstate the death penalty were cautious in using it. Texas did not begin using the death penalty again until 1982. But by the early 1990s Texas was using the death penalty much more than it ever had before and much more than any other state.

The debate in the Texas Legislature over whether and in what form to reinstitute the death penalty was both interesting and entertaining. The outcome was not really in doubt as all of the southern states eventually reinstituted the death penalty, but there was opposition. It was quelled by an appeal to Texas commonsense. Arguing in favor of the death penalty, a combative San Antonio attorney named Fred A. Semann made the point that while civilized states like Minnesota might get away without the death penalty, Texas could not. When first-term Texas House member Craig Washington (D-Houston) asked him whether he thought Texans were more violent than others, he answered yes, saying, "I don't think in Maine, New Hampshire, Vermont and those states people go to a beer joint the way some people do in Texas—sit there and drink beer, and because somebody goes up and puts a nickel in a jukebox and plays a tune that somebody else don't like, kill him for it. That's been done here!"[44] The logic was irrefutable; Texas House Bill 200 was approved (114 to 30 in the House and 27 to four in the Senate) and went into effect on June 14, 1973. Texas was one of the first states to reinstitute the death penalty, though it did not use it for nearly a decade.

Death penalty convictions in the U.S. peaked at 315 in 1996 and have since fallen steeply, to 223 in 2000, 114 in 2010, and just 30 in 2016. Texas averaged 34 death sentences a year throughout the 1990s, but just 9 in 2012, and 4 in 2016. Most analysts point to the passage in Texas in 2005 of the "life without parole" option to the death penalty. Since 2005, Texas has averaged between 8 and 9 death sentences annually. Still, Texas death row is backed up and executions, though also down, still ran at 20 a year from 2005 to 2010, but only 14 a year since.

Figure 8.9, covering the 1830s to the 2000s, shows the high proportion of minority executions prior to the 1970s and the somewhat smaller proportion following the Supreme Court's rulings in *Furman v. Georgia* and *Branch v. Texas*. Before the Civil War, blacks as property were rarely executed. After the Civil War, and, more particularly, after Reconstruction when whites were employing all tools to reestablish unchallenged sway, blacks were sent to the gallows and, after 1924, the electric chair, in numbers that did not begin to taper off until the 1950s. By the time Texas returned to execution in early 1982, lethal injection had replaced electrocution as the method of execution. The total number of executions soared, though for the first time since Reconstruction slightly more whites were executed than blacks. From 1982 through 2016, Texas executed 540 persons: 36 percent black, 45 percent white, and 17 percent Hispanic. Nonetheless, while whites and Hispanics were executed at rates lower than their presence in the population, blacks were executed at a stunning three times the rate that their presence in the population would suggest.

Figure 8.10 highlights Texas's modern avidity for the death penalty. The third quarter of the twentieth century saw widespread questioning of the death penalty, at least

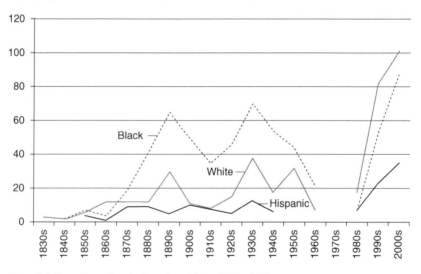

Figure 8.9 Texas Executions by Decade and Race, 1830s–2016

Source: Death Penalty Information, the Espy file and the Executions by state file. See www.deathpenaltyinfo. org/number-executions-state-and-region-1976.

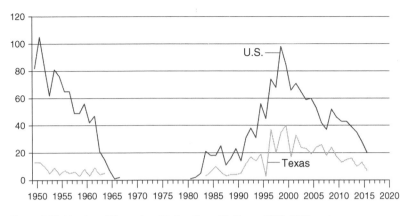

Figure 8.10 Number of Executions Nationally and in Texas, 1950–2016

Source: U.S. execution numbers, 1930–2010, Bureau of Justice Statistics. See also Death Penalty Information Center, Executions by State, www.deathpenaltyinfo.org and the U.S. Census Bureau, Statistical Abstract of the United States, Law Enforcement, Courts, and Prisons section, "Prisoners Executed under Civil Authority by States," various years.

in its application if not in its fundamental legitimacy. The number of executions in the U.S. came steadily down while a series of legal challenges to the implementation of the death penalty, its fundamental fairness, and its constitutionality made their way through the nation's courts. Though the Supreme Court did not declare a legal moratorium until 1972 and then began to lift the moratorium on a state-by-state basis in 1976, virtually all states halted use of the death penalty by the mid-1960s and did not return to it until the early 1980s. Texas carried out no executions between 1965 and 1981. In fact, executions in Texas remained generally in single digits into the early 1990s. However, from 1991 through 2016, Texas averaged 19 executions per year, fully 41 percent of all of the executions carried out in the U.S. during that period.

While the death penalty is under review in some states, it is not in Texas. Eighteen states and D.C. no longer have the death penalty and 15 more have used it ten or fewer times since 1976.[45] Since the death penalty was reinstated in 1976, six states—New York in 2004, New Jersey in 2007, New Mexico in 2009, Illinois in 2011, Connecticut in 2012, and Maryland in 2013—have abolished the death penalty.[46] About three-quarters of Texans support the death penalty and candidates for office generally voice full-throated support.

Exoneration in the U.S. and Texas

Many Americans and more Texans think of some crimes, horrific murders being the most obvious example, as worthy of the death penalty. Still, virtually all supporters of the death penalty presume that only the worst will be sentenced to death and that extraordinary care will be taken to assure that innocents are not mistakenly caught up in this terrible process. But many now wonder whether there is too great a possibility that an innocent person might be convicted, sentenced to death, and executed. Since 1973, 157 men who were tried, convicted, and sentenced to death have had their convictions reversed—they have been exonerated—and been released. Other men and women have been convicted of lesser crimes, later found innocent and released, but most of the attention revolves around those sentenced to death and later released because in these cases the state had come closest to irreversible error—executing an innocent person.

The posthumous pardon of Timothy Cole in March 2010 raised many troubling questions. Timothy Cole was convicted of raping a fellow Texas Tech student in 1985. He protested his innocence at trial and throughout his 11 years in prison. He died in prison of an asthma-induced heart attack in 1999. Meanwhile, another Texas inmate, Jerry Wayne Johnson, began admitting to various rapes and in 2007, unaware that Cole had died, wrote to Cole's mother admitting to that rape. Subsequent DNA testing confirmed Cole's innocence and Johnson's guilt. Governor Perry issued the state's first posthumous pardon, clearing Cole's name nearly two decades after his conviction and a decade after his death. Had Timothy Cole gone on to graduate from Texas Tech, rather than being wrongly imprisoned for more than a decade, it is highly unlikely that he would have died of complications from asthma. In 2015, Governor Abbott signed legislation establishing an 11-member Timothy Cole Exoneration Committee to recommend reforms to limit future mistakes.

Despite the posthumous pardon of Timothy Cole, Texas officials have remained resistant to the very idea of judicial error. Texas has so many people on death row, 254, and has executed so many people since 1976, 540, that most state officials are reluctant to allow even for the possibility that the death penalty has been used mistakenly. While Texas has executed 37.3 percent (540 of 1,446) of the persons executed in the U.S. over the past four decades, a little over 8 percent (13 of 157) of the death row inmates exonerated in the U.S. have been in Texas. Alternatively, Florida, which has more people on death row, 396, but has executed fewer, 92, has exonerated and released 26 people. Either Florida was much sloppier than Texas to begin with, sending people to death row who they later had to release, or they are being much more careful now. California provides another model. California has more people on death row, 741, and executed far fewer of them, just 13 since 1976, but has exonerated only three. California has not exonerated many people, but they are much less likely than Texas to make a mistake they cannot correct. Table 8.1 indicates that Florida and California are not alone in being more careful than Texas. Everyone is more careful. Ominously, Texas ranks 50th among the 50 states and D.C. in providing legal assistance to indigent defendants.

Table 8.1 Death Row Inmates, Executions, and Exonerations

States	*Death Row, 2016*	*Executions since 1976*	*Exonerations since 1973*	*Exonerations as % of Executions*
California	741	13	3	23%
Texas	254	540	13	2%
Florida	396	92	26	28%
Pennsylvania	175	3	6	200%
Alabama	194	58	6	10%
Ohio	142	53	9	17%
North Carolina	155	43	9	21%
Arizona	126	37	9	24%
Georgia	68	69	6	9%
Oklahoma	47	112	10	9%
Louisiana	77	28	10	36%
South Carolina	43	43	2	5%

Source: Death Penalty Information Center, www.deathpenaltyinfo.org.

We close with the ongoing controversy surrounding the execution of Cameron Todd Willingham. Willingham was executed by the state of Texas in 2004 for the 1991 house fire, judged to be arson by the initial investigation and at trial, that killed his three young children.

Willingham professed his innocence throughout and subsequent review of the evidence upon which he was convicted, sentenced, and executed has called much of it into question. Specifically, three separate reviews of the forensic evidence by a total of seven of the nation's leading arson experts led them to question whether arson had in fact occurred. If the house fire was not arson, then the children's deaths were not murder and the execution was unwarranted.

The controversy around the Willingham case had been percolating since before his execution on February 17, 2004, but did not become a national story until 2009.[47] As Willingham awaited execution in 2004, a nationally acclaimed fire expert named Gerald Hurst reexamined the trial evidence and declared that the fire had been accidental—not arson. Hurst wrote a report outlining his conclusions and submitted them to Governor Perry's office and the state Board of Pardons and Paroles. Neither took explicit note of his findings. As the execution date approached, Hurst said that "the most distressing thing is the state of Texas will kill an innocent man and doesn't care they're making a mistake."[48] The execution was carried out as scheduled. Hurst subsequently told the *Chicago Tribune* that "there's nothing to suggest to any reasonable arson investigator that this was an arson fire. It was just a fire."[49]

In 2009, Craig Beyler, another renowned arson investigator, compiled a report for the Texas Forensic Science Commission (TFSC), again finding no evidence of arson. Governor Rick Perry responded that he was "familiar with the latter-day supposed experts on the arson side of it. . . . I have not seen anything that would cause me to think that the decision that was made by the courts of the state of Texas was not correct."[50] Still, even jaded long-time political observers were stunned when Governor Perry abruptly replaced three members of the TFSC, including the chairman, just two days before the Commission was set to examine Beyler's findings. The new chairman, District Attorney John Bradley of Williamson County, promptly cancelled the meeting arguing that he and his new colleagues needed time to get up to speed on the case. Newspapers from Chicago to Houston, spurred by charges of cover-up issued by Barry Scheck of the Innocence Project, cried foul. The outgoing chairman, Sam Bassett, who Perry had named to his post two years earlier, said "In my view, we should not fail to investigate important forensic issues in cases simply because there might be political ramifications." And Senator Kay Bailey Hutchison, Perry's opponent for the Republican gubernatorial nomination in 2010, stirred the pot by asking, "Why wouldn't you at least have the hearing that the former member suggested, to find out what the facts are, when a man has been executed and now the facts are in dispute?" She closed, covering her Texas political bases, by declaring, "I am strongly for the death penalty, but always with the absolute assurance that you have the ability to be sure—with the technology that we have—that a person is guilty."[51] Governor Perry then sent the conspiracy theorists into further paroxysms of outrage when he refused to release the documents that were provided for his review (some question whether the documents really were closely reviewed) in the hours before Willingham was executed.

In the days following the reorganization the TFSC, Sam Bassett, the ousted chair, told the *Chicago Tribune* that top legal aides to the governor had tried to pressure him over the direction of the Willingham review. Bassett had been called to two meetings with lawyers from the governor's general counsel's office and representatives of that office had been attending the Commission's meetings. Bassett expressed concern for the future of the TFSC, saying "It's clear to me that the Willingham investigation is a lightning rod for the future of the commission. I'll never, ever say we shouldn't have taken on that investigation."[52] Beyler, the fire expert, called Perry "unethical." Beyler argued that "the governor had a conflict of interest because he approved the execution of Cameron Todd Willingham of Corsicana. His failure to recuse himself is both unethical and injurious to the cause of justice." Perry responded by forcefully declaring that Willingham was "a monster." "This was a guy that murdered his three children, who tried to beat his wife into an abortion—person after person has stood up and testified to the facts of this case that, quite frankly, you guys aren't covering," Perry said to the media. "This was a bad man."[53]

The state's newspapers were unsatisfied by Governor Perry's increasing emotional protestations. Lisa Falkenberg wrote a commentary in the *Houston Chronicle* noting that "being a bad man isn't a crime punishable by death, even in Texas." Falkenberg went on to say that,

> the fact that he was a "bad man," that he beat his pregnant wife, that he'd been convicted of low-level crimes, that he was fond of expletives, might have been enough, even a month ago to sow doubt about his innocence or simply deflect attention from the case of such an unsympathetic figure. But the story isn't about Willingham anymore. It isn't just about guilt or innocence. It isn't even about whether Perry did his homework before allowing Willingham's 2004 execution. It's about whether Perry is purposely trying to subvert the law in Willingham's case, and potentially obstruct justice in countless other arson cases that could benefit from the commission's review, all for political gain during a hotly contested primary.[54]

Governor Perry's newly named commission chair declared in early 2010 that the Commission's procedures for handling complex cases such as Willingham's needed to be refined before the case responsibly could be considered. Critics howled, but the process went underground for much of the year. Governor Perry easily survived the March 2010 Republican primary, beating Senator Kay Bailey Hutchison by 20 points, and then cruising to re-election later in the year. Just weeks prior to the general election, Chairman Bradley offered the Commission a draft report clearing arson investigators of any fault in the Willingham case. The Commission rejected the draft and members declared their intention to interview arson experts about the state of fire investigation science in 1994 and whether the investigators in the Willingham case appeared to have understood the science and applied it correctly. In other words, Perry's maneuver and Chairman Bradley's stalling left the Commission right where it had been a year earlier, needing to interview fire investigation experts. This did not go unnoticed. When Governor Perry nominated Bradley in 2011 for a full term as commission chair, the overwhelmingly Republican Texas Senate rejected the nomination. Perry's next nominee, Dr. Nizam Peerwani, the highly respected Chief Medical Examiner for Tarrant County, would have been expected to bring the Willingham case to a public resolution. Grizzled old veterans of Texas politics smiled when Texas Attorney General Greg Abbott declared in mid-2011 that the TFSC had no legal authority to investigate fires before the date of its founding in 2005. The TFSC did eventually issue a final report, but it took no position on Willingham's guilt or innocence. When Perry declared in 2013 that he would not seek re-election as governor, Abbott immediately declared for governor—the Willingham case, they thought, was well and truly buried. Until it wasn't!

With the arson evidence in the Willingham case largely discredited, prosecutors and politicians defending the legitimacy of the conviction and execution pointed to Johnny Webb, a jailhouse snitch who testified that Willingham had confessed to him that he set the fire. Prosecutors swore for two decades that Webb, who had sought to recant his testimony, did not receive a deal, a reduction in the charges he faced, in exchange for his testimony. Then in early 2014, Innocence Project lawyers working on a posthumous pardon for Willingham found a note in the prosecutor's files that Webb had received a deal in exchange for his testimony.[55] Over the course of the next year, evidence also showed that Webb had received tens of thousands of dollars in cash and support following his Willingham testimony. Today, Webb has fully recanted that testimony. Death penalty opponents claim that with the arson evidence and the supposed jailhouse confession compromised, Willingham represents an unambiguous case of an innocent man (or perhaps a bad man not guilty of this particular crime) wrongly executed. Likely so![56]

In 2012, the Texas State Fire Marshal, Chris Connealy, began working with the Texas Innocence Project and leading arson investigators to identify old cases in which outdated fire science might have led to wrongful convictions. One case, similar to the Willingham case in many respects, involved Ed Graf, convicted in 1988 of setting a fire in which his two step-sons were killed. Graf spent 28 years in prison, protesting his innocence, and got a new trial as part of the fire science reviews. As the jury deliberated his fate, Graf suddenly accepted a plea deal, admitting that he had killed his two step-sons, and accepting a sentence of 60 years, with the 28 already served making him eligible immediately to apply for parole. Don't expect to see Mr. Graf on the streets anytime soon. Still, the broader message is that criminal justice is a complicated business and can only work if all of the participants—police, courts, and prisons—are trying to do their very best. Sometimes they are, sometimes they are not.

Conclusion

Texas A&M sociology professor Ben Crouch, a close observer of the Texas prison system since the 1970s, noted that, "Institutionalized sanctions of serious criminal offenders mirror the society in which they are applied. . . . In turn, citizens whose behavior and lifestyle least reflect these values are invariably those most often subject to criminal sanctions."[57] Crouch's observations clearly apply to Texas; throughout the state's history, its traditional political culture bore most heavily on African Americans and Hispanics, but particularly African Americans. Once the Civil War ended slavery, blacks quickly became the majority of prisoners and have always, then to now, been represented in the prison population at two to three times their presence in the state's population. Still, the fact that Texas has always been particularly watchful of its minority populations does not fully explain the extraordinary rise of the state's prison population, incarceration rate, and use of the death penalty.

The 1960s were a period of social tumult that thrilled some and terrorized others. Many of those others were in Texas and they moved decisively to limit social change where they could. Between 1968 and 2005 the Texas prison system expanded by 1,350 percent, nearly twice as much as all U.S. prison systems. Robert Perkinson has noted that, "While the white prisoner population has increased eightfold since 1968, the African-American prisoner population has grown fourteen-fold; the Mexican-American prisoner population has jumped even faster, increasing twenty-five fold."[58] Sentences grew longer, early release harder to achieve, and cost rose from less than $30 million to $4.9 billion.

Though the growth of the Texas prison system peaked around 2010 at over 172,000 and has fallen by several thousand in recent years, it has not fallen at anything like the fall in the crime rate. Violent crime in Texas peaked in 1991 and has fallen by more than half since then. During precisely these years, the Texas prison system grew from 52,000 to 172,000 inmates. As a result, Texas is saddled with an overbuilt prison establishment that we have only begun to unwind. Texas officials congratulated themselves on closing the first prison in the state's history—the 102-year-old Central Unit in Sugar Land, in 2011. They have since closed seven more but there is much more to be done. Michelle Alexander of the Ohio State University has written of the U.S. prison system—and it applies to Texas in spades:

> If our nation [and Texas] were to return to the rates of incarceration we had in the 1970s, we would have to release 4 out of 5 people behind bars. A million people employed by the criminal justice system could lose their jobs . . . This system is now so deeply rooted in our social, political, and economic structures that it is not going to fade away without a major shift in public consciousness.[59]

Notes

1   Wilhelm Steinert, *North America, Particularly Texas, in the Year 1849*, Dallas, TX: DeGolyer Library, 2003, pp. 121–122.
2   Noah Smithwick, *The Evolution of a State*, Austin, TX: University of Texas Press, 1983, p. 54.
3   Douglas A. Blackmon, *Slavery by Another Name*, New York: Anchor Books, 2008, pp. 61–62.
4   Marilyn McAdams Sibley, *Travelers in Texas, 1761–1860*, Austin, TX: University of Texas Press, 1967, p. 120. See also Robert Wuthnow, *Rough Country*, Princeton, NJ: Princeton University Press, 2014, p. 7.
5   Ben M. Crouch and James W. Marquart, *An Appeal to Justice: Litigated Reform of Texas Prisons*, Austin, TX: University of Texas Press, 1989, p. 13.
6   Chad R. Trulson and James M. Marquart, *First Available Cell: Desegregation of the Texas Prison System*, Austin, TX: University of Texas Press, 2009, p. 78.
7   Steinert, *North America, Particularly Texas*, p. 93.
8   Randolph B. Campbell, *An Empire for Slavery*, Baton Rouge, LA: Louisiana State University Press, 1989, p. 104.
9   Sibley, *Travelers in Texas*, pp. 128–129.
10   Trulson and Marquart, *First Available Cell*, pp. 78, 29. See also Wuthnow, *Rough Country*, p. 164.
11   Robert Perkinson, *Texas Tough: The Rise of America's Prison Empire*, New York: Metropolitan Books, 2010, p. 8.
12   James W. Marquart, Sheldon Ekland-Olson, and Jonathan R. Sorensen, *The Rope, the Chair and the Needle*, Austin, TX: University of Texas Press, 1984, pp. x–xi.
13   Vesla M. Weaver and Amy L. Lerman, "Political Consequences of the Carceral State," *American Political Science Review*, vol. 104, no. 4, November 2010, pp. 817–833.
14   William Bollaert, *William Bollaert's Texas*, Norman, OK: University of Oklahoma Press, 1956, p. 146. So well-known was this code that Mark Twain described it in detail *Pudd'nhead Wilson*, New York: Book-of-the-Month Club, 1992, p. 166. Originally published in 1894.
15   Frederick Law Olmsted, *A Journey through Texas*, Dallas, TX: DeGolyer Library, 2004, p. 105.
16   James R. Arnold, *Jeff Davis's Own: Cavalry, Comanches, and the Battle for the Texas Frontier*, Edison, NJ: Castle Books, 2000, p. 50. See also Wuthnow, *Rough Country*, p. 23.

17 William Ransom Hogan, *The Texas Republic*, Norman, OK: University of Oklahoma Press, 1946, p. 255.

18 Marquart et al., *The Rope*, p. 2. See also Blackmon, *Slavery by Another Name*, p. 54.

19 Steve J. Martin and Sheldon Ekland-Olson, *Texas Prisons: The Walls Came Tumbling Down*, Austin, TX: Texas Monthly Press, 1987, p. 5.

20 Crouch and Marquart, *An Appeal to Justice*, p. 14.

21 Trulson and Marquart, *First Available Cell*, p. 78; Martin and Ekland-Olson, *Texas Prisons*, p. 12.

22 Frank R. Kemerer, *William Wayne Justice: A Judicial Biography*, Austin, TX: University of Texas Press, 1991/2008, p. 356.

23 Martin and Ekland-Olson, *Texas Prisons*, pp. 169–171.

24 Kemerer, *William Wayne Justice*, p. 379.

25 Martin and Ekland-Olson, *Texas Prisons*, pp. 113, 187.

26 Ibid., pp. 217, 232, 244–246.

27 Kemerer, *William Wayne Justice*, p. 416.

28 Douglas Martin, "William Wayne Justice, Judge Who Remade Texas, Dies at 89," *New York Times*, October 16, 2009, p. B11.

29 James R. Parrish, *Two-Headed Monster: Crime and Texas Prisons*, Austin, TX: Eakin Press, 1989, p. 32.

30 Texas Legislative Budget Board, *Fiscal Size-Up 2010–11*, pp. 62–63, 306, 313–321.

31 Erik Eckholm, "With Crime Down, U.S. Faces Legacy of a Violent Age," *New York Times*, January 14, 2015, pp. A1, A3.

32 Mike Shea, "Previews + Reviews: Books, Robert Perkinson," *Texas Monthly*, March 2010, pp. 60–62.

33 Bill Hobby, *How Things Really Work: Lessons From a Life in Politics*, Austin, TX: University of Texas Press, 2010, pp. 149–150.

34 Parrish, *Two-Headed Monster*, p. 32.

35 Hobby, *How Things Really Work*, p. 150.

36 Justice Center, the Council on State Governments, Justice Reinvestment State Brief: Texas, https://csgjusticecenter.org/wp-content/uploads/2012/12/TexasStateBrief.letter.pdf. See also Cindy Horswell, "Texas Says Rise in Paroles Gives State Bragging Rights," *Houston Chronicle*, August 15, 2012.

37 Cindy Horswell, "Texas Cuts Costs amid Prison Reforms," *Houston Chronicle*, December 15, 2009. See also Charlie Savage and Erica Goods, "A Major Shift on Crime," *New York Times*, August 13, 2013, pp. A1, A13.

38 Kemerer, *William Wayne Justice*, pp. 370–371; see also Martin and Ekland-Olson, *Texas Prisons*, p. 141.

39 Crouch and Marquart, *An Appeal to Justice*, p. 155.

40 Martin and Ekland-Olson, *Texas Prisons*, p. 238; Kemerer, *William Wayne Justice*, p. 396.

41 Veva Institute of Justice, "The Price of Prisons: Examining State Spending Trends, 2010–2015," May 2017, p. 8.

42 The Pew Center on the States, "One in 100: Behind Bars in America," 2008, p. 33.

43 Marquart et al., *The Rope*, pp. 12, 23.

44 Jon Sorensen and Rocky Leann Pilgrim, *Lethal Injection: Capital Punishment in Texas during the Modern Era*, Austin, TX: University of Texas Press, 2006, p. 22.

45 Death Penalty Information Center, "Facts about the Death Penalty," as of March 9, 2011.

46 "Death Penalty under Examination," *State Legislatures*, June 2009, p. 10.

47 David Grann, "Trial by Fire: Did Texas Execute an Innocent Man?" *The New Yorker*, September 7, 2009, pp. 42–63.

48 Dahlia Lithwick, "Innocent Until Executed: We Have No Right to Exoneration," *Newsweek*, September 14, 2009, p. 29.

49 Steve Mills and Maurice Possley, "Man Executed on Disproved Forensics," *Chicago Tribune*, December 9, 2004.

50 Todd J. Gillman, "Governor Defends Disputed Execution," *Dallas Morning News*, September 19, 2009, pp. A1, A2.

51 Christy Hoppe, "Perry Ousts Officials before Arson Hearing," *Dallas Morning News*, October 1, 2009, pp. A1, A2.

52 Steve Mills, "Cameron Todd Willingham: Former Head of the Texas Forensics Panel Probing 1991 Fire Says He Felt Pressured by Gov. Perry Aides," *Chicago Tribune*, October 12, 2009.

53 Christy Hoppe, "Fire Expert Calls Perry 'Unethical,'" *Dallas Morning News*, October 15, 2009, pp. A1, A3.
54 Lisa Falkenberg, "Commentary: Execution Controversy about More than 'Bad Man,'" *Houston Chronicle*, October 14, 2009.
55 John Schwartz, "Evidence of Concealed Jailhouse Deal Raises Questions on an Old Execution," *New York Times*, February 28, 2014, p. A17.
56 Marshall Possley, The Marshall Project, "Evidence Mounts that Death Penalty Witness Had Deal," *Dallas Morning News*, March 11, 2015, p. A7.
57 Trulson and Marquart, *First Available Cell*, "Foreword," p. ix.
58 Perkinson, *Texas Tough*, p. 365.
59 Michelle Alexander, "Opinion: In Prison Reform, Money Trumps Civil Rights," *New York Times*, May 15, 2011, p. Wk 9.

9 Good Roads, Highways, and Transportation in Texas

> I reached some plains so vast, that I did not find their limit . . . [It was as] if we had been swallowed up by the sea. . . . there was not a stone, nor bit of rising ground, nor a tree, nor a shrub, nor anything to go by.
>
> (Francisco Vazquez de Coronado, 1541)

The first Europeans into Texas were struck by the massive distances that spread out before them. The very first, Alvar Nunez Cabeza de Vaca, saw a great deal of Texas. Cabeza de Vaca was a member of a Spanish party of exploration that first came to grief in Florida before setting to sea in makeshift rafts which eventually came ashore on Galveston Island in late 1528. Soon Cabeza de Vaca was one of a handful of survivors and a captive slave of Indians. He remained in the Galveston area for four years before linking up with three other survivors and setting out on a journey that led him through South Texas and into northern Mexico and as far west as the Mexican Pacific coast before the tattered band showed up in Mexico City in 1536. Cabeza de Vaca's claim to have seen golden cities on his journey intrigued Antonio de Mendoza, the Spanish Viceroy of New Spain.

After further inquiries seemed to confirm Cabeza de Vaca's claim, Mendoza dispatched the Conquistador Captain Francisco Vazquez de Coronado with a force of 1,500 Spanish and Indians to find the seven cities of Cibola and their riches. What Coronado found when he crossed out of what is now New Mexico and into Texas was terrifying to most of his men if not to the captain himself. In the spring of 1541, Coronado's force descended onto the "stockade plain" of the Llano Estacado. The rimrock that marked the edge of the plain reminded the Spaniards of a stockade wall, but it was the 30,000 square miles of flat, virtually featureless, grasslands stretching out beyond the horizon that left them awestruck. Anglos later mistranslated Coronado's descriptive phrase as "staked plains" and that name stuck. Once out on the plain, nothing but grass as far as the eye could see in every direction, the Spaniards were reduced to navigating as if they were at sea.[1]

For the next three centuries, Anglos, whether Europeans or eventually Americans, found traversing Texas a challenge. Indians had regular travel routes but these did not constitute what Anglos recognized as roads. At best, Indian routes might be footpaths "deepened somewhat by the poles dragged by the Indian's canine beasts of burden. When the Indians acquired horses, the old footpaths became wider, deeper tracks routed through less dense timber and, in West Texas, running from water hole to water hole. The first American explorers and settlers followed these same tracks."[2] Oftentimes, however, there were no tracks to follow.

The Reverend Daniel Baker, an early evangelist in Texas, became lost in 1831. Baker wrote that, "Bewildered in the wild and trackless prairie, I was lost, *lost*, LOST! After wandering about in every direction . . . I began seriously to think that I should at last have to lie down and die in this untraveled wilderness, far away from my family and the habitation of men, without a friend to close my eyes, or dig my grave!" Just a year later, the American author and diplomat Washington Irving, famous for his "Rip Van Winkle" (1819) and "Legend of Sleepy Hollow" (1820) stories, toured Oklahoma and North Texas with a U.S. Commissioner of Indian Affairs survey party. In late 1832, Irving wrote, "here we have an immense extent of landscape without a sign of human existence. We have the consciousness of being far, far beyond the bounds of human habitation; we feel as if moving in a desert world."[3]

A Brief History of Texas Transportation

When Moses Austin crossed the Sabine into Texas in the fall of 1820, there were few roads. The Camino Real, or King's Road, began in Mexico City, passed through Monclova, crossed the Rio Grande at San Juan Bautista, ran north to San Antonio, and then northeast to Nacogdoches and Louisiana beyond. While the Camino Real was the most traveled route in Texas and Austin followed it into San Antonio, it was little more than a cart path across the prairie. The La Bahia road ran parallel to the Camino Real to the south. It ran from Monterrey, Mexico, crossing the Rio Grande at Laredo, then north and northeast through La Bahia to the Sabine. Most of the first settlers came overland by horse or wagon from Arkansas or Louisiana or they came by sea to Galveston. Those coming from the east by land, such as the planter Jared E. Groce from Alabama, guided their parties along the Camino Real before turning southwest across open land to the Austin colony.[4] Anglos soon came to call the Camino Real the Old San Antonio Road and the La Bahia Road came to be called the Opelousas Trail.

William Ransom Hogan's *The Texas Republic* includes a chapter on early roads entitled "Roads of Mud and Slush." Hogan reports that in early 1838 the new republic's distinguished president, Sam Houston, "wrote that he was unable to start on an intended trip from Houston to Nacogdoches because 'at this time the roads are most terrible and impossible in this section of the country.'"[5] The Texas Republic struggled financially throughout its decade-long history and so had no revenues to assist with road building or even improvement.

One of the most striking themes in the journal writing of the early Anglo immigrants and visitors to Texas is the difficulty and danger of simply trying to move around the state. The Englishman William Bollaert, traveling west from Houston to Columbus on the Colorado River, described the roads along Buffalo Bayou as treacherous. "During and after heavy rains," Bollaert wrote, "these creeks are not fordable and in some parts of the low country, what with the water in the bottoms swamps and creeks, the roads are rendered impassable for weeks." Not surprisingly, those who depended on the roads for their livelihood did not take the delays as gracefully as President Houston seemed to. Bollaert records that, "to swear like a bullock driver when bogged . . . is the concentrated essence of blasphemy."[6]

Wilhelm Steinert described the road from Fredericksburg to Austin in 1849 as "nothing more than field paths or tracks." After visiting Bastrop, La Grange, and Industry, Steinert reported that "we started for Columbus. The road went through meadows for many miles, broke up later in side roads, and gradually stopped altogether." Rain turned rutted wagon trails into axel deep mud and hard rain turned rivers and creeks into torrents that could not be crossed, occasionally requiring teamsters to camp by rivers for days, sometimes weeks, waiting for the water to recede. Steinert concluded that "Broken wagon parts lying along the roads give the best evidence of their condition."[7]

Every traveler commented on the lack of well-marked roads. In East Texas in the early 1850s, Frederick Law Olmsted reported that:

> The road could hardly be called a road. It was only a way where people had passed along before. Each man had taken such a path as suited him, turning aside to avoid, on high ground, the sand, on low ground, the mud. We chose, generally, the untrodden elastic pavement of pine leaves, at a little distance from the main track.

Similarly, on the broad, flat lowlands near the Texas Gulf, Olmsted again reported that "The road was a mere collection of straggling wagon-ruts, extending for more than a quarter of a mile in width, from outside to outside, it being desirable, in this part of the country, rather to avoid a road than to follow it." Finally, the Olmsteds were not simply eastern naïfs wandering aimlessly across Texas, they had a competent guide. Nonetheless, they frequently reported following the wrong cattle path or wagon track: "On the way from Trinity to Centreville. . . . At some fork in the indistinct road we have gone wrong, and are to the northward of our regular course. . . . Our road was little better than a cow-track, and once we followed a worn cattle-path for some two or three miles, and were obliged to follow it back again." On another occasion, "The road was very indistinct, and we followed some wagon tracks, at twilight, two hours out of our way."[8]

Even the army complained about the quality, really the absence, of Texas roads in the 1850s. With a string of frontier posts from Fort Belknap west of Dallas to Fort Clark just north of the Rio Grande, the army struggled with both troop movements and resupply. "The surgeon general complained that Texas's rough roads destroyed medicines and surgical instruments before they could be delivered to the garrisons. One passenger aboard an Overland Mail wagon reported that his coach overturned three times in the vicinity of Fort Belknap alone."[9] T.R. Fehrenbach reports that "Only a few miles of roadway in the entire state in 1860 were graded; exactly twenty miles in all was planked or similarly improved."[10]

Throughout the nineteenth century, first the Congress of the Republic of Texas and then the Texas state legislature made road building and maintenance a county responsibility. Robert Calvert has written that, "The state government entrusted internal improvements to the counties, but inadequate resources compelled local authorities to let bad roads languish. Besides the sorry shape of the roads, few bridges existed."[11] Counties were empowered to lay out and maintain roads and to authorize ferries and toll bridges. They were encouraged, but not required, to coordinate with adjoining jurisdictions. Counties also were empowered to require ten days of labor each year from every male resident between 18 and 45 and every slave between 16 and 50, though the political culture exempted wealthy whites and discouraged bothering citizens at all.[12] As late as 1879, the Texas Legislature renewed these county powers, adding exemptions for citizens willing to hire a substitute or pay a tax of a dollar a day up to their ten-day obligation. By the end of the nineteenth century, counties were authorized to levy property taxes to support road building and maintenance, but, again, they did so only rarely. Richard Morehead writes that in 1900 "Texas roads bore no semblance to an integrated system."[13]

Texas in the mid-nineteenth century was money poor and land rich. While the state could not fund road building, it could fund railroad construction with land grants. In 1854 and again in 1876, the legislature offered railroads a subsidy of 16 sections of public land, 10,240 acres, for every mile of mainline track it laid. Thin population and light demand outside the early cotton belt slowed construction. By 1860, less than 400 miles of track connected Galveston and Houston to the plantations along the Brazos, Colorado, and Trinity rivers. By 1870, the rail system had grown to just 583 miles, but a boom was building. Between 1876 and 1883, 40 railroad companies were awarded more than 32 million acres of public land in exchange for nearly 3,000 miles of new track. By the end of the century, Texas had nearly 10,000 miles of track; more than any other state.

Between 1875 and 1885, railroads connected Galveston and Houston to Corpus Christi, San Antonio, El Paso, Dallas, and Fort Worth. Unlike most public roads, railroads were owned and operated as private, profit-making corporations. Texas farmers were concerned from the beginning that railroads favored big custom-ers with lower rates and rebates while gouging the small shipper. The railroads also gave stock and free passes to legislators and other political friends to limit taxes, regulations, and oversight. Public outrage over the predations of the railroads led Attorney General James Stephen Hogg to force the return of 1.5 million acres of pub-lic land and to break up a railroad price-fixing scheme. In 1890, Hogg was elected governor and in the 1891 legislative session he sought and won approval of the Texas Railroad Commission (TRC). Texas was just the second state to form a regulatory com-mission to oversee railroad rates and services.[14]

The railroads that came to Texas after the Civil War helped, but roads, particularly farm-to-market roads in the vast rural reaches of the state, would wait another half century. Through the early decades of the twentieth century, it was common for Texas farmers to face a 100-mile wagon ride over unimproved dirt roads to get their crops to market. Historians Thad Sitton and Milam Rowold write that, "Rural transportation in Texas during the first three decades of the twentieth century was extremely primi-tive . . . Roads were usually just raw tracks across the land, unimproved by gravel or asphalt, and in certain seasons so deep in the mud that travelers had to take to nearby fields or fence rows."[15]

Though the automobile came late to Texas, its arrival changed everything. States in the east, led by Massachusetts and New Jersey, began providing state aid for road construction in the early 1890s. By 1915, all but three states—Indiana, South Carolina, and, you guessed it, Texas—had passed laws providing state funds to assist road building. Then Congress passed the Federal-Aid Highway Act of 1916 provid-ing for sharing the cost of highway construction between the states and the federal government. Texas, Indiana, and South Carolina all passed state highway fund-ing laws in 1917 so that they would be eligible for the federal matching funds. On April 4, 1917, Governor James Ferguson signed the bill creating the Texas Highway Department (THD) and the three-member Texas Highway Commission (THC) to oversee it. The THD assumed responsibility for road maintenance and arterial con-struction from the counties. By the end of the year, the THC had registered 194,720 vehicles, developed a plan for 8,865 miles of improved roadways, and raised the speed limit to 25 miles per hour. In 1923, the THD gained a dependable revenue stream when the legislature dedicated a fuels tax to fund highway construction. A decade later, when Texas adopted its first Drivers' License Law in 1935, "three million applicants received legal authority to operate motor vehicles." Despite the fact that the law required no exam to qualify for a license, "many Texans considered it an infringement on their independence and refused to obtain licenses."[16] Texans who needed no license to ride a horse or drive a wagon bristled at mandatory state licenses to drive motor vehicles.

Despite the creation of the THD and passage of the fuels tax, state funding of roads passed slowly from counties to the state over the course of 15 years. During their three terms as governor, James (Pa) and Miriam (Ma) Ferguson joined the county commissioners courts and rural legislators to oppose centralized or state control of road building. In 1932, the state assumed primary responsibility for funding and the legislature passed the State Assumption Act to pay off outstanding county road bonds but the struggle continued into the mid-1940s. The first farm-to-market road was completed in Texas in 1937 and in 1949 the Colson–Briscoe Act mandated an annual $15 million appropriation for farm-to-market and ranch-to-market roads. Though the Texas Legislature remained tight with the dollar, it did recognize that a large state of mostly scattered rural communities needed roads and it spent money to provide them.

Two men are credited with making the THD of the mid-twentieth century a national model. Gibb Gilchrist established the THD as an agency above politics, but not without a fight. Gilchrist took an engineering degree at the University of Texas in 1909 and served in the U.S. Army Corps of Engineers in World War I before joining the THD. In 1924, he was briefly state highway engineer, the department's top job, before resigning over political interference by the Fergusons. Gilchrist returned to lead the department from 1927 to 1937 before leaving to become dean of engineering at Texas A&M. Gilchrist is credited with shaping the THD into a highly professional organization.

DeWitt Greer became chief highway engineer and head of the THD in 1940 and built on the solid foundation that Gilchrist had left behind. Greer, a Texas A&M graduate, spent 55 years with the THD. Greer was head of the highway department from 1940 to 1972, when he moved over to spend another decade, 1972 to 1981, as a member of the THC. When Greer took over in 1940, Texas had 22,207 miles of road and when he finally retired in 1981 it had 72,945 miles. Fifty thousand miles of new Texas roads had been built under Greer's watchful eye. The current Texas Department of Transportation (TxDOT) headquarters on East 11th street in Austin is named in honor of DeWitt Greer.

The halcyon days of U.S. and Texas highway building were the late 1940s, 1950s, and 1960s and Texas led the way. Congress and the state highway departments began intensive planning for a national highway building program during World War II. In 1943, Congress passed a $1.7 billion highway bill that required state matching money. Greer's THD was ready with the plans and matching money in place when federal funds began to flow, receiving $30 million three years running from the initial allocation. In 1946, Texas passed the famous "Good Roads Amendment" to guarantee ongoing state revenues. The Good Roads Amendment, now Article VIII, section 7-a of the Texas Constitution, guaranteed that three-quarters of all road-user fees, including the gas tax, drivers' license fees, and vehicle registration fees, would go to roads, while the other quarter would go to education.[17]

The taxes and fees guaranteed to roads, with modest adjustments, kept the THD a pay-as-you-go operation into the late 1970s. Texas Governor Coke Stevenson (1941–1947), one of the most conservative and tight-fisted men ever to occupy the governor's mansion, demanded a balanced budget for roads. But DeWitt Greer shared his view. Greer believed that planning a massive road-building effort required stable funding flows not subject to the vagaries of political manipulation. Only dedicated funds would suffice.

Sam Waldrop, an Abilene businessman who served on the THC with Greer, observed that his "philosophy was that bonding and such were political traps. The politicians can spend a lot of money and vote a lot of expenses, but he doesn't have the courage to support the taxes necessary for this funding. The statesman does."[18]

By the late 1940s, "the Texas Highway Department emerged in the vanguard of states seeking federal assistance for massive road-building projects. Texas, in short, embraced federal policy in a way it would not in any other domestic policy area."[19] Fehrenbach notes that, "some Texas counties got their first paved roads in the 1940s—by the 1950s even the rural, farm-to-market roads in the underpopulated areas were superior to most U.S. highways in the East."[20] Finally, in 1962 at a ceremony celebrating DeWitt Greer's 35th anniversary with THD, THC member Charles Hawn declared, "We are so far ahead of other state highway departments, there is no comparison. . . . That sounds like Texas brag but it's on the record. . . . At the same time our average cost is way, way down . . . we get more for our tax dollar in our highway system than in most any other system or department."[21] Even adjusting just a bit for the standard hyperbole, Texas was making serious investments in roads by the mid-twentieth century, but, as with education and much else, it fell off thereafter.

THD bustled through the 1960s, but the 1970s, with Arab oil boycotts, a movement to smaller cars with higher gas mileage, 55 mile per hour speed limits, and double-digit domestic inflation brought tough times. THD reached an all-time high of 20,500 employees in 1972. By the end of the decade, gas tax revenues were still largely flat and THD employment was under 14,500, down 29 percent. Gas taxes were raised from 5 cents to 10 cents a gallon in 1984 and 15 cents a gallon in 1987, but by then the oil boom had collapsed and the state's property markets and banks had swooned as well. Texas's highway building and maintenance programs never recovered.

The Pace of Texas Population Growth, Road Building, and Vehicle Registration

In 1950, Texas was the nation's sixth most populous state, with 7.74 million residents, or 5.1 percent, of the nation's 151.87 million residents. In that same year, Texas had 196,426 miles of road, or 6.6 percent of the nation's 2.99 million miles of road. Texas is a big state with lots of lightly populated rural territory, so one would expect a higher proportion of road miles to population than the average state. By 2015, Texas was the nation's second most populous state, with 27.5 million residents, or 8.6 percent of the nation's 321.5 million residents. But in that same year, Texas had 315,000 miles of road, or 7.5 percent of the nation's 4.2 million miles of road. Since 1950, the population of Texas has increased by 255 percent while the road base has increased by just 60 percent. While the population of Texas has grown inexorably since 1950, its road building has lagged badly in recent years. Figure 9.1 highlights the steady growth of population and slower and slowing growth of roads.

Though Texas contains vast, lightly populated, rural areas, it has been a majority urban state since the 1940s. Hence, for decades Texas focused its road money on the economically critical urban road system within the triangle connecting Dallas-Fort Worth, Houston, and San Antonio. In the early 1950s, Texas matched the national average for percentage urban population at about 55 percent and then quickly pulled away. By 1960, Texas was 75 percent urban while the national average was 70 percent. That margin held remarkably steady at four to six points for more than half a century. The 2010 census showed Texas as 85 percent urban and the nation as 81 percent urban. From the early 1950s through the economic travails of the late 1980s, Texas maintained

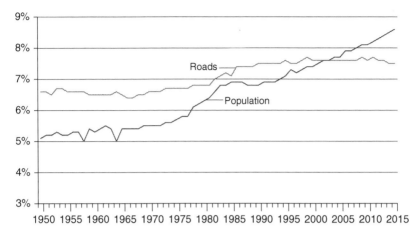

Figure 9.1 Texas Population and Road Mileage as a Percentage of U.S. Population and Road Mileage, 1950–2015

Source: U.S. Census Bureau, Statistical Abstract of the United States, Population section, various years, 1950 to present; Transportation section; "Highway Mileage by State—Functional Systems and Urban/Rural," various years, 1950 to 2015.

a greater share of urban roads than did the nation as a whole and the Texas proportion of urban roads grew faster. In the late 1980s, Texas urban road building faltered, at least as a percentage of total state roads, and though some sleight of hand has been used to mask the fact, it has remained stagnant since.

As Figure 9.2 shows, in 1953 (the first year for which we have data) 12.4 percent of Texas roads were urban compared to 10.5 percent of U.S. roads. By 1960, 16 percent of Texas roads and 12.1 percent of U.S. roads were urban. By 1980, 20.9 percent of Texas

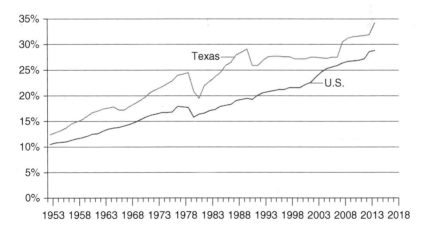

Figure 9.2 Urban Roads as a Percentage of Total Roads in the U.S. and Texas, 1953–2014

Source: U.S. Census Bureau, Statistical Abstract of the United States, Transportation section; various years, 1953 to 2014. The decreases, especially evident in the Texas data, reflect definitional changes. In 1976, the definition of an urban place was raised from 2,500 to 5,000, and in 1991 new legislation again adjusted the traditional definitions. Between 2007 and 2008 about 9,000 miles of Texas roads were reclassified from rural to urban.

roads were urban while just 15.8 percent of U.S. roads were urban. From 1991 through 2007, while the U.S. continued to add to its urban road system, Texas was absolutely flat. In 1991, the percentage of U.S. roads that were urban stood at 19 percent, and in 2007, it stood at 26. In 1991, the percentage of Texas roads that were urban stood at 25.9, and in 2007, it stood at 27.5. In 2008, Texas reclassified about 9,000 miles of rural roads as urban roads and jumped three full percentage points, to 30.5 percent. In 2014, another 8,000 road miles were reclassified from rural to urban, increasing the proportion of urban roads by more than two points, to 34.4 percent. In 2014, U.S. urban roads comprised 29 percent of all roads.

The results of Texas's underinvestment in roads is clear when we see that road building has not kept up with the number of vehicles on the roads. The road system in Texas is described in terms of both road miles and lane miles because, obviously, some roads are multilane. Widening a road from two lanes to four would double lane miles but would not increase road miles. Between 1950 and 2014 the road system in Texas grew from 196,426 road miles to 313,595 road miles, an increase of 60 percent. Over that same period, the number of vehicles on Texas roads rose from just under three million (2,968,143) to nearly 21 million (20,877,026), an increase of 603 percent. As a result, between 1950 and 2014, the number of vehicles per road mile increased from 15 to 67, an increase of 347 percent (Figure 9.3).

The data on lane miles go back only to 1980, so to get a good comparison of vehicle loads in relation both to road miles and to lane miles, we will need to look at both for the period 1980 to 2014. Road miles in Texas increased from 267,500 in 1980 to 313,595 in 2014, an increase of 17 percent. The number of vehicles on the roads increased from about 10.5 million (10,474,816) in 1980 to nearly 21 million (20,877,026) in 2014, an increase of 99 percent. And the number of vehicles per road mile increased from 39 in 1980 to 67 in 2014, an increase of 70 percent.

The number of lane miles in Texas increased from 561,408 in 1980 to 677,575 in 2014, an increase of 21 percent. The number of vehicles on the road, as we saw above, rose 73 percent. And the number of vehicles per lane mile increased from 18.66 in 1980

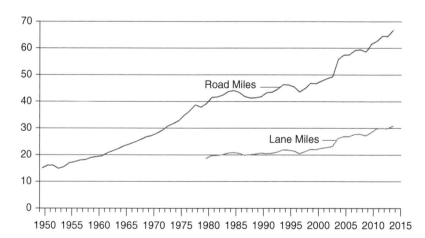

Figure 9.3 Licensed Vehicles per Road Mile and Lane Mile in Texas, 1950–2014

Source: Department of Transportation, Highway Statistics Publications, 1950–2014, www.fhwa.dot.gov/policy/ohpi/hss/hsspubs.cfm. The slight dip in 2009 is artificial. Texas reported an increase in road and lane miles in 2009 but no increase in licensed drivers.

to 30.8 in 2014, an increase of 65 percent. Clearly, whether you look at road miles or lane miles, the number of vehicles per mile on Texas roads has increased by 65 to 70 percent over the last three and a half decades. Texas has been losing the battle to provide adequate transportation infrastructure at least since the mid-1990s.

As with so many other policy areas, the fundamental fact is that Texas spends less of its own money, fewer state funds, on roads than do other states. Between 1950 and 2006, Texas per capita expenditure on roads from state funds amounted to just 86.3 percent of the national average for all of the states (Figure 9.4). As we have seen elsewhere, Texas was near the national average in 1950, spending $23.17 per capita on roads while the national average was $23.43. In 1959 and 1960, Texas exceeded the national average and for the entire decade of the 1950s Texas spent 94.2 percent of the national average for per capita road expenditures. In the 1960s, Texas spent 88.1 percent of the national average; in the 1970s, 74 percent; in the 1980s, 85.6 percent; in the 1990s, 78.1 percent; and from 2000 through 2004, Texas spent just 82.4 percent of the national average for per capita road expenditures. In 2005 and 2006, Texas matched the national average, and in 2007 and 2008, it was 128 and 143 percent of the national average before dropping back, probably due to debt exhaustion, to more historical averages of 85 percent of U.S. per capita highway spending in 2009 through 2011. New revenue streams dedicated by the 2013 and 2015 legislative sessions have put Texas back above the national average for per capita transportation spending, 141 percent of the national average in the most recent data, but the backlog for both road maintenance and building will take years to work through. From THD's founding in 1917 through 2001, Texas ran a pay-as-you-go highway department. Roads were built and maintained as funds became available. In 2001, Governor Perry and the legislature approved borrowing for road construction for the first time. Since then, Texas's credit card has been smoking.

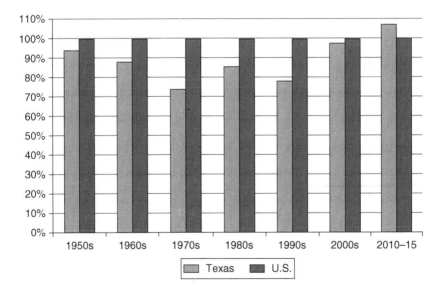

Figure 9.4 U.S. and Texas per Capita Expenditures for Roads by Decade, 1950–2015

Source: U.S. Census Bureau, Statistical Abstract of the United States, Population section, various years, 1950 to 2015; Transportation section; Highway Financing, "State Disbursements for Highways by States," various years, 1950 to 2015.

Looking at per capita spending on roads from an annual perspective, as we do in Figure 9.5, shows Texas struggling unsuccessfully to fund its road system. As with education and so many other policy areas, Texas leaders in the immediate post–World War II era felt the state's growth and momentum and moved decisively to build a solid infrastructure under it. If growth outruns infrastructure, growth must slow, but keeping infrastructure up with population and economic growth is not easy because funding flows follow rather than lead growth. In the late 1950s, Texas's spending on roads began to fall behind and stayed in decline until 1970. The saw tooth pattern of per capita expenditures between 1970 and 1990 shows politicians struggling, ultimately unsuccessfully, to keep up with the growth-driven demand for transportation improvements. The subdued saw tooth pattern between 1990 and the early 2000s suggests capitulation. Per capita spending fell and stayed low but new revenues, new solutions to the state's growing traffic woes, did not come to hand. In 2001, all that seemed to change. Texas moved away from pay-as-you-go to borrow, toll, and bluster. Texas per capita spending on roads increased dramatically after 2001, but it was all debt fueled. Authorized debt limits began bumping against their legal caps in 2008 and spending fell back to more normal levels. Unfortunately, those levels were barely sufficient to fund repair of existing roads with little left for new construction.

There are, of course, many practical results to inadequate funding of road maintenance and construction. In 2012, TRIP, a national transportation research group, reported that "Issues including traffic congestion, damage to vehicles from roads needing repair, and costs incurred in accidents caused by insufficient safety features on roadways cost drivers in Texas $23 bilion annually." By 2014, TRIP's cost estimate was up to $25.1 billion annually.[22] Let that number, $25 billion annually, sink in—it is twice the annual road construction budget of TxDOT. That means Texans are paying for excellent roads, $25 billion worth, but just are not getting them. The Texas response to congestion and inadequately maintained roads, typically enough, was to raise the state's maximum speed limit to 85 mph. Traffic engineers will determine which highways can handle the higher speeds.

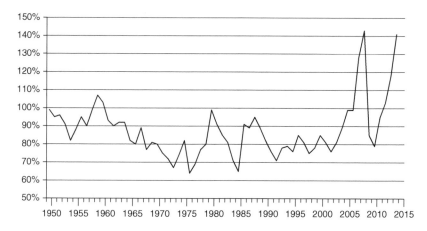

Figure 9.5 Texas per Capita Expenditures for Roads as a Percentage of Average U.S.
           Expenditures, 1950–2014

Source: U.S. Census Bureau, Statistical Abstract of the United States, Population section, various years, 1950 to 2014; Transportation section; Highway Financing, "State Disbursements for Highways by State," various years, 1950 to 2014.

Only Texas and Utah have speeds over 75 mph. The 2011 legislature also removed all lower night and truck speed limits. Hilariously, House Transportation Committee chair Larry Phillips (R-Sherman) explained the changes as a delicate "balance between protecting citizen's rights and their individual freedoms and protecting our citizens on our roadways."[23] Just off the top of your head—do you think they got the balance right?

Financing Texas Roads: The Federal and State Gas Tax

States fund their roads from a number of revenue streams, but the bulk of the funds traditionally have come from gas tax revenues they collect and from remittances to the states of gas taxes collected by the federal government. The federal government distributes gas tax funds to the states based on data that the states provide concerning motor fuel use.[24] States receive funds from federal gas taxes based on a formula that includes the cost of road building and maintenance, so that Alaska and Wisconsin, where winters are harsh and roads break up, receive proportionately more than states such as Texas where wear and tear on roads is less. Texas and other "donor" states wail incessantly about receiving less than their fair share of federal highway dollars.

Since 1950, the gas taxes charged by the federal government, Texas, and the average state gas tax have all risen from the low to mid-single digits to about 20 cents per gallon. The gas tax has been raised by different amounts at different times by the federal government and by each of the states including Texas (Figure 9.6). The federal gas tax of 1.5 cents per gallon in 1950 and 1951 was raised to 2 cents in 1952, 3 cents in 1957, and 4 cents in 1960, where it remained through 1982. In 1983, the gas tax was more than doubled to 9 cents a gallon, before being raised to 9.1 cents in 1987, 14.1 cents in 1990, and 18.4 cents in 1993, where it has remained ever since.

The U.S. Department of Transportation's Federal Highway Administration reports each year on how much of the Federal Highway Trust Fund is attributed to each state

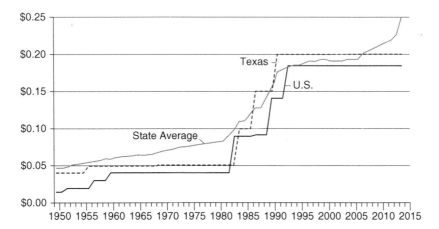

Figure 9.6 Federal Gas Tax Compared to Texas and Average State Gas Taxes, 1950–2015

Source: U.S. Census Bureau, *Statistical Abstract of the United States, 1950 to 2015*, "Federal and State Gasoline Tax, by states," www.census.gov/library/publications/time-series/statistical_abstracts.html. See also Department of Transportation, Federal Highway Administration, *Highway Statistics*, various years, www.fhwa.dot.gov/policy/ohpi/hss/hsspubs.cfm.

and how much each state is allocated from the fund. Congress supplements the Trust Fund with General Fund dollars, so that most states come out ahead. For example, in 2015 just seven states received less than they put in and overall the Trust Fund paid out 109 percent of what it took in. Between 1956 and 2015, the Trust Fund paid out 116 percent of what it took in and fully 45 states received more than they contributed. Five states have received less than they put in and Texas had the lowest return of any state. Between 1956 and 2015, Texas paid in a total of $78.9 billion dollars and received allocations totaling $74.4 billion dollars; for every Texas dollar into the Trust Fund Texas gets 94 cents out. The next lowest states are Indiana and South Carolina at 98, and Michigan and North Carolina at 99. Many of the federal funds made available to the states require matching funds and often Texas is reluctant.[25]

Champagne and Harpham argue that, "For over half a century, highway policy . . . stood as an exemplar of successful public policy in Texas."[26] Texas held its gas tax lower than most states for longer than most. Texas lagged the 48-state (later 50-state) average from 1950 through 1983, charging an average over that 34-year period of 4.82 cents per gallon, compared to the 50-state average of 6.69 cents per gallon. That might not sound like much of a difference, but in percentage terms it means that Texas charged just 72 percent of the 50-state average. Since 1984, Texas has charged slightly more than the national average, 17.92 cents compared to 17.11 cents.

The Texas Legislature set the gas tax at 1 cent per gallon in 1923. It was raised to 2 cents in 1929, 4 cents in 1934, 5 cents in 1956, and then held there for almost 30 years. By 1983, the Texas gas tax, at 5 cents, was just over half the 50-state average gas tax of 9.75 cents. In 1984, Texas raised its gas tax to 10 cents, still below the national average of 10.6 cents, and in 1987 they raised it again, to 15 cents, above the national average of 12.75. Texas fell behind the national average of 15.5 cents in 1990, though only briefly. In 1991, Texas reorganized THD, renaming it the Texas Department of Transportation (TxDOT), and raised the state gas tax to 20 cents per gallon, marginally above the national average. The Texas state gas tax has remained at 20 cents ever since. Some states, though not Texas, have added to their road funds by charging a sales tax on gasoline (in addition to the gas tax itself) and by allowing local governments to add their own gas taxes. These additional motor fuel taxes and fees averaged 9 cents per gallon across the 50 states and D.C. in 2017. Table 9.1 and Table 9.2 help make these points. They also show Texas at 44th in gas taxes per gallon.[27] Hence, with both the Texas and federal gas taxes stable since the early 1990s, inflation has steadily eaten away the buying power of those funds and road building in Texas has stagnated.[28]

Table 9.1 State Gasoline Motor Fuel Taxes by Region (cents per gallon)

Region	Basic Motor Fuel Tax	Other Motor Fuel Taxes	Total Sate Motor Fuel Taxes
Northeast	24.69	5.60	30.29
Mid-Atlantic	9.52	34.55	44.07
South Atlantic	17.85	12.83	30.68
Midwest	23.49	5.34	28.83
South	19.58	0.73	20.31
Mountain	25.71	0.29	26.01
West	28.69	7.73	36.42
U.S.	21.03	10.01	31.04

Source: American Petroleum Institute, www.api.org/oil-and-natural-gas/consumer-information/motor-fuel-taxes.

Table 9.2 State Gas Taxes and Related Fees

Pennsylvania	58.2	Nevada	33.5	Minnesota	28.6	Virginia	22.4
Washington	49.4	Maryland	33.5	Nebraska	28.2	Colorado	22.0
Hawaii	44.4	Idaho	33.0	Ohio	28.0	Arkansas	21.8
New York	43.9	Wisconsin	32.9	Montana	27.8	Tennessee	21.4
Michigan	40.4	W. Virginia	32.2	Massachusetts	26.5	Louisiana	20.0
Connecticut	39.9	Oregon	31.1	Kentucky	26.0	**Texas**	**20.0**
California	38.1	Georgia	31.1	Kansas	24.0	Arizona	19.0
New Jersey	37.1	U.S. Aver.	30.0	Wyoming	24.0	Mississippi	18.9
Florida	36.8	Iowa	30.7	New Hamp.	23.8	New Mexico	18.8
N. Carolina	34.6	Vermont	30.5	D.C.	23.5	Missouri	17.3
Illinois	34.0	Maine	30.0	N. Dakota	23.0	Oklahoma	17.0
Rhode Island	34.0	S. Dakota	30.0	Alabama	23.0	S. Carolina	16.8
Indiana	33.6	Utah	29.4	Delaware	22.9	Alaska	12.3

Source: American Petroleum Institute, www.api.org/oil-and-natural-gas/consumer-information/motor-fuel-taxes.

Though Texas gas taxes are among the nation's lowest, few Texas politicians have called for increasing them. Rather, Texas's former U.S. Senator Kay Bailey Hutchison (R-Dallas) introduced a bill to allow each state to retain 100 percent of the federal gas taxes raised in that state. Demonstrating Texas's characteristic denial of federalism, Senator Hutchison declared that "It's time for every state to be able to be on its own. We are very underfunded because we're a high growth state, and we need to be able to use our dollars in a more efficient way." Congress did not adopt Senator Hutchison's proposal and likely will reject similar proposals in the future. Only about one-quarter of the states represented in Congress would benefit by such a proposal, and, more importantly, it would help only at the margins. Even Texas Transportation Commissioner Ned Holmes, a Perry appointee who supported Hutchison in the 2010 governor's race, declared "If all we are doing is keeping the funding the same and pulling it from one state and giving it to another, then that is a pretty rough game to play. There needs to be more funding period. This is not just a big state, high growth state problem."[29] Hutchison lost the election and Holmes's term ended. He was not reappointed.

The deep recession of 2008–2009 depressed both the federal and Texas state gas taxes as Texas drivers cut back to save money. In late 2008 and early 2009, Texas state gas taxes were down 2.9 percent while the TxDOT budget had presumed a 1.5 percent increase. Worse, because federal gas tax revenues were lagging too, the state faced reduced funding in the coming years. Hence, one politician, Texas State Senator John Carona (R-Dallas), suggested the need to increase state gas taxes. Senator Carona introduced proposals to increase the gas tax in both the 2007 and the 2009 legislative sessions, to no avail. In late 2009, Carona told a Senate Transportation Committee meeting in El Paso that "We are in the critical position in this state where we are growing and will need more roads. But we have no money to build them and no more debt that we can issue." Absent new revenues, state Transportation Department executive director Amadeo Saenz has said "We'd be able to finish the projects that have already been funded, but no new dollars for construction will come our way."[30]

Transportation funding was discussed in the 2013 legislative session and in several special sessions that followed. Unfortunately, in the regular session, Governor Perry and many conservatives opposed raising taxes or fees, including gas taxes, transportation-related sales taxes, or vehicle registration fees, to fund new road building. Mass transit and high-speed rail were not even on the agenda. With no new revenues on the table, discussion flagged. In the special sessions, momentum built around proposals to rechannel about $2.5 billion annually from the rainy day fund (more about the rainy day fund in Chapter 11) to transportation. The Texas House and Senate sought the political cover of a statewide ballot measure to approve or disapprove the spending. In November 2014 voters approved the new funds but TxDOT claimed it was still several billion dollars a year short or maintaining existing roads and keeping up with growth. As we shall see below, Governor Greg Abbott made transportation funding a top issue in the 2015 legislative session.[31]

The Resort to Toll Roads and Debt

Toll roads, bridges, and ferries were not uncommon in nineteenth-century Texas. Tolls are a user fee, paid by those using the road, bridge, or ferry, and so attractive to those opposed to more general taxes. Once the automobile came into wide use and THD took over road building and maintenance, federal and state gas taxes and drivers' license and auto registration fees provided the bulk of the revenues. However, as early as 1954, toll fees were introduced to supplement gas taxes and to speed up the pace of road building. Between 1954 and 1957, the section of I-30 between Dallas and Fort Worth was constructed as a toll road. Once the costs of construction were paid off in 1977 and the tolls were removed, the road became, like most other roads, free to motorists.

More recently, "system financing" envisions permanent toll roads in which tolls from the system, including stretches no longer paying off bonds, remain tolled with revenues going to pay for new roads or to back new bonds for more toll roads. Victor Vandergriff, a past Chairman of the North Texas Tollway Authority, put the matter succinctly: "Tolling is the only way we are getting any new roads built at this point in time. Funding from the state of Texas is not available for roads."[32] This represents major change from the post–World War II period when Texas built the nation's most extensive road system on a pay-as-you-go basis to a system where borrow and toll seem the only tools available.

For more than a decade, Governor Perry sought to meet the state's transportation needs through a number of devices that would add capacity but still allow him to claim that he had not raised taxes. The state constitution and statutes until 2001 severely limited the issuance of bonds to fund transportation projects. No transportation bonds were issued in the 1950s. The 1960s saw a single issue of $33.65 million, while the 1970s saw two issues totaling $111.2 million. Since the early 1980s, almost every legislative session has approved transportation bonds and in ever increasing amounts. In the 1980s, there were four issues totaling nearly $706 million.[33] Nonetheless, as late as 1999, state and federal motor fuel taxes made up 76 percent of the State Highway Fund.

In 2001, Governor Perry and the Texas Legislature instituted a dramatic change in Texas's traditional pay-as-you-go system. Though that system had been under stress since at least the mid-1980s, Texas turned it on its head in 2001, making the state and federal gas tax revenues merely supplementary to the new revenue sources from bonds, private investors, and tolls. In 2001, Governor Perry proposed and the legislature approved the Texas Mobility Fund (TMF). The TMF went into effect when voters approved Proposition 15, adding Article 3, section 49k, to the Texas Constitution. TMF permitted the Texas Transportation Commission (TTC), for the first time, to issue bonds on its own authority, though within limits established by statute, to fund construction and maintenance of the state highway system. By the end of 2014, $7.4 in TMF bonds had been issued. The 2015 legislature ended TMF authority to issue new bonds.

In 2003, Governor Perry and the legislature increased its dependence on debt financing by again amending the Texas Constitution and Transportation Code to allow the TTC to issue bonds and related forms of public debt secured by the State Highway Fund. In 2007, the legislature set $6 billion as the aggregate bonding limit available to TTC in its State Highway Fund account. By 2008, the percentage of road building and maintenance funded from federal and state gas taxes was down to just 39 percent while the remaining 61 percent came from new sources, including bonds, tolls, and public/private comprehensive development agreements (CDAs).[34] The TTC's aggressive borrowing, tolling, and comprehensive development agreement activities fueled legislative concern and soon a political split between Governor Perry and the legislature in 2009. Transportation legislation in the 2009 regular legislative session, including renewal of TxDOT's legal mandate, as well as TTC's bonding and CDA authority, were held up until late in the session and then lost in the last minute scramble before adjournment. Governor Perry was forced to call a special session in July 2009 to salvage his transportation agenda.

In the 2009 special session, the legal mandate of TxDOT was renewed but the department's authority to negotiate CDAs was repealed. Governor Perry pushed hard for an extension but the legislature was adamantly opposed. CDA agreements allow public/private deals in which the private entity, usually a multinational construction company, puts up some or all of the money to build a road in exchange for the right to charge tolls for use of the road for up to 50 years. The state lays out modest amounts of money, a road gets built, Texans pay tolls, often rising at rapid rates, in perpetuity, but—and this is the best part—politicians get to claim that the road was free and no tax monies were required. TTC, knowing that the tide had turned against them, ordered that existing bonding authority be encumbered immediately. Texas also received $2.8 billion in highway-related federal stimulus money in 2009, so road building continued. While these monies were rapidly running out, a panel of experts appointed by the TTC estimated that the state would need an astounding $448 billion over the next 20 years to make up for past underinvestment and to meet the maintenance and new road construction needs of this rapidly growing state. Lower estimates have been offered, but most run into the many tens of billions of dollars.

Texas is not alone in struggling to pay for road building and maintenance. Many states are in the same boat, costs are rising fast and traditional funding mechanisms struggle to keep up. But Texas has more room to maneuver than others do, if it will take advantage of it. For example, as noted above, Texas collects about 10 cents per gallon less in gas and related taxes than does the average state. Some legislators have proposed increasing the state gas tax by as much as 10 cents, but that proposal has been rejected in the last several legislative sessions. Moreover, proposals by Regional Transportation Council leaders for a local option to allow cities, counties, and regions to raise funds for transportation improvement have been side-tracked in recent legislative sessions. Urban officials, particularly in Houston and Dallas-Fort Worth (DFW), feel a special urgency due to both traffic congestion and air pollution. In 2009, the local option tax provision was designed to allow regional transportation authorities to raise up to $25 billion by 2030 for transportation improvements. Late in the session, Governor Perry, never a fan of allowing tax increases even by local option, opposed the bill, calling it a "big huge monstrosity with lots of taxes and lots of areas of the state" involved.[35]

In the 2011 legislative session, Senator Tommy Williams (R-The Woodlands), chair of the Senate Transportation Committee, proposed debt service funding for the last $1 billion in bonds authorized in 2009 and $3 billion in new bonding authority for the 2012–2013 biennium. The new bonds allowed TxDOT contracting levels to remain above $4 billion annually for the next biennium.[36] By 2012, TxDOT had sold $17.3 billion in bonds for four major road building programs. Those bonds required annual loan payments of nearly $715 million, rising to $800 million in 2015.

Legislators know that road debt is prohibitively expensive over the long term. One major project, the $2.7 billion reconstruction of the LBJ Expressway and I-35 in Dallas, was funded with $2.2 billion in private funding from Centra, a Spanish construction firm. Centra also will maintain the project through 2061. Cool, right, Centra picks up 80 percent of the initial cost and project maintenance for half a century. Not so cool—in exchange, Centra gets a share of the toll revenues estimated by TxDOT at $18.1 billion over the life of the contract.[37]

Legislators seemed to approach the 2013 legislative session with new determination and new leadership. The third new Senate Transportation Committee chair in the last three sessions, Senator Robert Nichols (R-Jacksonville), said, "We don't need to use more debt to solve our transportation problem. We need to identify a long-term, predictable revenue source so TxDOT can actually plan."[38] In 2016, TxDOT officials reported to legislative leaders that it would take $30 billion to pay off construction debt on toll roads now operating or under construction and billions more if the bonds were paid off over time.[39]

In the 2013 and 2015 legislative sessions, Texas officials, backed by the voters, targeted new revenues to TxDOT. In 2013, the legislature proposed diverting some oil and gas revenue that previously had gone into a state savings account, called the "rainy day fund," to TxDOT. Voters approved the diversion of $2.5 billion into the State Highway Fund for 2016–17 and beyond. In the 2015 legislative session, legislators proposed that an additional $2.5 billion in general sales tax revenues and a share of motor vehicle sales and rental taxes be allocated to TxDOT. These new funds stabilized TxDOT's finances for a time.

The new revenues were most welcome, but two problems emerged quickly. First, while these revenues were new to TxDOT, they were not "new" revenues, they had merely been redirected from elsewhere in the state budget, leaving budgetary holes behind. And second, the legislative and constitutional language rerouting the money to TxDOT included bail-out clauses should tight budgets suggest the transfers were untimely. Sure enough, the 2017 legislative session faced budget shortfalls and members were soon discussing whether some or all of the approved TxDOT transfers might not need to be clawed back.[40] In the end, the new road money was just delayed, not taken back, but the legislature also continued the prohibition on new public/private partnerships and the tolls that they require. Road money will continue to be tight.

Urban Transit and High-Speed Rail in Texas

The dire problems faced by Texas's urban areas are worse than they first appear because not only have we fallen behind in road building, we have been even more laggard in regard to mass transit and high-speed rail. Texas railroads have always been commercial carriers little interested in passengers. Private railroad passenger services to Dallas stopped in 1969 and to Houston in 1974.[41] Since the 1980s only the federally subsidized Amtrak system has carried passengers in Texas. The Heartland Flier makes the short trip from Oklahoma City to Fort Worth. The Sunset Limited goes from New Orleans to Los Angeles via Houston, San Antonio, and El Paso. And the Texas Eagle originates in Chicago, stops in Dallas and San Antonio, before heading west to Los Angeles.

Even while borrowing heavily to build roads, Texas largely has ignored alternative transportation modes and funding sources. Over the past quarter century, the Urban

Mass Transportation Administration (UMTA), now the Federal Transit Administration (FTA), has funded urban bus, subway, light rail, and trolleys. The national average for per capita funding was $17 per year. Some states did much better: California received more than $22 annually per capita, New York, not surprisingly, got the most with almost $40 annually. Other states did worse than the national average: Florida got about $11, while Texas got just $9.45. Again, most federal programs involve matching funds, so energetic state programs, such as those in New York and California, draw generous matches while sleepy state programs draw much less.

Similarly, when the federal government offered $8 billion in 2009, with $5 billion more to follow over the next five years, for high-speed rail as part of the fiscal stimulus package, Texas was caught flat-footed. The first $8 billion was to go to high-speed rail projects that were ready to build or had completed feasibility and environmental studies so that federal funds could reasonably be committed. Texas has had some high-speed rail proposals on the table for years but has never funded the initial evaluations that would make them ready to go. Amadeo Saenz, executive director of the TTC in 2009, admitted that "Texas is really behind everyone else because we have not done the studies to see if high-speed rail corridors are feasible."[42] Making the same point, the *Dallas Morning News* editorial page admitted that "Texas has been neglectful in not exploring and advocating improved passenger rail as an intercity option. California has been at it for a while, investing its own money in planning a bullet train route along the coast. Trying to get up to speed, Texas lawmakers passed a bill [in 2011] calling for a passenger-rail strategy. It's about time."[43] The phrase "investing its own money" is key here: Texas rarely invests its own money to get ahead of the game, in fact, it only grudgingly puts up enough of its own money to leverage a federal match when that is available. Texas has been left behind on high-speed rail as it has been on public transportation in general.

Texas is home to three of the nation's ten largest cities, spaced far enough apart across ideal terrain to make high-speed rail clearly feasible. But because none of the planning that would have made Texas competitive for these federal grants had been done, Texas laid down a double-thick smoke screen. As Governor Perry's spokeswoman, Alison Castle, explained, TxDOT had requested federal funds for a study to "tell us the costs, benefits, use, etc. of HSR in the state—all of which are necessary before even deciding to pursue public or private investment in HSR." States best positioned to get federal awards had, of course, already completed feasibility studies on their own dime. To cover what everyone expected would be a denial of funds to Texas and awards to the better-prepared states, Castle said, "Perry isn't holding his breath, . . . Texas is routinely overlooked in federal transportation spending."[44] So the explanation of Texas being passed over was not that we were unprepared to compete, it was, once again, they hate us because we are a successful red state.

When the first round awards were made in early 2010, the big prizes went to Florida, Illinois, and California. Florida subsequently withdrew due to state budgetary constraints, but the other programs are proceeding. Texas got scraps, a mere $11 million, or about 1.3 percent of the funds available, for improvements to existing rail lines, but not for new high-speed rail. In the meanwhile, Texas appointed a new rail division chief within TxDOT, Bill Glavin, but remains in the early planning stages. In March 2010, *Fiscal Notes*, a publication of Texas Comptroller Susan Combs's office, wrote: "According to state rail officials, to attract significant high speed rail funding, Texas needs a unified rail plan supported by officials from all levels of government. Many other states, including those that received the rail stimulus funds, are far ahead of Texas in this process."[45] In August 2010, Texas submitted requests for a number of small rail projects in the second round of the competition.

In late 2012, using $9 million in federal grant funds and $1.4 million in state money (i.e., 87 percent federal money), TxDOT initiated a two-year feasibility study on rail services, perhaps high-speed rail, between Oklahoma City and Houston. Other plans are under way that would connect Austin and San Antonio to a rejuvenated rail grid. Bill Glavin said, "This is to define the parameters of what can be done." A bit more forthcoming, perhaps accidentally, was Jennifer Moczygemba, rail system sector director for TxDOT. She said, "What it does is it gets Texas caught up, as far as our planning level studies . . . that would put us in line for future funding."[46]

Meanwhile, private sector entrepreneurs have stepped into the breach. In 2015, a venture named Texas Central Partners (TCP) commissioned a study on the feasibility of constructing, with private money, a 215-mile bullet train from Dallas to Houston. At a cost of $12 billion, the train would deliver passengers from one city to the other in 90 minutes. By 2017, TCP had raised $115 million in initial funding and had plans on paper, but skepticism abounded. Rural Texans and their elected representatives lined up to oppose taking their land for the project, while others argued that raising $12 billion for such an uncertain venture would prove impossible. This project will bear close watching.

Conclusion

Transportation analysts suggest that while Texas is at the end of the "highway centric" phase of its development, it has not yet embraced the subsequent stage of urban mass transit and high-speed rail. Some argue that another possibility is to foster job growth in suburban and exurban areas so that people can more conveniently live and work outside the state's major urban centers and, therefore, not have to spend so much time on the roads. This would, they suggest, limit costs by reducing demand on the most expensive controlled access, high-speed roads—the freeways that have shaped modern Texas.

While urban mass transit and high-speed rail between the major urban centers of Houston, San Antonio, Austin, and DFW seem the most plausible, both are nearly as expensive as new freeways and, just as importantly, they fly in the face of Texan independence and individualism. Growing jobs in outlying areas is certainly an option and has to some extent been happening since the 1970s, but it misses the fact that modern Texas is intensely urban. The 2010 census declared that fully 86 percent of Texans live in urban settings and a related study by the *Dallas Morning News* found that two-thirds of Texans live within 20 miles of Interstate Highways 10, 35, and 45 that connect Houston, San Antonio, Austin, and the DFW Metroplex. Most transportation analysts in Texas, and in the nation for that matter, argue that the money to build huge new free roads on the model of the current interstate highway system is simply not there anymore. This, of course, begs the question—why not?[47]

Most pointedly, the Texas gas tax has been set at 20 cents per gallon since 1991. In the two decades between 1991 and 2017, cumulative inflation totaled 75 percent, meaning that goods purchased for $100 in 1991 would cost $175 in 2017. Road building and maintenance costs have risen faster than general inflation over this period. As a result, Texas's transportation revenues in 2011 almost equal the state's road maintenance costs with essentially no revenue for new road construction. One of the few elected officials to call for an increase in the gas tax during the 2009 legislative session was Senator John Carona (R-Dallas). Carona also called for ending diversion of transportation funds for other purposes, permitting local and regional referenda on increased funding options, and streamlining TxDOT management. For his trouble, Carona was removed as chairman of the Senate Transportation Committee for the 2011 regular session. Though Lieutenant Governor Dewhurst and the new Transportation Committee chair, Robert Nichols, both talked in the early days of the session about an increased vehicle registration fee, no new fees were passed. Senator Carona was defeated for re-election by a Tea Party challenger in 2014.

Unfortunately, the state's conservative leaders tend to ignore strong conservative arguments in favor of improved transportation systems. Transportation systems are designed, one hopes, to improve mobility in general—but specifically, mobility allowing people efficiently to get to work where they create value and earn wages and income upon which they pay taxes. The better the roads and the less time spent in gridlocked traffic, the more time spent on the job creating value. One clear sense of how costs to economic efficiency can rise is shown in commuter time lost to congestion presented by the Texas Transportation Institute (TTI) at Texas A&M University. TTI's "Annual Urban Mobility" study covers the period 1982 to the present. Over that nearly four-decade-long period, lost commuter time in Dallas increased from 7 hours per year in 1982 to 53 hours per year in 2016. Fifty-three hours is the equivalent of a very long work week lost to traffic congestion each year.[48] Much remains to be done.

Notes

1   Randolph B. Campbell, *Gone to Texas: A History of the Lone Star State*, New York: Oxford University Press, 2003, pp. 28–33. See also T.R. Fehrenbach, *Lone Star: A History of Texas and the Texans*, New York: Macmillan, 1968, pp. 25–27.
2   James R. Arnold, *Jeff Davis's Own: Cavalry, Comanches, and the Battle for the Texas Frontier*, Edison, NJ: Castle Books, 2007, p. 183. See also David G. McComb, *The City in Texas: A History*, Austin, TX: University of Texas Press, 2015, pp. 38–39.
3   The Baker quote is in Marilyn McAdams Sibley, *Travelers in Texas, 1761–1860*, Austin, TX: University of Texas Press, 1967, p. 51. The Irving quote is in Glenn Frankel, *The Searchers: The Making of an American Legend*, New York: Bloomsbury, 2013, p. 31.
4   Campbell, *Gone to Texas*, pp. 46, 80. See also Henderson K. Yoakum, *History of Texas*, New York: Redfield, 1856, p. 66.
5   William Ransom Hogan, *The Texas Republic*, Norman, OK: University of Oklahoma Press, 1946, p. 53.
6   William Bollaert, *William Bollaert's Texas*, Norman, OK: University of Oklahoma Press, 1956, pp. 180, 340.
7   Wilhelm Steinert, *North America, Particularly Texas in the Year 1849*, Dallas, TX: DeGolyer Library, 2003, pp. 41, 54, 70, 79, 116.
8   Frederick Law Olmsted, *A Journey through Texas*, Dallas, TX: DeGolyer Library, 2004, pp. 54, 150, 72, 80.
9   Arnold, *Jeff Davis's Own*, p. 184.
10 Fehrenbach, *Lone Star*, p. 319. See also, David B. McComb, *Texas: A Modern History*, Austin, TX: University of Texas Press, 2010, p. 113. Chris Tomlinson, *Tomlinson Hall*, New York: St. Martin's Press, 2014, p. 26.
11 Robert A. Calvert, Arnoldo De León, and Gregg Cantrell, *The History of Texas*, 5th ed., Malden, MA: Wiley Blackwell, 2014, pp. 114.
12 Randolph B. Campbell, *An Empire for Slavery*, Baton Rouge, LA: Louisiana State University Press, 1989, p. 95.
13 Richard Morehead, *DeWitt C. Greer: King of Highway Builders*, Austin, TX: Eakin Press, 1984, p. 31. See also, Hogan, *The Texas Republic*, p. 60.
14 Calvert et al., *History of Texas*, pp. 120, 204–206.
15 Thad Sitton and Milam Rowald, *Ringing the Children In*, College Station, TX: Texas A&M University Press, 1987, p. 24.
16 Morehead, *DeWitt C. Greer*, p. 39.
17 Calvert et al., *History of Texas*, p. 348.
18 Morehead, *DeWitt C. Greer*, p. 176.

19 Anthony Champagne and Edward J. Harpham, *Texas at the Crossroads: People, Politics, and Policy*, College Station, TX: Texas A&M University Press, 1987, p. 204.

20 Fehrenbach, *Lone Star*, p. 649.

21 Morehead, *DeWitt C. Greer*, p. 148.

22 Nick Swartsell, "Study: Inadequate Roads Cost Texans Billions," *Texas Tribune*, October 2, 2012. Brandon Formby and Michael A. Lindenberger, "Drivers Pay Price for Aging Highways," *Dallas Morning News*, July 24, 2014, pp. A1, A7.

23 Theodore Kim, "Many Highways Are About to Get Speedier," *Dallas Morning News*, August 29, 2011, pp. 1B, 2B.

24 For more detail on the system for attributing motor fuel tax revenues to states, www.fhwa.dot. gov/ohim/attrib.htm.

25 Highway Statistics 2015, Table FE 221, "Ratio of Apportionments and Allocations to Payments," www.fhwa.dot.gov/policyinformation/statistics/2015/fe221.cfm.

26 Champagne and Harpham, *Texas at the Crossroads*, p. 203.

27 www.api.org/oil-and-natural-gas/consumer-information/motor-fuel-taxes.

28 Legislative Budget Board, "Texas Highway Funding: Legislative Primer," April 2016, p. 4.

29 Todd J. Gillman and Michael A. Lindenberger, "Hutchison Bill Would Let Taxes Keep Gas Tax Funds," *Dallas Morning News*, April 28, 2009, p. 9A.

30 AP, "Lawmakers Weighing Increase in Gas Tax to Help Build Roads," *Dallas Morning News*, November 12, 2009, p. 6B.

31 Jamie Rall, "Pain at the Pump: Are Gas Taxes in the Future of Transportation Funding?" *State Legislatures*, June, 2013, pp. 26–29.

32 Michael A. Lindenberger, "NTTA Defends Permanent Tolls," *Dallas Morning News*, March 10, 2011, p. 5B.

33 www.fhwa.dot.gov/ohim/summary95/sb202i.pdf.

34 Highway Funding Primer, Legislative Budget Board, March 2011, p. 3; www.lbb.state.tx.us/ Documents/Publications/Primer/Highway%20Funding%20Primer%20312012.pdf.

35 Michael A. Lindenberger, "Local Tax Proposal Cut from Transportation Bill," *Dallas Morning News*, May 31, 2009, pp. A1, A25.

36 Peggy Fikac, "Woodlands Senator Seeks $3 Billion for Highways," *San Antonio Express-News*, April 11, 2011.

37 Aman Butheja, "Road Tolls Proliferate as State Financing Falls Short," *Texas Tribune*, in the *New York Times*, November 30, 2012, pp. A25A, A26A.

38 Ben Wear, "Highway Leader Says Time to Turn Away from Debt for Roads," *Austin American-Statesman*, November 25, 2012.

39 Madlin Mekelburg, "Paying Off Texas Toll Roads Could Top $30 Billion," *The Texas Tribune*, March 30, 2016.

40 Jim Malewitz and Brandon Formby, "With Money Tight Texas Budget Writers Eyeing Billions Approved for Roads," *The Texas Tribune*, February 13, 2017.

41 David G. McComb, *Texas: A Modern History*, Austin, TX: University of Texas Press, 2010, p. 160.

42 Michael A. Lindenberger, "Texas Is Lagging in Contest for High-Speed Rail Money," *Dallas Morning News*, June 25, 2009, p. 6A.

43 Editorial, *Dallas Morning News*, July 12, 2009, p. 2P.

44 Michael A. Lindenberger, "Most Rail Funds Likely to Bypass State," *Dallas Morning News*, January 19, 2010, pp. A1, A5.

45 Gerard MacCrossen, "Switching Tracks: Can Texas Ease Its Traffic Woes with Rail?" *Fiscal Notes*, February/March 2010, pp. 8–11.

46 Ben Wear, "TxDOT Looking at Passenger Rail along I-35 Corridor," *Austin American-Statesman*, October 16, 2012. See also Vianna Davila, "Is Texas on Track to High Speed Rail?" *San Antonio Express-News*, October 16, 2012.

47 Michael E. Young and Ryan McNeill, "Texas Triangle Holding Most of State's Growth," *Dallas Morning News*, March 6, 2011, pp. A1, A4.

48 https://mobility.tamu.edu/ums/national-congestion-tables/, see especially Table 7.

10 Energy and the Environment in Texas

> It has become customary . . . to damn the ancestral frame of mind that ravaged the world so fully and so soon. What I myself seem to damn mainly though, is just not having seen it . . . But God! To have viewed it entire, the soul and guts of what we had and gone forever now.
>
> (John Graves, 1991)[1]

To the frontier mind, the land and its resources were in endless supply—but time was wasting, others were coming, so the choice was to maximize profits today or share the bounty with others tomorrow. Individual initiative searched for opportunity and seized on it when found. With small government, low taxes, and light regulation, opportunity time and again produced feeding frenzies that burned out the resource before its time. Texas historian Robert Calvert has written that, "Intruders into the frontier often recklessly ravaged the natural resources of the region. This resulted in the decimation of the great buffalo herds, the overgrazing of the range, the stripping of timber lands without regard for the future, and the pollution of rivers, streams, and the Gulf."[2]

Fiction has made the same point somewhat more colorfully. The sweeping historical novel, *The Son*, published by Philipp Meyer in 2013, described Colonel Eli McCulloch, the founder of a majestic South Texas ranch, explaining the inevitable conflict between man and the land.

> I don't have to tell you what this land used to look like, . . . And you don't have to tell me that I am the one who ruined it. Which I did, with my own hands, and ruined forever. You're old enough to remember when the grass between here and Canada was balls high to a Belgian, . . . But this is the story of the human race. . . . It's all we know how to do.[3]

While Texans have always enjoyed the beauties of nature, the urge to preserve nature for its own sake has been suspect. John Graves, author of the iconic *Goodbye to a River* (1960) and of the headnote above, explained that his beloved Hill Country land, now mostly limestone and scrub cedar, once was covered with three or four feet of top soil. But two generations of intensive cotton farming scraped it down to rock and left him dreaming about what it once must have looked like. What made Graves, just days short of his 94th birthday when he died in 2013, a Texas treasure was that few Texans, then or now, took time to protect the landscape, let alone dream about what it looked like when it was pristine.

A Brief History of Texans and the Land

While the early Anglo settlers thought Texas a beautiful place, they saw a far greater beauty in the potential of its rapid economic development. T.R. Fehrenbach reports that, "Somewhere along the line, [Stephen F.] Austin . . . developed an obsession to 'redeem Texas from its wilderness state by . . . spreading over it North American population, enterprise, and intelligence.' . . . Destroying nature and creating civilization as they knew it was already a fetish in North American minds. Austin merely had more vision and far more ability than most."[4] Throughout the nineteenth century and well into the twentieth, Texans viewed their state as a starkly beautiful but harsh land that needed to be confronted and subdued if its riches were to be extracted and enjoyed. The land proved bountiful but fickle to generations of plantation owners and farmers, cattle and timber men, and oil and gas men. Until the mid-twentieth century, Texas was an extractive, colonial economy in which wealth drawn from land was processed elsewhere. Millions of bales of cotton left the Gulf Coast ports for the manufacturing centers of New York and Boston, London and Manchester. The millions of longhorns driven north to Kansas and Missouri railheads were slaughtered in Chicago for consumption in the East. Both are prime examples of the extractive Texas economy of the nineteenth century. The energy economy of the twentieth century began as a colonial enterprise, dominated by northern capital, but ultimately proved rich enough to draw the capitalists themselves south.

In the two decades following the end of the Civil War, not only were the great buffalo herds eliminated, but cattle herds were increased until overgrazing threatened the range. During the 1870s, the buffalo herds that had numbered in the many millions were slaughtered for hides, sport, and to deprive the remaining plains Indians of the principal resource around which their lives revolved. Texas Congressman James Throckmorton said, "It would be a great step forward in the civilization of the Indians . . . if there were not a buffalo in existence."[5] By 1880, the buffalo numbered only in the thousands and the last herd was sheltered in the new Yellowstone National Park. As the northern plains emptied, Texas ranchers sent six million longhorns to northern markets from the late 1860s through the 1880s. Half went to slaughter and half went to stock ranches in Colorado, Wyoming, Montana, and the Dakotas. Strong demand for Texas cattle led to overstocking and overgrazing. When U.S. Department of Agriculture representatives met with Texas ranchers to discuss the problem, the Texans, predictably, bristled. The cattlemen unanimously passed a resolution declaring, "That none of us know, or care to know, anything about grasses, native or otherwise, outside of the fact that for the present there are lots of them, the best on record, and we are after getting the most out of them while they last."[6] Environmentalism looked, to these Texans, like yet another form of federal meddling.

The timber men of East Texas took the same short-term, maximum utilization approach as the cattlemen of West Texas. Between the 1870s and 1930s, the old-growth pine forests of East Texas were decimated with little thought of conservation. Northern financiers and Texas entrepreneurs combined talents to bring the forests to market. Timber products led all other freight categories in tonnage carried on Texas railroads in the late nineteenth and early twentieth century. Timber production peaked at 2.2 billion board feet in 1907 and then began dropping.[7] Texas responded by establishing the state Forest Service (TFS) in 1917 as part of Texas A&M University. The TFS was to advise and assist private landowners in managing and improving forestry assets and products. The TFS's impact was modest and by the early 1930s production had fallen to 350 million board feet, the lowest levels since the 1880s: "Most of the virgin pine had been cut, and many operators had moved to new locations, often to the Pacific coast, leaving vast cut-over areas behind them."[8]

The energy industry, also an extractive industry, drove the development of modern Texas. Texas oil and gas, once it was out of the ground, was refined and marketed by Eastern and even European corporations, led by Royal Dutch Shell (the largest European oil company), Gulf Oil (owned by the Mellon family of Pittsburgh), and Sun Oil (owned by the Pew family of Philadelphia).[9] From the first big discovery at Spindletop near Beaumont in the Upper Gulf Coast field in 1901, through the discoveries in the Panhandle and Permian Basin in the 1920s, to discovery of the great East Texas field in October 1930, Texas increasingly became identified with oil.

For the first three decades of the twentieth century, Texas took a laissez-faire approach to the oil industry as well. The major oil companies controlled most of the production and they understood the importance of managing an oil field for long-term productivity. But the majors had ignored Northeast Texas and so the discoveries around Kilgore in 1930 set off a wildcatter scramble of epic proportions. Within a year, thousands of wells producing at maximum capacity had driven the price of oil to all-time lows and threatened to reduce pressure in the field and render vast reserves unrecoverable. In a rare case of state intervention, Governor Ross Sterling authorized state troops to seize the field and limit production and he empowered the Texas Railroad Commission to regulate future production in the interest of maximizing the long-term productivity of the field.[10]

Oil and gas continue to bulk large in the Texas imagination today. Though both production and reserves declined steadily from the early 1970s through 2005, the state's refinery and petrochemical industries continued to grow by supplementing Texas oil and gas stocks with imported oil. In recent years, both Texas and non-Texas U.S. production are up and rising while imports are down and falling. In 1972, Texas crude oil production peaked at 1.3 billion barrels annually. Texas production bottomed out at 388 million barrels in 2005, rising slowly to 404 million barrels in 2009, before jumping to 1.26 billion barrels in 2015. The daily capacity of Texas refineries was nearly twice that, 2 billion barrels annually. Just half of the oil refined in Texas is used in the state; the other half is exported to other states, mostly in the south and east through an extensive network of pipelines. Unfortunately, refineries and related petrochemical industries, critical to Texas's economic well-being, are heavy polluters. Texas is, by a wide margin, the heaviest U.S. producer of polluting gases, heavy metals, and fine particulates. Moreover, even as oil and gas production waned, Texas stuck doggedly with its historic energy sources. Only in the last decade or so, despite the abundant sun, wind, and agricultural plant wastes in Texas, have meaningful efforts been made to foster the development of renewable energy sources.[11]

In this chapter, we explore the history of the Texas energy and power industries, usually since 1950, though earlier where good data permit. As we shall see, Texas held a position of overwhelming dominance in the U.S. energy economy of 1950, producing nearly half of the oil and natural gas used in the U.S. As global oil supplies grew, particularly from the Middle East, U.S. domestic production fell and imports rose. Texas expanded its refinery capacity so that though it produced only about 21 percent of the oil used in the U.S., it refined and distributed about 30 percent of the oil used in the U.S. Texas has about 36 percent of the nation's proven oil reserves and 30 percent of its proven gas reserves. These are critically important state and national assets, but they tend to mesmerize, even blind, Texas officials. The state's ongoing commitment to the petroleum, natural gas, and petrochemical industries, whose beneficial products are distributed through much of the country and create good jobs in Texas, leave Texas heavily polluted. Worse, it leaves Texas officials in the position of denying the environmental impacts that flow from these industries and resisting national and international attempts to regulate their emissions.

Texas Oil and Gas Production and Reserves, 1935 to Present

Good data on U.S. crude oil production go back to 1859 but Texas did not become a major player until the early years of the twentieth century. On August 27, 1859, the Drake well in Titusville, Pennsylvania, marked the first commercially viable oil discovery in the U.S. U.S. production jumped from 2,000 barrels in 1859 to 500,000 barrels in 1860 and the race was on. Production increased steadily, to 5.3 million barrels in 1870, 26.3 million barrels in 1880, 45.8 million barrels in 1890, and 63.6 million barrels in 1900. Texas played a marginal role in the early development of the U.S. oil industry, though there were small strikes in Northeast Texas as early as the 1860s. During the nineteenth century, prior to the introduction of the automobile in the early decades of the twentieth century, the markets for petroleum products were limited mainly to industrial lubricants and kerosene for lighting.

On January 10, 1901, an Austrian engineer, Colonel Anthony Lucas, brought in the Spindletop well near Beaumont. Spindletop produced an unprecedented 100,000 barrels a day and brought entrepreneurs and would-be oil men from all over the country and the world to Texas to search for oil. Most failed, but a few struck it rich so that by 1929 Texas was the capital of the world oil industry, having produced 2 billion barrels since Spindletop. And then on October 3, 1930, Columbus M. ("Dad") Joiner brought in the Daisy Bradford #3 well in Northeast Texas near Kilgore. Within two weeks the soon-to-be-legendary H.L. Hunt of Dallas was drilling just south of Joiner's lease and by the end of November he owned Joiner's leases. The East Texas field, the largest field discovered in the world to that time, contained 5.5 billion barrels of oil. Over the next four decades, Texas stood astride the U.S. and global oil industries.

U.S. oil production increased from 63.6 million barrels in 1900, to 209.6 million in 1910, 442.9 million in 1920, and 898 million in 1930. The Texas share of that production probably ranged from one-third to one-half, but solid data on Texas production extend back just to 1935. In 1935, U.S. production was 994 million barrels, of which 376 million barrels, or 38 percent, came from Texas. Production in the U.S. and Texas grew slowly during the Depression years and then more rapidly as the nation plunged into World War II. Texas provided more than 40 percent of U.S. oil production every year from 1944 to 1957. By 1957, U.S. production was 2.6 billion barrels a year while Texas production was about 1.1 billion barrels. For the next two decades, Texas produced from 35 to 40 percent of U.S. oil, reaching 40 percent in both 1975 and 1976. Texas, of course, exulted in its extraordinary wealth, while the nation suffered under high oil price. Bumper stickers, reading SECEDE AND JOIN OPEC, adorned bumpers in the elite enclaves of Houston, Midland, and Dallas.[12] But the highpoint of both U.S. and Texas production (they were obviously closely related) had come in the early 1970s and, struggle as they might, production fell steadily from there. Just in the last couple of years, new discoveries and advanced drilling techniques have increased production to levels not seen in Texas for 40 years.

While production of U.S. oil began falling in 1972, U.S. oil consumption continued to rise and imports filled the gap (Figure 10.1). Oil imports did not comprise 10 percent of U.S. consumption until 1955 when we imported 285 million barrels. But imports soared from 15 percent in 1971, to 26 percent in 1973, and a stunning 44.5 percent in 1977.

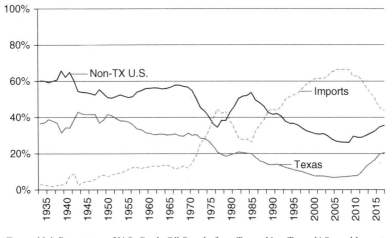

Figure 10.1 Percentage of U.S. Crude Oil Supply from Texas, Non-Texas U.S., and Imports, 1935–2015

Source: For U.S. crude oil production, see www.eia.gov/dnav/pet/hist/LeafHandler.ashx?n=pet&s=mcrfpus 2&f=a. For imports, see www.eia.gov/dnav/pet/hist/LeafHandler.ashx?n=pet&s=mcrimus1&f=a. For Texas production, see www.rrc.state.tx.us/data/production/oilwellcounts.php.

During the late 1970s, the U.S. imported about 2.3 billion barrels of oil each year. Oil embargoes, price shocks, and conservation measures held imports around 2.5 billion barrels until the early 1990s when they began rising again. The U.S. imported 3 billion barrels in 1997, cresting at 3.7 billion barrels in 2006. By 2015, it had fallen back to 2.7 billion and is expected to fall further.

In 2015, Texas produced 1.26 billion barrels of oil, near its 1970 peak production, while the U.S. (including Texas) produced 3.4 billion barrels, also its 1972 peak production. In 2015, Texas provided 37 percent of U.S. oil production and 28.6 percent of the oil consumed in the U.S. In 2015, the U.S. imported 2.7 billion barrels of oil, or 43.9 percent of the oil it consumed. From Spindletop in 1901 through the 1960s, Texas producers and regulators largely set international oil prices. From the 1970s through the beginning of this century, the Saudis and OPEC largely held that role. But the rapid run-up in Texas and U.S. production since 2000 has produced a worldwide oil glut and driven prices down sharply. Low oil prices are bemoaned in Texas but cheered nationally. This divergence of U.S. and Texas interests in regard to the price of oil has long fueled tension.

As with crude oil, Texas is the largest U.S. producer of natural gas, but, unlike with crude oil, domestic production is nearly sufficient to serve the U.S. market. In 2015, domestic production of natural gas fulfilled 90 percent of domestic consumption with most of the remainder being piped in from Canada. Relatively small amounts of liquefied natural gas (LNG) arrived by ship before being re-vaporized and moved into the national distribution system. In 2015, the U.S. produced and marketed 28.8 billion cubic feet (bcf) of natural gas. Texas produced 7.9 bcf, 27 percent of U.S. domestic production. Texas natural gas travels through an extensive system of pipelines to serve markets from California, through the Midwest, to the East Coast and New England.

During the first half of the twentieth century, natural gas was treated as a nuisance in the search for oil. Untold billions of cubic feet of natural gas were flared, or burned off, at the wellhead. A few towns near the oil and gas fields used the gas for energy and some was re-injected to extend the life of depleted oil fields, but most was simply flared. After World War II, Texas passed legislation banning flaring and producers were forced to search for more productive and profitable uses for the gas. Two pipelines, the "big inch" (24 inch) and the "little big inch" (20 inch), built in 1942 and 1943 to deliver oil to the East Coast during World War II, were sold to the Texas East Transmission Corporation (TETCO) after the war. TETCO converted and extended the pipelines to move natural gas to the Midwest and East Coast. The El Paso Corporation built a new pipeline to carry natural gas from West Texas's Permian Basin to Southern California. As these markets grew, Texas production increased to serve them.[13]

In 1950, the natural gas market was just getting organized and Texas was by far its dominant player. In 1950, the U.S. produced nearly 6.3 bcf of natural gas, of which 3.1 bcf, almost exactly half, were produced in Texas. Texas's neighbors, Louisiana and Oklahoma, produced 832 and 482 million cubic feet, respectively, another 13 percent and 8 percent. By 1960, U.S. production doubled to 12.8 bcf, Texas's production nearly doubled to 5.9 bcf, as did Oklahoma's to 0.8 bcf, and Louisiana's production tripled to 3 bcf. In 1960, Texas produced 46 percent of the U.S. total while Louisiana produced 23 percent and Oklahoma produced another 6 percent (Figure 10.2). Between 1960 and 1990, Texas, Louisiana, and Oklahoma provided three-quarters of the nation's natural gas. As late as 2010, Texas, Oklahoma, and Louisiana were still producing half of U.S. production, though increasingly they were supplemented by gas fields in New Mexico, Montana, the deep Gulf, and the Rocky Mountains.

Recent finds, some of them huge, in Texas, Louisiana, Arkansas, and Pennsylvania have rejuvenated the natural gas market. More importantly, new drilling techniques combining fracturing shale formations (called "fracking") by pumping water, sand, and chemical gels into them at high pressure, and horizontal drilling to follow the formations underground have enhanced production dramatically.[14] The Barnett Shale near Fort Worth, where these techniques were developed, produced 2 billion cubic feet of

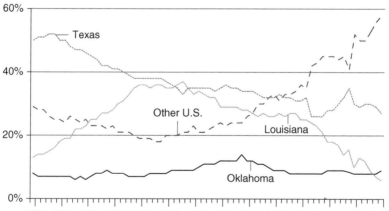

Figure 10.2 Percentage of U.S. Natural Gas Supply from Texas and Other U.S. Sources, 1950–2015

Source: Department of Commerce, Bureau of the Census, Statistical Abstract of the United States, Natural Resources, Mining and Mineral Products, various years, 1950–2015. See also U.S. Department of Energy, Energy Information Administration, Annual U.S. Natural Gas Marketed Production, http://tonto.eia.doe.gov/dnav/ng/hist/n9050us2a.htm.

gas a day in 2012, making it one of the most productive fields in the U.S. Similar finds—the Marcellus fields in Pennsylvania, the Fayetteville Shale in northern Arkansas, and the Haynesville Shale in northern Louisiana—pushed natural gas reserve estimates to a 90-year supply. They also created a natural gas glut that saw prices drop from nearly $13 in 2008, to $9 in early 2009, to $2 in 2012 and again in 2016. Many companies scaled back production.[15] Given the secure long-term supply and moderate prices, most experts and policymakers now see natural gas as an increasingly important energy source and as a likely transition fuel as the nation moves away from coal toward more climate-friendly energy sources.

Even after more than a century of intense oil production and three-quarters of a century of concerted gas production, Texas has almost 36 percent of the nation's proven oil reserves and 26 percent of its proven gas reserves. Still, Texas reserves have trended downward for decades and just a decade ago it appeared that the depletion of Texas reserves would continue apace, but new discoveries and new techniques are renewing the productivity of older fields and opening up new fields. In 1950, Texas claimed 53 percent of the known U.S. reserves for both oil and natural gas. Those estimates remained above 40 percent through the 1960s before declining rapidly in the 1970s, holding at around one-quarter of both oil and gas reserves from 1980 through 2010. Even though new reserves of oil and gas are discovered regularly, Texas has been more extensively explored than other places.

In 1950, U.S. oil reserves were estimated to be 25.3 billion barrels of oil, more than half of which, 13.5 billion barrels, were in Texas (Figure 10.3). In 2015, U.S. oil reserves were estimated to be 32.3 billion barrels, more than one-third of which, 11.8 billion barrels, were in Texas. Similarly, U.S. natural gas reserves in 1950 were estimated to be 185.6 trillion cubic feet, of which more than half, 99.2 trillion cubic feet, were in Texas. Texas gas reserves fell to just one-fifth of U.S. totals by the late 1990s, but have rebounded in the wake of recent discoveries. In 2015, U.S. gas reserves totaled 307.7 trillion cubic feet, of which about 26 percent, 79 trillion cubic feet, were in Texas.

Figure 10.3 Texas Oil and Gas Reserves as a Percentage of U.S. Reserves, 1950–2015

Source: U.S. Energy Information Administration, U.S. and Texas Crude Oil Proved Reserves.

The sharp drop in Texas's share of total oil reserves from 1969 to 1970 reflects the Prudhoe Bay, Alaska, discoveries of 1968. Nonetheless, the drop in the price of oil from its mid-2014 peak highlighted a number of problems likely to plague the future of the oil patch. First, by 2016, Texas had more than 10,000 abandoned wells. Abandoned wells pose environmental hazards both above and below ground. Each well costs about $17,000 to cap and with dozens of drillers going bankrupt since 2014, the costs fall on underfunded state regulators. No one will be surprised to hear that the bond drillers must post to insure cleanup has not been raised since 1991.[16] Second, the Texas oil and gas sector shed about 100,000 jobs during the recent downturn. These high paying jobs are unlikely fully to return. Tight budgets and new technology have forced efficiencies and sped-up automation so that fewer workers per rig are needed. Moreover, new jobs in the industry are likely to be geoscientists, engineers, and computer operators, often many miles from the fields, rather than the roustabouts of yore.[17]

Energy Consumption in the U.S. and Texas, 1980 to Present

Texas not only produces a substantial share of U.S. energy, it consumes a great deal of energy as well. In fact, Texas uses more energy than any other state, including California which is half again as populous (in 2015 California had 39.1 million residents compared to 27.5 million for Texas). Although Texas uses more energy than any other state, a few small states use more energy per capita. Since 1980, Texas has been the fourth most intensive energy-consuming state, behind only Alaska, Wyoming, occasionally North Dakota, and Louisiana. The cold states use a great deal of energy to heat homes and businesses in the winter, while warm states use lots of energy to cool homes and businesses in the summer. But heavy energy use by Texas is not explained by hot summers; all of the South and Southwest have hot summers and most use far less energy. As we will see, Texas uses a great deal of energy to create electricity to run industrial processes such as turning petroleum into gasoline, chemicals, and plastics.

Figure 10.4 highlights two key facts about energy usage in the U.S. State energy profiles are both stable, they do not change much over time, and quite different, some states use more energy per person than other states do. In 2014, Texas used 478 million British thermal units (BTUs) of energy annually per resident, while the U.S. average was 309 million BTUs. Even more strikingly, Texas's 478 million BTUs per capita more than doubled California's 196 million BTUs and Florida's 207 million. California and Florida are garden spots with fairly temperate climates and sea breezes, but New York, no garden spot in most estimates, uses only 190 million BTUs annually per capita. Georgia and Ohio, both with substantial industrial usage, consume 282 million BTUs and 329 million BTUs per capita, respectively.

Not only does Texas use more energy than almost any other state, its energy use is more carbon intensive than most other states and more of that energy is used for industrial purposes than in most other states. Hence, as we shall see below, Texas creates more pollution, more carbon dioxide (CO_2), more toxic emissions, and more fine particulates than any other state. In fact, with just 8.2 percent of the nation's population, Texas has produced fully one-third of the nation's hazardous waste over the last two decades. As the U.S. responds to the threat of global warming by transitioning to less carbon-intensive sources of energy, Texas's traditional dependence on carbon fuels and its historically loose approach to pollution control have come under tremendous pressure.

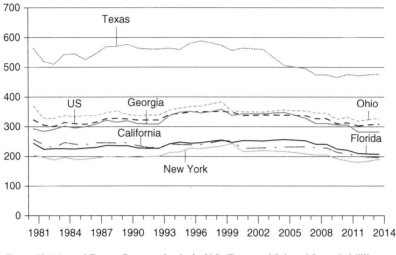

Figure 10.4 Annual Energy Consumption in the U.S., Texas, and Selected States in Million
BTUs per Capita, 1980–2014

Source: U.S. Census Bureau, Statistical Abstract of the United States, "Energy Consumption—End Use Sector
and Selected Source, by State," 1981 to 2014.

Historically, the U.S. has been heavily dependent on carbon fuels, petroleum, natural gas, and coal. Hydroelectric power became an option for some states in the middle third of the twentieth century, nuclear power came online in the 1960s, and in the last two decades, biomass, solar, and wind have begun to contribute to our energy requirements. Each state, depending on their natural advantages, has drawn on a distinctive fuel mix and that mix has changed over time, albeit slowly, as fuel options have evolved. In 1980, the U.S. used about 45 percent petroleum, 27 percent natural gas, 20 percent coal, and 4 percent each of hydropower and nuclear power. By 2014, petroleum had declined to 36.7 percent, natural gas held steady at 27.9 percent, as did coal at 18.3 percent, hydropower was at 2.45 percent, while nuclear power was just over 8 percent and biomass, solar, and wind added the last six points. But those numbers are just averages; different states, by accident of history and by policy design, meet their energy needs with different amounts and mixes of fuel.

California and Texas, the two largest states in the nation, have taken predictably different approaches. Given its own history and resources, Texas has taken a carbon-intensive approach to meeting its energy needs. In part, this was inevitable: Texas petroleum and natural gas are prepared for market in Texas plants and refineries. In 1980, Texas depended on fossil fuels (petroleum, natural gas, and coal) for 100 percent of its energy needs. The U.S. depended on fossil fuels for 92 percent of its energy needs, using hydropower and nuclear to meet the rest. California, on the other hand, used fossil fuels for 86 percent of its energy needs, using hydropower for 5 percent, and a diverse mix of nuclear, biomass, wind, and solar for the rest. In 2014, Texas used 92 percent fossil fuels to meet its energy needs; the U.S. used 83 percent fossil fuels, while California used just 76 percent fossil fuels. Figure 10.5 shows that while the U.S., Texas, and California have all reduced their dependence on fossil fuels, Texas began from a much higher base and has moved more slowly. By far the greatest difference between Texas

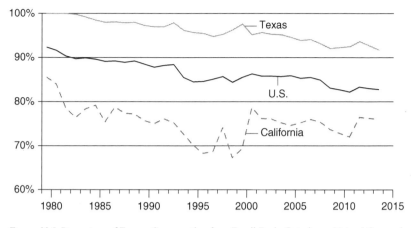

Figure 10.5 Percentage of Energy Consumption from Fossil Fuels (Petroleum, Natural Gas, and Coal), 1980–2014

Source: U.S. Census Bureau, Statistical Abstract of the United States, "Energy Consumption—End Use Sector and Selected Source, by State," 1981 to 2014.

and California is that Texas used coal, the dirtiest fossil fuel, to meet an average of 14 percent of its energy needs while California has averaged less than 1 percent since 1980.

The U.S. Energy Information Administration tracks the purposes to which energy is put throughout the U.S. Four broad categories of energy use—residential, commercial, industrial, and transportation—have been tracked since 1981. Texas's energy problem is made more complex by the fact that a larger portion of the state's energy consumption goes to more polluting industrial uses, and less to less polluting residential, commercial, and transportation uses than in most other states. For example, in 2014, U.S. energy usage was 32.2 percent industrial, 21.9 percent residential, 18.4 percent commercial, and 27.5 percent transportation. California energy usage was 24.4 percent industrial, 18.3 percent residential, 18.6 percent commercial, all three at or below the national average, and 38.7 percent transportation. California freeways burn up a lot of gas, but California battled the Bush and Obama Environmental Protection Agencies (EPAs) in the 2000s to allow it to demand better gas mileage and more robust pollution controls than demanded by national standards. Texas, on the other hand, devoted 48.8 percent of its energy usage to industrial purposes, 13.2 percent to residential, 12.7 percent to commercial, and 25.3 percent to transportation. And Texas battled the Obama EPA (the Bush administration did not bother Texas) over demands that Texas take a harder line toward industrial pollution. As with energy mix, Figure 10.6 shows that energy use has changed only slowly since 1980.

The form of energy that most people know best is the electricity that flows into their homes to insure that the lights come on when they flip the switch. Electric power came late to much of Texas. LBJ famously championed rural electrification for the Hill Country during the Depression. But the war initiated changes in Texas, especially urbanization and industrialization, which dramatically changed the state over the next several decades. In 1950, Texas was the nation's sixth most populous state, with 7.7 million residents, 5.1 percent of the total U.S. population of 152 million. But Texas produced just 3.9 percent of the electricity produced in the U.S. (Figure 10.7). Within a decade, Texas had caught up and was producing 5.2 percent of the nation's electricity for 5.3 percent of its population and by 1970 Texas was producing 7.6 percent of the

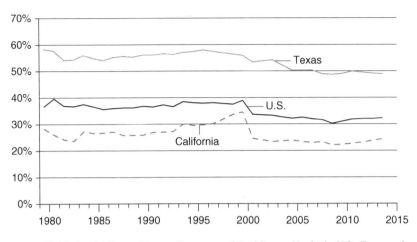

Figure 10.6 Industrial Energy Use as a Percentage of Total Energy Use in the U.S., Texas, and California, 1980–2014

Source: U.S. Census Bureau, Statistical Abstract of the United States, "Energy Consumption—End Use Sector and Selected Source, by State," 1981 to 2014. Note that the bursting of the tech bubble in 2001 hit California industrial energy use particularly hard.

nation's energy for 5.5 percent of its population. As late as 2014, Texas was producing 10.7 percent of the nation's electricity for 8.5 percent of its population.

The explosive build out of Texas electricity production was meant to serve industrial customers at least as much and probably more than residential and commercial consumers. Between 1950 and 1979, U.S. electricity production grew from 329 billion kilowatt hours (kWh) to 2,319 billion kWh, an increase of 605 percent. Texas, starting from further back, grew faster. In 1950, Texas produced 12.7 billion kWh and in 1979 produced 197 billion kWh, an increase of an astounding 1,454 percent. But since 1980, growth in the production of electric power in the U.S. and Texas has been much slower. U.S. electricity production has grown just 80 percent (from 2,286 billion kWh to 4,128 billion kWh) while Texas electricity production has grown just 103 percent (from 203 billion kWh to 412 billion kWh). And industry, because it uses power in bulk when compared to commercial and residential users, pays less. Commercial users pay about 70 percent of what residential users pay per kilowatt hour, while industrial users pay about 52 percent.

Finally, slow growth of electricity production capacity in Texas after 1980 has put increasing pressure on electricity prices for all classes of users. Throughout the 1990s, electricity prices in Texas were well below the national average. In 1990, Texas electricity prices were 29th in the nation (with 1 being the most expensive) and in 1999 they were 27th in the nation. By 2001, they were 14th in the nation and in 2006 they were 11th. As Figure 10.8 shows, Texas electricity prices were stable through the 1990s and took a sharp upward spike between 2000 and 2006. They did not fall back to the national average until 2010. What happened? Texas public policy happened.[18]

Enron was a major player in Texas politics and energy policy in the 1990s and they pushed hard for deregulation. Republican Senator David Sibley introduced Senate Bill 7 early in the 76th Texas legislative session (1999) and Governor George W. Bush signed the bill into law on June 18, 1999. Senator Sibley declared that the goal of SB7 was to bring down the cost of electric power. He said "We want this bill to bring down the cost of electricity for all Texans. If we don't get consumers lower rates, then we

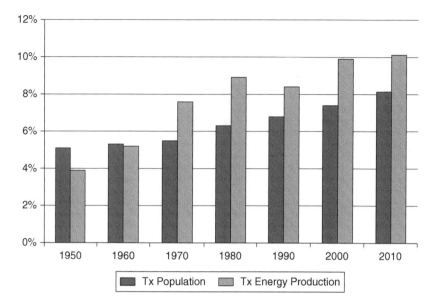

Figure 10.7 Texas Population and Energy Production as a Percentage of U.S. Population and
Energy Production by Decade, 1950–2014

Source: U.S. Census Bureau, Statistical Abstract of the United States, Population section, 1950 to 2014; Electric
Power Industry, Net Generation section, 1950 to present.

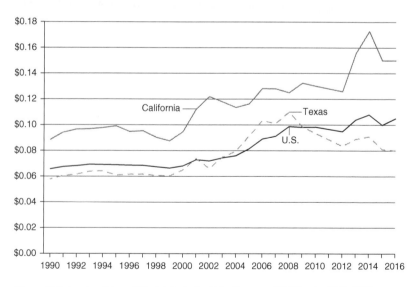

Figure 10.8 Average Price of Electricity in the U.S., Texas, and California, 1990–2016

Source: U.S. Department of Energy, Energy Information Administration, see www.eia.doe.gov/cneaf/electricity/
epa/average_price_state.xls, Average Price of Electricity by state.

have been a failure—I'll be the first to say it." However, rates did not fall below the national average until 2010, though they have remained there since.[19] Is this a win?

How we create electricity raises as many complex issues as whether we will have enough of it at prices that we can afford. First, electricity is generated by using fuel stocks, mostly fossil fuels, but also nuclear and renewable stocks, to heat water, creating steam that is forced past a turbine's blades to turn a shaft connected to a generator. The generator converts mechanical to electrical energy for distribution and use. In 2015, coal (31.1%) and natural gas (35.1%) were the principal fossil fuel feed stocks used in electric generation in the U.S. Of renewable fuels, nuclear power (19.5%), hydroelectric power (6.3%), and other renewables (including biomass, wind, and solar; about 8%), were the most productive. In 2015, Texas used less coal (29%) and more natural gas (48%) than the U.S. in general, but also used less nuclear power (11%), and more renewables, at about 11 percent.[20]

While Texas's heavy use of natural gas for electricity production is decidedly a good thing, as it is less polluting than coal, Texas has not pushed residential and commercial use of natural gas nearly as aggressively. Natural gas has long been used to heat about half of the nation's homes. But residential use of natural gas in Texas has been falling against the national average for more than half a century. In 1955, Texas accounted for 5.2 percent of the U.S. population, but Texas's 1.8 million residences served by natural gas accounted for 6.4 percent of total U.S. residences served by natural gas. In 2015, Texas accounted for 8.5 percent of U.S. total population, while the 4.47 million Texas residences served by natural gas still accounted for just 7.4 percent of total U.S. residences served by natural gas. California, on the other hand, with a 2015 population half again as large as Texas's had many more homes (10.37 million residences) served by natural gas. With 12.2 percent of the U.S. population, California had 17.2 percent of homes served by natural gas. Interestingly, California served its 10.37 million residential customers with 19 gas utilities, while Texas served its 4.47 million residential customers with 162 gas utilities.[21] Heavier use of natural gas in Texas homes and businesses should be an obvious step in the direction of reducing the state's carbon footprint.

Coal presents U.S. policymakers with a major dilemma. On the one hand, the U.S. has about 27 percent of the world's known coal reserves, more than any other nation. The U.S. has a demonstrated reserve base of 477 billion short tons (don't ask, they call them short tons, but they are regular tons of 2,000 pounds), of which over 255 billion short tons are recoverable with current technology, a 250-year supply at current rates of usage. Over the past 15 years, the U.S. has produced an average of 1.1 billion short tons a year.[22] On the other hand, coal is a dirty form of energy, producing twice as many pollutants as natural gas.

Texas's demonstrated coal reserves account for just 2.5 percent of U.S. reserves. In 2015, Texas produced 36,101 short tons of coal from 13 surface mines, mostly in East Texas, but brought in more than 55,173 short tons by rail from Wyoming and another 798 short tons from elsewhere. Texas lignite coal is low in energy content but it is also low in sulfur, which makes it less polluting than the more efficient subbituminous coal from Wyoming. As a result, Texas consumes more coal than any other state and its emissions are the highest in the nation. And as late as 2007, Texas authorities seemed on the verge of doubling down on coal. Texas then had 17 coal-fired power plants. In early 2007, Texas power companies proposed 18 new coal-fired plants, 11 for a single company, Dallas's TXU. Governor Rick Perry ordered the Texas Environmental Quality Commission to "fast-track" the approval process, but a coalition of local officials, led by Dallas Mayor Laura Miller, business people, and environmentalists, got in the way. Eventually, TXU was acquired in a leveraged buyout and 8 of the 11 proposed coal plants were cancelled, no thanks to Texas political authorities. However, due to the recession and the declining price of natural gas, only 4 new plants had been built in Texas by 2015.[23] No new coal-fired plants are planned and older plants continue to slow production or shut down entirely.

Nuclear power plants began contributing to the nation's electricity supply in the 1960s. More than 100 plants were built nationwide before the first nuclear power plant in Texas came online in 1988. When Texas brought its first plant online, California already had six units producing 25 percent of the state's electricity. Since 1993, Texas has had four units, two each at Comanche Peak southwest of Dallas and the South Texas Project southwest of Houston, producing about 10.1 percent of the state's electricity. But concerns about the safety and cost of nuclear power have hobbled the industry for decades, nowhere more so than in Texas. Today, the U.S. has 104 nuclear plants, down from 111 in 1990, producing a steady 21.9 percent of the nation's electricity. The 2011 nuclear catastrophe in Japan further chilled the industry in the U.S. and globally. And like coal, the prospects of new nuclear plants are undercut by the low price of natural gas.

While Texas's preference for traditional fossil fuels has made it skeptical of nuclear power, in a jaw-dropping decision in early 2011, Texas agreed to become a permanent storage site for low-level nuclear waste. The 1,340-acre Waste Control Specialists (WCS) site in West Texas, near Andrews, is the only facility in the nation to accept federal and out-of-state low-level nuclear waste products, such as clothing, rags, cleaning materials, syringes and the like from nuclear power plants, chemical plants, and hospitals. The last such site, in South Carolina, closed in 2008, leaving on-site storage as the only option for those who create such waste. WCS won a 15-year license in 2009 to store 2.31 million cubic feet of waste. Opponents worried that Waste Control would move to expand its licensed storage capacity because the 36 states eligible to deposit waste created about 2 million cubic feet per year. Opponents also pointed to the $600,000 contribution that Waste Control's board chairman Harold Simmons made to Rick Perry's 2010 gubernatorial re-election campaign ($1.12 million since 2001) and $430,000 in lobbying fees as typical of Texas politics and environmental policymaking.[24]

Just as opponents feared, WCS sought almost immediately to expand the sources and kinds of nuclear waste products that could be accepted. Initially, the only out-of-state waste that could be accepted was from Vermont, but everyone knew it would be opened to waste from 35 other states. However, in 2014, the state environmental agency unanimously approved a WCS request to accept depleted uranium, a more radioactive by-product from nuclear power plants and nuclear weapons facilities. In early 2015, WCS sought a license from the Nuclear Regulatory Commission (NRC) to build a facility that could accept high-level nuclear waste, including spent fuel rods, from around the country. Opposition arose immediately, but the company promised to push through to construction beginning in 2019 with the goal of accepting shipments of high-level nuclear waste by 2021.

Renewable energy generally refers to energy produced from sources that, unlike coal, petroleum, and natural gas, are not used up but occur and recur naturally. The oldest renewable energy source is wood and wood waste, which does replenish through new growth but which can be overwhelmed if harvested too quickly. Hydropower is another old source of renewable energy, used throughout history, but employed as a major source of electrical power only since the early decades of the twentieth century. Though concentrated heavily in New York and the West Coast states of Washington, Oregon, and California, hydropower still provides 46 percent of renewable electric energy supplies.

Newer sources of renewable energy are biomass, including corn for ethanol, but plant wastes more generally, as well as wind and solar power.

U.S. consumption of renewable energy is about 10 percent of total energy consumption. Texas is still a bit below the national average. Texas has little hydro-power, so its renewable energy bets have been placed elsewhere. In 2000, Texas, with 7.4 percent of the nation's population, produced just 2.2 percent of the nation's non-hydro renewable power, but by 2005, now with 7.7 percent of the nation's popu-lation, that contribution was up to 6.1 percent, mostly from a growing wind energy industry. In 2005, Texas adopted a law requiring that 5,880 megawatts of additional renewable generation capacity be built by 2015 and 10,000 megawatts be built by 2025, of which 500 megawatts are to be non-wind renewable energy. In 2006, Texas surpassed California to become the nation's largest producer of wind energy. In 2015, Texas produced fully one-quarter of the nation's wind energy. More than 85 percent of Texas's renewable energy production came from wind, which accounted for 14.5 percent of the state's total electricity usage. Texas has been quite friendly to production of wind power, investing $5 billion in new transmission lines to carry power from West Texas to the urban centers of the state, though opposition from landowners and environmentalists has been difficult to overcome.[25] Texas policy-makers have not yet provided incentives to solar power energy production.

While Texas has led on wind energy, informed observers argue that a coordinated state plan to foster renewable energy has been lacking. Amy Jaffe of the Rice University's energy program has argued that "We're stuck in 30-year-old thinking, not only in the companies, but in our politicians, and we are not understanding that there is a sea change that is coming." Jeff Morris, head of the Dallas refining company Alon USA has made a similar point, saying, "They need a statewide strategy, not a little piece here, a little piece there kind of thing." Austin Mayor Will Wynn said "I'm disappointed to see the state leadership either diving under the table or, worse, pounding their chest, instead of taking part in the energy discussion." As if on cue, then-Governor Perry said, "If the answer is Washington, D.C., then I would suggest to you that most people in America would rather go it alone. My argument here is that we have, by our own volition, by our own innova-tion, led the country in a lot of the alternative energy side of things."[26]

Pollution Consequent to Energy Production and Consumption in Texas

Fossil fuels are of little use until they are converted into usable energy, usually in the form of electricity, transportation fuels, or chemical products. But those conversion processes, making coal into electricity, oil into gasoline, or natural gas into fertiliz-ers and plastics, leave undesirable residuals or wastes in their wake. Because Texas produces and consumes more energy than any other state, it would have to work very hard not to produce more waste products and pollutants than any other state. Not only does Texas not work very hard to control pollution, but it also habitually resists national pressure, let alone mandates, to limit the pollution that accompanies energy production and consumption. The Obama administration and its EPA argued that cleaner air and water were important to human health and to a healthy environment more generally. The Perry and Abbott administrations and their Texas Commission on Environmental Quality (TCEQ) argue that tougher rules are unnecessary and unachievable, will limit economic growth, and cost jobs. The Trump administration and the EPA, now headed by former Oklahoma Attorney General Scott Pruitt, have been much friendlier to Texas, just as the Bush administration was before Obama.

The mission of the EPA "is to protect human health and the environment." It has a $8.2 billion budget and 15,078 employees. While its mandate is broad, its focus is defined by authorizing legislation, including the Clean Air Act of 1970, the Clean Water Act of 1972, the Resource Conservation and Recovery Act of 1976, and the Federal Hazardous and Solid Waste Amendments of 1984. The mission of the TCEQ is "to protect our state's human and natural resources consistent with sustainable economic development." TCEQ has a budget of $456 million and 2,780 employees. Both EPA and TCEQ have taken substantial budget cuts in recent years and the EPA remains under heavy pressure in the Trump administration.

Critics argue that the TCEQ is too business-friendly to be a credible defender of the environment. They argue that "in decision after decision, the Texas agency that is supposed to protect the public and the environment has sided with polluters." Texas leaders of course disagree. Former TCEQ Chairman Buddy Garcia, said "'From what you read and what you hear, it would almost appear we have little or no interest in taking care of the environment. . . . It's very frustrating' . . . Texas actually should be viewed as a 'model for the country.'"[27] Governor Perry describes Texas's light regulatory regime as, "the right way. We refer to it as the Texas way."[28]

The data seem to be on the side of the critics as opposed to the TCEQ. The EPA and U.S. Department of Energy's Energy Information Administration have tracked

Table 10.1 CO_2 Emissions from Energy Consumption at Conventional Power Plants in the U.S., Texas, and California, 1990–2014

	U.S. CO_2	TX CO_2	TX/U.S.	CA CO_2	CA/U.S.
1990	1,931,248	211,045	10.9%	52,338	2.7%
1991	1,928,035	210,362	10.9%	49,786	2.6%
1992	1,949,594	209,309	10.7%	57,646	3.0%
1993	2,033,139	244,931	12.0%	54,130	2.7%
1994	2,063,900	219,803	10.6%	61,887	3.0%
1995	2,083,509	220,223	10.6%	49,976	2.4%
1996	2,161,258	230,508	10.7%	46,847	2.2%
1997	2,232,709	237,181	10.6%	49,834	2.2%
1998	2,324,139	246,845	10.6%	52,882	2.3%
1999	2,338,660	252,540	10.8%	57,551	2.5%
2000	2,441,722	262,280	10.7%	67,411	2.8%
2001	2,389,745	253,227	10.6%	71,258	3.0%
2002	2,395,048	255,890	10.7%	59,669	2.5%
2003	2,415,680	255,073	10.6%	55,983	2.3%
2004	2,456,934	256,725	10.4%	59,820	2.4%
2005	2,513,609	258,661	10.3%	54,680	2.2%
2006	2,459,800	257,552	10.5%	59,389	2.4%
2007	2,516,580	255,092	10.1%	62,780	2.5%
2008	2,484,012	252,710	10.2%	62,548	2.5%
2009	2,269,508	242,864	10.7%	59,428	2.6%
2010	2,259,000	235,000	10.4%	45,000	2.0%
2011	2,222,000	250,000	11.3%	37,000	1.7%
2012	2,156,875	222,000	10.3%	47,940	2.2%
2013	2,168,284	226,230	10.4%	45,650	2.1%
2014	2,021,600	224,840	11.1%	46,300	2.3%

Source: U.S. Department of Energy, Energy Information Administration, www.eia.gov/cneaf/electricity/epa/emission_state.xls.

emissions from conventional, meaning non-nuclear, power plants since 1990. The principal pollutants emitted during the production of electric power, usually using natural gas and coal, are carbon dioxide (CO_2), sulfur dioxide (SO_2), and nitrogen oxides (NOx). CO_2 is by far the largest pollutant, totaling 2 billion metric tons in 2014. Table 10.1 shows that Texas is by far the largest producer of CO_2, producing four times as much each year over the past two decades as California. As we shall see below, Texas has been in a long-running struggle with the EPA over CO_2 emissions in the state.

The EPA also has published biennial reports on generation of hazardous wastes by states since 1991. EPA defines hazardous wastes as liquids, solids, gases, or sludges, such as cleaning fluids, pesticides, and by-products of manufacturing processes that are dangerous or potentially harmful to the environment or human health. In 12 of the 13 EPA reports produced since 1991, Texas ranked number 1, producing more hazardous waste materials than any other state, usually by a wide margin (Table 10.2). For example, in 1991, the first year for which data are available, Texas produced fully 34 percent of the nation's hazardous waste materials, and in 1997, Texas produced nearly half, 46.6 percent, of the nation's hazardous wastes. In the 2007 report, Texas slipped to number 2, not because Texas had a particularly good year but because neighboring energy state Louisiana had a particularly bad year, nearly tripling 2005 hazardous waste totals. In 2007, Louisiana produced 34 percent of the nation's hazardous wastes while Texas contributed another 28.4 percent. Together the two oil producing and refining states produced nearly two-thirds of the nation's total hazardous waste output. California, more populous than Texas and Louisiana combined, produced just 1.3 percent of the nation's hazardous wastes. In 2009 Texas came roaring back to capture the number 1 spot. Texas has since built a formidable lead, producing fully 45.7 percent of the nation's hazardous waste in 2011, 46.2 percent in 2013, andc 48.4 percent in 2015. In 2015, Texas, with more than 16 million tons of hazardous waste produced, smoked number two Louisiana with just over 5 million tons. Who is the big dog?

Table 10.2 Hazardous Waste Generated by State: Comparing the U.S., Texas, and California, 1991–2015

	U.S.	Texas	TX/U.S.	TX Rank	Calif.	CA/U.S.	CA Rank
1991	305,709	104,079	34.0%	1	12,925	4.2%	8
1993	258,449	63,436	24.6%	1	14,056	5.4%	7
1995	214,093	68,513	32.0%	1	11,110	5.2%	6
1997	40,676	18,973	46.6%	1	673	1.7%	12
1999	40,026	14,924	37.3%	1	427	1.1%	16
2001	40,821	7,555	18.5%	1	807	2.0%	16
2003	30,176	6,585	21.8%	1	445	1.5%	16
2005	38,347	15,224	39.7%	1	747	1.9%	13
2007	46,693	13,272	28.4%	2	609	1.3%	11
2009	35,331	13,462	38.1%	1	700	2.0%	11
2011	34,835	15,683	45.7%	1	335	1.6%	11
2013	33,816	15,628	46.2%	1	381	1.1%	12
2015	33,641	16,289	48.4	1	307	0.9	13

Source: Environmental Protection Agency, Biennial Hazardous Waste Report, various years

Note: As of 1997, all wastewater treatment data contained in previous reports are excluded, which makes cursory comparison before and after that date potentially misleading.

Texas vs. the EPA: Greenhouse Gases (CO_2)

The battle between the EPA and TCEQ has been particularly intense over air pollution, especially in and around Houston. The EPA is responsible for setting national limits on ground-level ozone, the principal cause of smog, while TCEQ is responsible for developing the state compliance plan, though the plan must be approved by the EPA. Smog is caused by a cocktail of transportation and industrial pollutants interacting in the atmosphere. Houston's millions of cars and trucks, together with its nine oil refineries and over 100 chemical plants, have left the city out of compliance with national rules for decades. In 2009, Houston met the 1997 EPA standard of .084 parts per million. Unfortunately for Houston, the Bush administration had lowered the standard to .075 parts per million in 2006 and the Obama administration announced plans to lower it still further, to between .06 and .07.

Texas politicians, mostly but not exclusively Republicans, have long opposed both national energy and environmental policy, especially the particular form of policy preferred by the Democrats in Washington. Led by Governors Rick Perry and Greg Abbott, Texas Republicans have questioned the science behind global warming and the economic impact that regulations or taxes on fossil fuels might have on the Texas economy. Perry said "I think the science is still out there and it's not settled yet." Barry Smitherman, former chairman of the Texas Public Utility Commission, declared I am "more concerned about climate change legislation than I am about climate change."[29] Governor Perry's spokesperson, Alison Castle, argued that "Governor Perry has proven that stifling government mandates are not the answer to our state's energy and environmental challenges. Texas has proven it is possible to balance sound environmental policies with pro-growth economic efforts that have produced the best business climate in the country."[30]

On December 7, 2009, the U.S. EPA issued an "endangerment finding" which held that carbon dioxide emitted from automobiles, power plants, and oil refineries constituted a public health threat subject to federal regulation. Governor Perry immediately issued a 38-page rebuttal, declaring that "It is unconscionable that unelected bureaucrats at the EPA have declared carbon dioxide a public danger despite a lack of scientific evidence to support their ruling."[31] Ten days later Governor Perry was still complaining that federal regulation of greenhouse gases would "kill jobs and raise the cost of living . . . It's time for them to take a look at the way we do things here in Texas."[32] The TCEQ called the proposed levels "arbitrary, unnecessary, and unachievable" and Debbie Hastings, a spokesperson for the Texas Oil and Gas Association, said, "I really don't think we can meet the standard." Houston Mayor Annise Parker "supported the stricter rules to protect the health of city dwellers, though she cautioned the city would need years to reach the goals."[33]

Though Texas continued to aggressively protect its petrochemical industry from national regulation, this was a fight that Texas increasingly seemed bound to lose. The EPA's endangerment finding cleared the way for EPA rule-making to set limits for CO_2 from vehicles, power plants, refineries, and other large emitters. As if speaking directly to the political and business leadership of Texas, EPA administrator Lisa Jackson said, "We know that skeptics have and will continue to try to sow doubts about the science. . . . But raising doubts—even in the face of overwhelming evidence—is a tactic that has been used by defenders of the status quo for years."[34]

Nonetheless, the EPA probably underestimated Texas's tenacity. In February 2010, Attorney General Greg Abbott, with Governor Perry's support, filed suit in federal court to halt implementation of greenhouse gas rules, claiming the rules were based on bad science. Governor Perry declared that, "This legal action is being taken to protect the Texas economy . . . and protect Texas's successes against federal overreach." EPA regional administrator Al Armendariz responded, "Texas, which contributes up to 35 percent of the greenhouse gases emitted by industrial sources in the United States, should be leading the way in this effort."[35] Abbott sued twice more in 2010, once in July and again in September, still claiming the proposed rules were based on faulty climate change data and would unnecessarily slow economic activity and cost jobs. By the end of the year, Texas stood alone as the other 49 states, many grudgingly, prepared to implement the new rules. When a federal appeals court ruled for the EPA and against Texas in December 2010, Governor Perry responded, "Texas will do everything in its power to defeat the threat that these misguided policies impose on our state's energy industry and the thousands of jobs it sustains."[36] The new rules went into effect on January 2, 2011.

As Texas pinned its hopes on the courts to halt the imposition of stricter air pollution rules, the EPA increased the pressure on Texas by challenging its overall process and standards for issuing operating licenses to oil, gas, and chemical plants. The EPA challenged Texas's "flexible permitting" standards whereby Texas sets limits on emissions for entire facilities rather than for individual units and smokestacks within large facilities. Only Texas used the flexible permitting system and EPA claimed that it allowed more pollution overall than the provisions of the Clean Air Act permitted. On December 23, 2010, just two weeks after the federal appeals court rejected Texas's challenge to the new greenhouse gas standards, EPA seized the industrial permitting process for 167 of the state's largest facilities, mostly oil refineries and chemical plants on the Gulf Coast, from Texas and promised not to return it until the state brought its permitting system into compliance with EPA mandates.

In 2012, the U.S. Court of Appeals for the District of Columbia again found that the EPA was "unambiguously correct" in developing regulations to limit greenhouse gases from vehicles and smokestacks. The court also held that the EPA was entitled to use climate science as a basis for its regulations despite opponents' claims that the science was flawed or in dispute. Attorney General Abbott, undaunted, declared that the court had "failed to rein-in the unelected bureaucrats at the [EPA] who are holding our country's energy independence and fragile economy hostage to a radical environmental agenda."[37] Despite this defeat, Texas won a round when the Fifth Circuit Court of Appeals held that the EPA had overstepped its bounds in taking over the state's air permitting program.

Even in the last year of the Obama administration, the EPA continued announcing new regulations and Texas continued to resist. In late 2015, the EPA announced new emissions requirements designed to push power plants from coal to natural gas. Governor Greg Abbott immediately declared that, "Texas will lead the fight against an overreaching federal government that seems hell-bent on threatening the free-market principles this country was founded on."[38]

Over the course of the Obama administration, Texas sued the federal government 39 times and more than half of those suits challenged the EPA. Altogether, the suits cost Texas taxpayers more than $5 million and more than 14,000 staff hours, mostly in the attorney general's office. Texas officials thought this money and time well-spent as it did slow and in some cases defer EPA action. These Texas officials breathed a deep sigh of relief when Donald Trump won the presidency and an even deeper sigh when he appointed Oklahoma Attorney General Scott Pruitt to the EPA.

No doubt Texas officials were correct to think they would face less pressure from the Trump EPA than they had from the Obama EPA, but they soon found that there was no going back to the pre-Obama status quo. Obama EPA requirements and low natural gas prices already had changed the Texas energy mix. Between 2010 and 2015, the amount of coal used to produce Texas electricity fell from 39.5 percent to 27.3 percent while the amount of natural gas rose from 38.2 percent to 48.4 percent and the amount of wind power rose from 7.8 percent to 11.4 percent. Both natural gas and wind are much cleaner than coal and likely will continue to grow their share of the fuel mix at coal's expense.

Texas vs. the EPA: Hazardous Waste

Two of the longest running hazardous waste pollution disputes in Texas history concern the Asarco copper smelter in El Paso and the cement plants around Midlothian. In both cases, the TCEQ tenaciously protected the polluters until the EPA forced them to change course. The American Smelting and Refining Co. (later Asarco) opened a lead smelter in El Paso in 1887. The facility was sued by the city as early as 1970 in an attempt to limit pollution and its impact on nearby neighborhoods. The smelter shut down in 1999 amid a global copper glut and law suits charging Asarco with extensive pollution throughout the Southwest. Asarco hired the prominent Houston law firm of Baker Botts in 2002 to try to get the smelter reopened to improve their leverage during a struggle with Mexican billionaire Carlos Slim for control of the company. In 2005, Asarco filed for chapter 11 bankruptcy protection from as much as $25 billion in environmental and asbestos claims. Staggering toward liquidation or takeover, Asarco stepped up its appeal to the TCEQ to get its environmental permits renewed so that it could reopen the mothballed plant. Opponents argued that the plant had pumped 7,000 tons of pollution, of which 2,000 tons were lead, into the environment when it was in good shape and would certainly do worse after eight years of deterioration and rust. Asarco made $1.6 million in contributions to Texas-elected officials between 2000 and 2008, and on February 13, 2008, the TCEQ voted to approve Asarco's permit to reopen the smelter.

Texas State Senator Eliot Shapleigh (D-El Paso) and a host of Texas environmental groups were outraged and called on the EPA to intervene. Over the course of the next year the EPA did exactly that. On February 3, 2009, the EPA told the TCEQ that Asarco did not qualify under federal law for renewal of the operating permit that had been granted in 2008. EPA said that because the El Paso smelter had been shut down for eight years, it considered the shut down to be permanent and a whole new emissions permit process would be required. EPA said further that if TCEQ did not revoke their recent approval, "EPA might be forced to formally object to the permit, order any work on the smelter stopped, and initiate enforcement action."[39] The same day the EPA announced its intention to intervene Asarco withdrew its petition to reopen the plant and said that instead it would tear it down. Plant demolition took place in 2013, though cleanup continued into 2015. Clearly, both TCEQ and EPA see the trade-off between business interests and environmental interests, but it is just as clear that they see them very differently.

A similar contest between citizens, state regulators, industry, and the EPA has been raging for decades around three huge cement plants near Midlothian. The three plants, with their ten kilns, constitute the largest complex of cement plants in the nation. Each plant has a strip mine nearby for limestone which is the principal raw material for cement. The limestone and other materials are heated to 2,700 degrees Fahrenheit in kilns fed by coal, natural gas, shredded shingles and old tires, and hazardous waste materials. Given the noxious inputs, it should come as no surprise that cement plants are big polluters. All three are among the top 40 pollution sites in Texas, with particularly high levels of mercury, sulfur dioxide, and fine particulates. For decades, the TCEQ has held that there is no evidence that the plants and their effluents harm public health or the environment.

To assure they get a fair hearing from the political authorities of Texas, the cement industry and its political action committees (PACs) have spread a lot of money around. Industry PACs have contributed more than $2 million to Texas politicians since 2000, while their lobby firms have been paid another $12.6 million. Governor Perry alone received $921,714 from cement industry PACs. U.S. Representative Joe Barton (R-Arlington), whose district includes Midlothian, has received $103,500 since 2000. Barton has frequently tried to protect the cement plants from additional EPA regulation, though not always successfully. Both industry spokesmen and their political allies argued that additional regulation would cost jobs and force cement production overseas. Nonetheless, in April 2009 the EPA proposed new rules for the nation's 100 cement plants, including those at Midlothian, setting the first limits on mercury and tighter limits on particulates. Though the rules did not take effect until 2013, they were expected to cut mercury emissions by 81 to 93 percent over time. The relationship between Texas and the EPA had shifted to one in which the agency is more likely to push past Texas objections than to be dissuaded by them.[40] Though the Trump administration will moderate EPA enforcement, whatever enforcement they do pursue will be resisted by Texas.

Conclusion

Edna Ferber's *Giant* is one of the premier literary depictions of Texas in transition from the farming and ranching, cotton and cattle, pursuits of the late nineteenth and early twentieth centuries to the oil and urban business pursuits of the mid-twentieth century. Jordan "Bick" Benedict was deeply and blindly Texan, a third generation rancher, running the Benedict family's 2.5 million acre Reata ranch. During a business trip to Washington, after a whirlwind romance, Bick married Leslie Lynnton of the beautiful northern Virginia hunt country. Returning to Texas by train with his new bride, Bick's pride in all things Texan was wounded by his new wife's initial reaction to the state. As Texas passed by out the train window, Leslie said, "It's sort of frightening, isn't it—like something that defies you to conquer it? So huge. Why, we've been riding in it for days. And ugly, too, isn't it! I thought it would be beautiful." At Bick's pained reaction, she said, "Oh, now, don't be sulky. I'm not talking about your ancestors or something, dearest."[41]

Generations of Texans worked hard to conquer the rough land and never took time to wonder or worry that it was not beautiful in the way of more temperate latitudes. In fact, they assaulted its assets, the soil, the range, the timber, and, ultimately, the minerals that lay beneath the surface. The first major discovery of oil in Texas came at Spindletop, near Beaumont on the upper Gulf Coast, in 1901. That discovery made Texas the center of the U.S. and global oil industry for almost 75 years as the original discoveries were supplemented by discoveries in the Permian Basin, the Panhandle, and the huge East Texas field discovered in 1930. After World War II, extensive natural gas discoveries broadened the energy industry in Texas. New techniques have pushed the oil industry out into the Gulf and fracking has released a 90-year supply of new natural gas from rocks thousands of feet below the surface. Texas still accounts for more than 37 percent of U.S. oil production and 27 percent of natural gas production annually. Texas claims 36 percent of U.S. oil reserves and 26 percent of gas reserves.

But along with the blessings of abundant natural resources have come the environmental challenges of extracting those resources from the ground and processing them into usable energy and products. Texas leads the nation in greenhouse gas emissions, both because Texans love their cars and trucks and because coal continues to play a big role in electricity production. Texas also leads the nation, by a large margin, in the production of hazardous wastes.

Texas officials have long argued that Texas refineries and chemical plants produce not just for Texas but for the nation. Texas refineries produce one-quarter of the nation's gasoline products. The argument is that the nation should be grateful that Texas is willing to produce these beneficial, even critical, products and to be exposed to the consequent pollution. The nation, speaking, or sometimes mumbling, through the Congress, the administration, and the EPA, agrees that it needs the products but wants them to be produced with less environmental impact. Texas has resisted, arguing that Texans will lose business, jobs, and income if pollution regulations are too strict. The Congress, President Trump, and the EPA might be more willing to listen than was the Obama administration, but any regulation not arising out of Texas itself will rankle state officials.

Notes

1   John Graves, *Self-Portrait, With Birds*, Dallas, TX: Chama Press, 1991.
2   Robert Calvert, Arnoldo De León, and Gregg Cantrell, *The History of Texas*, 5th ed., Malden, MA: Wiley Blackwell, 2014, p. 211.
3   Philipp Meyer, *The Son: A Novel*, New York: Harper Collins, 2013, p. 165.
4   T.R. Fehrenbach, *Lone Star: A History of Texas and the Texans*, New York: Macmillan, 1968, pp. 145–146.
5   PBS, "American Buffalo: Spirit of a Nation," Introduction, 1998.
6   David G. McComb, *Texas: A Modern History*, Austin, TX: University of Texas Press, 2010, pp. 84, 86.
7   Mary Lasswell, *John Henry Kirby: Prince of the Pines*, Austin, TX: The Encino Press, 1967.
8   Robert S. Maxwell, "LUMBER INDUSTRY, Handbook of Texas Online," https://tshaonline.org/handbook/online/articles/drl02, accessed July 24, 2017. Published by the Texas State Historical Association.
9   Bryan Burrough, *The Big Rich: The Rise and Fall of the Great Texas Oil Fortunes*, New York: Penguin Press, 2009, p. 11.
10 David F. Prindle, *Petroleum Politics and the Texas Railroad Commission*, Austin, TX: University of Texas Press, 1981, pp. 21–32.
11 See the U.S. Energy Information Administration's Texas State Energy Profile at http://tonto.eia.doe.gov/state/state_energy_profiles.cfm?sid=TX
12 Robert Bryce, "Barreling Ahead on Oil Production," *Dallas Morning News*, October 2, 2016, pp. 1P, 4P.
13 Prindle, *Petroleum Politics and the Texas Railroad Commission*, pp. 56–69.
14 Anna Kuchment and Steve Thompson, "State Won't Admit Fracking Tie," *Dallas Morning News*, November 20, 2016, pp. A1, A16–A17.
15 Floyd Norris, "Off the Charts: Two Directions for the Prices of Natural Gas and Oil," *New York Times*, February 26, 2011, p. B3. See also Max B. Baker, "No Rigs Active in Barnett Shale," *Dallas Morning News*, April 26, 2016, p 3D.
16 Paul J. Weber, AP, "Well Clean-Up Too Big for States," *Dallas Morning News*, July 10, 2016, pp. 1D, 7D.
17 Clifford Krauss, "Oil Recovers, But Not Its Jobs," *New York Times*, February 20, 2017, pp. A1, A13.
18 Kate Galbraith, "Has Electric Deregulation Helped or Hurt Texans?" *Texas Tribune*, July 12, 2010, pp. 2–5.

19 A Special Report by Cities Aggregation Power Project, Inc., "The History of Electric Deregulation in Texas: The Unfulfilled Promise of Utility Restructuring," 2009, see https://tcaptx.com/downloads/HISTORY-OF-DEREGULATION.pdf.

20 See http://tonto.eia.doe.gov/energyexplained/index.cfm?page=electricity_in_the_united_states, and www.eia.gov/state/index.php?sid=TX.

21 American Gas Association (AGA), state profiles, www.aga.org/knowledgecenter/facts-and-data/state-profiles-natural-gas?state=TX.

22 U.S. Department of Energy, U.S. Energy Information Administration, Coal Reserves, www.eia.doe.gov/cneaf/coal/reserves/reserves.html.

23 James Osborne, "Expected Coal Plant Closings Cut," *Dallas Morning News*, October 17, 2015, pp. A1, A19.

24 Asher Price, "Importing Low-Level Radioactive Waste to Texas OK'd," *Austin American-Statesman*, January 4, 2011. See also Ramit Plushnick-Masti, "Commission Lets 36 States Dump Nuke Waste in Texas," *Houston Chronicle*, January 4, 2011.

25 Kate Galbraith, "Cost of Texas Wind Transmission Lines Nears $7 Billion," *Texas Tribune*, August 24, 2011.

26 Elizabeth Souder and Dave Michaels, "Texas Lags as Nation Shifts to Green Policies," *Dallas Morning News*, June 1, 2009, pp. A1, A8.

27 Forrest Wilder, "Agency of Destruction," *The Texas Observer*, May 28, 2010, pp. 6–12.

28 Anna M. Tinsley, "Perry Touts 'the Texas Way' as He Signs Three Energy Bills," *Fort Worth Star-Telegram*, July 15, 2011.

29 Souder and Michaels, "Texas Lags as Nation Shifts to Green Policies," pp. A1, A8.

30 Randy Lee Loftis, "EPA, Texas Activists in Sync," *Dallas Morning News*, June 24, 2009, pp. A1, A8.

31 Dave Michaels, "EPA Plan Targets Emissions," *Dallas Morning News*, December 8, 2009, pp. A1, A14.

32 Gromer Jeffers, "Perry Jabs Gore on Climate," *Dallas Morning News*, December 17, 2009, p. B4.

33 James C. McKinley Jr., "In Texas, Resistance over Stricter Smog Limits," *New York Times*, February 3, 2010, p. A19. See also Ana Campoy, "Smog Fight Clouds Houston Cleanup," *Wall Street Journal*, January 20, 2010, p. A3.

34 John M. Broder, "Greenhouse Gases Imperil Health, E.P.A. Announces," *New York Times*, December 12, 2009, p. A16.

35 James Drew, "Texas Sues EPA," *Dallas Morning News*, February 17, 2010, pp. A1, A6.

36 Dave Michaels, "State Loses in Appeal to Halt Federal Emissions Regulation," *Dallas Morning News*, December 12, 2010, p. 6D.

37 Randy Lee Loftis, "EPA Climate Action Upheld," *Dallas Morning News*, June 27, 2012, pp. A1, A2.

38 Michael A. Lindenberger and James Osborne, "Texas May Speed Change," *Dallas Morning News*, August 4, 2015, pp. A1, A9. See also Hiroko Tabuchi, "What's at Stake in the Cuts Proposed for the EPA," *New York Times*, April 11, 2017, p. A21.

39 Randy Lee Loftis, "Company Gives Up on Smelter," *Dallas Morning News*, February 4, 2009, p. A4.

40 Randy Lee Loftis, "Public, Industry Clash on EPA Plan," *Dallas Morning News*, June 18, 2009, pp. A1, A11.

41 Edna Ferber, *Giant*, Garden City, NY: Doubleday & Company, 1952, p. 106.

Part III
The Coming Reality

11 The Way Forward

It's a low-tax, low-service state—so shoot us. The only depressing part is that, unlike Mississippi, we can afford to do better. We just don't.

(Molly Ivins)

One of the striking episodes in twentieth-century Texas history occurred at John Connally's Floresville ranch in January 1988. Connally was an iconic Texan; born into rural poverty, he became a protégé of Lyndon Johnson as a young man, Democratic governor of Texas in 1963, and he was seriously wounded in the Kennedy assassination later that year. After six years as governor, Connally served as Secretary of the Navy and Secretary of the Treasury in the Nixon administration, switched to the Republican Party, and made an unsuccessful run for the presidency in 1980. By 1982, Connally was in partnership with Ben Barnes as—what else?—a developer. Texas was booming and Connally declared that, "We're beginning an era of prosperity like America hasn't dreamed of, and Texas will be at the forefront of it."[1] But within a very few years the price of oil collapsed and the Texas property markets and the banks that funded them went down as well. Connally declared personal bankruptcy in 1987 and he and Nellie sat through five days of public humiliation as their worldly goods passed under the auctioneer's gavel.

John Connally's biography, *In History's Shadow*, was published soon after his death in June 1993. The very last page of that biography registered his warning, born of the booms and busts in his own Texas life, that "The real question for us in Texas, as in the nation, is whether or not we have the insight and the courage to restructure our government in time to meet the changing conditions that will touch each of our individual lives."[2] As we shall see below, we have had the insight for quite some time, but not yet the courage. In fact, as Connally's goods were being auctioned off, Texas was in the process of responding to the late 1980s economic crisis in the state by lightening the tax burden on the oil and gas industry and increasing it on consumers. This was business as usual in Texas.

More than three decades later, the state's fiscal problems remain unresolved. As population grew and demographic change continued apace, state revenues tightened and unaddressed problems in education, health care, transportation, and the environment festered. Ominously, Robert Calvert, Arnoldo De León, and Gregg Cantrell close their prominent book, *The History of Texas*, by warning that "almost all the challenges facing Texans in the twenty-first century will hinge upon a rethinking of how they will pay for state and local government."[3] The reason that Texas seems paralyzed in the face of growing problems is that the state's leadership has painted itself and us into a fiscal corner over the past half century. First, we ask how that happened and then we look for ways out.

A Brief History of Tax Policy in Texas

The first Anglo settlers into Texas were lured by free land and tax exemptions. Texas pioneer Noah Smithwick described this lure in the very first paragraph of his famous memoir. Smithwick, then an 18-year-old Kentuckian, heard the Texas empresario Sterling C. Robertson praise the new country and urge immigration. Like his competitor, Stephen F. Austin, Robertson promised new immigrants "177 acres of farming land . . . and 4,428 acres of pasture land for stock; colonists to be exempted from taxation six years from the date of settlement, with the privilege of importing, duty free, everything they might desire for themselves and their families."[4] Texans were early trained to expect low, preferably no, taxes.

From independence in 1836 through the first half of the twentieth century, Texans supported a small government with a hodgepodge of minor taxes intended to nibble a little here and there but not to bite anywhere too hard. The Texan attitude in the early days was famously expressed by an anonymous land commissioner from Nacogdoches who declared, "Come what may I am convinced that Texas must prosper. We pay no taxes, . . . get our land at cost, and perform no public duties of any kind."[5] This remains the Texan view: prosperity comes from individual effort unconstrained by public imposition upon one's time, choices, or income.

Texas was born in revolution, so existing political institutions and any funds that they might possess belonged to the enemy until they could be wrestled from them. Hence, the framers of the Constitution of 1836 authorized the provisional government to seek loans and issue promissory notes to fund an army and navy. Following the victory at San Jacinto and the elections of 1836, the provisional government passed a $1.25 million debt to President Sam Houston and the new Congress. Houston had an instinct for frugality and a republican's fear of an idle army, so he was happy to reduce the army and most other expenses of government. Nonetheless, with scant revenues, debt continued to grow.[6]

The first Congress passed a series of taxes on imports, businesses, and property, but members knew that with little real money in the republic revenues would arrive in a trickle. The mainstays of the republic's tax system were tariffs on imported goods ranging from 1 to 10 percent on staples such as bread and flour, 50 percent on luxuries such as silk, and 25 to 75 percent on wine and liquor. More than half of Texas revenue during the republic came from import fees.[7] Minor taxes on businesses, professional licenses, land fees, and voting brought some revenue, but general taxes on land, livestock, and slaves were nearly uncollectable given the tenuous state of the economy. Hence, political authorities tried to keep the tax burden low and to be neighborly about collections.[8]

Texas remained in debt throughout the life of the republic. President Sam Houston ran an extraordinarily frugal administration, but he was still reduced to asking the Texas Congress to issue a paper currency. The first issue of "star money," so-called for the star featured on the bills, circulated at par for a time but subsequent issues quickly depreciated. By the end of Houston's term, star money was trading at eight to one American dollar. Despite the fiscal stringency faced by the new government, Texas's second president, Mirabeau B. Lamar, had visions of empire. He formed a navy to patrol the Gulf and sent military expeditions against Mexico and its territories to the west as far as Santa Fe. Unable to secure loans abroad, Lamar and the Congress issued "redback" dollars, named for the color of the currency's reverse side, which very quickly lost their value.[9] By the time Houston returned to office in 1842, the attempt to annex New Mexico had failed—Mexican armies had twice captured San Antonio, and the republic was $7 million in debt. Houston sought to calm relations with Mexico, gain admission to the American Union, and restore financial stability. To show how serious he was about controlling costs, he ordered the navy to port, withheld further appropriations, and put it up for sale. Citizens of Galveston, the navy's home port, blocked the sale but the ships remained in port.

Despite Houston's frugality, revenues came in so slowly that by the end of his second term the republic's debt was approaching $10 million.[10] The German immigrant Wilhelm Steinert observed in 1849, by which time Texas was a U.S. state and Houston was serving in the U.S. Senate, that, "Taxation remains poorly regulated. . . . Every man makes his own estimates of the profits of his business enterprise. Real estate values are set by a board of equalization. Only a few percent tax must be paid in general, . . . I spoke with some people who owned farms and farmhouses but were not made to pay taxes." Steinert did say that trade licenses for "merchants, innkeepers, and tavern owners" were very expensive, but, in general, one sees a regime of light taxes lackadaisically collected.[11]

Accession to the Union did not change the Texan attitude toward government and taxation, though it did provide what many saw as another outside, meaning non-Texan, source of revenue. When Texas entered the Union in 1845, it retained title to 150 million acres of unclaimed lands within the state. Other American states, entering the Union after a period of territorial status, entered with unclaimed lands retained by the federal government. Unfortunately, too much of anything, including land, drives down its price, so the present cash value of Texas's vast landholdings was limited. Land could be given away or disposed of at "fire sale" prices to attract immigrants or railroads, but it could not be sold for cash to support the government. Slaves, on the other hand, had a substantial and rising value. "After statehood," the historian Randolph Campbell writes, "the value of slaves constituted more than one-third of the state's total tax assessment during the 1850s."[12] The obvious incentive of the ruling class of shareholders was to limit the cost of government and, hence, its need for tax revenues.

Fortunately, Texas had tenuous claims to parts of New Mexico and Colorado and, though that land could not be sold either, it provided a valuable bargaining chip. In 1850, Texas renounced these broader claims, assuming its current boundaries, in exchange for $10 million from the federal treasury. The U.S. kept $5 million to settle the currency debts of the Republic of Texas and Texas used some of the rest to pay off non-currency debts incurred for goods and services prior to statehood. The remainder was dedicated to public buildings, infrastructure, and education. Texas's path to temporary fiscal stability taught lessons good and bad. Fehrenbach wrote that:

> The net result of the boundary bill was that Texas during the 1850s was financed publicly almost entirely by federal money. . . . But as Rupert Richardson [a Texas historian of the 1940s] observed, "the system may have worked injury as well as benefit. The people learned to look to outside sources rather than to taxation as the means of supporting their government and were not prepared for the day when windfalls would cease."[13]

As the Civil War loomed, Texas was back in debt to the tune of $1 million and the war itself cost mightily in blood and treasure. Once Governor Sam Houston was pushed aside in favor of Lieutenant Governor Edward Clark, Texas prepared for war. Governor Clark increased the ad valorem land and property tax from 12.5 cents to 16.5 cents and then to 25 cents, raised the poll tax from 50 cents to one dollar, and reinstituted professional taxes on doctors, lawyers, and dentists. Other taxes were levied on financial transactions and liquor.[14] These revenues, as well as control over the state's future, were lost with the Civil War.

Despite the economic conditions in the war-ravaged state, the Reconstruction administration of Republican Governor Edmund J. Davis pushed education and economic recovery programs that required unprecedented revenues. White conservatives, the ashes of defeat in their mouths, thought that the little wealth they had remaining was being expropriated to educate and otherwise advantage their former slaves. They protested vigorously, holding a "Tax Payers' Convention" in Austin in September 1871. Convention leaders charged that tax rates had risen from 15 cents per $100 of assessed value before the war to $2.175 in the Davis administration. Levies to pay off railroad bonds, license taxes, and poll taxes added to the post-war tax burden.[15] These charges by Davis's opponents have passed into Texas history as proof of his administration's profligacy. True or not, as soon as Texas statehood was restored and whites in their full numbers returned to the electorate, Democrats moved quickly to restore the antebellum fiscal order. That was, of course, a fiscal order of small government and low taxes because an abundance of cheap land limited revenues from land sales and property taxes. In 1874, Texas was selling prime land for $1.50 an acre.

Governor Oran M. Roberts, citing the slow sale of land and the need to raise state revenue, encouraged the legislature to lower prices. In 1879, the legislature revised land sale policy to allow lands set aside to support public schools to be sold for $1 an acre for up to four sections (a section is 640 acres or one square mile) and to sell all other unclaimed land for 50 cents an acre with no limit on the amount to be purchased. These prices drove down all land prices in Texas, bankrupting railroads and land-holding companies and creating widespread public concern. In 1883, a state land board was empowered to reclassify

> the remaining public domain into agricultural, timber, and pastoral areas. The first two categories sold for $3, the pastureland for $2. Payment periods lasted from ten to forty years, and interest rates ranged from 5 to 10 percent. Until 1899 a married man could claim a 160-acre homestead with proof of three-year residence; a single man could obtain half that amount.[16]

Throughout the nineteenth century, Texas had so much land that its value stayed low and it produced little revenue from land sales or property taxes.

The Specialty Sales and Petroleum Tax Regime, 1900–1960

As the populist and progressive eras unfolded nationally and in Texas during the last two decades of the nineteenth century and the first two decades of the twentieth century, Texas elites generally resisted. The federal government and many states sought to deal with urbanization and industrialization by expanding government services and funding them with new revenues, including inheritance, income, and sales taxes. New York adopted an inheritance tax in 1885 and President Theodore Roosevelt, a former governor of New York, campaigned for a federal inheritance tax for a decade before it became law in 1916. Wisconsin adopted a personal income tax in 1911 and President Woodrow Wilson campaigned for passage and adoption of the Sixteenth Amendment in 1913 permitting a federal income tax. Other states were slow in adopting the income tax until the Great Depression hit, reducing property values and property tax revenues, and then 16 states adopted an income tax between 1931 and 1937. Mississippi was first to adopt a general sales tax in 1932 and by 1937 half the states had a general sales tax.[17]

Texas monitored these trends, discussed their relevance to the state, and a few people even advocated for one or another of them, but generally Texas sniffed socialism on the winds of change. Nonetheless, Texas did begin to edge away from property taxes toward a series of modest new business and consumer taxes. As early as 1905, Governor S.W.T. Lanham successfully urged the legislature to approve a severance tax of 1 cent on each barrel of oil, a franchise tax on capital investment, and gross receipts taxes on railroads and insurance companies. In 1907, Governor Thomas M. Campbell proposed both an income tax and an inheritance tax. Campbell lost the fight for the income tax, but won a modest inheritance tax and higher licensing fees for liquor dealers. The Lanham–Campbell reforms were an important reorganization of the Texas tax structure. The arrival of the automobile in numbers in the second decade of the twentieth century brought new taxes on vehicles, drivers, and fuels. Texas governors and legislatures from the 1920s through the 1950s tinkered with but did not fundamentally reform a diffuse mélange of small, narrow, targeted taxes and levies on natural resources, capital investment, professional licenses, auto license fees, gas taxes, and other specialty sales taxes.

Under the pressure of the Great Depression, some Texas leaders proposed tax reform, but their overtures were usually rejected. Governor Ross Sterling got little support when he proposed a state income tax in 1931. Governor Miriam "Ma" Ferguson proposed a sales tax as well as corporate and personal income taxes in 1933 but the legislature refused them all. They approved a severance tax increase to 2 cents on each barrel of oil and a small tax on pari-mutuel betting on horse races. Governor James V. Allred (1935–1939) was a supporter of FDR and the New Deal and sought to follow in its policy footsteps, but the Texas Legislature could only rarely be persuaded to go along. In a special session in 1935, Allred won an increase in taxes on natural resources and a modest new tax on chain stores. The legislature also passed the Texas Liquor Control Act and set taxes and fees on package store sales.[18] Governor Allred, worried that good Texans might be led astray by betting on horse races, had pari-mutuel betting repealed in a 1937 special session.

Wilbert Lee "Pappy" O'Daniel, one of the great characters in Texas political history, was elected governor in 1938 and 1940. He urged the 1939 and 1941 regular sessions of the Texas Legislature to pass a "transactions tax" of 1.6 percent on all manufacturing, wholesale, and retail transactions, except the first sale of agricultural products, to replace the ad valorem property tax. Legislators recognized the transactions tax as a sales tax and declined to go along. Instead, the 1941 regular session of the Texas Legislature passed an Omnibus Tax Bill that "placed new taxes on motor vehicle sales, stock transfers, cosmetics, and radios. It increased existing levies on oil, natural gas, utilities, insurance company premiums, and a few other items."[19] While Texas was struggling to pass narrowly targeted levies on cosmetics and radios, the rest of the nation and most of the South had adopted a new tax regime. They had supplemented the traditional property tax with state income and sales taxes. As Numan V. Bartley explained, "by 1945 all the southern states but Florida and Texas had enacted personal and corporate income taxes, and six states had adopted general sales taxes as well."[20] The southern states were poor, so they tended to keep their tax rates low even when measured as a proportion of personal income, but their systems had a balance and flexibility that they had not enjoyed before.

Population growth in the 1940s and a post-war decline in oil prices and oil revenues soon exposed the limits of Texas's revenue system. Governor Allan Shivers, a wealthy landowner, businessman, and staunch fiscal and social conservative, called a special session of the legislature in 1950 to resolve a $26 million budget deficit. Some in the legislature called for increasing taxes on business or on natural resources, but the business lobby convinced Shivers to again back increases in a number of targeted consumer taxes.[21] While this resolved the short-term budget crisis it did nothing to put Texas tax and revenue policy on a sounder footing. By 1951, all of the southern governments but Kentucky, Texas, and Virginia had adopted a general sales tax. Only Texas eschewed both the state income tax and a general sales tax. Texas was able to maintain its traditional tax system because a rise in the price of oil, and the Eisenhower administration's decision to honor Texas claims to oil-rich "tidelands" in the Gulf, buoyed revenues. By the mid-1950s, severance taxes and related fees accounted for one-third of state tax revenues in Texas.[22]

By the end of the decade, increased oil production in the Middle East had reduced prices and Texas oil wells were allowed to produce for only nine days a month to avoid a further glut and even lower prices. With severance tax revenues down, the Texas Legislature met in January 1959 facing a $90 million dollar projected shortfall in its general revenue budget. Talk of a general sales tax was rampant but Governor Price Daniel, a moderate who had replaced the conservative Shivers in 1957, was opposed. It took three special sessions to craft a true Texas solution. Governor Daniel pushed through a "beneficiary tax" on out-of-state users of Texas natural gas, as well as increases in selective sales taxes and in fees and licenses on utilities and corporations. Unfortunately, the Supreme Court quickly struck down the beneficiary tax because it was not levied against in-state and out-of-state users—but that, after all, had been the whole point. Nonetheless, once the Supreme Court acted, the issue of Texas's tax structure was teed-up for the 1961 regular session of the Texas Legislature.

The General Sales Tax Regime: 1960 to Present

By 1961 the business lobby realized that tinkering with the traditional tax system was no longer an option and they were ready for change, as long as it was the right change. Teacher salaries and other government costs were rising, so a sizable tax increase seemed necessary. Governor Daniel opposed a general sales tax as unduly regressive and hard on the common people, but he did not have an attractive solution of his own. Instead, he proposed "a continuation of omnibus tax bills, including so-called sin taxes on tobacco and alcohol, and a larger share of taxes on business interests."[23] He was opposed by the Texas Manufacturing Association and the powerful oil and gas lobby, as well as by members, conservative and moderate, who saw the sales tax as the broadest path to badly needed new revenues. In his first term in the House, future Speaker Ben Barnes (1965–1969) explained that "as a conservative he preferred" the sales tax "over a corporate tax or state income tax as a way to raise much needed funds for Texas."[24] Rayford Price, another future speaker (1972–1973), "saw the sales tax as a practical necessity. 'Oil had carried the state for many years, but the economy was changing, and we needed to draw from a new tax base. . . . The sales tax, I think, was the correct place to go at that time.'"[25] Though it took three contentious special sessions, the legislature adopted a general sales tax of 2 percent, excluding food, prescription drugs, and a few other necessities. With no viable alternative source of revenue on the horizon, Governor

Table 11.1 Texas General Sales Tax Rates

	State %	*Municipal %*
1961–1967	2	
1968	3	1
1969–1970	3.25	
1971–1983	4	
1984–1985	4.125	
1986	5.25	
1987–1989	6	
1990–Present	6.25	
1992		2

Source: The Handbook of Texas Online, "Sales Tax," www.tshaonline.org/handbook/online/articles/mpszr.

Daniel allowed the sales tax to go into effect without his signature. The general sales tax became the workhorse of the Texas tax system.

Revenues from the new sales tax and rising prices for oil and natural gas, as well as a brief willingness to consider additional revenues, especially for public schools and colleges and universities, made governing seem easier in the 1960s and 1970s. John Connally served three terms as governor from 1963 to 1969. In the 1963 legislative session, Connally sought almost $33 million in new revenue for a higher education coordinating board, university libraries and research, vocational education, and teacher salaries. In Connally's final term, he asked the legislature to authorize $125 million for teacher pay raises and he recommended that it be funded by a 1 percent increase in the general sales tax and that cities be allowed to impose a 1 percent addition to the state sales tax. Teachers got a pay raise and, as Table 11.1 shows, the sales tax was increased to 3 percent and the cities got the option of adding a local sales tax which most did quickly.[26]

When Connally declined to run for a fourth term in 1968, Lieutenant Governor Preston Smith moved up to governor and Ben Barnes, speaker of the Texas House and the protégé of both LBJ and Connally, moved up to lieutenant governor. Their desire to keep the momentum of the Connally years going brought general sales tax increases to 3.25 percent in 1969 and 4 percent in 1971. Not surprisingly, Texans soon became wary that LBJ, Connally, and Barnes had led them down the path to big government, high taxes, and liberal social experimentation.

When Governor Preston Smith, Barnes, and Speaker Gus Mutcher were all caught up in an influence-peddling scandal, Texas voters went in search of honest leadership. The 1972 governor's election featured the liberal Democrat Sissy Farenthold and the conservative Democrat Dolph Briscoe. Briscoe, a wealthy cattle rancher from Uvalde and one of the largest landowners in the state, won on a platform of honesty, transparency, and no new taxes. Meanwhile, Florida's Governor Reuben Askew "pushed through Florida's legislature a corporate income tax. With that, only Texas [among the southern states] assessed no income taxes at all."[27]

In launching his 1972 campaign, Briscoe declared that "there was no need for new taxes and that the state could operate within the income generated by the existing tax structure." Briscoe's analysis of the state's fiscal situation was both correct and shortsighted. He wrote that, "it was obvious in 1972 that the state's energy-based economy would continue to increase our tax revenue for years to come. I realized that state services would have to expand to meet the challenge of a larger population, but

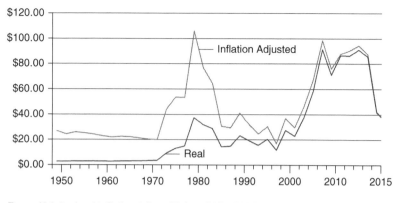

Figure 11.1 Real and Inflation-Adjusted Price of Oil, 1950–2016

Source: InflationData.com, Historical Crude Oil Prices, www.inflationdata.com/inflation/inflation_rate/historical_
oil_prices_table.asp

the increase in revenue from existing taxes would be sufficient to do the job well."[28]
Briscoe was right, Texas oil and gas revenues went on a steep upward climb during the
1970s, but he was shortsighted because it could not and it did not last. While the sales
tax, corporate licenses and fees, the gas tax, and most other taxes and fees produce more
revenue in a strong economy and less in a weak economy, few large revenue sources are
as volatile as post-1970 oil and natural gas taxes.

Figure 11.1 shows both the real and the inflation-adjusted price of oil from 1950
through the present. The difference between the two is not difficult to understand.
The real price of a barrel of oil in 1950, $2.77, is its actual cost that year. The 2010
inflation-adjusted price of that 1950 barrel of oil, $26.80, is what it would cost in
today's depreciated currency to have bought that same barrel of oil. Adjusting for
inflation isolates the real changes in the relative price of oil over time. Note four
things in particular about Figure 11.1. First, note that the real price of a barrel of oil
from 1950 to 1970 was so stable, barely rising from $2.77 to $3.39, that the inflation-
adjusted price steadily fell. Second, note the extraordinary rise in the real price of
oil from $3.39 in 1970 to $37.42 in 1980. In inflation-adjusted terms, the rise is a
fivefold increase from $21.04 to $109.51. Third, in 1981 the price of oil began a slow
fall that picked up speed in the mid-1980s. Finally, oil prices bounced around in the
1990s until they took off again about 2005 and they remained high for a decade—
and then they fell hard. The rollercoaster ride, up in the 1970s and down hard in the
1980s, led to broad changes resulting in a more diverse and stable Texas economy.
Unfortunately, it also led to changes in the Texas tax and revenue system that left it
less efficient and more brittle.

Dolph Briscoe had the good fortune to serve as governor of Texas from 1973 to
1979. Political scientists Anthony Champagne and Edward Harpham explain that,

> As the value of oil produced in Texas rose from $4.1 billion in 1970 to $21.3
> billion in 1980 and the value of natural gas rose from $3 billion in 1970 to
> $10.7 billion in 1980, the state budget rose from $3 billion in 1970 to $10.2
> billion in 1980. In constant dollars, this translates into a real increase of 65%,
> an astounding number in light of Texas's history of fiscal austerity.

Energy taxes rose from 13 percent of total tax collections in 1973 to one-quarter by the end of the decade.[29] Briscoe reported that throughout his three terms as governor, "Increased revenue made it possible for us to enhance essential services, especially our highway system, and to raise the average teacher's salary more than 50 percent without increasing the state tax burden."[30] Former Lieutenant Governor William Hobby (1973–1991), the longest serving lieutenant governor in Texas history by far, offered a different take on the state of the state as Governor Briscoe gave way to Governor William Clements, the first Republican governor in Texas in more than a century. Hobby wrote that at the start of Clements's first term in 1979, "Texas ranked forty-fifth among the states in state and local tax collections and lowest among the top industrial states. . . . There were critical unmet needs in mental health, education, prisons, and the state police. The state of Texas is as big a tax break as there is."[31] But just as federal monies had lulled Texans of the 1850s into thinking they could fund state government without local taxes, the steady increase of oil and gas revenues convinced Texans in the 1970s, including the governor, that existing taxes were sufficient.

Energy prices and the revenues they generated dipped modestly in the early 1980s. Comptroller Bob Bullock began warning in 1982 that future severance tax revenues were uncertain. Nonetheless, Governor Mark White pushed a $5.5 billion tax bill through a special session of the legislature in 1984 to fulfill campaign promises of continued increases in teacher pay, more equitable school funding, and transportation improvements. This was the first tax increase in Texas in 13 years and Governor White and scores of legislators declared that they saw no further need for tax increases. Throughout 1985, as the price of oil continued a slow downward slide, Bullock talked about the looming prospect of wholesale tax reform in Texas. Late in the year, he said, "We need new revenue. Yes, I'm talking about an income tax. It is political death to everyone who mentions it, but you have to think about it."[32] As oil price declines steepened and Texas property and financial markets began to totter, Governor White called a special session of the legislature in August 1986. White was in a tough re-election battle, but he had no choice but to call the legislature to Austin because Bullock was projecting a deficit of $2.3 billion in the current fiscal year. State leaders discussed every way imaginable to increase state revenues, including a lottery, horse racing, sin taxes, program cuts and wage and hiring freezes for state workers, and increases to the sales tax and the franchise tax. Talk of an income tax grew louder. In the end, leaders settled on budget cuts totaling nearly $600 million and an increase in the general sales tax from 4.125 percent to 5.25 percent. Not surprisingly, Mark White was beaten for re-election by Bill Clements, the man he had defeated for re-election four years earlier.

Governor Clements took office just as the 1987 regular session of the legislature convened facing more deficits. Clements proposed a budget totaling $36.9 billion and toured the state calling for fiscal stringency. The Texas House called for $39.4 billion in spending and the Senate called for $40 billion. In the middle of the legislative session, state district judge Harley Clark declared the Texas school funding system unconstitutional because it was too stingy toward poor districts. When Clements agreed to consider broadening the sales tax and other revenue increases, Republican Party state chair George Strake was livid. In a meeting with the governor, Strake declared:

> We have the legislature about to break, and you're giving in, right here at the end. I know they're threatening to open the prisons and close the schools and quit building roads, but this is when you get something done. You have all the Republicans in the legislature hanging on at the end of the limb and you're sawing it off for them.[33]

Despite the partisan pressure to demand more budget cuts, Clements compromised with the Democratic majorities in the legislature, though a special session was required to seal the deal. In late July, Clements signed a $38.3 billion budget and a bundle of related tax increases totaling $5.7 billion. The sales tax was increased to 6 percent and broadened to include a range of services not previously covered and increases were made to the gas taxes, tobacco taxes, and corporate franchise fees.[34] Gib Lewis, Democrat of Fort Worth and speaker during the 1987 regular and special sessions, lauded Clements for his willingness to compromise, saying, "It takes a lot of courage to make a hard decision. . . . But there comes a time and place to keep government services functioning, that you have to bite the bullet."[35]

The compromise struck by Clements and Democrats to help weather the fiscal storms of the late 1980s was courageous, but not courageous enough. Bullock continued to believe that only an income tax would allow state revenues to grow with the economy. Shortly after being elected lieutenant governor in 1990, Bullock again declared for an income tax and tried, unsuccessfully, to push it through the 1991 regular session of the legislature. The blow-back was sufficiently intense that he had to reverse field completely to insure his own political survival. Bullock proposed a constitutional amendment to prohibit an income tax unless voters approved it by referendum. As a result, the Texas Constitution now prohibits an income tax unless supported by a majority of each house of the legislature and approved by statewide vote. Moreover, two-thirds of the revenues from an income tax would have to go to property tax relief and the remaining one-third to education.

Governor George W. Bush unsuccessfully sought broad reform of the Texas tax system. Bush was first elected in 1994 and then overwhelmingly re-elected in 1998. In Bush's first term, he proposed reductions in property taxes and elimination of the franchise tax, to be funded by a 0.5 cent increase in the sales tax and a European style value-added tax. The 1997 legislature scrapped Bush's plan and produced one of their own which contained little tax relief and no new revenue. In 1999, with a presidential campaign in immediate prospect, Governor Bush pushed a smaller property tax cut and a somewhat larger cut in corporate franchise fees through the legislature. The result, of course, was that when the economy again turned down, in 2003, more devastatingly in 2011, and again in 2017, revenue shortfalls required ever deeper budget cuts. As we shall see, in the absence of an income tax, the revenue gap left by the decline in severance tax receipts has been closed by relentless budget cutting.

The Changing Sources of Texas Revenues

The main sources of Texas state government revenues have changed in substantial and worrisome ways. First, by the early 1950s, specialized sales taxes were already the main source of state revenues, providing 35 percent of total revenues, followed by severance taxes at 25 percent, federal transfers at 24 percent, and licenses and fees at 10 to 15 percent. Second, sales tax revenues (the top line) jumped sharply from 35 to 45 percent of total revenues with passage of the general sales tax in 1961 and rose to around 50 percent over the next three decades, reflecting increases to the sales tax rate. Third, federal transfer payments accounted for a fairly steady 25 to 30 percent of total revenues until the early 1990s, 35 to 40 percent for the next decade, and 45 to 50 percent from 2004 to 2011 before settling down into the low 40s in the most recent data. Fourth, licenses and fees declined to a steady 8 to 10 percent of total revenues. Finally, severance tax revenues fell from 25 percent to single digits by the early 1970s, rebounded to 20 percent of total revenues by the early 1980s, before going into a steady decline.

Figure 11.2 Total Texas Revenues by Source, 1950–2015

Source: *The Book of the States*, The Council of State Governments, Lexington, KY, vol. 48, 2016, "State Government Tax Revenue, By Selected Types of Tax," pp. 410–411, 420–421. See similar tables in previous editions back to 1942.

Figure 11.2 shows that the mid-1980s, with the collapse in the price of oil and the subsequent declines in the state's property values and banking sector, changed the sources of Texas revenues. Between 1981 and 1990, sales tax income jumped from 45 percent to 56 percent while revenues from the severance tax fell from 20 percent to 5 percent. Over the space of a decade, the 1980s, 15 percent of total state revenues were shifted from the oil and gas industry to consumers. This was done in two ways, one far more visible than the other. First, a quick series of increases in the general sales tax were enacted, from 4.125 percent in 1984 to 6.25 percent by 1990, with an additional 2 percent permitted to local governments. From 1990 through the early 2000s, general and selective sales taxes provided more than half of Texas state government revenues. Federal revenues rose steadily from a third toward 40 percent. Second, and much less remarked upon, is the precipitous fall in the share of Texas revenues provided by severance taxes on oil, natural gas, and other natural resources. To the extent that this decline is remarked upon, it is attributed to the late 1980s collapse in oil prices, but that is only half the story.

To get a better picture of the Texas tax system, it will be helpful to set aside federal transfer payments. This will allow us to focus directly on how Texas has chosen to raise tax revenues and how those revenue streams have changed over time. Figure 11.3 presents Texas tax revenues from 1950 to the present. In the early 1950s, Texas's selective sales taxes on automobiles, fuels, alcohol, tobacco, and other designated products produced almost half the state's tax revenues. Once the general sales tax was passed in 1961, the proportion of Texas revenues from the general and specialized sales taxes rose to 60 percent, increases in the Connally years pushed it to 70 percent, and further increases in the late 1980s and early 1990s pushed it to 80 percent of state tax revenues. Licenses and fees provided as much as 20 percent of state tax revenues around 1960, declining to 10 percent by the 1980s and remaining in a tight 10 to 15 percent band thereafter. Severance tax revenues provided a third of state tax revenues in the 1950s and a quarter as late as the early 1980s.

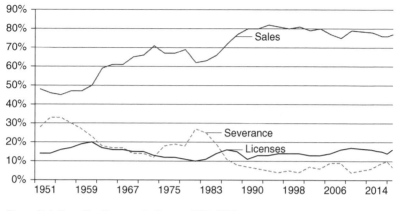

Figure 11.3 Texas Tax Revenues by Source, 1950–2015

Source: *The Book of the States*, The Council of State Governments, Lexington, KY, vol. 48, 2016, "State Government Tax Revenue, By Selected Types of Tax," pp. 410–411. See similar tables in previous editions back to 1942.

However, by the early 1990s severance tax revenues accounted for less than 10 percent of tax revenues and have averaged 4 to 10 percent for the last two decades. Figure 11.3, highlighting just Texas-raised revenues, shows how dependent the state is on the sales tax and, glancing back at Figure 11.2, federal transfer payments. Licenses, fees, and severance taxes are important, but they don't float the boat.

Texas was the first state to levy a severance tax on oil in 1905, just four years after the Spindletop discovery. The initial tax was 1 percent of market value (the adjusted commodity price paid at the wellhead) and has been increased eight times, most recently in 1951 when it was set at 4.6 percent. The severance tax on natural gas was established in 1931 at 2 percent of market value and after several changes it has been at 7.5 percent since 1969. No other major taxes in Texas have remained unchanged for so long. Three-quarters of severance tax revenues from oil go into the state General Fund and the remaining one-quarter goes to support public education. Most of the severance tax revenues from natural gas go into the state's "rainy day" fund.

What accounts for the volatility and, more importantly, the sharp decline in severance tax revenues since 1950? Texas severance tax revenues were just about $100 million in 1951. They grew steadily, but not spectacularly, reaching $200 million in 1965, before tripling to $667 million in 1975. In Figure 11.4 we show total severance tax revenues from 1951 through 1975 and then we break out oil and natural gas severance taxes. In the late 1970s, both oil and gas severance taxes rose from $500 million to more than a billion before falling back to $500 million by the mid-1980s. Oil revenues slightly outpaced gas revenues until 1985, from 1986 to 2010 gas jumped ahead, and since 2010 oil has been back in the lead. Gas revenues held up when oil revenues began to slide in the mid-1980s, jumping dramatically after 2001 as the impact of the Barnett Shale discoveries began to be felt. Unlike oil, which is an international market on which Texas supplies until recently had little impact, natural gas is a North American market where large increases in supply can drive down prices. The recovery of severance tax revenues from oil in the mid-2000s was a function both of sharp increases in the international price of oil and of the application of fracking techniques to oil shale formations, especially in South Texas. Increases in

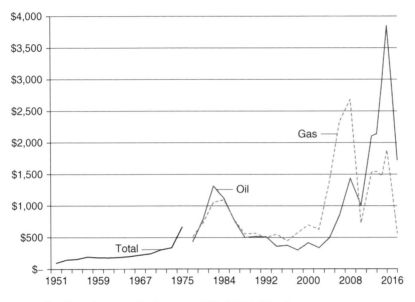

Figure 11.4 Texas Severance Tax Revenues, 1950–2016 (millions)

Source: Data for 1951 through 1975 is from *The Book of the States*, The Council of State Governments, Lexington, KY, vol. 42, 2010, "State Government Tax Revenue, By Selected Types of Tax," pp. 426–427. See similar tables in previous editions back to 1942. The data from 1978 to 2016, which breaks out severance taxes for oil and natural gas are from the Texas Comptroller at http://comptroller.texas.gov/transparency/reports/revenue-by-source/history.php.

natural gas supplies and the deep recession of 2008 and 2009 drove down gas prices but eroded oil prices relatively little until large and steady increases in supply drove prices down hard. However, and this is critical, what looks in Figure 11.4 like big increases in severance revenues in the mid-2000s and big declines after 2015 hardly moved the needle in Figure 11.2's description of total revenues. Changes in Texas public policy will help explain why.

Naturally, as the price of oil collapsed, slowly in the early 1980s and then much more rapidly in 1986 and 1987, severance tax revenues declined. The severance tax is a wellhead tax on the value of oil and gas being extracted from the ground and as the value of the product goes down so do tax revenues. But the dramatic drop in severance tax revenues had political as well as economic causes. In the late 1980s, Texas political authorities decided that the recovery of the oil and gas industry would be aided by lifting or reducing taxes on some producers. The Texas Railroad Commission, which oversees oil and gas production in the state, reports on its website that, "The reduction or elimination of state severance taxes provides an economic incentive to operators to undertake activities that produce oil and gas resources that might otherwise remain unrecovered. Texas recognized back in the late 1980s that incentives to increase the state's oil and gas production were extremely valuable."[36] Tax relief undoubtedly helped the oil and gas industry recover in the 1990s, but for much of the last decade the price of oil was strong, sometimes over $100 a barrel, and the natural gas industry has been so productive, discovering new fields such as the Barnett Shale, that prices have been driven down; still the reductions and exemptions remained in place.

Critically, the reduction in severance tax revenues was partly a reflection of production and price declines, but also a reflection of changes in Texas tax policy. Just as Texas was rapidly increasing its general sales tax, it was simultaneously, but much more quietly, reducing its severance taxes. In 1989, the legislature passed the Enhanced Oil Recovery (EOR) Act which cut the severance tax rate of 4.6 percent in half for eligible wells for up to ten years. EOR wells use the injection of water or chemicals to enhance production or extend the life of the well. The program was extended in 1997 and remains in effect today. In 1993, the legislature passed the Inactive Well Program declaring that any oil or gas well not active for more than one month in the past three years would get a ten-year exemption from severance taxes if brought back online. In 1997, the period of inactivity was reduced to two years and the program has been extended and remains in effect. Most importantly, in 1989, the legislature passed the High-Cost Gas Well program. Gas production was languishing and it was thought that deeper (more than 15,000 feet) and more difficult (horizontal) drilling would be required to increase production. High-cost wells were made exempt from the severance tax until 2001, but subsequent revisions have produced a sliding scale of taxation and extended the exemptions indefinitely. Everyone realizes that techniques like deep and horizontal drilling that were thought exotic in the late 1980s and early 1990s are common today, but the exemptions remain in place and at a high cost to taxpayers. Exemptions have also been extended to oil and gas wells defined as marginal or low producing.

A study by the Texas Legislature's LBB, author unknown and, in fact, actively suppressed, told a fascinating story. In preparation for the 2011 legislative session, a study entitled "Overview of Natural Gas Tax Structures" was conducted by the LBB for the information of members. The study was not intended for public release, but was, in fact, posted to the internet by an apparently disgruntled member. Its unchallenged findings were incendiary. While this study applied just to natural gas severance taxes, one can reasonably assume that the oil lobby has been at work too. The take-away line from the study was striking: "Natural gas production in the state is taxed at 7.5 percent of market value; however, deductions, exemptions, and rate reductions have reduced many producers' tax liabilities to zero and reduced the overall effective rate to between 1.1 and 1.9 percent in recent years." The LBB study also reported that the value of high-cost gas reductions averaged $1.23 billion from 2004 through 2009, for a total of $7.4 billion. Over the same period, natural gas severance tax payments averaged $1.9 billion, for a total of $11.4 billion. In 2009 alone, the last year covered by the study, 55 percent of all gas produced in Texas was designated high-cost gas and the effective tax rate on that gas was 1.5 percent. In 2009, natural gas severance taxes totaled $1.4 billion and exemptions and deductions cost the state $1.2 billion.[37] Every dollar that does not come in through severance taxes has to come in through sales taxes or be accounted for by deeper budget cuts.

Clearly, Texas has been moving for two decades toward reducing and perhaps eliminating the severance tax without the kind of public discussion that one would expect. Several reasons for the silence readily occur. First, the oil and gas industry is very well represented in Austin and it has always been effective in protecting its interests. Second, the public would be aroused if it were obvious that the tax burden was further being shifted from this wealthy industry to consumers. But third, the public demise of the severance tax might open a broad discussion of the efficiency of the state's tax structure. Let's have that discussion now.

Reform of the Texas Tax Regime

Texas political authorities have painted themselves into a fiscal corner. Over the course of the twentieth century, most states, even most southern states, supplemented their traditional dependence on property taxes, first with sales taxes, and then eventually with corporate and individual income taxes. Even with these new revenue sources, southern states kept their tax revenues below the national average of all 50 states, but they enjoyed the flexibility and the stability provided by the "three-legged stool" of property, sales, and income taxes. Drawing on all three sources of revenue means that each can be low and still produce a moderate but flexible and sufficient amount of revenue.

Figure 11.5 presents Texas tax collections compared to average tax collections in 14 southern states and the U.S. U.S. average tax collection for the 50 states is fixed at 100 percent, meaning half the states pay higher taxes and half pay lower, and the southern and Texas tax collections are presented as percentages of the U.S. average. For example, in 1951 the U.S. per capita state tax collection was $59.59, while the southern average was $55.69 (93 percent of the U.S. average) and the Texas per capita tax collection was $45.68 (77 percent of the U.S. average). The comparisons for 1961 and 1971 are very similar; the southern rate of state tax collection is about 90 percent of the national average while the Texas rate is 75 to 80 percent. In 1981, at the height

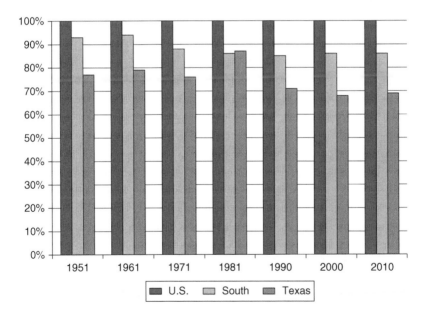

Figure 11.5 Texas Tax Collections per Capita Compared to the U.S. and the South

Source: *The Book of the States*, The Council of State Governments, Lexington, KY, 1951 from "State Tax Collections, by State," column labeled "1951 amount per Capita," vol. 9, p. 212; similar table and column for 1961, at vol. 14, p. 237; 1971 from "Summary of State Tax Revenue," column labeled "Per Capita" 1971, vol. 19, p. 238; 1981 from similar table and column, vol. 24, p. 409; 1990 from similar table and column, vol. 29, p. 411; 2000 from vol. 34, p. 300; 2010, "State Government Tax Revenue," vol. 44, pp. 432–433.

Note: Southern states are the ten Confederate states other than Texas and Kentucky, Missouri, West Virginia, and Oklahoma Territory. Hence, alphabetically, Alabama, Arkansas, Florida, Georgia, Kentucky, Louisiana, Mississippi, Missouri, North Carolina, Oklahoma, South Carolina, Tennessee, Virginia, and West Virginia.

of an oil boom, Texas edged ahead of the rest of the South, collecting $574.48 (87 percent of the U.S. average) compared to the southern average of $571.50 (86 percent of the national average). The late 1980s collapse of the international price of oil, followed by Texas property and financial markets, forced changes to taxes and revenues. Figure 11.5 shows clearly that Texas per capita tax collections fell in relation to both the national and the southern averages in 1990 and thereafter. Prior to 1980, Texas tax collections averaged 77 percent of average U.S. state tax collections, while after 1990 it has averaged just 70 percent. Prior to 1980, the southern tax collection average was 92 percent of the U.S. average, while after 1990 it was 88 percent. Texas's fiscal options lie between steady as she goes, taxing and spending about 70 percent what other states do, and moving toward the average spent by the southern states.

Before we begin talking about new sources of revenue, let's really nail down the fact that Texas is a low-tax state. This will require no great effort. In 1977, the Tax Foundation, a well-respected but clearly anti-tax think tank, began publishing state rankings on what they and others call "tax effort." Tax effort is generally defined as the percentage of per capita personal income taken in state and local taxes. The Tax Foundation reports that from 1977 through 2010, Texas had a state and local tax burden averaging 7.9 percent, 45th among the 50 states. Only five states had a lower state and local tax burden. The Tax Foundation also presents data on per capita personal income and on the dollar amount of taxes paid per capita. While Texas has among the lowest state and local tax rates in the nation, Texas per capita income has averaged 25th in the nation since 1977, so Texans pay more in state and local taxes than the low rate might initially suggest. From 1977 through 2012, Texans ranked 25th in per capita income, 38th in amount of taxes paid, and 45th in state and local tax rate. As we shall see below, the space between 25th and 45th provides room to think about how additional revenues might be used to improve education, health care, transportation, and much else in Texas. Increasing taxing and spending to the southern average would still mean that half the southern states and nearly four-fifths of the states in the nation had higher taxes.

Texas entered the 2011 legislative session with one of the lowest tax burdens in the nation and a budget deficit of $15 billion from current spending levels and $27 billion accounting for population growth and inflation. Large Republican majorities in both chambers of the legislature cut billions from public schools, higher education, health care, transportation, and much more. Legislators faced a less challenging environment in 2013, but even then they were unable to restore all the cuts made in 2011. The 2015 session was easier as oil prices were high, but once prices fell by two-thirds later in the year, the budgetary forecasts for the 2017 session were foreboding. Given the ongoing budget difficulties, Texans must eventually ask what additional revenues might be available. As that discussion begins, it is important to note that Texas has a regressive tax system, meaning that it bears more heavily on the poor than on the wealthy. The Austin-based Center for Public Policy Priorities (CPPP), drawing on data from the Comptroller's Office, reported that the bottom fifth of income earners in 2017 paid 17.2 percent of their income in state and local taxes while the top fifth paid just 4.5 percent.[38]

Texas has relatively high property taxes and sales taxes, but no corporate or personal income tax. The Tax Foundation reports that in 2010 Texas had the fourth highest property taxes as a percentage of home value in the nation. Texans paid a rate of 1.90 percent of home value as opposed to a national average of 1.14 percent. Not much room for increase there. Texas has the 12th highest state and local sales tax in the nation at 8.19

percent. Eleven states have sales taxes of 8.25 to Louisiana's 9.98. There is some room for a modest increase here, perhaps 0.5 percent, but certainly no more than 1 percent. In fact, as the 2011 regular session of the Texas Legislature faced big deficits, the CPPP suggested that a temporary 0.5 cent increase in the sales tax would raise $1.5 billion a year. They also proposed sin taxes on alcohol, tobacco, and high-sugar beverages. CPPP estimated that this "Healthy Texas Revenue Package" would raise more than $2.5 billion a year.[39]

Alternatively, Lori L. Taylor, a public finance specialist in the Bush School of Government and Public Service at Texas A&M, argued that the sales tax is honeycombed with exemptions and exclusions. Food and medicine, as well as gas, electricity, and internet access, are big exemptions. And there are dozens of smaller exemptions, "Massages are taxable, but manicures, facials, and other spa services are not. . . . Dishwasher repair is a taxable service, but auto repairs are not. . . . Laundry services . . . are taxable, but the car washing industry is tax exempt. . . . The list goes on and on." Taylor cites estimates from the Comptroller's Office to the effect that eliminating most sales tax exemptions on food and medicine, even while exempting the poor, could raise as much as $4 billion and more broadly cancelling exemptions could raise another $2 to 3 billion annually.[40]

Political leaders could also review dozens of other tax rebates, exemptions, and deductions that reduce state government revenues each year. In fact, the Comptroller provides the governor and legislature at the beginning of each regular session with a book-length analysis entitled "Tax Exemptions and Tax Incidence." The February 2017 report declared that "the value of each exemption, exclusion, discount, deduction, special accounting method, credit, refund, and special appraisal" totaled $55.5 billion.[41] The $55.5 billion total for exemptions, exclusions, and discounts includes $43.7 billion in items excluded from the sales tax and $11.8 billion in school property tax exemptions. Many of the exemptions are, of course, worthwhile. For example, governments and non-profits are exempt from the sales tax. But there are dozens more, totaling $10 to 15 billion, some of which undoubtedly merit scrutiny.[42]

One exemption that has drawn some scrutiny, but not enough to bring change, is the exemption for "high-cost gas" from the gas severance tax. The exemption for high-cost gas was passed in 1989 with the support of Tom Craddick, a future speaker, as temporary assistance to gas producers during hard times. But temporary benefits have a way of becoming permanent. The exemption for high-cost gas was extended in 1995 and again in 1999 and then, after Craddick became speaker in 2003, the provision was made permanent in a "technical corrections" bill that few legislators read. Former Senator Ken Armbrister, the bill's sponsor on the Senate side, later said, "I can guarantee you that nobody in the Legislature knew that was in the bill."[43] Of course, Armbrister was not speaking literally—someone knew, several people knew, and they were acting quite deliberately. The exemption remains law today and costs the Texas treasury $1 billion a year.

It could well be that in response to the collapse of oil prices in the mid-1980s, deep reductions in oil and gas severance taxes in the late 1980s were needed to nurse that critical industry back to health. As Texas entered the 1980s, severance taxes provided 20 percent of total revenues and 27 percent of Texas-raised revenues. By the early 1990s, those severance tax revenue totals had fallen to 5 percent and 7 percent, respectively. They have remained in that range, always under 10 percent of Texas-raised revenues, for the past two decades, even as oil and gas prices, especially oil prices, have hit all-time highs. Clearly, severance tax revenues could be restored, even if only on a sliding scale, so that the industry paid more during good times and less during hard times. Paying reduced taxes during good times, when the price of oil and gas are high, given the frequency of tight budgets in Texas, makes no sense.

The biggest items on any list of potential new sources of revenue to Texas state government are corporate and personal income taxes. Texas is one of only five states (Nevada, South Dakota, Texas, Washington, and Wyoming) that have neither a corporate nor a personal income tax. Two others (Alaska and Florida) have a corporate income tax but no personal income tax. Let's look first at the corporate income tax. Forty-four states tax business capital, capital gains, gross receipts, or profits in one way or another. Some have a flat tax rate, some have tax brackets, some allow federal taxes as a deduction, and most tax financial institutions at higher rates than retail businesses. Though Texas has no corporate income tax per se, it does levy taxes on business activity. For example, Texas has for a century taxed insurance companies and utilities. The oil and gas industry certainly consider the severance tax to be a tax on their businesses. More importantly, Texas long had a corporate franchise tax, which it described as a privilege tax on corporations operating in the state. The tax was 0.25 percent of taxable capital (value of the corporation) or 4.5 percent of earned income (federal taxable profits). Limited partnerships and professional services, including most legal, accounting, and financial management firms, were not subject to the franchise tax.

The spring 2006 special session of the Texas Legislature revised the way business is taxed in the state. It replaced the franchise fee with a broad new "margins tax" (many continue to refer to the margins tax as the franchise fee, so be alert). The margins tax is 1 percent on gross receipts, minus either the cost of employee compensation or the cost of goods sold, whichever is greater. Retailers and wholesalers pay 0.5 percent. Sole proprietors, general partnerships, and businesses grossing less than $1,100,000 annually are exempt. The margins tax provided $9.4 billion in 2014–2015, about 4.5 percent of total revenues. It had been expected to generate nearly twice that.

The best way to think about the revenue potential of corporate and personal income taxes in Texas without getting down in the weeds of hypothesized tax rates, tax brackets, standard deductions, and personal exemptions is to look at the Tax Foundation figures for per capita tax revenues for the U.S. and the 14 southern states that levy such taxes. All 14 of the southern states that we have been using as a comparison group (see Figure 11.5 for the list of states), for Texas had a 2017 corporate income tax averaging 5.9 percent. North Carolina at 3 percent, Mississippi and South Carolina at 5 percent, and Florida at 5.5 percent are the lowest. Nine states are between 6.0 and 6.5 percent, while Louisiana at 8.0 percent is the highest. Ten states have a flat tax while four vary their tax rate across three to six tax brackets. For example, Kentucky taxes corporate income at 4 percent on the first dollar, 5 percent over $50,000, and 6 percent over $100,000. Moreover, 11 of the 14 also have a corporate franchise fee, usually ranging from $1.20 to $2.50 per $1,000 of taxable capital, a tax on deployed capital, or a gross receipts tax in addition to the corporate income tax. Given the business tax regimes of comparable states, Texas might consider a corporate income tax at the regional average of 6 percent in addition to the margins tax. In 2012, the 14 southern states took in $107 per capita in corporate income taxes. If Texas had a corporate income tax at the southern average, the $107 per person times Texas's population of 27 million, it would produce

$2.84 billion. A corporate income tax at the national per capita average of $140 would produce $3.78 billion.

All but one (Florida) of the 14 southern states we have been comparing to Texas have a personal income tax. Tennessee does not tax wage income but does have a flat tax of 6 percent from the first dollar after a personal exemption of $1,250 on interest and dividend income. The other 12 states have three to six tax brackets and most offer both standard deductions and personal exemptions. Most states start with a tax of 1 or 2 percent on low incomes rising to 6 or 7 percent on higher incomes. Most states take the brackets for single filers and simply double them for married couples filing jointly. Standard deductions are usually doubled for married couples and personal exemptions are multiplied by the number of dependants. Standard deductions range from $2,000 ($4,000 for couples) to $5,400 ($10,800 for couples) and personal exemptions range from $1,000 to $3,000 per dependant. Obviously, the higher the standard deductions and personal exemptions are set, the higher one's income has to be to be subject to taxation.

Virginia provides a reasonably simple example of a state income tax system. The standard deduction is $3,000 for single filers and $6,000 for couples and the personal exemption is $930 per dependant. Virginia charges 2 percent on the first $3,000 of taxable income, 3 percent on taxable income from $3,000 to $5,000, 5 percent on income between $5,000 and $17,000, and 5.75 percent above $17,000. South Carolina shields the very poor by providing standard deductions of $6,300 for singles and $12,600 for couples and $3,000 for each dependant. On the other hand, South Carolina levies higher taxes on income above the deductions and exemptions. While Virginia's top bracket is 5.75 percent on taxable income above $17,000, South Carolina has a 6 percent bracket that kicks in at $11,680 and a 7 percent bracket beginning at $14,600.

Virginia's personal income tax took in $1,318 per capita in 2013 while Mississippi's took in just $587 per capita. The average per capita income tax revenue for the 12 southern states (excluding Florida and Tennessee) in 2013 was $880. If Texas adopted a personal income tax at the southern average (multiply per capita income tax revenue by Texas population), the 2011 revenue would have been $23.8 billion annually. An income tax set at the average of the 50 states would generate $29.8 billion. Texas is and has always been a low-tax state, so it is likely any income tax would have generous deductions and exemptions and modest rates. Moreover, a constitutional amendment adopted by voters in 1993 requires that the revenue from any future income tax go two-thirds to reduce existing property taxes with the remaining one-third going to support public education. Clearly, an income tax that lowered the existing property tax would result in a more balanced revenue system and public education could certainly use an infusion of funds.[44] Although one might tinker elsewhere to some good effect, the Texas tax system cannot be thoroughly revised without adopting a state income tax.

The last serious discussion of a personal income tax in Texas was held at the behest of Texas Comptroller and then Lieutenant Governor Bob Bullock. As noted, the pushback was so strong that Bullock sponsored a constitutional amendment prohibiting an income tax unless approved by a majority vote of both houses of the legislature and a statewide voter referendum. Even then, two-thirds of the income tax revenues would have to go to property tax reductions and one-third to public education. Despite the obvious fact that Texas property taxes are among the highest in the nation and school funding is among the lowest in the nation, state leaders do not mention an income tax even under their breath.

So What Does the Future Hold?

If broad scale tax reform designed to enhance state revenues would almost have to include a tax on personal income and neither party, certainly not the ruling Republican Party, will so much as mention it, what are our prospects? The short answer is bleak— underfunded schools and universities, large numbers of people without health insurance or reliable care, and thin social services—and the long answer is, long, at least a couple of decades long. The long answer is that Texas politics and policymaking will not change until competitive two-party politics returns to the state—as I said, a couple of decades.

Let us close by looking at two sets of numbers that should give us some sense of when two-party politics—sometimes called Purple Texas—might be restored in the state. As with much else, this discussion starts with demographic change and, more pointedly, the rise of the Hispanic population in the state. Close political observers note that the century long dominance of the Democratic Party in Texas broke up in the decades after World War II. In its place came a Republican Party ascendancy, clearly visible in the late 1970s and 1980s, and unchallenged since the late 1990s. The last Democrats to win statewide office in Texas did so in 1994, were swept aside in George W. Bush's blowout re-election victory in 1998, and few Democrats have been competitive statewide since. In 2014, the entire Republican ticket for statewide offices, from Greg Abbott for governor to George P. Bush (yes, Bush) for Land Commissioner, won by 20 points. As the 2018 statewide races loom, Republican incumbents confidently declare that they will stand for re-election, while Democrats step forth tentatively if at all.

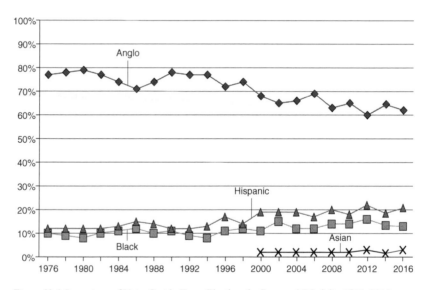

Figure 11.6 Percentage of Votes Cast in Texas Elections by Race and Ethnicity, 1976–2016

Source: Derived by the author from U.S. Census data. Go to Census, click on "V" in the alphabetical list. Data for 1976 come from "Registration and Voting in 1976—Jurisdiction Covered by the Voting Rights Act Amendments of 1975," Table 1. Data for later years come from "Reported Voting and Registration, by Race and Spanish Origin (Hispanic Origin after 1986), for States," 1980, Table 5; 1982, Table 4; 1988, Table 4; 1990, Table 4; 1992, Table 4; 1994, Table 4a; 1998, Table 4a; 2000, Table 4a; 2002, Table 4a; 2004, Table 4a; 2006, Table 4b; 2008, Table 4b; 2010, Table 4b; 2012, Table 4b; 2014, Table 4b.

Note: Data are unavailable for 1978 and 1984. Average of votes cast by race and ethnicity in the previous and subsequent election has been inserted.

So, whether you view the prospects of a Democratic Party return to competitiveness with glee or disdain, how can we think about its likelihood and its timing? Both Republicans and Democrats understand that they must address the coming Hispanic majority in Texas. Republicans believe that they can compete for Hispanic votes and, while they might not win a majority of them, can continue to win elections for a long time with 35 or 40 percent of that vote. Democrats bank heavily on a rising Hispanic vote and on winning at least two-thirds of it. Historically, Democrats usually do win two-thirds of the Hispanic vote, but Republicans point to elections from Senator John Tower in the 1960s, to George W. Bush in the 1990s and 2000s, to Greg Abbott in 2014, where their candidates won 40 to 50 percent of the Hispanic vote.

To get a good sense of the role that the Hispanic vote might play going forward, we can look back several decades to see what role it has played so far. Figure 11.6 presents a demographic breakdown of votes cast by race and ethnicity in the four decades between 1976 and 2016. In 1976, Anglos cast about 80 percent of votes in Texas statewide elections, while blacks and Hispanics cast about 10 percent each. By 2016 the Anglo share of the vote had dropped about 12 percent, to about two-thirds of votes cast. The black vote remained very stable at 10 to 12 percent. The Hispanic vote, where all the attention is focused, slowly rose from 10 percent of votes cast in 1976 to 20 percent of votes cast in 2016. It is an increase, but a slow one, and few Democrats would find acceptable a similarly slow rise over the next 40 years.

Not surprisingly, most Democrats are cautious about their near-term prospects in statewide races. Congressman Joaquin Castro's 2017 response to a question posed by *The Texas Observer*'s Kolten Parker was informative: Parker said, "Texas Democrats have been shut out in statewide races for more than two decades. . . . Is the Democratic Party here in disarray?" Castro's response, accurate I think, was, "No, it's in a comeback mode. And the comeback period is obviously a long one."[45]

Before we consider how long the "comeback" might take, we must remind ourselves that not all Texas residents are eligible to vote and not all of those who are eligible are equally likely to register and to vote. In Chapter 3, "Demographic Change and Its Implications," Figure 3.2 showed that in the mid-1970s Anglos were 70 percent of the total population (casting 80 percent of the votes), blacks were 10 to 12

Table 11.2 Projecting Texas Partisan Vote Shares from 2016 to 2030

	Anglo	*Hispanic*	*Black*	*Asian*	*GOP Vote Share*
% Tx Pop 2016	42	40	12	5	
% CVAP 2016	53	29	13	4	
% Votes by Race	65	20	13	2	
GOP Vote Share	.65 × .72	.20 × .35	.13 × .10	.02 × .3	
% GOP Votes	46.8%	7%	1%	.6%	55.4%
% Tx Pop 2030	36	46	11	7	
% CVAP 2030	45	39	12	5	
% Votes by Race	55	30	11	4	
GOP Vote Share	.55 × .75	.30 × .35	.11 × .10	.04 × .30	
% GOP Votes	39.6%	10.5%	1%	1%	52.1

Source: Texas State Data Center, Estimates of Population by Age, Sex, Race and Ethnicity, 2015. Citizen Voting Age Population, U.S. Census, Voting and Registration Tables, 2016, Texas.

percent of the population (casting about that proportion of votes), and Hispanics about 15 percent of the population (casting about 10 percent of votes). Forty years later in 2016, blacks, at a little more than 10 percent of the population continued to cast their proportionate share of the total vote. Anglos were 44 percent of the population (casting 65 percent of the votes) and Hispanics were 39 percent of the population (casting 20 percent of the votes).

Some reasons, evident in Table 11.2, that Anglos vote in proportions larger than their share of the population and Hispanics vote in proportions smaller than their share of the population are evident. First, about 98 percent of Anglos and blacks in Texas are citizens, while only 70 percent of Hispanics are citizens, and only citizens are allowed to register and vote. Second, Hispanics are a younger population than blacks and Anglos, especially Anglos. One-third of Hispanics in Texas are under 18 and, therefore, ineligible to vote, while just under one-quarter of blacks and less than one-fifth of Anglos are under 18. And third, we saw in Chapters 4 through 6 that Anglos have higher average incomes and more education than blacks and Hispanics and more income and education translate into higher voter registration and turnout. So—couple of decades.

Conclusion

Texas taxed property, business and professional licenses, and luxury goods throughout the nineteenth century. Texas adopted its first severance taxes and automobile sales and fuels taxes soon after the turn of the twentieth century. Taxes on tobacco products, alcohol, insurance companies, and public utilities also were enacted. After 1950, Texas public officials regularly nudged up selective sales taxes, licenses, and fees, but the potential revenue gains in most instances were modest. The introduction of the general sales tax in 1961 created the potential for great change because it applied to a wide range of economic transactions and, as everyone understood, additional transactions could be made taxable and the rate itself, initially 2 percent, could be raised as economic circumstances seemed to demand. In fact, into the early 1980s, the Texas tax system did seem to provide sufficient revenue to meet the state's small government needs.

The second half of the 1980s was a traumatic period for Texas, its citizens, and its political authorities. After nearly two decades of strong economic growth and expanding tax revenues, the extended downturn of the late 1980s elicited dramatic policy reforms that have not been well understood. Even before the general sales tax was adopted in 1961, selective sales taxes provided nearly half of state tax revenues. As late as the early 1980s, sales taxes provided about two-thirds of state tax revenues, licenses and fees provided one-tenth, and severance taxes provided a quarter. As the economic problems in Texas gathered in the 1980s, political leaders increased the sales tax and other sources of income several times, and they provided a range of rebates, exemptions, and deductions to the energy industry to help them weather the downturn. What few Texans realized was that those incentives to the oil and gas industry were not temporary as advertised, but became permanent and increasingly expensive to the state.

Over the past two decades, Texas state government revenues have declined as a proportion of both average southern state revenues and average U.S. state revenues. Over that same period of time, the Texas Republican Party, the majority party in Texas now and for some years to come, has adopted an increasingly rigid no new taxes ideology. Hence, while there are sources from which new revenues might be drawn, in both large and small amounts, the prospects for doing so seem slim. Perhaps the most likely possibility, because it has been done so many times before, is an increase in the general sales tax of perhaps 0.5 cent. Also possible is a thorough review of the sales tax with an eye to broadening its base to cover more of the modern service economy and closing loopholes. The problem with this tack, of course, is that it would increase the regressivity of a tax regime that already bears down hard on the poor.

Bigger changes, such as the institution of corporate or personal income taxes, are less likely but, if adopted, could be mitigated by reductions in other taxes. For example, if Texas were to adopt a broad corporate income tax, it might well reduce or eliminate the franchise fee or margins tax. The result would still be a broader, more equitable tax on Texas businesses. Similarly, adoption of a personal income tax would, by constitution, require that two-thirds of the revenues be dedicated to property tax reductions and the remaining one-third to public education. Even in the face of structural budget deficits, the search for new revenues is unlikely to lead to major tax reform unless the state and federal courts force the issue. They have in the past and they might well again.

Notes

1 John Connally, with Mickey Herskowitz, *In History's Shadow: An American Odyssey*, New York: Hyperion, 1993, p. 304.
2 Ibid., p. 361.
3 Robert A. Calvert, Arnoldo De León, and Gregg Cantrell, *The History of Texas*, 4th ed., Wheeling, IL: Harlan Davidson, Inc., 2007, p. 465.
4 Noah Smithwick, *The Evolution of a State*, Austin, TX: University of Texas Press, 1985, p. 1.
5 D.W. Meinig, *Imperial Texas: An Interpretive Essay in Cultural Geography*, Austin, TX: University of Texas Press, 1969, p. 34.
6 James P. Bevill, *The Paper Republic: The Struggle for Money, Credit, and Independence in the Republic of Texas*, Houston, TX, Bright Sky Press, 2009.
7 John G. Johnson, "Tariff Policies of the Republic of Texas," Handbook of Texas Online (www.tshaonline.org/handbook/online/articles/mpt01), accessed June 6, 2011. Published by the Texas State Historical Association. See also Stanley Seigel, *A Political History of the Texas Republic, 1836–1845*, Austin, TX: University of Texas Press, 1956, pp. 62–63, 201.
8 T.R. Fehrenbach, *Lone Star: A History of Texas and the Texans*, New York: Macmillan, 1968, p. 253. See also Wilhelm Steinert, *North America, Particularly Texas in the Year 1849*, Dallas, TX: DeGolyer Library, 2003, p. 61.
9 David G. McComb, *Texas: A Modern History*, Austin, TX: University of Texas Press, 2010, p. 53. See also Smithwick, *The Evolution of a State*, pp. 157, 171, and 201.
10 Robert A. Calvert, Arnoldo DeLeon, and Gregg Calvert, *The History of Texas*, 5th ed., Malden, MA: Wiley Blackwell, 2014, pp. 83–90.
11 Steinert, *North America, Particularly Texas*, p. 124.
12 Randolph B. Campbell, *An Empire for Slavery*, Baton Rouge, LA: Louisiana State University Press, 1989, pp. 94–95.
13 Fehrenbach, *Lone Star*, p. 278.
14 Kenneth E. Hendrickson Jr., "The Confederate Governors of Texas," in Kenneth W. Howell, *The Seventh Star of the Confederacy*, Denton, TX: The University of North Texas Press, 2009, pp. 228–245.
15 C.E. Evans, *The Story of Texas Schools*, Austin, TX: The Steck Company, 1955, p. 87; see also Fehrenbach, *Lone Star*, p. 422.
16 McComb, *Texas: A Modern History*, p. 79.
17 Dennis L. Dresang and James J. Gosling, *Politics and Policy in American States*, 6th ed., New York: Longman, 2008, p. 546.
18 Richard Morehead, *50 Years in Texas Politics*, Burnet, TX: Eakin Press, 1982, pp. 15, 23.
19 Ibid., pp. 35, 42.
20 Numan V. Bartley, *The New South, 1945–1980*, Baton Rouge, LA: Louisiana State University Press, 1995, p. 147.

21   Ricky F. Dobbs, *Yellow Dogs and Republicans: Allan Shivers and Texas Two-Party Politics*, College Station, TX: Texas A&M University Press, 2005, pp. 54–55.

22   Bartley, *The New South, 1945–1980*, p. 150.

23   Calvert et al., *The History of Texas*, 5th ed., p. 346.

24   Ben Barnes, *Barn Burning, Barn Building*, Albany, TX: Bright Sky Press, 2006, p. 45.

25   Patrick L. Cox and Michael Phillips, *The House Will Come to Order*, Austin, TX: University of Texas Press, 2010, p. 83.

26   Connally and Herskowitz, *In History's Shadow*, pp. 224–225. See also Morehead, *50 Years in Texas Politics*, p. 201.

27   Bartley, *The New South, 1945–1980*, p. 402.

28   Dolph Briscoe, *Dolph Briscoe: My Life in Texas Ranching and Politics*, Austin, TX: University of Texas Press, 2008, pp. 171, 256.

29   Anthony Champagne and Edward J. Harpham, *Texas at the Crossroads: Politics, People, and Policy*, College Station, TX: Texas A&M University Press, 1987, p. 7.

30   Briscoe, *Dolph Briscoe*, p. 249.

31   Bill Hobby, *How Things Really Work: Lessons From a Life in Politics*, Austin, TX: University of Texas Press, 2010, p. 82.

32   Dave McNeely and Jim Henderson, *Bob Bullock: God Bless Texas*, Austin, TX: University of Texas Press, 2008, pp. 175, 179.

33   Carolyn Barta, *Bill Clements: Texian to His Toenails*, Austin, TX: Eakin Press, 1996, pp. 352–354.

34   Barta, *Bill Clements*, pp. 360–361; see also Hobby, *How Things Really Work*, p. 132.

35   Barta, *Bill Clements*, p. 362.

36   www.rrc.state.tx.us/oil-gas/publications-and-notices/texas-severance-tax-incentives-past-and-present/.

37   LBB, "Overview of Natural Gas Tax Structures," www.lbb.state.tx.us/Documents/Publications/Primer/Natural%20Gas%20Tax%20Overview.pdf.

38   Center for Public Policy Priorities, "Who Pays Taxes in Texas," March, 2015.

39   Center for Public Policy Priorities, letter from William P. Hobby and F. Scott McCown to "Dear Business Leader," dated February 1, 2011, p. 3.

40   Lori L. Taylor, "Digging in the Wrong Places," *Dallas Morning News*, February 6, 2011, p. 6P.

41   https://comptroller.texas.gov/transparency/reports/tax-exemptions-and-incidence/.

42   Louise Story, "Lines Blur as Texas Gives Industries a Bonanza," *New York Times*, December 2, 2012.

43   Patricia Kilday Hart, "Commentary: Tax Cut Comes at High Cost," *Houston Chronicle*, March 27, 2011.

44   For a similar analysis in more detail, see Dick Lavine, Center for Public Policy Priorities, "The Best Choice for a Prosperous Texas: A Texas-Style Personal Income Tax," June 3, 2008.

45   Kolten Parker, "The Interview: Joaquin Castro Says Texas Democrats are Poised for a Comeback," *Texas Observer*, April 4, 2017.

Index

Note: References in *italics* are to figures, those in **bold** to tables.:

Taylor & Francis eBooks

Helping you to choose the right eBooks for your Library

Add Routledge titles to your library's digital collection today. Taylor and Francis ebooks contains over 50,000 titles in the Humanities, Social Sciences, Behavioural Sciences, Built Environment and Law.

Choose from a range of subject packages or create your own!

Benefits for you

» Free MARC records
» COUNTER-compliant usage statistics
» Flexible purchase and pricing options
» All titles DRM-free.

REQUEST YOUR FREE INSTITUTIONAL TRIAL TODAY

Free Trials Available
We offer free trials to qualifying academic, corporate and government customers.

Benefits for your user

» Off-site, anytime access via Athens or referring URL
» Print or copy pages or chapters
» Full content search
» Bookmark, highlight and annotate text
» Access to thousands of pages of quality research at the click of a button.

eCollections – Choose from over 30 subject eCollections, including:

Archaeology	Language Learning
Architecture	Law
Asian Studies	Literature
Business & Management	Media & Communication
Classical Studies	Middle East Studies
Construction	Music
Creative & Media Arts	Philosophy
Criminology & Criminal Justice	Planning
Economics	Politics
Education	Psychology & Mental Health
Energy	Religion
Engineering	Security
English Language & Linguistics	Social Work
Environment & Sustainability	Sociology
Geography	Sport
Health Studies	Theatre & Performance
History	Tourism, Hospitality & Events

For more information, pricing enquiries or to order a free trial, please contact your local sales team: www.tandfebooks.com/page/sales

Routledge
Taylor & Francis Group

The home of
Routledge books

www.tandfebooks.com